PEOPLE, MARKETS, GOODS:
ECONOMIES AND SOCIETIES IN HISTORY
Volume 16

Globalized Peripheries

T0386148

PEOPLE, MARKETS, GOODS:
ECONOMIES AND SOCIETIES IN HISTORY

ISSN: 2051-7467

Series editors
Steve Hindle – The Huntington Library
Jane Humphries – University of Oxford
Willem M. Jongman – University of Groningen
Catherine Schenk – University of Glasgow
Nuala Zahedieh – University of Edinburgh

The interactions of economy and society, people and goods, transactions and actions are at the root of most human behaviours. Economic and social historians are participants in the same conversation about how markets have developed historically and how they have been constituted by economic actors and agencies in various social, institutional and geographical contexts. New debates now underpin much research in economic and social, cultural, demographic, urban and political history. Their themes have enduring resonance – financial stability and instability, the costs of health and welfare, the implications of poverty and riches, flows of trade and the centrality of communications. This paperback series aims to attract historians interested in economics and economists with an interest in history by publishing high quality, cutting edge academic research in the broad field of economic and social history from the late medieval/ early modern period to the present day. It encourages the interaction of qualitative and quantitative methods through both excellent monographs and collections offering path-breaking overviews of key research concerns. Taking as its benchmark international relevance and excellence it is open to scholars and subjects of any geographical areas from the case study to the multi-nation comparison.

PREVIOUSLY PUBLISHED TITLES IN THE SERIES ARE
LISTED AT THE BACK OF THIS VOLUME

Globalized Peripheries

Central Europe and the Atlantic World, 1680–1860

Edited by

Jutta Wimmler and Klaus Weber

THE BOYDELL PRESS

First published 2020
The Boydell Press, Woodbridge

ISBN 978-1-78327-475-8

The Boydell Press is an imprint of Boydell & Brewer Ltd
PO Box 9, Woodbridge, Suffolk IP12 3DF, UK
and of Boydell & Brewer Inc.
668 Mt Hope Avenue, Rochester, NY 14620–2731, USA
website: www.boydellandbrewer.com

A catalogue record for this book is available
from the British Library

The publisher has no responsibility for the continued existence or accuracy of URLs for
external or third-party internet websites referred to in this book, and does not guarantee
that any content on such websites is, or will remain, accurate or appropriate

This publication is printed on acid-free paper

Contents

Illustrations

Figures

Tables

Contributors

Torsten dos Santos Arnold is a Ph.D. candidate who worked on the DFG-project, 'The Globalized Periphery: Atlantic Commerce, Socioeconomic and Cultural Change in Central Europe (1680–1850)', at the European University Viadrina in Frankfurt (Oder). He is currently employed at Justus-Liebig-University Gießen. **Publications**: 'Portugal and the Hanseatic League c. 1450–1550', *Portugal e a Europa nos Séculos XV e XVI. Olhares, Relações, Identidade(s)*, ed. P. C. Lopes (Lisbon, 2019); 'Central Europe and the Portuguese, Spanish and French Atlantic, Fifteenth to Nineteenth Centuries', *European Review* 26/3 (2018), pp. 421–9.

Friederike Gehrmann completed her MA at the European University Viadrina in Frankfurt (Oder) in early 2020 with a thesis on Russian economic modernization in the eighteenth century. **Publications**: 'Der Fall Therese Hirschfeld: Eine Berliner Jüdin als Opfer der nationalsozialistischen Krankenmorde', *Berlin in Geschichte und Gegenwart: Jahrbuch des Landesarchivs Berlin* (2018), pp. 121–35; 'Aryzacja': *Uwagi do kwestii wywłaszczenia wrocławskich Żydów w okresie Trzeciej Rzeszy*, online publication on Wirtualny Sztetl, ed. POLIN Museum of the History of Polish Jews (2018), https://sztetl.org.pl/pl/miejscowosci/w/642-wroclaw/104-teksty-kultury/182310-aryzacja-uwagi-do-kwestii-wywlaszczenia-wroclawskich-zydow-w-okresie-trzeciej-rzeszy.

Alexandra Gittermann works in Hamburg as an independent historian. **Publications**: 'El *Glückshafen* de Johann Gaspar de Thürriegel en el contexto del reclutamiento de colonos por parte de los monarcas europeos después de la Guerra de los Siete Años', *Actas del Congreso Internacional Nuevas Poblaciones de Sierra Morena y Andalucía y otras colonizaciones agrarias en la Europa de la Ilustración* (Jaén, 2018), pp. 637–55; *Die Ökonomisierung des politischen Denkens: Neapel und Spanien im Zeichen der Reformbewegungen des 18. Jahrhunderts unter der Herrschaft Karls III.* (Stuttgart, 2008).

Klemens Kaps is Senior Lecturer at the Institute for Modern and Contemporary History at the Johannes Kepler University Linz. **Publications**: 'Cores and Peripheries Reconsidered: Economic Development, Trade and Cultural Images in the Eighteenth-Century Habsburg Monarchy', *Hungarian Historical Review*

7/2 (2018), pp. 191–221; *Merchants and Trade Networks between the Atlantic and the Mediterranean (1550–1800): Connectors of Commercial Maritime Systems*, co-edited with Manuel Herrero Sánchez (New York, 2017); 'Centers and Peripheries Revisited' (with Andrea Komlosy), *Review Fernand Braudel Center* 36, 3/4 (2013), pp. 237–64.

Josef Köstlbauer is a postdoctoral researcher in the ERC Consolidator Grant project 'German Slavery' at the University of Bremen. **Publications**: 'Validation and the Uniqueness of Historical Events', *Computer Simulation Validation – Fundamental Concepts, Methodological Frameworks, and Philosophical Perspectives*, ed. C. Beisbart and N. Saam (Cham, 2019), pp. 881–97; co-editor of *Weltmaschinen: Digitale Spiele als globalgeschichtliches Phänomen* (Vienna, 2018); co-editor of *Grenzen – Kulturhistorische Annäherungen* (Vienna, 2016).

Anne Sophie Overkamp is a postdoctoral researcher in the project 'Landhäuser im Wandel' at the University of Tübingen. **Publications**: 'A Hinterland to the Slave Trade? Atlantic Connections of the Wupper Valley in the Early Nineteenth Century', *Slavery Hinterland: Transatlantic Slavery and Continental Europe, 1680–1850*, ed. F. Brahm and E. Rosenhaft (Woodbridge, 2016), pp. 161–85; 'Of Tape and Ties: Abraham Frowein from Elberfeld and Atlantic Trade', *Europeans Engaging the Atlantic: Knowledge and Trade, 1500–1800*, ed. S. Lachenicht (Frankfurt/New York/Chicago, 2014) pp. 127–50.

Göran Rydén is Professor in Economic History, based at the Institute for Housing and Urban Research, Uppsala University. **Publications**: *Sweden in the Eighteenth-Century World: Provincial Cosmopolitans* (Farnham, 2013); '"Voyage Iron": An Atlantic Slave Trade Currency, its European Origins, and West African Impact' (with Chris Evans), *Past & Present* 239/1 (2018), pp. 41–70; 'Balancing the Divine with the Private: The Practices of Hushållning in Eighteenth-Century Sweden', *Cameralism in Practice: The Principles of Early Modern State Administration*, ed. Marten Seppel and Keith Tribe (Woodbridge, 2017), pp. 179–201.

Margrit Schulte Beerbühl is Associate Professor of Modern History at Heinrich Heine University, Düsseldorf. **Publications**: *Deutsche Kaufleute in London: Welthandel und Einbürgerung 1660–1818* (Munich, 2007); co-editor of *Dealing with Economic Failure: Between Norm and Practice (15th to 21st Century)* (Frankfurt, 2016); *The Forgotten Majority: German Merchants in London, Naturalization and Global Trade 1660–1815* (New York, 2015).

Anka Steffen is a Ph.D. candidate who worked on the DFG-project, 'The Globalized Periphery: Atlantic Commerce, Socioeconomic and Cultural Change in Central Europe (1680–1850)', at the European University Viadrina in Frankfurt (Oder). She is currently a visiting scholar at the Weatherhead Initiative on Global History at Harvard University, USA. **Publications**: 'Spinning and Weaving for the Slave Trade: Proto-Industry in Eighteenth-Century Silesia' (with Klaus Weber), *Slavery Hinterland: Transatlantic Slavery and Continental Europe, 1680–1850*, ed. F. Brahm and E. Rosenhaft (Woodbridge, 2016), pp. 87–108; 'A Cloth that Binds: New Perspectives on the Eighteenth-Century Prussian Economy', *Slavery & Abolition* (forthcoming, 2021).

Bernhard Struck is Associate Professor of Modern History and founding director of the Institute for Transnational and Spatial History at the University of St Andrews. **Publications**: *Révolution, guerre, interferences 1789–1815* (Paris, 2013); co-editor of the series *Peripherien: Beiträge zur Europäischen und Globalgeschichte* (Cologne/Weimar/Vienna); co-editor of *Grenzräume: Ein europäischer Vergleich vom 18. bis 20. Jahrhundert* (Frankfurt, 2007); *Nicht West – nicht Ost: Frankreich und Polen in der Wahrnehmung deutscher Reisender zwischen 1750 und 1850* (Göttingen, 2006).

David K. Thomson is Assistant Professor of History at Sacred Heart University in Fairfield, Connecticut, USA. **Publications**: 'Financing the War', *The Cambridge History of the American Civil War*, Vol. 2, ed. A. Sheehan-Dean (Cambridge, 2019), pp. 174–92; '"Like a Cord through the Whole Country": Union Bonds and Financial Mobilization for Victory', *The Journal of the Civil War Era* 6/3 (2016), pp. 347–75.

Klaus Weber is Professor of European Economic and Social History at the European University Viadrina in Frankfurt (Oder), and director of the DFG-project, 'The Globalized Periphery'. **Publications**: *Deutsche Kaufleute im Atlantikhandel 1680–1830: Unternehmen und Familien in Hamburg, Cádiz und Bordeaux* (Munich, 2004); *Schwarzes Amerika: Eine Geschichte der Sklaverei* (with Jochen Meissner and Ulrich Mücke) (Munich, 2008); *Jean Potocki (1761–1815): au-delà des frontières entre disciplines et cultures | Jan Potocki (1761–1815): ponad granicami dyscyplin i kultur | Jan Potocki (1761–1815): Grenzgänger zwischen Disziplinen und Kulturen*, co-edited with Erik Martin and Lena Seauve (Berlin, 2019).

Jutta Wimmler is a research group leader at the Bonn Center for Dependency and Slavery Studies. She previously co-directed the DFG-project, 'The Globalized Periphery' at the European University Viadrina in Frankfurt (Oder). **Publications**: 'From Senegal to Augsburg: Gum Arabic and the Central European Textile Industry in the 18th Century', *Textile History* 50/1 (2019), pp. 4–22; *The Sun King's Atlantic: Drugs, Demons and Dyestuffs in the Atlantic World, 1640–1730* (Leiden/Boston, 2017); *Centralized African States in the Transatlantic Slave Trade: The Example of 18th Century Asante and Dahomey* (Graz, 2012).

Acknowledgements

This book concludes the research project, 'The Globalized Periphery: Atlantic Commerce, Socioeconomic and Cultural Change in Central Europe (1680–1850)', generously funded by the German Research Foundation from 2015 to 2019. The idea for this project dates back much further, however. We want to thank Hans Medick and Jürgen Schlumbohm for encouraging Klaus Weber long ago to further investigate the entanglements between the production of commodities in Central Europe and the distant regions of their consumption. For Jutta Wimmler, the credit for strengthening her interest in the subject goes to Renate Pieper, with a previous research project about the role of France and Spain as mediators for the Habsburg Empire's access to the Atlantic World.

We are lucky to have received valuable insights from a great number of excellent scholars. We can mention only a few by name: in alphabetical order, we are indebted to Sven Beckert, Loïc Charles, Tamira Combrink, Guillaume Daudin, José da Silva Horta, Werner Plumpe, Friederike Sattler, Kim Siebenhüner, John Styles, and our colleagues at the Viadrina Center B/ORDERS IN MOTION for critical comments and further encouragement and advice. We also thank the participants of the conference, 'Globalized Peripheries: New Approaches to the Atlantic World, 1680–1850', hosted at the European University Viadrina in Frankfurt (Oder) in July 2018. We could not include all of the papers presented there in the present volume, but we believe that we have all mutually benefited from the discussions.

We thank the team at Boydell & Brewer as well as the anonymous reviewer(s) for backing this book project. Finally, we are grateful for the support of our student assistants Friederike Gehrmann and Felix Töppel in editing the volume.

Abbreviations

ACEB	Admiralitäts- und Convoygeld- Einnahmebücher
AHPC	Archivo Histórico Provincial de Cádiz
ASG	Archivio di Stato di Genova
ASTS	Archivio di Stato di Trieste
BPP	British Parliamentary Papers
CLRO	City of London Record Office
CRS	Cesarea Regia Suprema
DFG	Deutsche Forschungsgemeinschaft (German Research Foundation)
DK StAbt	Diplomatische Korrespondenz Staatenabteilung
ERC	European Research Council
FCA	Frowein Company Archive
FHKA	Finanz- und Hofkammerarchiv
HHStA	Haus-, Hof- und Staatsarchiv (Vienna)
HSP	Historical Society of Pennsylvania
HZW	Historisches Zentrum Wuppertal
NARA	National Archives and Records Administration (Washington, DC)
NARA II	National Archives and Records Administration II (College Park, Maryland)
NHK	Neue Hofkammer
ÖStA	Österreichisches Staatsarchiv (Vienna)
RAC	Royal African Company (in Chapter 3)
RAC	Russian America Company (in Chapter 5)
STRO	Sound Toll Registers Online
TNA	The National Archives (London)
UA	Unity Archives (Herrnhut)

Constructing Atlantic Peripheries:
A Critical View of the Historiography

JUTTA WIMMLER AND KLAUS WEBER

As a field, Atlantic history developed primarily in Anglo-American academia and has consequently produced more information on certain Atlantic regions (and subjects) than on others. The early modern Atlantic World, with its flows of bullion, of free and unfree laborers, of colonial produce and of manufactures from Europe and Asia, with its mercantile networks and rent-seeking capital, has to date been described as a preserve almost entirely of the Western sea-powers. Central and Eastern Europe have been notably absent from the narrative, with few exceptions.[1] The reluctance of the historical profession in these very regions to engage with Atlantic history, and of 'Western' scholars to engage with these more eastern regions, has certainly contributed to this state of affairs. In 2009, when Jack P. Greene and Philip D. Morgan published their still very readable critical appraisal of the field of Atlantic history, hardly anyone would have regarded Central and Eastern European history as an area of study for the Atlantic historian. In their introduction, they proclaimed that 'developments in Central and Eastern Europe ... may well be less tightly linked to those in the Atlantic and better approached through other perspectives'.[2] The notion that this part of Europe was not an integral part of the early modern Atlantic economy continues to be prominent in the field to this day.[3]

---

1 For example, R. R. Palmer, *The Age of the Democratic Revolution*, 2 vols (Princeton, 1959 and 1964).
2 P. D. Morgan and J. P. Greene, 'Introduction: The Present State of Atlantic History', *Atlantic History: A Critical Appraisal*, ed. J. P. Greene and P. D. Morgan (Oxford, 2009), pp. 3–34, here p. 9.
3 For example, D. Armitage, 'The Atlantic Ocean', *Oceanic Histories*, ed. D. Armitage, A. Bashford and S. Sivasundaram (Cambridge, 2018), pp. 85–110; N. Canny and P. Morgan, eds, *The Oxford Handbook of the Atlantic World 1450–1850* (Oxford, 2012).

This attitude is not just characteristic of Anglophone scholarship. Already in 1994, Hans-Heinrich Nolte proclaimed that German scholarship was too 'self-centered' to be occupied with such global narratives.[4] In 2002, Sebastian Conrad remarked that German historiography had hardly been touched by globalization and showed a continuing tendency to write history from the perspective of the nation. This tendency, he continued, had in fact intensified after 1989.[5] This is all the more curious, considering that contemporaries in past centuries were perfectly aware of Central and Eastern Europe's dense entanglements with the Atlantic World. For Abbé Raynal (1713–1796), editor of the *Histoire des deux Indes* (1770), it was evident that the maritime expansion not only stimulated the economies of European sea-powers, but that more continental territories like those of Prussia and even Russia were also closely involved.[6] For the German historian Arnold H. L. Heeren (1760–1842), the history of Europe as a whole could only be understood against the background of its colonial dimension, as the title of his *Geschichte des Europäischen Staatensystems und seiner Colonien* (1809) illustrates. Approaches like that of Heeren – whose works were translated into various European languages shortly after publication – were forgotten in the course of the nineteenth and twentieth centuries.[7] The tradition of *Universalgeschichte* that had also considered these global dimensions, and that was particularly strong in Germany, experienced a brief revival during the 1950s and 1960s, but was then discredited as too Eurocentric and teleological.[8] At the same time, attempts at writing global

4   H.-H. Nolte, 'Zur Rezeption des Weltsystemkonzepts in Deutschland', *Comparativ* 5 (1994), pp. 91–100, here p. 92.

5   S. Conrad, 'Doppelte Marginalisierung: Plädoyer für eine transnationale Perspektive auf die deutsche Geschichte', *Geschichte und Gesellschaft* 28 (2002), pp. 145–69, here p. 145.

6   G. T. Raynal, ed., *Histoire Philosophique et Politique des tablissements et du Commerce des Européens dans les Deux Indes* (Amsterdam, 1770), Vol. 2, Book 5. More examples of eighteenth- and early nineteenth-century scholars who realized these connections are Alexander von Humboldt (1769–1859) and Samuel Buchholtz (1717–1774), as well as the writers Heinrich von Kleist (1777–1811) and Johann Heinrich Daniel Zschokke (1771–1848).

7   A. Hermann and L. Heeren, *Handbuch der Geschichte des Europäischen Staatensystems und seiner Colonien* (Göttingen, 1809). [English edition: *A Manual of the History of the Political System of Europe and its Colonies: From its Formation at the Close of the Fifteenth Century to its Re-establishment upon the Fall of Napoleon* (Oxford, 1834).] For a discussion of Heeren's approach, see G. T. Molin, 'Internationale Beziehungen als Gegenstand der deutschen Neuzeit-Historiographie seit dem 18. Jahrhundert: Eine Traditionskritik in Grundzügen und Beispielen', *Internationale Geschichte: Themen – Ergebnisse – Aussichten*, ed. W. Loth and J. Osterhammel (Munich/Oldenburg, 2000), pp. 3–30, here pp. 24ff.

8   See e.g. A. Landwehr, *Die anwesende Abwesenheit der Vergangenheit: Essay zur Geschichtstheorie* (Frankfurt, 2016), pp. 44f; W. Hardtwig and P. Müller, eds, *Die Vergangenheit der Weltgeschichte: Universalhistorisches Denken in Berlin 1800–1933* (Göttingen, 2010); M. Middell and K. Naumann, 'The Writing of World History in Europe from the Middle of the Nineteenth Century to the Present: Conceptual Renewal and Challenge to National Histories', *Transnational Challenges to National History Writing*, ed. M. Middell and L. Roura (Basingstoke, 2013), pp. 54–139.

histories in the Soviet Bloc were either rejected for their ideological baggage or simply went unnoticed in Western scholarship. Examples are the works of the Polish historian Marian Małowist (1909–1988), the Czech Miroslav Hroch (*1932), or the Hungarian Zsigmond Pál Pach (1919–2001) in the 1960s and 1970s, each of whom also published in English and German.[9] After the fall of the Iron Curtain, Central and Eastern Europe were occupied with very different historiographical problems that seemed much more pressing than an attempt at assessing the role of these regions in the early modern world-economy.

Increasing numbers of researchers (especially in Germany, Austria and Switzerland) now tackle the question as to how the territories of the Holy Roman Empire (and beyond) engaged with Africa, America and Asia during the early modern period.[10] Our own research project, 'The Globalized Periphery: Atlantic Commerce, Socio-Economic and Cultural Change in Central Europe 1680–1850', funded by the German Research Foundation (DFG) from 2015 to 2018, understood itself as a part of these broader efforts. The contributions to this volume originated with this project's concluding conference, entitled 'Globalized Peripheries: New Approaches to the Atlantic World 1680–1850'.

The chapters of this book look at the trading practices and networks of merchants established in Central and Eastern Europe, investigate commodity flows between these regions and the Atlantic World, and explore the production of export commodities, migration back and forth, and financial exchanges in this space. The book's title – *Globalized Peripheries* – is intentionally provoking: the case studies presented here do not intend to introduce the new analytical category of the 'globalized periphery', to be distinguished from the

---

9   J. Batou and H. Szlajfer, eds, *Western Europe, Eastern Europe and World Development, 13th–18th Centuries: Collection of Essays of Marian Małowist* (Leiden, 2009); M. Hroch, 'Die Rolle des zentraleuropäischen Handels im Ausgleich der Handelsbilanz zwischen Ost- und Westeuropa 1550–1650', *Der Außenhandel Ostmitteleuropas 1450–1650*, ed. I. Bog (Cologne/Vienna, 1971), pp. 1–27; Zsigmond Pál Pach, 'The East-Central European Aspect of the Overseas Discoveries and Colonization', *The European Discovery of the World and its Economic Effects on Pre-Industrial Society, 1500–1800: Papers of the Tenth International Economic History Congress*, ed. H. Pohl (Stuttgart, 1990), pp. 178–92.
10   See e.g. S. Lachenicht, ed., *Europeans Engaging the Atlantic: Knowledge and Trade 1500–1800* (Frankfurt/New York, 2014); F. Brahm and E. Rosenhaft, eds, *Slavery Hinterland: Transatlantic Slavery and Continental Europe, 1680–1850* (Woodbridge, 2016). A recent issue of the journal *Atlantic Studies* (No. 14/4, 2017) was entitled 'German Entanglements in Transatlantic Slavery'; the ERC-funded project 'The Holy Roman Empire of the German Nation and its Slaves' at the University of Bremen is currently planning a publication. A research project directed by Roberto Zaugg (Zurich) entitled 'Atlantic Italies: Economic and Cultural Entanglements (15th–19th Centuries)' is being funded by the Swiss National Science Foundation from 2018 to 2022. For the encounter with Asia, see J. Osterhammel, *Unfabling the East: The Enlightenment's Encounter with Asia* (Princeton, 2018); original German edition: *Die Entzauberung Asiens: Europa und die asiatischen Reiche im 18. Jahrhundert* (Munich, 1998).

'non-globalized periphery'.[11] Instead, the book aims to show, on the basis of empirical findings, that the historiography of the Atlantic World has created a misleading image of apparent 'centers' and 'peripheries' of the early modern world-economy that should be called into question.

Central and Eastern Europe in Atlantic and global history

In 2014, Martin Aust and Julia Obertreis took the observation that Eastern Europe had been marginalized in global history as a starting point for their edited collection – which, however, focused on the nineteenth and twentieth centuries, typically the subject of global history in German academia.[12] Indeed, introductions to global history (especially in the English language) do not usually refer to Central and Eastern Europe at all.[13] Katja Naumann has pointed to the connection between the rise of world and global history and the neglect of Central and Eastern Europe in this context. The antidote to Eurocentric historiography was seen in increasing the study of non-European histories and cultures, which in turn led to a continued prominence of Western Europe in the narrative, while Central and Eastern Europe remained outside the field's radar.[14] Her plea is to integrate Eastern Europe into global history, by putting processes in this region in the relevant context and analyzing the nature of the global from this perspective (instead of moving the other way around and imposing the existing categories and narratives of global history on Eastern Europe).[15] The same appeal can and should be made for Atlantic history: instead of simply writing Central and Eastern Europe into the existing narratives, we should investigate if and how regional developments had global dimensions, and how they in turn affected this global context.

Of course, the terms 'Central Europe' and 'Eastern Europe' are ambivalent, and they lack clear-cut boundaries. In one single book, Immanuel Wallerstein considered Bohemia and Silesia as parts of Central Europe in one instance, and

11   In Wallerstein's understanding, a 'non-globalized periphery' is utterly impossible, because all peripheries are intertwined with the globalizing 'core'.
12   M. Aust and J. Obertreis, 'Einleitung', *Osteuropäische Geschichte und Globalgeschichte*, ed. M. Aust and J. Obertreis (Stuttgart, 2014), pp. 7–23, here p. 8.
13   For example, M. Berg, ed., *Writing the History of the Global: Challenges for the 21st Century* (Oxford, 2013). The tendency is somewhat different in transnational history, which often figures as a synonym for global history – as A.-C. Knudsen and K. Gram-Skjoldager have pointed out. This field, however, also has a stronger tradition in the writing of nineteenth- and twentieth-century history. A.-C. Knudsen and K. Gram-Skjoldager, 'Historiography and Narration in Transnational History', *Journal of Global History* 9 (2014), pp. 143–61, here p. 147.
14   K. Naumann, 'Osteuropäische Geschichte und Globalgeschichte: Ein Kommentar', *Osteuropäische Geschichte und Globalgeschichte*, ed. Aust and Obertreis, pp. 317–30, here pp. 319f.
15   Naumann, 'Osteuropäische Geschichte', p. 321.

as parts of Eastern Europe in another.[16] As Marcin Moskalewicz and Wojciech Przybylski have recently pointed out, the ambivalence of the term 'Central Europe' stems from the fact that it not only connotes a geographic region, but an idea.[17] This idea was initially connected to politics, dominance, and the Cold War divide. During the Cold War, 'Eastern Europe' was a term usually employed in the West to refer to the Soviet satellite states; but afterwards, this space was reconceptualized as 'Central Europe' ('Mitteleuropa'), indicating a position between West and East. Today, many Germans and Austrians see themselves as 'Central European', but they may be perceived as 'Western' in Poland or Hungary (who see themselves as 'Central') – in turn perceived as 'Eastern' by their neighbors to the west.[18] Then, of course, there is the curious term 'East-Central Europe' ('Ostmitteleuropa'), which appeared in the 1980s and hardly makes the issue of definition easier.[19] For our purposes, we can nicely circumvent the issue of definition: we roughly understand Central and Eastern Europe as those regions stretching from the German-speaking lands to the European provinces of the Russian Empire. What all of them have in common is that they have been neglected by the scholarship of European expansion, which has emphasized the maritime powers along Europe's Atlantic shoreline.

This emphasis dates back to stereotypes of an Enlightenment that discursively constructed Eastern Europe as a 'demi-orientalized Other'.[20] As described by Larry Wolff, this discourse turned Eastern Europe into a region between the Orient and the Occident and was firmly established by the nineteenth century. Wolff also pointed out that Immanuel Wallerstein's construction of Eastern Europe as a periphery depending on the core region of his Modern World-System

16   I. Wallerstein, *The Modern World-System, Vol. 1: Capitalist Agriculture and the Origins of the European World-Economy in the Sixteenth Century* (New York/London, 1974), pp. 94, 307.

17   M. Moskalewicz and W. Przybylski, 'Making Sense of Central Europe: Political Concepts of the Region', *Understanding Central Europe*, ed. M. Moskalewicz and W. Przybylski (New York, 2018), pp. 1–22, here p. 1.

18   See in detail L. R. Johnson, *Central Europe: Enemies, Neighbors, Friends* (Oxford/New York, 2002), pp. 6–9; T. Serrier, 'Veröstlichung der Barbaren: Die symbolische Verwerfung des Anderen hinter Rhein und Oder im deutsch-französischen und deutsch-polnischen Kontext', *Europa Vertikal: Zur Ost-West-Gliederung im 19. und 20. Jahrhundert*, ed. R. Aldenhoff-Hübinger, C. Gouseff and T. Serrier (Göttingen, 2016), pp. 102–20.

19   For the discussion of the terms in the historiography of the 1980s, see e.g. J. Szücs, *Die drei historischen Regionen Europas: Mit einem Vorwort von Fernand Braudel* (Frankfurt, 1994; Hungarian original published in 1983); A. Mczak, H. Samsonowicz and P. Burke, eds, *East-Central Europe in Transition: From the Fourteenth to the Seventeenth Century* (Cambridge, 1985); G. Dalos, I. Eörsi et al., *Die andere Hälfte Europas* (Berlin, 1985); K. Schlögel, *Die Mitte liegt ostwärts: Die Deutschen, der verlorene Osten und Mitteleuropa* (Berlin, 1986).

20   L. Wolff, *Inventing Eastern Europe: The Map of Civilization on the Mind of the Enlightenment* (Stanford, 1994), pp. 4ff. For a deeper analysis of this discourse's legacy in the twentieth and twenty-first centuries, see T. Zarycki, *Ideologies of Eastness in Central and Eastern Europe* (London/New York, 2014) (who, however, employs Wallerstein very uncritically alongside his discursive approach).

was a projection of this rather modern idea of Eastern Europe into earlier times. Scholars have criticized Wolff on similar grounds, pointing out that he superimposed the twentieth-century spatial concept of 'Eastern Europe' on to his eighteenth-century sources, which do not use the term at all.[21] Arguably, the 'orientalization' of Europe's East only became possible after such a spatial concept had been developed. Until well into the eighteenth century, many of the regions we are concerned with in this book (notably the German lands east of the Elbe River, Poland and Russia, but also Scandinavia) were commonly conceptualized as the 'North'. Only after the Congress of Vienna (1815) did a vertical line – running roughly from Turku on the Eastern Baltic to Trieste on the Adriatic Sea and separating East from West – replace previously dominant horizontal lines, partitioning Europe into 'North' and 'South' (or even using a tripartite model).[22]

As scholars have highlighted, the idea of Eastern European backwardness was also taken over by the 'peripheralized' themselves, especially by intellectuals in the East.[23] Indeed, if one peruses library catalogues, one finds that the term 'periphery' overwhelmingly appears in the titles of books concerned with Central and Eastern Europe, followed by Africa, Asia and Latin America. It is thus probably not a coincidence, as Anna Veronika Wendland has noted, that the field of Eastern European history has dominated discussions about peripheries within Europe.[24] Even more interesting is the fact that large numbers of books carrying the term 'periphery' in their title do not define this term in any way – it is assumed that the status of these regions as 'peripheral' is a given.[25] This kind of 'self-peripheralization' is a phenomenon typically ascribed to formerly colonized peoples, and it has increasingly been reinterpreted as a source of agency for the colonized, who use their 'peripheral' status rhetorically to position themselves against a political 'center'. In a similar manner, scholars of Central and Eastern Europe are appropriating the label 'periphery' for the regions they are studying, sometimes reaffirming the accuracy of the label, but increasingly in order to challenge it.

21   F. B. Schenk, 'Lemberg and Wolff Revisited: Zur Entstehung und Struktur des Konzepts "Osteuropa" seit dem späten 18. Jahrhundert', *Europa Vertikal*, ed. Aldenhoff-Hübinger, Gouseff and Serrier, pp. 43–62, here p. 43.
22   Schenk, 'Lemberg and Wolff', p. 48.
23   See e.g. E. Haid, S. Weismann and B. Wöller, 'Einleitung', *Galizien: Peripherie der Moderne – Moderne der Peripherie?*, ed. E. Haid, S. Weismann and B. Wöller (Marburg, 2013), pp. 1–10, here p. 3.
24   See A. V. Wendland, 'Randgeschichten? Osteuropäische Perspektiven auf Kulturtransfer und Verflechtungsgeschichte', *Osteuropa* 58/3 (2008), pp. 95–116, here p. 100.
25   For example, I. T. Berend, *Central and Eastern Europe 1944–1993: Detour from the Periphery to the Periphery* (Cambridge, 1996); G. Hausmann, *Universität und städtische Gesellschaft in Odessa, 1865–1917: Soziale und nationale Selbstorganisation an der Peripherie des Zarenreiches* (Stuttgart, 1998); I. Röskau-Rydel, *Kultur an der Peripherie des Habsburger Reiches: Die Geschichte des Bildungswesens und der kulturellen Einrichtungen in Lemberg von 1772 bis 1848* (Wiesbaden, 1993).

While the case studies presented in this book are thus relevant for historiographies of East and Central Europe, they can also prove fruitful for the field of Atlantic history. For one thing, the question whether our understanding of Central and Eastern European history can benefit from a specifically Atlantic (instead of a global) perspective can have repercussions for the debate about the relationship between Atlantic history and global history.[26] Is Atlantic history a sensible perspective only for an analysis that focuses, in one way or another, on maritime powers whose institutional settings differentiated between Atlantic and Indian Ocean trade (notably through the East and West India Companies)? Do we then, as Morgan and Greene suggested, indeed need a different framework when studying (global) actors and trade flows in Silesia or Westphalia? Or does this have little to do with the region one is studying, but more with the topic? More importantly, the common equation of north-western European historical experience with the development of modernity is arguably a constitutive element of Atlantic history. This narrative was not just built on the 'peripherialization' of the African, American or Asian experience that has increasingly been called into question by Atlantic and global history, but also builds on the 'backwardness-narrative' employed not only for certain parts of Europe (including Central, Eastern and southern Europe), but also for rural regions in its west and north.[27] By challenging this narrative, the contributions in this book also challenge the fields of Atlantic and global history to rethink some of their foundations.

Beyond Wallerstein

Although we have seen that the peripherialization of Central and Eastern Europe dates back much longer, we cannot omit the impact of Immanuel Wallerstein's concept of the Modern World-System on the definition of the term 'periphery', and especially on the identification of Central and Eastern Europe as 'peripheries' of his Modern World-System. Scholars have since identified this as one of the major empirical problems in the model: Wallerstein is inconsistent when it comes to identifying specific regions as core, periphery and semi-periphery, and his concept of the 'strong state' that allegedly characterizes core regions is ill defined.[28] Scholars often use the examples of Prussia and the Habsburg

26   For example, N. Canny, 'Atlantic History and Global History', *Atlantic History*, ed. Greene and Morgan, pp. 317–36.

27   For the place of Central and Eastern Europe within the 'narrative of modernity', see also C. Dejung and M. Lengwiler, 'Einleitung', *Ränder der Moderne: Neue Perspektiven auf die Europäische Geschichte (1800–1930)*, ed. C. Dejung and M. Lengwiler (Cologne/Weimar/Vienna, 2016), pp. 7–35, here pp. 18f, 21ff.

28   For a strong critique, see e.g. P. Imbusch, *'Das moderne Weltsystem': Eine Kritik der Weltsystemtheorie Immanuel Wallersteins* (Marburg, 1990), pp. 51f.

monarchy to illustrate weaknesses in his concept.[29] Peter Imbusch has also pointed out that Wallerstein attributes peripheral status to all regions east of the Elbe River as a matter of fact, while it is entirely unclear to what category the regions west of the Elbe (amongst them many other German states) belong.[30] Charles Tilly coined his own set of categories, but in the outcome there is some overlap with Wallerstein's conclusions: Tilly saw Prussia (but also the interior provinces of Spain) as an example of the 'coercion-intensive' path of state-building, and Great Britain and the Netherlands as examples of the 'capital-intensive' path.[31] This division of the German lands along the Elbe is a classic modern trope,[32] and it ignores the economically important Prussian exclaves in Westphalia and in the Rhineland.

This is not the place to delve into an in-depth critique of Wallerstein's concept of the Modern World-System. Indeed, confirming or disproving this model (let alone the approach of world-systems analysis) is not the aim of the book. Instead, our point is this: Wallerstein of necessity draws on the existing historiographical narrative. He read the works available to him, both in terms of the languages he could read and in terms of access. Although the important Polish economic historian Marian Małowist figures as prominently in Wallerstein's reading as Fernand Braudel or Michel Morineau, his conclusions do not always conform to Małowist's more nuanced findings. As noted, such a lack of a proper inclusion of scholarship concerned with early modern Central and Eastern Europe into Wallerstein's model has been one of the major points of criticism since the 1970s.[33] Hermann Kellenbenz, for example, stressed the connection between Wallerstein's treatment of these regions and his failure to consider developments in metal (and linen) production, in which these regions played a major role.[34]

Thereafter, the history of European expansion and of the transatlantic slave trade – in short, Atlantic and global history – continued to be dominated by a north-west European (and mostly a North Atlantic) perspective. In part, this also has to do with a lack of interest in these issues within proper Central and Eastern European scholarship. We have already mentioned the observations Hans-Heinrich Nolte and Sebastian Conrad made in 1994 and 2002 respectively.[35] Three years later, Matthias Middell could still make a similar

---

29 For example, Imbusch, 'Das moderne Weltsystem', pp. 54f.
30 See Imbusch, 'Das moderne Weltsystem', p. 65.
31 C. Tilly, European Revolutions 1492–1992 (Cambridge, 1993).
32 See e.g. Aldenhoff-Hübinger et al., Europa Vertikal.
33 H. Kellenbenz, 'Review of Immanuel Wallerstein: The Modern World-System, Vol. 1', Journal of Modern History 48/4 (1976), pp. 685–92; H.-H. Nolte, 'The Position of Eastern Europe in the International System in Early Modern Times', Review 4/1 (1982), pp. 25–84; Nolte, 'Zur Rezeption des Weltsystemkonzepts'.
34 Kellenbenz, 'Review', p. 692.
35 Nolte, 'Zur Rezeption des Weltsystemkonzepts', p. 92; Conrad, 'Doppelte Marginalisierung'.

point when he diplomatically suggested that Central and Eastern European historiographies simply faced other problems after 1989, and thus focused on rediscovering national histories after the end of the Soviet Union and of the dogmatic Marxist historical narratives imposed on its satellites.[36]

Researchers in Western Germany who had investigated proto-industries (notably Peter Kriedte, Hans Medick and Jürgen Schlumbohm) and who could have linked Central European metal and linen production with wider Atlantic regions were reluctant to apply spatial categories, because the German term 'Raum' had been thoroughly contaminated by Nazi ideology. Many of the more eastern regions had been prominent topics of 'Ostforschung', a strand of research established during the 1920s and further developed between 1933 and 1945 for a revisionist approach to the history of Germany's eastern border-lands. Hermann Aubin, one of its most prominent protagonists, his brother Gustav Aubin, and Arno Kunze had carried out pioneer studies on the cottage industries in these lands, but for Kriedte and his colleagues it was difficult to tie in with their work.[37] Considering these historiographical imbalances, we urge that more empirical work on the position of Central and Eastern Europe in the early modern world needs to be done.

If the 'self-centered' nature of Central and Eastern European history – its proclivity towards national history – is a consequence of its twentieth-century experiences, a similar conclusion may be drawn regarding Wallerstein's theories. It is not a stretch to understand his Modern World-System as a narrative intended for his own present: a narrative that sympathized with the suppressed people of his day and tried to advocate for them by explaining their position historically, simultaneously attacking modernization and development theories dominant at the time. Andreas Leutzsch has argued that Wallerstein's (as well as Braudel's) theories originated in a 'crisis of the center', and he emphasized the importance of Wallerstein's own experiences in Africa in the wake of decol-onization for his understanding of the Modern World-System.[38] Others have pointed out that Wallerstein's categories of core, semi-periphery and periphery fulfill the same function as (and are essentially substitutes for) categories of

36 M. Middell, 'Universalgeschichte, Weltgeschichte, Globalgeschichte, Geschichte der Globalisierung – ein Streit um Worte?', *Globalisierung und Globalgeschichte*, ed. M. Grandner, D. Rothermund and W. Schwentker (Vienna, 2005), pp. 60–82, here p. 63.
37 P. Kriedte, H. Medick and J. Schlumbohm, *Industrialization before Industrialization: Rural Industry in the Genesis of Capitalism* (Cambridge/Paris, 1981); M. Raeff, 'Some Observations on the Work of Hermann Aubin', *Paths of Continuity: Central European Historiography from the 1930s to the 1950s*, ed. H. Lehmann and J. Van Hörn Melton (Cambridge, 1994), pp. 239–49; M. Burleigh, *Germany Turns Eastwards: A Study of Ostforschung in the Third Reich* (Cambridge/New York, 1988).
38 A. Leutzsch, *Geschichte der Globalisierung als globalisierte Geschichte: Die historische Konstruktion der Weltgesellschaft bei Rosenstock-Huessy und Braudel* (Frankfurt/New York, 2009), pp. 227f.

class: upper, middle and lower class.[39] Social stratification became spatial stratification in Wallerstein's model, which corresponds to a growing awareness of
the forces of globalization, even before this category entered historiographical
discourse in the early 1990s.

'"Truth" changes because society changes,' wrote Wallerstein in the introduction to the first volume of *The Modern World-System*: 'everything is
contemporaneous, even that which is past.'[40] Indeed, Wallerstein was very aware
of his own position as a researcher, and conceded that his theories may prove
insufficient in a future setting – a fact not often acknowledged in scholarship.
We trust we are following in his spirit, when questioning his own narrative.
And what is true for Wallerstein is also true for us. Most of us write from a
continental European perspective that witnesses a continuing East-West (and
North-South) divide within the European Union, where the North and West are
imagined as 'advanced' and 'modern', while the South and East are considered
'underdeveloped' and sometimes even 'anti-modern'.[41] The dominant historical
narrative, we claim, legitimizes these notions and contributes to the idea of
Western 'superiority' and 'development' over the backwardness of the East
(in keeping with the narrative established during the Enlightenment). Central
Europe – and Germany in particular – occupies an ambivalent position, both
in the historical narrative and in the current socio-political landscape, with
Germany having its own East-West divide that 'peripherializes' those parts of
the country previously forming the GDR.

This book may also be understood critically as taking part in a discursive
shift that pushes the Other further to the east by extending the borders of
Europe to include EU countries like Germany, Austria and Poland in the overall
historical narrative of European modernity.[42] While this is not our intention
(and we would caution the reader against drawing such conclusions), this
example illustrates why we maintain with Wallerstein that the past is indeed
contemporaneous – our own time requires us to adjust our historical narratives
and also influences the way we write history. That is not to say, however, that
the historical narrative is a work of fiction. It just means that the questions we
ask about the past – the things we consider 'relevant' – are influenced by the
time in which we ask them.[43] By unearthing and interpreting previously ignored
sources and questioning existing narratives, we want to exemplify what Achim

39   See e.g. Imbusch, '*Das moderne Weltsystem*', pp. 64f; also acknowledged by Wallerstein in
his paper, 'Hold the Tiller Firm: On Method and the Unit of Analysis', *The Essential Wallerstein*
(New York, 2000), pp. 149–59.
40   Wallerstein, *Modern World-System*, Vol. 1, p. 9.
41   For the prevalence of these stereotypes among the bureaucrats of the European Union, see
P. Lewicki, *EU-Space and the Euroclass: Modernity, Nationality and Lifestyle among Eurocrats
in Brussels* (Bielefeld, 2017).
42   For this conceptual shift, see Moskalewicz and Przybylski, 'Making Sense', p. 4.
43   See also Landwehr, *Die anwesende Abwesenheit*, pp. 151ff.

Landwehr calls 'forgotten histories' – stories that could have been told but have previously not been found useful for the dominant narrative.[44] By changing perspective in this way, we intend not only to contribute to but also to challenge some assumptions about both the past and the present. Currently, scholars are discovering a great many such 'forgotten histories' – blind spots, if you will – in existing scholarship, and indeed quite a few mistakes. The scholars contributing to this book all identified one or the other such lacunae.

Periphery and dependence

In his book about the European Renaissance, Peter Burke explains his decision to use the subtitle 'Centers and Peripheries' in a way that approaches our understanding of the terms. The book, Burke explains, started with his intention to include peripheral regions in the narrative, acknowledging that the location of such peripheral regions always depends on time and context (e.g. the scientific discipline or the art style under discussion). The goal of such an approach is essentially to question our current narrative of the Renaissance; by including references to Sweden, Poland or Portugal, as well as to Asian or African art, we can come to a fuller understanding of styles that the cultural center would have classified as deviations from a presumed original or complete style. Consequently, Burke also urges us to consider where and how contemporaries located the cultural center in their own time, and which regions they perceived as being far removed from this cultural center.[45]

While employing the terminology of hegemonic discourse to challenge that discourse certainly has merit, it also seems necessary to go beyond the use of the term 'periphery' as a *Kampfbegriff* with a postcolonial touch. In order to illustrate that the regions and peoples we are studying are not in fact 'peripheral' to the early modern world-economy, the term has to be defined in a way that makes it useful for an empirical case study. In most definitions of the term, dependence plays a major role – especially (but not exclusively) if they invoke Wallerstein. The periphery is that which is 'weak' and is thus influenced by a 'core'. The core, in turn, profits from its dominance of the periphery, making the latter attractive and contested.[46]

This kind of definition does not necessarily have to be used in the way ascribed to it by development theory. Since the point of our endeavor is to question the narrative of 'development' and 'backwardness', such an approach

---

44   Ibid., p. 234.

45   P. Burke, *Die europäische Renaissance: Zentren und Peripherien* (Munich, 1998), p. 27. [English edition: *The European Renaissance: Centres and Peripheries* (1998)].

46   For example, M.-L. Recker, ed., *Von der Konkurrenz zur Rivalität: Das britisch-deutsche Verhältnis in den Ländern der europäischen Peripherie 1919–1939* (Stuttgart, 1986), pp. 1f.

would be less than fruitful in our case (which is why we opted against the more loaded term 'dependency' and in favor of 'dependence'). It may nevertheless be prudent to ask ourselves, in each individual case study: who depends on whom for what – and how? If the Western European sea-powers needed reasonably priced high-quality products in order to trade on the West African coast, do they depend less on the Central and Eastern European producers than these producers depend on them? If both sides depend on each other, then what justifies describing one as the center and the other as the periphery? This calls into question the added value of an approach that works with simple oppositions such as the core-periphery binary. Pointing out the major contribution of postcolonial theories that strive to dissolve such simple dichotomies, Klemens Kaps and Andrea Komlosy write: 'the postcolonial approach emphasizes the relationship between centers and peripheries as one of entangled interaction, which deactivates the dual scheme'.[47] The chapters of this book confirm that we need to question established tendencies of thinking in such dichotomies.

To offer a few illustrative examples: if producers of household knives, cutlasses and sabers from the Rhenish town of Solingen, or of brassware from Nuremberg, had created markets for their products on the Iberian peninsula and in Africa from the late medieval period,[48] and if they managed to expand the distribution of their products into the New World and to maintain these new markets at least through the nineteenth century, are these producers to be considered actors of the semi-periphery, or of the core? If linen from Silesia (a province that Wallerstein saw as a periphery until its conquest by Prussia) had become indispensable as a barter commodity on African coasts and as work-wear on plantations all over the Americas, are the linen merchants (who maintained a truly global correspondence, but also oversaw rural spinning and weaving on their estates) really peripheral? And how about merchants from linen-producing Westphalia or from Bremen or Hamburg, who migrated to London and, in the course of the eighteenth century, rose to become leading financiers in the City of London and directors of the East India Company?[49]

47   K. Kaps and A. Komlosy, 'Centers and Peripheries Revisited: Polycentric Connections or Entangled Hierarchies?', *Review* 3/4 (2013), pp. 237–64, here p. 254.
48   M. Małowist, 'The Foundations of European Expansion in Africa in the 16th Century: Europe, Maghreb, and Western Sudan', *Western Europe, Eastern Europe and World Development, 13th–18th Centuries: Collection of Essays of Marian Małowist*, ed. J. Batou and H. Szlajfer (Leiden, 2009), pp. 339–69; M. Małowist, 'Portuguese Expansion in Africa and European Economy at the Turn of the 15th Century', ibid., pp. 373–93.
49   Wallerstein, *Modern World-System*, Vol. 1, p. 94; A. Steffen and K. Weber, 'Spinning and Weaving for the Slave Trade: Proto-Industry in Eighteenth-Century Silesia', *Slavery Hinterland*, ed. Brahm and Rosenhaft, pp. 87–107. M. Schulte Beerbühl and K. Weber, 'From Westphalia to the Caribbean: Networks of German Textile Merchants in the Eighteenth Century', *Cosmopolitan Networks in Commerce and Society 1660–1914*, ed. A. Gestrich and M. Schulte Beerbühl (London, 2011), pp. 53–98.

According to Wallerstein, incorporating a previously external region 'into the orbit of the world-economy ... involves "hooking" the zone into' it, 'in such a way that it virtually can no longer escape'. The subsequent process of 'peripheralization' is 'referred to as the deepening of capitalist development'.[50] Wallerstein depicted these regions as prey, falling into the hands of the powers at the core. Being a passive actor fits well with the demi-orientalizing image of Eastern Europe described by Larry Wolff, but it does not fit with the observation that certain protagonists from the external, the peripheral and the semi-peripheral sphere made efforts themselves to have their regions incorporated into this world-economy – with some of them eventually becoming major players in the core.

'Dependence' as a guideline may help us to see these entanglements more clearly, especially if we distinguish between different kinds of actors and detach the term from the purely spatial. Individual actors in a given region can have a very strong position towards actors located in other (seemingly less peripheral) regions, as well as towards other actors in their own region. Similarly, some actors may depend more strongly on other local actors (who in turn were inter-mediating with the wider world) than on global actors at a larger distance. Global developments may also affect local processes without anyone immediately noticing – and they may have unintentional effects. It can easily be the other way around as well. As we shall see, the individual case studies make it difficult to confirm the location of a clear 'core' and 'periphery' of the early modern world-economy as seen through the lens of dependence.

We hope that the book as a whole, with authors from Britain and North America looking east, and with authors from Central Europe looking west, will offer a nuanced picture. The view from the 'periphery' or 'semi-periphery' certainly offers new insights, because this view is less tainted by the existing historiography on the Atlantic World – which to a wide extent is national historiography. An outstanding feature and achievement of Wallerstein's work is that it offers an analysis of the world-economy explicitly in its phase before the emergence of the nation state. Looking at this economy through the lens of quantitative and qualitative source material from its eastern '(semi-)peripheries' perfectly corresponds with this approach. Hamburg's seventeenth- and eighteenth-century customs records, for example, were produced in a polit-ically weak but economically important neutral city-state, which aimed at maintaining trade with as many partners as possible. Possibly even more than material from Britain, France, the Iberian Peninsula or the Netherlands, these records reflect the shifts within the commodity flows between the Atlantic basin and Central Europe, in particular during wartime and blockades.[51] This also

50   I. Wallerstein, *The Modern World-System, Vol. 3: The Second Great Expansion of the Capitalist World-Economy, 1730–1840s* (San Diego, 1989), p. 130.
51   F. Hatje, 'Libertät, Neutralität und Commercium: Zu den politischen Voraussetzungen für Hamburgs Handel', *Hamburger Wirtschafts-Chronik* 7 (2007/08), pp. 213–47; K. Weber, 'Les

applies to the Danish Sound Toll Registers, which reflect most of the commerce between the Atlantic basin and the commercially and strategically important Baltic regions. In a similar way, the networks of merchants from Central Europe were probably more mobile and cosmopolitan than those from the Western European 'core'. The former had no colonial empire of their own, and therefore penetrated the commercial systems of the latter.

The transnational character of these entrepreneurs, of their commercial networks, and of the commodity chains and commodity flows they controlled resembles those of the transnational protagonists in the present day's globalized world. Saskia Sassen describes how, in the shift to an increasingly 'borderless world', established regimes are complemented with new regimes which allow for certain flows of commodities and capital, immigration of privileged and exclusion of non-privileged individuals, extraterritorial jurisdiction (albeit for mercantile issues only), et cetera. It is not always clear whether this 'constitutes a new form of state authority', or rather a 'private authority [that] replaces established forms of state authority'. In any case, 'these entrees have given rise to a proliferation of specialized, semi-autonomous regulatory agencies and the specialized cross-border networks they create, which are taking over fictions once enclosed within national legal frameworks'.[52] David Hancock noted similar parallels between current and early modern trade networks, both characterized by a remarkable 'openness and porousness'.[53] Seen from this perspective, developments of the twenty-first century may have more in common with early modern frameworks than one might assume.

The contributions in this book

The book consists of several case studies, moving from the north (Prussia, the Baltic, Hamburg) to the south (Trieste) to the center (Westphalia and Saxony) and across the Atlantic Ocean (North America). The case studies begin with Bernhard Struck's question in Chapter 2, asking why the partition of Poland-Lithuania happened in 1772. He provides the provocative answer that this fundamental event in Polish history had a decidedly global dimension. Struck illustrates that the crisis years between the Seven Years' War and the Revolutionary Wars provide the framework to explain this course of events. While the seaborne empires of Western Europe were distracted, Prussia, Russia

livres douaniers de l'Amirauté de Hambourg au XVIIIe siècle: une source de grande valeur encore inexploitée', *Bulletin du Centre d'Histoire des Espaces Atlantiques, Nouvelle Série* 9 (1999), pp. 93–126.

52   S. Sassen, 'Bordering Capabilities versus Borders: Implications for National Borders', *Michigan Journal of International Law* 30/3 (2009), pp. 567–95, here pp. 569, 574, 579, 582.

53   D. Hancock, 'The Intensification of Atlantic Maritime Trade (1492–1815)', *The Sea in History: The Early Modern World*, ed. C. Buchet and G. Le Bouëdec (Woodbridge, 2017), pp. 19–29.

and the Habsburg Empire seized the opportunity to grab large territories – and with them, a considerable number of subjects to be taxed in order to alleviate their debts, caused by the inter-war crisis. Amongst other things, this illustrates that Prussian expansion in the eighteenth century cannot be separated from global developments.

Chapter 3 demonstrates that Struck's premise can also be applied to earlier events in Prussian history. When the Habsburg ruler died in 1740 without leaving a male heir, Prussia's King Frederick II saw an opportunity to take Silesia from the struggling new archduchess of Austria and queen of Hungary and Bohemia. Anka Steffen illustrates why this expansion was economically vital: Silesian linens had become increasingly popular in Western Africa, where they rivaled Indian cottons by the 1720s. Using the invoice books of the English Royal African Company, Steffen questions the widely established assumption of a dominance of Indian cottons in the African barter trade, as well as the common misconception that Silesian linens were generally of poor quality. Steffen also suggests a connection between the expansion of the slave trade and the intensification of serfdom (*Leibeigenschaft*) in the regions of Silesia, where serfs not only worked the land, but also produced these fabrics. The Silesian Wars that started in the 1740s were a struggle for control of a region of vital importance in Atlantic trade.

Chapter 4 focuses on the consequences of yet another of Prussia's major territorial expansions of the eighteenth century: the acquisition of Western Pomerania and its port of Stettin in 1720. Before the Polish partitions, which resulted in a direct link between Brandenburg (the Prussian heartland) and East Prussia with its port of Königsberg, Stettin provided the only direct connection between the capital Berlin and a growing overseas trade, previously channeled through the foreign port of Hamburg. Using the Sound Toll Registers as a source, Jutta Wimmler argues that the Prussian state's investment in the port and in the transport infrastructure from Stettin to Berlin made overseas products more accessible, which in turn affected Prussian industries as well as consumer practices in the kingdom – or rather, parts of the kingdom. These developments increased access to consumer products like sugar or rice, or to colorful textiles produced with the help of dyestuffs from overseas. Once again, Prussian territorial expansion had a decidedly global dimension.

From Stettin, we move further east. In Chapter 5, Friederike Gehrmann investigates the rhubarb trade in an attempt to debunk the myth that Russian trade policies of the eighteenth century were an expression of the country's 'backwardness'. She explores how the quest for furs – amongst other things an important exchange product for the China trade that prominently included rhubarb – fueled not only Russian expansion to Siberia, but also its contact with the American mainland. Using the Sound Toll Registers as a source, she establishes that the monopoly on high quality rhubarb garnered significant profits for the crown, who exploited European demand for this product. The

chapter questions common conceptions about the role of monopolies – not only
in Russia, but also in other European countries in the early modern period –
and pushes the boundaries of Atlantic history by highlighting the connections
between this space and China, as well as the Pacific.

Chapter 6 brings us back to Hamburg, which remained an important point
of transit for many cargos that made their way to Central European markets
via the Elbe River or through the Sound – despite Prussian attempts to establish
Stettin as an alternative to Hamburg. Torsten dos Santos Arnold investigates
Hamburg's imports of sugar and the people who traded in this popular
merchandise. While Wimmler and Gehrmann critically engaged the Sound
Toll Registers, dos Santos Arnold scrutinizes the usefulness of the Admiralty
Toll Books, Hamburg's major trade statistics from the early modern period.
Amongst other things, he concludes from these records that Hamburg not only
imported raw sugar to be processed in local refineries, as is usually assumed.
Refined or otherwise processed sugar also arrived in the Hanseatic port on a
regular basis. He also concludes that a small number of large firms controlled
most of this trade and that these firms were able to switch suppliers relatively
easily, if necessary (e.g. from Bordeaux to London during the Seven Years'
War, or to Cádiz during the French Revolution). This clearly speaks to the very
strong and diverse business ties of Hamburg's merchant elite, and to the crucial
importance of its status as a neutral city-state.

From Hamburg, the Holy Roman Empire's prime gateway to trade in
the north, we move to Trieste, its southern point of access. Klemens Kaps
investigates Trieste as a gateway to Spanish Atlantic trade for the eighteenth-
century Habsburg Empire. He argues that Trieste connected the empire to
Mediterranean as well as Atlantic trade from the second half of the century
until around 1830, although the Atlantic connection is difficult to grasp. As
Kaps argues convincingly, this has to do with the fact that ships moving between
Trieste and Spanish ports stopped at several Mediterranean ports on their way,
especially in Genoa. Trieste outward-bound cargo consisted of merchandise
typically used in Atlantic trade, namely copper and copper ware, ironware, linen,
or glass arriving from Upper and Lower Austria, Carinthia, Styria, Bohemia
and Carniola. Kaps further investigates the attempts of Trieste merchants to
establish direct trade with Spanish ports, illustrating the interest of Habsburg
merchants in accessing and profiting from Atlantic trade, and in circumventing
the long-established position of Genoa in the Spanish-Atlantic trade.

Profiting from Atlantic trade was not just the goal of merchants located
in port cities, however. With Chapter 8, we move away from coasts and ports
and far into continental hinterlands. In seemingly landlocked Elberfeld in the
Wupper Valley, Anne Sophie Overkamp reveals the scheme of tape merchants
to fix the prices of their valuable merchandise, which was also sought after in
the Americas. Conceptualizing this scheme as the formation of a cartel, she
argues that the structural preconditions in that region necessitated this type

of co-operative capitalism. The merchants co-operated to fix prices in order to protect themselves, and thus actively shaped their own position in the global economy.

While Overkamp's cartel members had little desire (or necessity) to leave the Wupper Valley, Margrit Schulte Beerbühl investigates the migration of merchant families from the Duchy of Berg and Westphalia to London. Chapter 9 analyzes migration from different angles: Schulte Beerbühl points out that many merchants who migrated to London from the Holy Roman Empire came from linen-producing regions, and she highlights the role of Bremen as a stepping point (she calls this 'step-and-chain migration'). She illustrates how these merchants established global networks reaching from Elberfeld and London to Amsterdam, Hamburg, St Petersburg, Boston, Carolina, Jamaica and Barbados.

Schulte Beerbühl focuses on actors moving within economic networks, whereas Josef Köstlbauer analyzes migration within a religious network. From its eighteenth-century base in today's Saxony, the Moravian Church established communities all over the world, but especially in Europe and the Americas (notably the Caribbean). As Köstlbauer points out in Chapter 10, people traveled within this space, including non-Europeans who often ended up in one of the European communities. The social and legal status of these individuals was often unclear, in particular in the case of former slaves. Köstlbauer proposes that this lack of definition concealed their status as slaves, rather than actually abolishing it. He thus argues that the commonly held view that there was no slavery in the Holy Roman Empire needs to be revisited, and that scholarship must move beyond legal definitions and take a closer look at these people's social realities.

The line between slavery and freedom is also blurred in Chapter 11, where Alexandra Gittermann deals with the approximately 100,000 people from German territories who were actively recruited for North American settlements during the eighteenth century, in an effort to further develop the cultivation of land in the British colonies. Gittermann investigates the recruitment strategies, the logistics of carrying these people from German hinterlands to North America, and the economic rationale of those who drew profit from this trafficking business. She particularly highlights the fact that migrants often served as living cargo or ballast on outbound ships, in order to operate them at full capacity. All of this led, Gittermann argues, to a commodification of humans who, in addition, usually had to work off the costs of their passage for years after their arrival in the Americas. Gittermann compares these mechanisms not only to those present in the movement of other types of indentured servants, but also to the logistics of the slave trade.

Chapter 12 delves deeper into the ties between the German states and North America, bringing us into the nineteenth century. Using the financing of debt as an example, David K. Thomson argues that the poorly investigated connections between German and North American financiers help to explain the rise of both economies in the course of the century. Exploring the US Civil War from the perspective of international finance, Thomson points to the crucial role of the growing financial ties between the US and German states in reorienting transatlantic banking structures, and in supporting the Union cause. He argues that this also had ideological reasons, namely the belief in the wake of the 1848 European revolts that the United States was a haven of political freedom – a symbol nevertheless stained by the existence of slavery in its southern states. The fact that the German states became the prime market for Union bonds thus needs to be seen in this context – as does the fact that economic ties between the two regions continued to grow stronger after the Civil War.

In his afterword, Göran Rydén pulls the threads together. He puts them into the wider context of research on global history as it has evolved since the 2000s, and of Wallerstein's model. For each of the contributions, he highlights the points in which they question the often-generalized characterization of Central and Eastern European regions and of actors from these regions as peripheral or semi-peripheral.

Flows of capital are less visible than flows of migrants and merchandise, but from the first chapter (referring to the debt of crowns) to the last (referring to modern bonds), the book illustrates that Central Europe was an integral part of the western hemisphere – and that this applied to the financial sector as well. Prominent merchant bankers in eighteenth-century London, such as the Barings and Schröders, complete this picture with their family origins in Westphalian linen regions. We end our case studies on the note that Germany and the United States had become two 'economic powerhouses' by the end of the nineteenth century. The history of early modern Europe (especially of Central and Eastern Europe) and nineteenth-century history are too often disconnected in scholarship. Yet it is no coincidence that many German-speaking historians from the early nineteenth to the early twentieth centuries wrote early modern history of Central and Eastern Europe as global history, almost as a matter of course. While this of course happened from a different historiographical and ideological angle, this perspective was gradually lost from the middle of the twentieth century onwards, and we are only now beginning to rediscover and move beyond it.

2

Did Prussia have an Atlantic History?
The Partitions of Poland-Lithuania,
the French Colonization of Guiana, and
Climates in the Caribbean, c. 1760s to 1780s

BERNHARD STRUCK[1]

Introduction: lands in the east – storms in the west

Brandenburg-Prussia is a long way from the Atlantic, particularly by late eighteenth-century standards. The journey from Berlin to La Rochelle would have taken some two weeks around 1770, provided that the weather was fair and the road conditions were good. After arriving on the French Atlantic coast, a traveler could embark on a transatlantic journey from La Rochelle to French Saint-Domingue or Guiana. Whatever the destination, the journey across the Atlantic would have taken around four to six weeks, again largely depending on weather conditions. Given the long distance and the perils of an overseas voyage – not to mention the turmoil the French empire experienced overseas after the Seven Years' War – not many Prussian travelers ever made such a journey across the Atlantic. Around 1770, there were not many direct connections between Brandenburg and Guiana. Yet there were some links.

Between the later 1760s and the early 1770s, newspapers across the German lands reported repeatedly about the distant transatlantic world. Some of these were weather reports – and not good ones. In February 1769, the *Münchner Zeitung* informed its readers that a storm in mid October the previous year had devastated large parts of Spanish Cuba. Havana was hit particularly hard, as '96 noble houses' and '4,048 common houses' had been destroyed. The article conveyed that the Spanish monarch had given orders for financial support, and

1   I would like to thank Klaus Weber, Jutta Wimmler, Anka Steffen, Anne Sophie Overkamp, Fabricio Prado, Klemens Kaps, Tom Cunningham, Jordan Girardin, Pol Dalmau, and Gregor Thum for feedback and suggestions. I would also like to thank the Fritz Thyssen Foundation for their support that initiated this research.

that measures would be taken to rebuild Havana and to support the suffering population. Overall, the damage was estimated at around 'six million piasters'. This excluded the loss of ships.[2]

The importance of the latter might easily be overlooked by a reader in landlocked Berlin. The wooden ships that crossed the Atlantic were highly specialized and very precious vessels. And so was the cargo, including cotton, sugar, grain, and tobacco. Not to mention the human loss: slaves, normally around 200 per vessel, plus the crew of some 30 to 50 men – carpenters, navigators, sailmakers, botanists. These ships were the arteries of transatlantic trade, commerce, and thus overseas empires. They were not only very costly, but also highly vulnerable in storms, before coal-powered steamships – and the weather was severe.

The Caribbean basin was hit particularly hard between 1768 and 1778 by recurring hurricanes,[3] which devastated large parts of the Spanish, French, and British overseas colonies, and the slave and settler plantations with their sugar and tobacco production. The hurricanes disrupted commodity chains and the slave trade during a prolonged inter-war crisis between the Seven Years' War and the War of American Independence. The exceptionally volatile weather effects that haunted the wider Caribbean lasted from around 1760 to 1800, with a peak around 1770.[4] Today, environmental historians concur that the severe weather conditions that affected parts of South America, the Atlantic, the Caribbean, and the southern coasts of North America marked the end of the 'Little Ice Age' around 1800.[5]

News did not travel fast in those days, but in steady concentric circles from the margins of the European overseas empires back to the metropoles and into the continental hinterlands. In October 1772, the *Reichs-Postreuter* reported that Spanish trade ships had gone missing in yet another storm in October 1772.[6] What this news conveyed was that maintaining overseas empires was a tremendous political, economic, and financial challenge in those far-away regions at the time.

The prolonged series of El Niño-La Niña, beginning roughly with the Seven Years' War, occurred during a time of repeated slave rebellions in the Caribbean and a crisis of overseas empires in the Americas, which ultimately led into the age of 'Atlantic Revolutions'.[7] This was a prolonged crisis of empires and old

---

2   *Münchner Zeitung*, 21 February 1769 (unpaginated).
3   S. Johnson, *Climate and Catastrophe in Cuba and the Atlantic World in the Age of Revolution* (Chapel Hill, 2011).
4   C. N. Caviedes, 'Five Hundred Years of Hurricanes in the Caribbean: Their Relationship with Global Climate Variabilities', *GeoJournal* 23/4 (1991), pp. 301–10, here p. 304.
5   On the seventeenth-century global environmental crisis and its entanglement with social, political, and economic issues, see G. Parker, *Global Crisis: War, Climate Change and Catastrophe in the Seventeenth Century* (New Haven, 2013).
6   *Beytrag zum Reichs-Postreuter*, 17 December 1772 (unpaginated). See also *Münchner Zeitung*, 31 October 1771 (unpaginated).
7   See for instance Richard B. Sheridan, 'The Jamaican Slave Insurrection Scare of 1776 and the American Revolution', *The Journal of Negro History* 61/3 (1976), pp. 290–308; Manuel Barcia,

regimes between c. 1760 and 1840.[8] It also coincided with events in distant landlocked Central Europe, including the partitions of Poland-Lithuania in 1772, 1793, and 1795. Not only did news about the scale of destruction and disaster reach Central Europe from Havana and Jamaica. As this chapter suggests, these events may have had long-distance ripple effects far beyond their immediate impact in the western Atlantic.

At the heart of this chapter lies a simple question: why partition Poland-Lithuania in 1772? It suggests that it was not a coincidence that the Hohenzollern monarchy, Tsarist Russia, and Habsburg Monarchy struck a deal and grabbed large swathes of territories, villages, towns, peasants, and craftsmen, all of whom were welcome taxpayers, at the very moment when storms in the Caribbean sent Western European powers into turmoil. A severe crisis across the Atlantic had the empires struggling to hold their overseas territories together. Sovereign debt is what all European powers shared after 1763, whether they were maritime or continental empires.[9] Tax revenues and other financial resources such as loans were needed.[10]

Linking the first partition of Poland-Lithuania and territorial reconfigurations in East-Central Europe to hurricanes and changing environmental, economic, territorial, and political climates in the Caribbean and across the Atlantic may seem far-fetched. Yet the moment to grab large swathes of Polish-Lithuanian territories in 1772 seemed ideal, or even consequential.

This chapter is, first and foremost, a historiographical exercise that seeks to bring East-Central Europe into the discussion about global history. For the period under investigation – the latter half of the eighteenth century – the chapter asks how East-Central Europe can be linked to global frameworks and themes. It takes the first partition of Poland-Lithuania in 1772 as a thinking tool, to consider how distant events that are traditionally narrated in the framework of more established area studies (such as Eastern or East-Central Europe, the Caribbean, or the Atlantic) can be drawn together. All too often the histories

---

'"A Not-so-Common Wind": Slave Revolts in the Age of Revolutions in Cuba and Brazil', *Review Fernand Braudel Center* 31/2 (2008), pp. 169–93.

8   C. S. Maier, 'Transformations of Territoriality, 1600–2000', *Transnationale Geschichte: Themen, Tendenzen und Theorien*, ed. G. Budde, S. Conrad and O. Janz (Göttingen, 2006), pp. 32–55.

9   J. C. Riley, *The Seven Years' War and the Old Regime in France: The Economic and Financial Toll* (Princeton, 1986), pp. 162ff. Britain's debt alone almost doubled from £74 million to £133 million between 1756 and 1763, before it reached an unprecedented level of £245 million by 1783. See J. Brewer, *The Sinews of Power: War, Money and the English State 1688–1783* (London, 2002).

10   C. Gibson, *Empire's Crossroads: A New History of the Caribbean* (Basingstoke/Oxford, 2014), p. 137. On war, public debt, and finance – also in comparison between Britain and France to serve debt – see R. B. Wong, 'Possibilities of Plenty and the Persistence of Poverty: Industrialization and International Trade', *An Emerging Modern World 1750–1970*, ed. S. Conrad and J. Osterhammel (Cambridge/London, 2018), pp. 251–409, here p. 259; J. H. Makin and N. J. Ornstein, *Debt and Taxes* (Washington, 1994), p. 54.

of Eastern and Western Europe are written separately. East-Central Europe thus far is largely left out of narratives of the Atlantic World, the 'age of global revolution', or global history altogether.[11] This chapter takes inspiration from transnational history and its call for rethinking spatial units of investigation and periodization. Drawing on the metaphor by Kiran Patel of transnational history as an 'onion model', it approaches the partition of Poland from the outer layers of Western European overseas empires across the Atlantic.[12]

It will first zoom into the Kourou project of the 1760s, where France sought to establish a new overseas settler colony in Guiana. This serves to highlight the challenges Western European states faced in building and running their overseas territories after 1763. From there, the chapter will move north into the Caribbean. Due to the severe hurricane seasons around 1770, all Western European powers were confronted with numerous difficulties in running their transatlantic political and economic operations. From the crisis in the Caribbean, the chapter finally turns to East-Central Europe and the first partition of Poland-Lithuania. The latter was linked to the complex situation far away, via the shared themes of debt, territory, resources, population, and imperial expansion in times of severe and changing climate.

Kourou: Enlightenment colony turned nightmare

The concept of empire evokes power. A mighty metropole with an administrative apparatus and a trained bureaucracy is in control of distant people and territories, and oversees the extraction of resources and taxes. The reality, however, was often rather different in the later eighteenth century. In order to flesh out the manifold challenges overseas empires faced, French Guiana between 1762 and 1765 may serve as an example.

By the end of the Seven Years' War, the French government sought to rebuild its overseas empire in this inhospitable corner of South America. The dream was to build a cultured European white-settler colony. The Kourou colony was a true Enlightenment project. Figure 2.1 helps us to see how Enlightenment thinkers, bureaucrats, and ministers – and not forgetting Louis XV himself – envisioned the future of the French empire overseas.

The scene could hardly be more idyllic. A river is winding through the landscape with rolling hills. Small vessels are navigating upstream and

---

11   See C. A. Bayly, *The Birth of the Modern World, 1780–1914: Global Connections and Comparisons* (Oxford, 2004), pp. 27–41. On the 'age of global revolution', see D. Armitage and S. Subrahmanyam, eds, *The Age of Revolutions in Global Context, c. 1760–1840* (Basingstoke, 2009).
12   K. K. Patel, 'An Emperor without Clothes? The Debate about Transnational History Twenty-Five Years on', *Histoire@Politique* 26 (2015), pp. 1–16, here p. 6. Similarly, on the notion of stretching our spatial imagination in transnational history, see P.-Y. Saunier, *Transnational History* (Basingstoke, 2013), pp. 118–21.

Figure 2.1. 'Vue de la Rivière de l'Isle de Courou dans la Guyane françoise où débarque les Européens pour l'Isle Cayenne, c. 1765'

downstream; a small barque or fishing boat is crossing the river. Further upstream, somewhat vague in the distance, the spectator sees another settlement and industry, a larger building, perhaps a warehouse with a chimney indicating productivity and industriousness. In front of the slightly elevated spectator's view, a small settlement unfolds on both sides of the river. To the very left stands a larger wooden house, surrounded and sheltered by trees. In the shade, groups of men and women discuss, socialize, or do business. The women are dressed in typical late eighteenth-century fashion. Neither peasant nor aristocrat, their dresses indicate that they are middle-class. One of the three women seems to be handing over a book.

Two men are in discussion over plans or commerce, one of them pointing back to the developing settlement with a few houses across the river. Small as it is, the colonial settlement seems to be prospering. Carpenters and woodworkers are cutting wood, and two more buildings are under construction. Goats and cattle are being herded nearby. Commerce and trade are under way. A group of men is transporting grain or another foodstuff down to the river. Two of them are loading grain bags onto a barque, ready to be shipped off.

The depicted pastoral scene that shows *la France équinoxale* in Guiana appears to be the perfect dream of any eighteenth-century colonial administrator, physiocrat, tax collector, and monarch. The problem was that it was a dream indeed: a pipe dream and a colonial fantasy. What the image does not show was the harsh reality behind the disastrous French project in Guiana between 1762 and 1765.[13]

By 1762 it became ever more obvious that France's fortunes in the Seven Years' War were slipping away. France fought a very costly war that devastated the country's finances. While other European states faced similarly high military, fiscal, and human costs, France fought on three fronts: in Europe, South Asia, and across the Atlantic. The territorial costs France had to pay overseas were far higher than those of any other belligerent party. While Frederick II managed to cling on to Silesia (the industrious and highly profitable province that Prussia had wrought from the Habsburg Empire in the Silesian Wars in the early 1740s), France saw its Canadian territories slip away.[14] This came as a blow after the French had already been defeated by the East India Company at the Battle of Plassey in 1757 and had lost their trading opportunities in Bengal.[15]

The Peace Treaty of Paris in 1763 confirmed the French loss of Quebec, Grenada, Dominica, and Tobago. France held on to Saint-Domingue, with its profitable sugar production. The treaty set the Atlantic World and the Caribbean economy in motion and, with a number of territories being transferred from one empire to another, it carved out 'the new world of the 1770s', as Emma Rothschild observed.[16] Yet – and this is the point this chapter seeks to make – these changes did not only affect the Atlantic World, but equally territories and economies between Quebec, Manila, Bengal, and East-Central Europe.

By the end of the war, the only French territory left on the American continent was Guiana. In the face of military disaster, the French government sought to seize the opportunity that the post-war period offered. After all, there was potentially a lot to gain. After 1763, tens of thousands of people were on the move. These included returning soldiers and sailors, many of whom returned home only to find their villages devastated. With territories trading hands and new imperial regimes in control, many French settlers left Quebec or were deported under the new British rule in Acadia.[17] The war was not only a military conflict, but also one over resources, territories, and people. The British deported some 11,500 Acadians to their colonies in Maryland and Massachusetts, and to Britain. Others left the former French colonies and

13   E. Rothschild, 'A Horrible Tragedy in the French Atlantic', *Past & Present* 192/1 (2006), pp. 67–108. The following section follows Rothschild's study of the Kourou expedition closely.
14   On Silesia, see the chapter by Anka Steffen in this volume. On the fiscal problem through agrarian productivity, tax reforms, and the removal of personal servitude in East-Central Europe, see C. S. Maier, *Once within Borders: Territories of Power, Wealth, and Belonging since 1500* (Cambridge/London, 2016), pp. 134f.
15   S. Bandyopādhyāÿa, *From Plassey to Partition: A History of Modern India* (New Delhi, 2004), p. 44.
16   Rothschild, 'A Horrible Tragedy', pp. 69f.
17   C. Hodson, *The Acadian Diaspora: An Eighteenth-Century History* (Oxford, 2017).

settled in Spanish Louisiana and French Saint-Domingue.[18] With thousands of people on the move, various empires competed for these people, who were potential landholders, craftsmen, and taxpayers.

In this moment of defeat and opportunity, the French government under Louis XV put all its hopes and substantial resources into the Kourou project. In 1763 the Duc de Choiseul, minister of the French navy and the colonies, appointed Étienne-François Turgot as governor of French Guiana and head of the Kourou expedition. The idea was to build a model white-settler colony, following Enlightenment principles. At a moment when slave rebellions erupted elsewhere and early abolitionists made themselves heard, the number of slaves was to be kept to a minimum. Rather than planning a future based on slavery, the aim was to attract as many settlers as possible from France and elsewhere in Europe. Religious freedom was granted, so that the French authorities freed Protestants who had hitherto worked on the galleys of Marseille in order to settle them in Kourou. Jews, who would only be granted full rights as French citizens in 1790, were equally welcome. Ideally, the project leaders hoped to tap into the pool of countless uprooted people who were on the move during this early inter-war period.

In order to attract settlers, the French authorities printed brochures and maps in French and other languages. Emissaries visited Alsace and the German states to advertise the settlement project.[19] Overall, some 17,000 individuals signed up. The new settlers came from France, the Rhineland, Alsace, Baden, from Russia and Hungary. They arrived in Rochefort and were shipped over to Guiana. This was one of the largest human cargos crossing the Atlantic in such a short period of time.

The French granted their new settlers land and tax exemption, as well as food supplies for two and a half years until the colony would be self-sustaining. People received clothing and rewards for the birth of children. In cases of severe illness, settlers would be shipped back to France at the expense of the state. Doctors and surgeons were recruited for the physical wellbeing of the newcomers. In order to turn Guiana into a profitable colony, natural scientists and botanists were attracted who would know how to introduce European crops, vegetables, and livestock.[20]

Kourou was an ambitious, well-planned project. In its early planning stage in 1762/63, Guiana was an impoverished and insignificant territory on the margins of the French overseas empire. Territorially speaking, it was small compared to Brazil or the Spanish colonies. In 1763, only 575 white settlers lived in Kourou, with around 7,000 slaves as the backbone of the colony, and various indigenous

---

18   G. Plank, *An Unsettled Conquest: The British Campaign against the Peoples of Acadia* (Philadelphia, 2003); C. Hodson, 'Exile on Spruce Street: An Acadian History', *The William and Mary Quarterly* 67/2 (2010), pp. 249–78.

19   The recruitment of German settlers for American settlements is also discussed by Alexandra Gittermann in this volume.

20   Rothschild, 'A Horrible Tragedy', pp. 72ff.

groups. Boosting the potential economic output from Guiana by an additional
17,000 settlers would have been a great success.

Competing for people made perfect sense within the mercantilist and physio-
cratic economic thinking of the time. Before Adam Smith and before industrialization in full swing, agricultural production was still the backbone of national
and imperial economies. The more people who could turn barren land into
fertile fields and produce agricultural surplus for the metropole or for trade,
the higher the economic output. All European states were in competition over
land and people.

What was so carefully planned quickly turned into complete disaster.
Thousands of people died of disease, starvation, or despair within months of
their arrival in Kourou. Once settlers landed, food that had arrived earlier was
already rotting on the shores. Wood and timber to build shelter had not yet
arrived, nor had the medicine necessary to treat the sick or weakened passengers.[21] Some 3,000 settlers tried to make their way out of the colonial misery and
returned to Rochefort, where many of them perished shortly after their return.

By 1765, it became evident that the French Kourou project had failed. Instead
of bringing the badly needed resources and taxes from its settlers back to the
metropole, it had literally sent resources, money, ships, and people down to the
bottom of the Atlantic. In 1770, only some 1,178 settlers lived in Kourou. It was
arguably the greatest disaster in France's colonial enterprises.[22]

History is full of ifs and buts. With a bit of luck, more favorable winds,
perhaps even better planning, *la France équinoxale* might have become the new
Massachusetts, a flourishing colony with a surplus in grain and rice production.
Food supplies were desperately needed a few hundred miles further north in the
Caribbean, when a far more severe crisis hit all the Western European overseas
colonies. Perhaps French Guiana could have tapped into this crisis scenario,
which opened up unexpected trade and economic opportunities. Yet Kourou
had little or nothing to offer when hurricanes haunted the Caribbean.

Havana: storms in the Caribbean,
trade co-operations, and imperial rivalries

Hurricanes are nothing unusual in the wider Caribbean basin: they occur on
a regular basis between July and early October and contain an element of
geographical coincidence (it may be sheer luck when a hurricane just passes

21   J. R. McNeill, *Mosquito Empires: Ecology and War in the Greater Caribbean, 1620–1914*
(Cambridge, 2010), p. 131.
22   C. de Castelnau-L'Estoile and F. Regourd, *Connaissances et Pouvoirs: Les Espaces Impériaux
(XVIe–XVIIIe siècles): France, Espagne, Portugal* (Bordeaux, 2005), p. 233; Rothschild, 'A Horrible
Tragedy', p. 69.

any of the Caribbean islands or only scrapes the coast of Florida). However, when one of the most severe hurricane seasons occurred in the early inter-war period, the frequency and violence were unusual: six major storms swept across the entire Caribbean basin from mid August onward in 1766.[23] All European powers who held territories in the region were affected. France's most populated islands (including Saint-Domingue with its rich sugar production, Martinique, and Saint Kitts) were severely hit. So was British Jamaica, where the hurricanes destroyed homes, people's lives, and crops. In September 1766, storms reached Puerto Rico and swept across the eastern parts of Cuba. Spanish ships with supplies drifted off or sank. The hurricanes affected territories as far north as Louisiana. With ship routes disrupted, the Spanish – who had taken over Louisiana in 1762 – struggled to establish their rule over the former French colony and to bring French settlers under control.[24]

Colonial economies were, according to the logic of the time, closed systems. However, no imperial power managed to cope on its own in such a crisis. In order to deal with the subsistence crisis in 1766, local French officials allowed foreign food (flour in particular) to be imported. In a similar *ad hoc* measure, the Spanish governor of Louisiana opened trade to local settlers who purchased flour from neighboring British settlements in Illinois. Such courses of action happened without permission from the metropole, of course, as there was simply no time. Rulers back in Europe and their colonial apparatuses could only sanction those local *ad hoc* measures weeks if not months later. The volatile Caribbean climate thus *de facto* opened the otherwise closed mercantilist systems, leading to a certain degree of open markets and trade, if only for a short period of time as an emergency measure.[25] Humans were not in the driving seat – they were acted upon. It was the climate that put people, trade, economic thought, and political action in motion.[26]

While newspapers across the Atlantic reported about lost Spanish ships and destruction in Havana in 1769, Cuba (the epicenter of Spanish rule and its economy) faced a longer spell of particularly severe climatic conditions that led to crop failures between 1772 and 1776. The prolonged subsistence crisis sent ripple effects to other parts of the Spanish empire, such as Mexico, Puerto Rico, and Louisiana.[27]

---

23   S. Johnson, 'El Niño: Environmental Crisis, and the Emergence of Alternative Markets in the Hispanic Caribbean, 1760s–1770s', *The William and Mary Quarterly* 62/3 (2005), pp. 365–410, here pp. 367f.
24   Ibid., p. 381.
25   Ibid., pp. 370ff. On the idea of free trade and the political economy of merchant empires, see Wong, 'Possibilities of Plenty', p. 259.
26   B. Struck, K. Ferris and J. Revel, 'Introduction: Space and Scale in Transnational History', *The International History Review* 33/4 (2011), pp. 573–84.
27   Johnson, 'El Niño', pp. 386, 397.

While the British, Dutch, and French had opened their ports to other empires for trade in the climatic crisis of the mid to late 1760s, the Spanish authorities, fearing that smuggling might undermine the mercantilist closed system, were the most reluctant to do so. In fact, they tried to hold on tight to Cuba after the Seven Years' War, as British troops had occupied Havana between August 1762 and July 1763.[28] In the immediate aftermath of the war, the Spanish monarchy put substantial resources into the fortification of Havana, which by then had a population of around 35,000. This was far bigger than Philadelphia, with its 23,000 people, or New York with a population of around 18,000.[29] Further troops were sent to Havana and thousands of workers were needed. There was a constant demand for labor, which came from slaves, freed slaves, and Europeans. In this post-war scenario, empires were forced to co-operate while simultaneously competing for land, territories, and people.[30]

Havana's population rose quickly between 1763 and 1765. The Spanish slave trade was operated via Cádiz and the *Compañia Gaditana de Negros*, with a direct transfer of slaves from Africa. Shipping the workforce over the Atlantic was not feasible for the *Compañia*. Labor was in such demand that the Spanish authorities opened the closed system, to import slaves from British ports in Jamaica and Barbados. The numbers of imported slaves jumped quickly from 258 in 1761 to 1,289 the following year, before reaching some 2,342 in 1763.[31] Once troops and slaves had arrived in Havana, the next challenge arose. People had to be fed, and there was simply not enough food to go around. As long as the only slaves imported came from the Spanish *Compañia*, there was a fixed ratio of how much food was imported along with each individual slave. The arrival of additional slaves from the British Caribbean created an imbalance.

In order to deal with the food shortage, the Spanish *Compañia* received permission to bring in foreign supplies. Yet this arrangement was also constantly undermined, or at least under threat from contraband. Smugglers came from Jamaica, and Spanish authorities had no other choice than to turn a blind eye during the crisis. And even though the Spanish monarchy and local authorities were reluctant to open markets to foreign goods, the *Compañia*

---

28   E. A. Schneider, *The Occupation of Havana: War, Trade and Slavery in the Atlantic World* (Chapel Hill, 2018).
29   Gibson, *Empire's Crossroads*, pp. 134f; J. H. Elliott, *Empires of the Atlantic World: Britain and Spain in America 1492–1830* (New Haven/London, 2006), p. 262.
30   F. Prado, *Edge of Empire: Atlantic Networks and Revolution in Bourbon Río de la Plata* (Oakley, 2015), p. 137; D. Alden, 'The Undeclared War of 1773–1777: Climax of Luso-Spanish Platine Rivalry', *Hispanic American Historical Review* 41/1 (1961), pp. 55–74. More generally: P. K. Liss, *Atlantic Empires: The Networks of Trade and Revolution, 1713–1826* (Baltimore, 1983).
31   Johnson, 'El Niño', pp. 373ff; on the British slave trade, see Gibson, *Empire's Crossroads*, pp. 135, 146. On Cádiz as a key port connecting the Atlantic World as well as Spanish, Dutch, and Baltic ports see S. A. Crespo, *Mercaderes atlánticos: Redes del comercio flamenco y holandés entre Europa y el Caribe* (Córdoba, 2009). On the Spanish Atlantic slave trade see J. M. Fradera and C. Schmidt-Nowara, eds, *Slavery and Antislavery in Spain's Atlantic Empire* (New York, 2013).

used its monopoly and turned to new trading opportunities. Maize, flour, and other foodstuffs were imported from neighboring empires and their outposts, including French Guadeloupe, Martinique, and Saint-Domingue. In times of rebellion against London, merchants in Philadelphia and New York took any opportunity to trade with Spain and to open markets beyond the British imperial system. Climate change and the subsequent subsistence crisis in the wider Caribbean thus had a domino effect, opening the possibility of economic independence for the 13 colonies.

Similar to the French government in Guiana, the Spanish had invested enormous financial, human, and infrastructural resources in rebuilding parts of its overseas empire during the early inter-war period. All these efforts were largely disrupted when another hurricane struck Cuba in 1768. While Havana largely escaped unscathed, the most important subsistence crop, the plantain, was completely destroyed. Large supplies of rice and maize were lost, along with salt pans that were crucial for food preservation.[32]

At the worst possible moment, French settlers in Louisiana rebelled against Spanish rule in October 1768. The Spanish governor, Ulloa, had to flee before another 2,000 Spanish troops could be sent to reinforce Spanish rule in early 1769. But this proved difficult in times of constant rebellion, volatile climate, and hunger, as the food crisis was also felt in Louisiana between 1770 and 1772. It was at the same time felt in distant Prussia and Poland, due to a prolonged cold spell in Europe.[33]

The Spanish had no other option than to allow local merchants to trade food supplies with the neighboring British colonies. Some merchant families used their widespread trans-imperial networks between Cádiz, London, Philadelphia, and Puerto Rico. Others (including former French Acadian settlers who had been deported from Canada after 1763) now also tapped into these unexpected opportunities to trade with the Spanish colonies from places like Philadelphia.[34] As these new trade opportunities between settlers in the British colonies and Spanish merchants undermined London's trade monopoly with its colonies, the British government raised protests, leading the country to the brink of warfare with Spain over the Falkland Islands in 1770.[35]

What this section has outlined can only scratch the surface of what was a prolonged overseas imperial crisis, when German newspapers reported storms, destruction, and lost ships. The crisis was by no means over by 1770, when storms struck the Caribbean again, followed by a prolonged drought in Cuba.

32 Johnson, 'El Niño', p. 380.
33 D. Collet, *Die doppelte Katastrophe: Klima und Kultur in der europäischen Hungerkrise 1770–1772* (Göttingen, 2019), pp. 350ff.
34 Hodson, 'Exile on Spruce Street'.
35 Johnson, 'El Niño', pp. 385f. On the turmoil in the Atlantic, British colonies and Caribbean, and on the entanglements of the Spanish, French and British empires, see L. D. Ferreiro, *Brothers in Arms: American Independence and the Men of France and Spain who Saved It* (New York, 2016).

Rebuilding overseas empires was a tremendous challenge in the post-1763 world. In a region with often unpredictable (if not lethal) climate conditions, it was almost impossible. French, Spanish, British as well as other minor colonial empires struggled throughout the 1760s and early 1770s to hold their overseas territories together. The maintenance, rebuilding, and securing of colonies between Saint-Domingue, Kourou, Cuba, and Louisiana consumed vast sums and provided little to no returns.[36] This was also true elsewhere, when the Bengal famine of 1769 and 1770 cost the lives of around 10 million people.[37] Troops, men, and food supplies were needed across the Atlantic, but often the hands of the metropolitan governments were tied. At best, they could react *post factum* to whatever local authorities had already done to somehow alleviate the often local and regional (yet simultaneously trans-imperial) post-war crisis. This was hardly the time to look over one's shoulder and face eastwards.

West Prussia: poor land of riches in the east

When Frederick II ascended to the Hohenzollern throne in 1740, he penned his first Political Testament. He later updated these visions for the future in 1758 and 1762. In terms of territory and population, Prussia was the smallest and most vulnerable of the major European powers. From the start of his reign, Frederick II envisioned the expansion of the Hohenzollern territorial base, as he saw Russia expanding east and south. He was equally aware of the colonial expansions and maritime opportunities of Spain, France, and Britain. In addition, there was the rivalry with the Habsburg dynasty within the Holy Roman Empire.

As he expressed repeatedly in his Political Testaments, the most viable way to expand in order to compete militarily and economically was by seizing territories from the neighbors. In the Silesian Wars of 1740 to 1742, Frederick II seized Silesia from Habsburg rule; this rich and industrious region added people, wealth, and taxes to his kingdom. During the Seven Years' War, Silesia once again became the main focus of territorial conflicts in Europe, and Prussia survived the war only by the skin of her teeth.[38]

---

36 At least not in the near future, as the world economy – plantations in the Caribbean, in particular – was highly vulnerable to climate change, bad weather, and poor harvests. See Wong, 'Possibilities of Plenty', p. 255.

37 V. Damodaram, 'The East India Company: Famine and Ecological Conditions in Eighteenth-Century Bengal', *The East India Company and the Natural World*, ed. A. Winterbottom (Basingstoke, 2015), pp. 80–102, here p. 81; D. Clingingsmith and J. Williamson, 'Deindustrialisation in Eighteenth and Nineteenth-Century India: Mughal Decline, Climate Shocks and British Industrial Ascent', *Explorations in Economic History* 45/3 (2009), pp. 209–34.

38 C. Clark, *Iron Kingdom: The Rise and Downfall of Prussia, 1600–1847* (Cambridge, 2006), pp. 1ff.

In his Political Testament from 1752, Frederick II stated his intention of seizing Polish territories, should the opportunity arise.[39] Territories in the east were vital to compete internationally, both economically and militarily. By that time, the Hohenzollern state was still a patchwork monarchy with no territorial bridge between the eastern provinces around Königsberg and the Brandenburg core territory. Brandenburg itself was not a particularly fertile region for agriculture, and it took major efforts to drain swamps around the Oderbruch east of Berlin to turn barren into agricultural land.[40] Other Hohenzollern territories like Kleve, Jülich-Berg, Tecklenburg, Mark, or Frisia all contributed to Brandenburg-Prussia's overall economic production and exports – as for instance metal production in Mark. Yet they were distant, detached exclaves, and relatively small in territory and population compared to the core territories.[41]

In terms of population, Brandenburg-Prussia was far smaller than the Habsburg Empire, France, Russia, and Britain. So, should the chance arise to swallow Polish territories along with their population, this would not only be a major boost for its standing in the overall balance of power. Equally, if not more importantly, it would allow Brandenburg-Prussia to grow economically. Crucially, an agricultural hinterland at the expense of Poland would bridge the gap to eastern Prussia without any external borders, tariffs, and tax barriers.[42]

Poland-Lithuania was a vast territory, yet sparsely populated with its roughly 10 to 11 million inhabitants. But it offered extensive areas of fertile agricultural land and forests, as well as access to the Baltic. During the early eighteenth century, the Polish Noble Republic had suffered enormously from the Great Northern War. Some areas had lost more than 30 per cent of their population, towns had been devastated, and it had never fully recovered from the war. It was a poor country, yet potentially rich. Due to the loss of population, there was a lack of husbandry and forests were neglected. Either there were not enough peasants to work the land or they were poorly trained, as travelers reported.[43] Some observers commented on the problem of serfdom. The latter

---

39   Frederick II, 'Das politische Testament von 1752', *Die Werke Friedrichs des Großen*, 10 vols, ed. G. Volz (Berlin, 1912), here Vol. 7.

40   D. Blackbourn, *The Conquest of Nature: Water, Landscape, and the Making of Modern Germany* (London, 2006).

41   See for instance K. H. Kaufhold, *Das Metallgewerbe der Grafschaft Mark im 18. und frühen 19. Jahrhundert* (Dortmund, 1976); W. Reininghaus, 'Wirtschaft, Gesellschaft und Staat in der alten Grafschaft Mark', *Preußen im südlichen Westfalen*, ed. E. Trox (Lüdenscheid, 1993), pp. 11–41; H. Kisch, 'The Textile Industries in Silesia and the Rhineland: A Comparative Study in Industrialization', *The Journal of Economic History* 19/4 (1959), pp. 541–64.

42   See F. Schui, 'Prussia's "Trans-Oceanic Moment": The Creation of the Prussian Asiatic Trade Company in 1750', *The Historical Journal* 49/1 (2006), pp. 143–60, here pp. 145f on Frederick II's economic policies, mercantilism, trade, and overseas ambitions.

43   B. Struck, *Nicht West – nicht Ost: Frankreich und Polen in der Wahrnehmung deutscher Reisender 1750 und 1850* (Göttingen, 2006), pp. 256ff.

was regarded as inhumane, but there was also the utilitarian argument that forms of unfree labor were less productive compared to free landholders.[44] The criticism of serfdom in East-Central Europe overlapped in its arguments with early abolitionist voices elsewhere.[45]

What needed to be done, as some observers suggested, was to increase the rural population in order to work the land more effectively, as well as to introduce agricultural reforms. This is precisely what the Polish-Lithuanian Commonwealth attempted during the early eighteenth century and again in the 1760s, by attracting settlers from elsewhere in Europe, distributing free land for freeholders, and offering some tax exemptions for colonists.[46] These measures followed the same rationale as the French Kourou project. Travelers in the 1760s and 1770s reported about the vast territories and literally hundreds of villages owned by the magnates.[47] Some of these (such as the Potockis) had recently freed their peasants. These actions were part of the reform era under Stanisław August Poniatowski in the 1760s and 1770s. He himself had freed the peasants on his own crown lands and experimented with agricultural reforms in order to increase output and improve the economy.

The Polish-Lithuanian Commonwealth had been a major political and economic factor during the early modern period. In the sixteenth and seventeenth centuries, it had been Europe's grain chamber with a huge surplus in grain, timber, and other products. The surplus of grain was historically traded across the Baltic, and from there to Western Europe with its higher and growing population.[48] It was a 'second colonial zone' (as Eric Hobsbawm observed) that exported raw materials such as flax, timber, and grain surplus to Western Europe.[49]

The moment for Prussia, the Habsburg Empire, and Russia to tap into these under-used resources and potential riches and to integrate this colonial zone as their own economic hinterland came in 1772. While the second and third partitions of Poland (in 1793 and 1795 respectively) happened against

44   Maier, *Once within Borders*, pp. 136f.
45   F. Brahm and E. Rosenhaft, eds, *Slavery Hinterland: Transatlantic Slavery and Continental Europe, 1680–1850* (Woodbridge, 2016); R. von Mallinckrodt, 'Verhandelte (Un-)Freiheit: Sklaverei, Leibeigenschaft und innereuropäischer Wissenstransfer am Ausgang des 18. Jahrhunderts', *Geschichte und Gesellschaft* 43 (2017), pp. 1–34; M. Cerman, *Villagers and Lords in Eastern Europe, 1300–1800* (Basingstoke, 2012).
46   Struck, *Nicht West – nicht Ost*, p. 262.
47   Ibid., pp. 256–9.
48   On the role of Polish Baltic trade and access to the sea, see H. Bagiński, *Zagadnienie Dostępu Polski do Morza* (Warsaw, 1959).
49   E. Hobsbawm, *Age of Revolution 1789–1848* (London, 1999), p. 32. See also K. Olszewski, 'The Rise and Decline of the Polish-Lithuanian Commonwealth due to Grain Trade', *Munich Personal RePEc Archive*, Paper No. 68805, posted 13 January 2016, pp. 2f. As an example of the rich Polish historiography on this, see H. Samsonowicz, *Późne Średniowiecze Miast Nadbałtyckich: Studia nad Dziejami Hanzy nad Bałtykiem w XIV–XV w* (Warsaw, 1968).

the backdrop of the French Revolution and the threat of revolution in Poland after the 1791 constitution, the timing of the first partition in 1772 raises some questions that are relatively under-explored. At times, the first partition is interpreted as yet another territorial trade, not unusual in European politics.[50] Yet the sheer size of territories seized by all three partitioning powers surpassed all other border alignments and territorial disputes by far.

Brandenburg-Prussia alone took a territory of some 36,300 square kilometers and a population of around 680,000. The former Royal or Polish Prussia became known as Western Prussia and was the missing patchwork territory to bridge Brandenburg and East Prussia. Furthermore, it allowed the Hohenzollern monarchy further access to the Baltic – beyond Stettin, which it had acquired in 1720 – via Elbing, Thorn, and Bromberg (later Danzig after 1793), and potentially from there into the Atlantic, as timber and iron underpinned the infrastructure of Atlantic trade.[51] Frederick II had all the right reasons to refer to the newly seized territories as 'our Canada', his colonial project, in a letter in 1775.[52]

In very crude numbers, and in comparison to overseas colonies, a population of 680,000 equaled 20 Havanas in terms of population. Some 600,000 peasants working the land – if we deduct the small urban population – equaled some 2,000 slave voyages across the Atlantic, with slaves working on sugar, cotton, or tobacco plantations. Of course, such comparisons are crude. Yet they show the dimension of what the integration of Polish territories meant economically. Plus, one did not need ships. There was no Atlantic that needed to be crossed. And there were no hurricanes. Logistically and in terms of administration, Polish territories were far easier to control and integrate politically, socially, and economically than Guiana, Jamaica, or Cuba.[53] Via news and correspondence networks, the Prussian monarch and his administration were well aware of the challenges of overseas trade and imperial projects. Well before turning towards Polish territory, he had tasted it for himself.

In 1750, Frederick II had chartered an Asiatic trade company in the port of Emden in East Frisia. Ultimately, the trade company was short-lived and failed. Yet the project attests to Prussia's aspiration to participate in maritime trade

---

50   P. W. Schroeder, *The Transformation of European Politics, 1763–1848* (Oxford, 1994), pp. 10f.

51   C. Evans and G. Rydén, *Baltic Iron in the Atlantic World in the Eighteenth Century* (Leiden, 2007). For Prussia's access to the Baltic via Stettin, see Jutta Wimmler's chapter in this book.

52   Frederick II, *Correspondance de Frédéric II Roi de Prusse*, Vol. 10 (Berlin, 1856), pp. 17f. See also G. Thum, 'Die kulturelle Leere des Ostens: Legitimierung preußisch-deutscher Herrschaft im 19. Jahrhundert', *Umkämpfte Räume: Raumbilder, Ordnungswille und Gewaltmobilisierung*, ed. U. Jureit (Göttingen, 2016), pp. 263–86.

53   H.-J. Bömelburg, A. Gestrich and H. Schnabel-Schüle, eds, *Die Teilungen Polen-Litauens: Inklusions- und Exklusionsmechanismen – Traditionsbildung – Vergleichsebenen* (Osnabrück, 2013); J. Hackmann and M. Kopij-Weiß, *Nationen in Kontakt und Konflikt: Deutsch-polnische Verflechtungen 1806–1918* (Darmstadt, 2014).

and commerce. The Asiatic trade company also prompts questions concerning Frederick II's economic visions and ambitions at the time. Often regarded as economically inflexible and dogmatically mercantilist, the Emden project suggests that Frederick II was open to naval and commercial enterprise. And while short-lived, the Asiatic trade company plans did indeed raise concerns among Dutch and British traders and politicians. It was clearly regarded as a threat to their own commercial interests.[54]

Lastly, the Prussian project of 1750 calls into question the geographical framework of Atlantic and, more broadly, oceanic history. The latter is often written from a British, French, Spanish and Dutch perspective, and along a narrow stretch of coast and port cities, yet merchants operating out of places like Bremen or Hamburg had far-reaching links back to the hinterland.[55] In the case of the Emden project of 1750, the initiative to take part in oceanic trade came from landlocked Brandenburg. This leads back to the initial question: why Poland in 1772? Why at this moment, some nine years after the Seven Years' War? Why did the opportunity to expand Prussia's territory that Frederick II had eyed as early as 1752 arise then? From an East-Central European as well as from a national Polish perspective, various interpretations have been offered.[56]

The national perspective can be described as a history of the relative decline of the Polish-Lithuanian Commonwealth since the mid to late seventeenth century. The political and partly federal structures of the electoral monarchy became ever more dysfunctional. Factions among Polish noblemen and their *liberum veto* paralyzed decision-making. This was also evident during the ambitious reform years under Poniatowski since 1764. Some nobles openly operated against the monarch and co-operated with Russia or Prussia. Russia, in particular, had started to influence Polish politics *de facto* during the latter half of the eighteenth century, with troops stationed on Polish territory. Around 1770, the Polish Noble Republic stood on the brink of civil war. This decline took place during a period when other states in the region (including Russia, the Habsburg Empire, and Brandenburg-Prussia) expanded and established more centralized forms of absolutism, standing armies, and a more efficient fiscal-military apparatus.

---

54   Schui, 'Prussia's "Trans-Oceanic Moment"', pp. 143f.
55   On the geographical scope of Atlantic history, see P. Emmer and W. Klooster, 'The Dutch Atlantic, 1600–1800: Expansion without Empire', *Itinerario* 2 (1999), pp. 48–69, here p. 48. More broadly on German trade in the Atlantic, see K. Weber, *Deutsche Kaufleute im Atlantikhandel, 1680–1830: Unternehmen und Familien in Hamburg, Cádiz und Bordeaux* (Munich, 2004).
56   The literature on the partitions, in particular from Polish historians, on internal and external factors as well as on economic, political, social, and constitutional aspects is complex. See for instance O. Halecki, 'Why was Poland Partitioned?', *Slavic Review* 22/3 (1963), pp. 432–41. Halecki is among the historians who focused on both internal factors (e.g. Polish magnates) and external factors (e.g. missing solidarity among other European powers). See also J. Łukowski, *The Partitions of Poland: 1772, 1793, 1795* (London, 1999); P. S. Wandycz, *The Lands of Partitioned Poland, 1795–1918* (Seattle, 1974); T. Kizwalter, *O Nowoczesności Narodu: Przypadek Polski* (Warsaw, 1999).

Economically, the Polish-Lithuanian Commonwealth had suffered many setbacks since the later seventeenth century. While not directly involved in the Great Northern War and while neutral during the Seven Years' War, the territories of the Noble Republic had repeatedly been the battleground of international warfare. The traditional Polish grain and timber trade via the Baltic declined when more and more grain, foodstuffs, and raw materials were shipped over the Atlantic from the British colonies. Once reliant on East-Central European grain and timber, Western Europe had become less dependent on this 'second colonial zone'.[57] At the same time, grain and agricultural products were desperately needed in the region itself. While droughts and repeated hurricanes led to food and subsistence crises across the Atlantic, a severe hunger crisis raged across East-Central Europe with a peak around 1770 to 1772.[58]

All these internal – national and regional – factors and interpretations are valid and needed. Yet the prolonged crisis of overseas empires across the Atlantic ultimately opened the window of opportunity for Brandenburg-Prussia, the Habsburg Monarchy and Russia to eventually execute the plan to partition Poland. The hands of the British empire were tied due to rebellion in the colonies. Transatlantic trade was disrupted, and British grain imports suddenly ended up in Cuba – not in Liverpool. The Spanish monarchy struggled to feed its colonial subjects between Louisiana and Cuba. The French had failed dramatically in Kourou. Both France and Spain were now fully enmeshed in supporting the cause of the rebellious British colonies.[59] When the moment of partition came in 1772, Stanisław August Poniatowski called for support from France and Britain. Given the tumultuous situation across the Atlantic, support for Poland, perhaps unsurprisingly, never came.

Conclusion: inter-war crisis and the quest for land, people, and taxes – east and west

Why partition Poland in 1772? This chapter does not claim to *prove* the point that events across the Atlantic had a direct causal relation to the partition. Yet in the light of global history, it seeks to *make* the point that there may have been direct links – as well as indirect parallels along themes from climate, hunger, population, territories, tax, and sovereign debt, to discourses on free and unfree labor.[60]

---

57 On the economic importance and east-west trade of the Polish-Lithuanian Commonwealth, see Samsonowicz, *Późne Średniowiecze Miast Nadbałtyckich*.
58 Collet, *Die doppelte Katastrophe*, pp. 350ff.
59 Ferreiro, *Brothers in Arms*.
60 Since making this point was the primary objective of this chapter, I have been brief on the complex and rich historiography, in particular by Polish historians, on the period of the partitions.

The hurricanes in the Caribbean around 1770 did not cause the partition of 1772. Neither did the failed French Kourou project. There are no straightforward, mono-causal relations in history. Both transnational and global history are critical of mono-causal or single country explanations. The purpose of outlining these distant events and crisis scenarios is to think about the history of East-Central Europe and how to relate it to global history, as the latter tends to turn a blind eye to the region.[61] Unintentionally, the tendency to see global history almost exclusively via expanding maritime empires during the 'age of revolutions' reinforces the long-established historiographical division between liquid-maritime Western Europe on the one hand, and territorial Eastern Europe on the other.[62]

The chapter suggests that political and territorial events between Poland, Prussia, the Habsburg Empire, and Russia that are normally interpreted as national histories or as a regional history were indeed related to wider and interconnected themes. As such, it attempts to overcome the long-established disconnection between Eastern and Western European history.

In addition to reconsidering the spatial units we operate in as historians, global and transnational history invites us to rethink established periodizations. We need 'to identify periods of conjunctural moments of crisis that shaped the future context within which others necessarily had to operate'.[63] Following this imperative, this chapter suggests that the period between c. 1760 and the 1780s ought to be seen as an inter-war period in crisis that tied all major European states – east and west – together. Some were directly entangled in co-operation and competition across the Atlantic between Guiana, Cuba, Philadelphia, and Louisiana. Others – like Poland, Prussia, or the Habsburg Empire – were indirectly related by the common threads of debt, severe weather conditions, hunger, the quest for territories, population, and taxes.[64] No European power in the later eighteenth century was able to escape these problems. Some sought to overcome the crisis by (re)building their overseas empires. Others, such as Brandenburg-Prussia, could not but face eastwards for expansion.

---

61   See for instance S. Conrad and J. Osterhammel, eds, *An Emerging Modern World 1750–1870* (Cambridge/London, 2018).

62   Among the few exceptions to overcome and question this divide are: Brahm and Rosenhaft, eds, *Slavery Hinterland*; C. Dejung and M. Lengwiler, 'Einleitung', *Ränder der Moderne: Neue Perspektiven auf die Europäische Geschichte (1800–1930)*, ed. C. Dejung and M. Lengwiler (Cologne, 2016), pp. 7–35, here pp. 14f, 32.

63   E. Burke III, 'Modernity's Histories: Rethinking the Long Nineteenth Century, 1750–1950', *World History Workshop e-Repository* (June 2004), pp. 1–12, here p. 5.

64   Wong, 'Possibilities of Plenty', p. 260.

3

A Fierce Competition!
Silesian Linens and Indian Cottons on the West African Coast in the Late Seventeenth and Early Eighteenth Centuries

ANKA STEFFEN[1]

European-made linens and woollens figured prominently among the foreign textiles exchanged at the very beginning of the African trade, as Colleen E. Kriger points out.[2] Indian cottons joined the product range shipped on European vessels to the coast of Africa, when the English and their European rivals became aware that they could become an inexpensive substitution for linens during the first years of the seventeenth century.[3] As Bernhard Struck has convincingly shown in the previous chapter, it is no longer possible to exclude Eastern Europe from global histories.[4] By implication, his conclusion also means that global history cannot be told by ignoring Eastern European actors or the supply of essential manufactures from this region for global trade. One particularly noteworthy commodity from East-Central Europe within the Atlantic trade system was Silesian linen textiles.

In recent years, scholars have come to agree on the central importance of African consumer preferences for the consistently high level of textile exports by European or Asian merchants to the western or eastern shores of Africa.[5]

1   Research for this chapter was funded by the German Research Foundation (WE 3613/2–1, 'The Globalized Periphery: Atlantic Commerce, Socioeconomic and Cultural Change in Central Europe, 1680–1850'). I would like to express my special thanks to Franziska Steffen and Jody Benjamin, who shared their thoughts in the early stage of the text. I am grateful to Carolyn Taratko for thoroughly ironing out my English. All remaining errors are mine.
2   C. E. Kriger, '"Guinea Cloth": Production and Consumption of Cotton Textiles in West Africa before and during the Atlantic Slave Trade', *The Spinning World: A Global History of Cotton Textiles, 1200–1850*, ed. G. Riello and P. Parthasarathi (Oxford, 2009), pp. 105–26, here p. 120.
3   J. Irwin and P. R. Schwartz, *Studies in Indo-European Textile History* (Ahmedabad, 1966), pp. 11f.
4   See previous chapter of this volume.
5   J. Thornton, *Africa and Africans in the Making of the Atlantic World, 1400–1800* (Cambridge, 1999); C. E. Kriger, *Cloth in West African History* (Lanham, 2006); J. Prestholdt, *Domesticating*

Strikingly, however, only Indian cottons have received a high degree of scholarly attention, whereas woollens and linens brought to Africa have been almost completely overlooked.[6] This situation is puzzling, considering that preferences of Africans for textiles not only dictated the type of cotton cloths that were traded, but also determined what kind of fabrics in general were transported to the West African coast and in what quantities.

It is time to pull woollens and linens out of the shadow cast upon them by the longstanding spotlight directed on cottons. Thus, the major part of this chapter brings into the limelight the competition between these three types of textiles on the West African coast during the decades just before and after the turn of the seventeenth to the eighteenth century. First, I explore the role played by the Royal African Company of England (RAC) as one major 'delivery service' for Silesian linens, based on extensive research in the company's invoice books. The chapter then provides a short introduction to the nature of the textiles. Since Silesian linens still lack an adequate definition, I survey their portrayal in contemporary travel accounts. Lastly, a quantitative comparison of all textiles shipped by the RAC (based on its invoice books) is introduced, and the narrative of the dominance of Indian cottons is called into question. The conclusion of this chapter probes the connection between two important Atlantic 'peripheries' and the link between the take-off phase of proto-industrialization in Silesia and the expanding slave trade around 1700 from the west coast of Africa.

'[F]or God sake lett us have them': the demand for textiles on the West African coast

In January 1681, a seemingly anxious Arthur Wendover at James Fort (Accra, Ghana) wrote a letter to Cape Coast Castle (Cape Coast, Ghana), the English Royal African Company's headquarters on the coast of West Africa. In this letter, Wendover tried to convey his urgent need for various textiles, which he had requested many times to no avail. Linen and cottons were among the

the World: African Consumerism and the Genealogies of Globalization (Berkeley, 2008); P. Machado, Ocean of Trade: South Asian Merchants, Africa and the Indian Ocean, c. 1750–1850 (Cambridge, 2014); E. A. Alpers, 'Indian Textiles at Mozambique Island in the Mid-Eighteenth Century', Textile History 48/1 (2017), pp. 31–48.
6   B. Lemire, Fashion's Favorite: The Cotton Trade and the Consumer in Britain, 1660–1800 (Oxford, 1991); G. Riello and T. Roy, eds, How India Clothed the World: The World of South Asian Textiles, 1500–1850 (Leiden, 2009); G. Riello and T. Roy, eds, The Spinning World: A Global History of Cotton Textiles, 1200–1850 (Oxford, 2009); G. Riello, Cotton: The Fabric that Made the Modern World (Cambridge, 2013); S. Beckert, Empire of Cotton: A Global History (New York, 2015); R. S. DuPlessis, The Material Atlantic: Clothing, Commerce, and Colonization in the Atlantic World, 1650–1800 (Cambridge, 2016).

goods he desired most: 'course [coarse] sletias', a linen fabric of Silesian origin, should be sent 'a many as cann bee spared', followed by Indian cottons such as 'allijars' and 'long cloths'.[7] Two weeks later, the warehouse of James Fort still did not seem to be sufficiently stocked, since Wendover felt compelled to stress his wishes again in a subsequent letter hoping finally to get hold of the required items. A delayed supply of coarse sletias might prove especially prejudicial for trade, as he put it.[8] In March his anxiety had turned into sheer despair. The reader of the third letter might have flinched a little at Wendover's outcry:

> If there be any goods that can be spared for God sake lett us have them, as sayes, perpetuanos blews [and] greens, bralls, carpetts, blanketts, pewter baisons, allijars, sletias course or fine, sheets, or any sorts of linnens, as long cloths good ones.[9]

The demand for Indian cottons, European woollens and linens – especially those from Silesia – remained high during the following decades. Whereas Indian cottons and English woollens could be purchased in London, linens had to be imported from the continent to match the quantities desired by the RAC. English domestic production of this sort of cloth was not yet sufficient to satisfy overseas demand and, for this reason, the linen exporters Halsey & Cressener of Hamburg received very specific orders from London. The directive from September 1723 was very clear:

> [We] desire you will provide Twenty Chests more of Sleazies each to q[uantity] 200 p[ieces] to come on board 5/9 to 6/3 pp [Shilling/Pence per piece] w [which] you are not to exceed [,] the assortment of Sleazies most for the Companys purpose are those that are fine thin and Good coloured their being strong & substantiall … & to send them over by the first opportunity …[10]

Even though the two Hamburg merchants were eager to fulfill the request as quickly as possible, they informed their client one month later that they had managed to purchase only 3,800 pieces of the needed linens, packed into 19 chests. Unfortunately, even those trunks were not immediately brought on

---

7   'Allijars' refers to either a cotton or a mixed silk-cotton cloth made in India. 'Long cloth' is a long-pieced cotton cloth from India. For further details on various Indian cottons, see R. Law, ed., *The English in West Africa: The Local Correspondence of the Royal African Company of England 1681–1699*, Vol. 1 (Oxford, 1997), pp. xviiif.
8   Ibid., p. 154.
9   'Sayes' are fine woollen cloths, 'perpetuanos' a sturdy kind. 'Bralls' [Brawls] are coarse cotton cloths made in India. Ibid., pp. xviiif. For the quotation, see ibid., p. 156.
10   The National Archives (Kew, London) [hereafter: TNA], T 70/25, letter from Wapler on behalf of the RAC (London) to Halsey & Cressener (Hamburg) dated 19 September 1723.

board any ship, since it was uncertain which of the three vessels currently lying at anchor in the port would set sail first.[11]

The ready and speedy supply of linens became even more urgent when the number of people considered for sale into captivity around the English forts began to decline. At William's Fort (Ouidah, Benin) the slave shortage seems to have been very severe from 1727 to 1728.[12] Abraham Duport complained in his letter to Cape Coast Castle in October 1727 that the late governor did not leave him properly supplied with cowries, sletias, gunpowder, rum and French brandy, and that especially 'without the three first Articles [he] can do nothing in Trade or anything else'.[13] In December he emphasized his claims, writing that: 'I'd make no Contract for Slaves till this Fort is well stockt with merchandize, and more particularly cowries and Sletias which are always a staple Commodity.'[14] Even in April of the following year, 'the small Quantity of Slaves that are purchased now are only for Cowries and a few Sletias … [When] you do send a supply [and] it don't consist in Boogies [cowries], Sletias and Powder it will signifie nothing'.[15]

Apparently, cowries, sletias and guns, as well as the necessary powder for firearms, were in demand even as other merchandise on the Gold and Slave Coasts lost its value as fungible goods. Interestingly, these requests always included linen fabrics produced in Silesia, a landlocked region in East-Central Europe, far removed from any port and without direct access to efficiently running distribution channels provided by a state company for overseas trade.

The Royal African Company as a delivery service for textiles

During the height of its power, the RAC was equipped with the monopoly of trade to Africa and to the American colonies. From its foundation in 1672[16] to the early 1720s, the company deprived up to 150,000 Africans of their freedom

11   TNA T 70/25, letter from Halsey & Cressener (Hamburg) to [?] on behalf of the RAC (London) dated 9 November 1723.
12   In 1727 began the Dahomean conquest of the Hueda Kingdom that had been the major supplier of slaves. The capital of Hueda, Savi, was destroyed and with it the main trading center on the Slave Coast prior to the return of Ouidah to full working order by the Dahomeans. J. Wimmler, *Centralized African States in the Transatlantic Slave Trade: The Example of 18th Century Asante and Dahomey* (Graz, 2012), p. 50.
13   R. Law, ed., *Correspondence of the Royal African Company's Chief Merchants at Cabo Corso Castle with William's Fort, Whydah, and Little Popo Factory, 1727–1728: An Annotated Transcription of Ms Francklin 1055/1 in the Bedfordshire County Record Office* (Madison, 1991), pp. 8f.
14   Ibid., pp. 16ff.
15   Ibid., pp. 25ff.
16   The pioneering 'Company of Royal Adventurers Trading to Africa' had already been founded by Charles II in 1660.

and carried them across the Atlantic to the developing plantation areas in the Caribbean. Already in the 1690s, independent traders successfully took over some of the company's market share in the African trade, but only in 1712 was the monopoly of the RAC enterprise revoked completely. Even though the company managed the English forts on the West Coast until its liquidation in 1752, one can safely say that its decline in relevance started during the 1720s, at the latest.[17]

The 'Brandenburgisch-Africanische Compagnie' was the weakest competitor in the waters off the African shores surrounding its base of operation, in Gross-Friedrichsburg on the Gold Coast, and – unlike the other European overseas companies – it never fulfilled its role as a major dealer in Central European finished goods. The company abandoned its trade completely in 1721.[18] Hence, in the absence of a German equivalent to the RAC, the English monopoly enterprise functioned as a major sales institution for Silesian linens within the maritime trading sphere; it is, therefore, much more suitable to illustrate the presence of Silesian linens in this part of the world during the late seventeenth and the early eighteenth centuries. The RAC dispatched its vessels along the entire West African coastline, stretching from the shoreline of modern Ghana in the west down to mid Angola in the south.[19]

The complexity of the European textile trade to the west coast of Africa cannot be sufficiently described, because of the unsatisfying nature of the sources.[20] However, the generally consistent and detailed invoice books of the RAC[21] offer rare insights into the trade, though these sources are not without problems. The scribes employed by the company were well acquainted with the several dozen varieties of textile types purchased by the company in London, and they listed them accordingly in the account books before dispatching them onto the ships. One can therefore assume that the (piece-)amounts of fabrics summed up under repeatedly used categories of traded goods reflect the actual (piece-)quantities of these fabrics sent to Africa over a longer period of time. However, estimating the full scale of the trade remains problematic, since the piece-measurements for particular articles are not mentioned anywhere in the books. Thus, exported quantities can only be expressed in quantities of pieces and value attributed in pound sterling, but cannot be easily compared in more incontestable units such as yards or meters.

17   Law, *Correspondence*, p. 1; W. A. Pettigrew, *Freedom's Debt: The Royal African Company and the Politics of the Atlantic Slave Trade, 1672–1752* (Chapel Hill, 2013), pp. 1ff.
18   K. G. Davies, *The Royal African Company* (London, 1957), p. 2; E. Schmitt, 'The Brandenburg Overseas Trading Companies in the 17th Century', *Companies and Trade*, ed. L. Blussé and F. Gaastra (Leiden, 1981), pp. 159–76, here p. 167.
19   In the sources, these regions were called 'Windward Coast of Ginny', 'Cabo Corso Castle' (Cape Coast Castle) or 'Coast of Angola'. TNA, T 70/911, T 70/912, T 70/923.
20   Kriger, 'Guinea Cloth', p. 120.
21   TNA, T 70/909–935.

Other sources offer such information on size for particular fabrics at specific times and, as will be explored later, the size of cloth pieces might explain why linens from Silesia were appreciated in Africa. Yet, to be sure, the significance of Silesian linen or of its woollen and cotton competitors for the African trade is not just a question of numbers. The fact alone that all sorts of textiles were exported to Africa invites questions about the economic role and social function of Silesian linens and their place among the various traded textiles. Since the cargos of all vessels sent to Africa contained similar contents, the example explored here can illustrate the general contours of the European textile trade in this period. Consequently, the RAC's textile exports can provide insights into the overall European textile trade to Africa and can help us to understand the relative importance of linens in this trade.

The lack of textile samples makes it particularly hard to form a picture of the fabrics mentioned in the letters of the main handlers, quoted earlier in this chapter and listed in the invoices. Nevertheless, this chapter will refer mainly to eight fabrics that seem to have been essential for successful transactions with African dealers during favorable and not so fortunate times: sletias, Silesian linens in their fine and coarse qualities, English fine and sturdy woollens such as sayes and perpetuanos, as well as Indian cottons known as 'Guinea stuff', long cloths, allejars and brawls.

In view of the broad literature on Indian textiles and the English maritime trade, it is much easier to describe the cotton and woollen cloths than it is to define the linen fabrics produced in Silesia and traded on the African Gold and Slave Coasts. According to the 'Master List' compiled by Stanley B. Alpern, 'Indian fabrics were popular in Africa for their cheapness, durability, attractive patterns, and bright colors that resisted repeated washings and tropical sunshine'. Correspondingly, allejars were either cotton-silk mixes or pure cotton fabrics, usually striped red and white or blue and white, less frequently checked, flowered, or dyed plain red or blue. Brawls were a coarser kind of cotton, usually striped blue and white, whereas Guinea stuffs were similar to brawls, but smaller (18 yards x 1 yard). In contrast, long cloths were solely distinguished by their exceptional piece-length of about 37 to 40 yards. Sayes, in turn, have to be envisioned as fine woollen fabrics produced and dyed in different colors, not only in England but also in Holland, Flanders and German-speaking territories, while perpetuanos were apparently a coarser kind of wool that was more durable.[22]

---

22   S. B. Alpern, 'What Africans Got for their Slaves: A Master List of European Trade Goods', *History in Africa* 22 (1995), pp. 5–43, here pp. 6f, 9. Similarly, the Indian cottons were characterized by Irwin and Schwartz, *Studies*, pp. 12, 24ff, 57ff. 'Guinea stuff', though, is understood by them as a generic term used for various lowest-priced Indian textiles, a view shared by Kriger: see Kriger, 'Guinea Cloth', p. 123. According to the textile database established by the research project 'Europe's Asian Centuries: Trading Eurasia 1600–1830' at the Global History and Culture Center

With respect to sletias, Alpern quotes the Dutch traveler to West Africa, Pieter de Marees, who described this type as 'the most popular cloth' for clothing in his memoirs, first published in 1602. Alpern also suggests that the English word 'sleazy' might have evolved because of the inherent flaws in quality of the sletias, sometimes pronounced as 'sleazies'.[23]

Sleser Lywaet, Silitias, Slaseys and Sletias

Descriptions like those offered by Alpern, in tandem with the established notion that linen was only used to clothe slaves, undoubtedly contributed to the image of Silesian linens as cheap products of inferior quality. Statements by historians according to which '[c]oarse linen garb and bare feet became two of the most potent markers of enslavement', or 'the "slave uniform" that emerged in the Atlantic World was distinguished by its coarseness', and 'the manufacture of coarse linen profited diverse regions of Europe',[24] find echoes in present-day generalized views about the production of only coarse linens in Silesia.[25] Even if Indian cottons were too valuable to dress African slaves on the plantations, while 'coarse European brown linens and rough woollens were dirt cheap and readily available',[26] it does not necessarily follow that only cheap and coarse linen textiles existed.

African consumers would not have favored Silesian linens if they had been worse than African-woven fabrics made from bark, bast or raffia fibres, or other imported foreign textiles. On top of that, 18 pieces of 'sleas. Linnen' were amongst the goods selected in July 1663 as gifts for local African rulers, 'for theirs good will to lett us [the English] settle at Cape Coast'. Surely the negotiators would not have dared to offend the kings of 'Fettoe', 'Saboe' and 'Fantine' by presenting tributes unfit for a king's court.[27] The repeated requests made by employees of the company to their Hamburg suppliers, asking to be sent only wares of thin but firm weave and of good color, would

---

of the University of Warwick, long cloths measured 36 yards x 1¹/₁₆ or 1⅛ yards; the dimensions of Guinea stuffs were 18 yards x 1 yard when ordered by the English in India.

23 Alpern, 'What Africans Got', p. 9.

24 B. Lemire, 'Distant Cargoes and Local Cultures in the Material Atlantic', *William and Mary Quarterly* 73/3 (2016), pp. 543–8, here p. 544; T. J. Shannon, 'Uniformity and Fashion in the Atlantic World', ibid., pp. 549–54, here p. 551.

25 L. Clarkson, 'The Linen Industry in Early Modern Europe', *The Cambridge History of Western Textiles*, ed. D. Jenkins (Cambridge, 2003), pp. 473–92, here p. 488; B. Collins and P. Ollerenshaw, 'The European Linen Industry since the Middle Ages', *The European Linen Industry in Historical Perspective*, ed. B. Collins and P. Ollerenshaw (Oxford, 2003), pp. 1–41, here p. 9.

26 J. Styles, 'An Ocean of Textiles', *William and Mary Quarterly* 73/3 (2016), pp. 531–7, here p. 535.

27 TNA, T 70/909.

have made no sense businesswise if inferior products would have done just as well, or if the sole purpose of the cloth was to cover the nakedness of enslaved Africans.

Sadly – and I believe unjustly – the fact that the written sources mention Silesian linens mainly in connection with slavery and the slave trade has led historians to picture these products as being both of humble appearance and of low quality. Instead, we should imagine them as they were described by contemporaries: thin, bleached, and well-fitting articles of clothing in hot and humid climates. It was precisely these characteristics that caught the attention of Africans and Europeans alike. Otto Friedrich van der Gröben, for example, began to appreciate the advantages of linen clothes in the tropics. In 1682, he noted in his travel account that '[w]hen we left Sinnegal it became very hot and we were obliged to take off our German clothes and put on linen ones'.[28]

Different terms denoting Silesian linens in European reports or travel accounts written in the seventeenth and eighteenth centuries, and the lack of their proper allocation to geographical places, probably factored into the difficulties historians have faced in determining the kind of cloth their sources referred to.[29] The manifold spelling variations – Sleser Lywaet,[30] Silitias,[31] Slaseys[32] – are only the tip of the iceberg. The 'glaaser' linen, which the editor of the Brandenburg sources relating to West African history, Adam Jones, furnished with a question mark, might actually refer to the fabric processed in the Silesian town of Glatz (Kłodzko). This is even more likely, because it is also referred to as 'chilesisen', possibly yet another phonetic rendering of 'Silesian'. Jones' assumption that the term referred to 'glass linen' (in other words, linen material with glass powder attached to it) is not very convincing when taking into consideration the context of its appearance. Listed among other textiles unloaded from a ship at Gross-Friedrichsburg in 1685, it would make more sense to consider it as a fabric intended as clothing material and not for polishing soft metals, as the author suggests.[33]

Despite the difficulties resulting from spelling variations, which sometimes make it hard to identify the item under discussion, travel accounts contain rich information about the demand for Silesian linens on the West African coast, as well as about their usage and value. As early as 1602, the travel memoirs of Pieter de Marees about his journey to the Guinea Coast mention that the Dutch

---

28 A. Jones, *Brandenburg Sources for West African History 1680–1700* (Stuttgart, 1985), p. 23.
29 Similar thoughts were already considered in 1964 by M. Małowist, 'Śląskie Tekstylia w Zachodniej Afryce w XVI i XVII Wieku', *Przegląd Historyczny* 55 (1964), pp. 98–9, here p. 98.
30 P. de Marees, *Beschryvinghe ende Historische verhael vant Gout Koninckrijck van Guinea* (Amsterdam, 1617), p. 25.
31 F. Moore, *Travels into the Inland Parts of Africa* (London, 1738), p. 154.
32 London Metropolitan Archives, A/FH/A/9/1/114. Foundling Hospital Billet Book, 1758. I would like to thank John Styles for providing me with this source.
33 Jones, *Brandenburg Sources*, pp. 132, 315.

brought great quantities of 'Sleser Lywaet' to the Gold Coast.[34] He described African noblemen (Edelman) being dressed in fine linen cloaks, while African merchants (coopman) could be met dressed either in cottons or in linens.[35] The Swabian Andreas Josua Ulsheimer traveled to West Africa shortly after de Marees and noted that in the village of Komenda 'is a great trade in linen, basins, cauldrons, knives, iron, glass beads of many sizes and colors, copper rings, coarse woollen cloth, mirrors and similar articles'. He observed men bringing gold from the interior of the continent to the coast and exchanging their valuable cargo for 'mainly linen'.[36] While reading numerous accounts, it is striking that linens nearly always appeared at the very top of the list of traded items.[37] While there is no evidence proving that the listing followed a specific hierarchy that revealed their trading ratio, it is fair to assume that merchandise sold in large quantities or generating great profits made a profound impression on people writing down their experiences.

It is also interesting that some Africans seem to have been dressed in linens throughout their lives, from birth until burial. During the seventeenth century, Wilhelm Johann Müller observed that newborns were wrapped in linen cloth before being presented to their mothers.[38] A couple of years earlier, Samuel Brun (or Braun) described a bridegroom dressed in white linen, the African having considered it an elegant garment.[39] During the funeral ceremonies, the body was wrapped in cloth made out of linen or 'say' (sayes) before it was laid to its final rest.[40] Müller reported that 'men of very slender means may perhaps buy … poor-quality coarse linen … Others, who are very poor … take just an ell of linen.' In contrast, 'distinguished men adorn themselves in splendid clothes and precious ornaments. They wear not only fine undergarment of rash, precious linen or silk stuff … but also a precious over-garment, which reaches from the shoulders down to the feet.'[41]

These reports support the assertion that clothes made from linen were not solely bought by ordinary people or forced on underprivileged laborers, but that the African elite also purchased them. Hence, linens were sold in *various* qualities.

Furthermore, whiteness was a repeatedly noted feature of linen fabrics, and of sletias in particular. It is quite possible that the association of white cloth

34 De Marees, *Beschryvinghe*, p. 25.
35 Ibid., p. 16.
36 'Andreas Josua Ulsheimer's Voyage of 1603–04', *German Sources for West African History 1599–1669*, ed. A. Jones (Wiesbaden, 1983), pp. 18–45, here pp. 29, 34.
37 'Wilhelm Johann Müller's Description of the Fetu Country, 1662–69', ibid., pp. 134–259, here pp. 246f, 252.
38 Ibid., p. 218.
39 'Samuel Brun's Voyages of 1611–20', ibid., pp. 44–96, here pp. 86f.
40 'Wilhelm Johann Müller's Description', here p. 257.
41 Ibid., pp. 203f.

with 'spirit cloth' is not limited to the mid nineteenth- and twentieth-century social life of the Bùnú (Nigeria), but had already spread much earlier along the coast of the Gulf of Guinea. The brighter the cloth worn during spirit possession dances or during rituals promoting conception or healing, the easier it was to bridge 'the gap between the heavens, the spirit world, and earth', as the Bùnú believe(d).[42] Religious faith and practices might have advocated the purchase of purely white linen fabrics, by both the well-off and the less-wealthy Africans.

Of course, not all of these travel accounts specified whether the linens serving all these purposes were of Silesian origin – but it is quite likely, since sletias appeared frequently as a valued trade commodity in the correspondence between representatives of the RAC, as illustrated earlier in this chapter. The content of these letters and the written accounts of contemporary witnesses provide a vivid picture of the supply and demand for this type of cloth on the West African coast. In the context of the early African trade, therefore, 'coarse' did not necessarily point to bad quality or sloppy weave, but referred to a durability that also characterized the English perpetuanos, described as coarser than sayes but durable (even perpetual), making them desired trade objects. What ought to have become abundantly clear is that historians should not hastily draw conclusions about the appearance and utility of linens on the coast of Africa from their usage in the Americas as dress material for enslaved Africans. Whether coarse or fine, Silesian linens should be envisioned as an eminently suitable cloth, serving various purposes and available in correspondingly diverse qualities.

For the sake of completeness, it should not be forgotten that some linens produced in Bohemia and Lusatia resembled Silesian fabrics. While arranging the cargos for their foreign clients, Silesian merchants purchased linens produced in the neighboring provinces from time to time, especially if the volume supplied by Silesian weavers proved insufficient. Additionally, Hamburg merchants might have sold some linen wares under the prominent brand of 'sletias', simply because of their selling advantages on the market.[43] The share of non-Silesian linen wares among the labeled sletias is impossible to estimate, but an exclusive tagging of specifically Bohemian or Lusatian linen products is completely lacking in all sources alluding to the linen trade. Only the brand 'garlix', perhaps hinting at cloth woven originally in the city of Görlitz (Upper Lusatia, Electorate of Saxony), is specified in the records of the RAC. However, the name could just as well refer to 'Guliksche linnens', a cloth produced mainly

---

42   E. P. Renne, *Cloth That Does Not Die: The Meaning of Cloth in Bùnú Social Life* (Seattle, 1995), pp. 24ff.
43   W. von Westernhagen, *Leinwandmanufactur und Leinwandhandel der Oberlausitz in der zweiten Hälfte des achtzehnten Jahrhunderts und während der Kontinentalsperre* (Görlitz-Biesnitzbell, 1932), p. 5; J. Ludwig, *Der Handel Sachsens nach Spanien und Lateinamerika 1760–1830: Warenexport, Unternehmerinteressen und Staatliche Politik* (Dresden, 2014), p. 21.

in the Rhine region, with Krefeld and Gladbach (Mönchengladbach) as centers of manufacture.[44] Despite these exceptions from other regions, one can assume that textiles of genuinely Silesian origin were of great importance on African markets and shipped there in corresponding quantities.

Silesian linens, English woollens and Indian cottons in direct competition

It is undeniable that Indian cottons made up the biggest percentage of textile exports to the west coast of Africa, considering the long duration of this trade,[45] which might explain why linens and woollens are marginalized in this field of research. However, the sole consideration of cotton cloths prevents a more holistic view of the role of textiles in the so-called 'era of European expansion' and the profound effects of their circulation in different parts of the globe. A comparison between the volumes of Silesian linens and the amounts of other fabrics within one of the leading trading zones of Western Africa, brought there by vessels of the RAC during a time span of 50 years (1674 to 1723), will add a new facet to this hitherto one-sided perspective.

The company's invoice books provide ample evidence of the pre-eminence of Silesian linens. While quantities of linen types such as 'crocus', 'garlix', 'hessian', 'holland' or 'Polish linen' were indeed negligible,[46] 'annabasses' and explicitly sletias were transported to Africa in substantial quantities. 'Annabasses' usually denote a blue-and-white striped linen cloth, chiefly produced in France and Holland.[47] This kind of pattern was also well known at the latest in mid seventeenth-century Silesia, and it was imitated in the Eastern European province early on, as the correspondence between merchants from Breslau (Wrocław), Glatz, Hirschberg (Jelenia Góra), Hamburg and London confirms.[48] It is likely that a substantial quantity of these fabrics had been woven in Silesia, but had entered English vessels under a different label. Therefore, the number of Silesian linen pieces might actually have been larger than indicated in Figure 3.1, which was created based on the listed sletias in the account books alone.

The general picture that emerges is as follows: until the end of the seventeenth century, Silesian linens were shipped in similar quantities to English woollens and the so-called 'Guinees', a cotton cloth produced on the Coromandel Coast and

---

44   J. G. van Bel, *De Linnenhandel van Amsterdam in de XVIIIe Eeuw* (Amsterdam, 1940), p. 37.
45   P. D. Curtin, *Economic Change in Precolonial Africa: Senegambia in the Era of the Slave Trade* (Madison, 1975), p. 92; Kriger, 'Guinea Cloth', p. 120.
46   Those linen types taken together never exceeded more than 1,400 pieces per year (except in 1683); in 1722 only 14 pieces of them were transported.
47   C. G. Ludovici, *Eröffnete Akademie der Kaufleute, oder vollständiges Kaufmanns-Lexicon*, Vol. 1 (Leipzig, 1767), p. 711.
48   TNA, C 104/126, 128, 129.

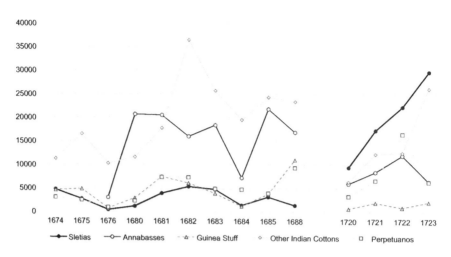

Figure 3.1. Textile exports of the English Royal African Company (1674–1723)

Source: TNA, T 70/910–923. 'Other Indian Cottons' are: allejars, baftas, brawls, calicos, chintz, cuttannees, longees, long cloth, niccannees, panthaes, photaes, pintados, saccerguntes, salampores, tapseils. The discrepancies between the number of pieces counted by the author of this chapter and the numbers offered by Kenneth G. Davies for the time period 1674 to 1704 are minimal. Compare Kenneth G. Davies, *The Royal African Company*, pp. 350ff. The years included in the graph recorded ships sailing from London to West Africa during at least six months of the respective year. The time between 1688 and 1720 saw the Glorious Revolution in England (1688–1689), the so-called Komenda Wars (1694–1700) and the War of the Spanish Succession (1701–1714), which essentially interrupted the seaborne trade of the RAC.

Gujarat specifically for the African market. Only linens labeled as annabasses and all other Indian cottons lumped together were transported in significantly higher numbers. The individual graphs of the various other types of Indian cottons would approach those in the lower part of the chart, if counted separately.

The chart presented here differs from previous statistical visualizations of textiles traded by the English to Africa, and it has two major advantages. First, it goes beyond the common practice of classifying textiles simply as linens, woollens and cottons. As a result, the presence of specifically Silesian linens is visible for the first time. Second, the chart covers a crucial period in which sletias became so prominent that their piles under deck must have pushed all other textiles on board out of the crew's eyes. In contrast, previous studies such as that of Marion Johnson covered a time frame starting in 1699, while Kenneth Gordon Davies considered only the time span until 1704.[49] Thus,

49 M. Johnson, *Anglo-African Trade in the Eighteenth Century: English Statistics on African Trade 1699–1808*, ed. J. T. Lindblad and R. Ross (Leiden, 1990), pp. 54f; Davies, *The Royal African Company*, pp. 350ff.

neither of them became aware of the quantum leap of Silesian linens during the time the RAC successfully relaunched its trade operations to Africa after the disturbances in shipping created by prolonged warfare. Unlike the chart created by Johnson, in which Indian cottons and English-imitated cottons clearly dominate the picture for the period from 1699 to 1808, the chart above demonstrates that in terms of pieces, only annabasses stand out against all other sorts of cloth, before linens of Silesian origin started to take off. Hence, the turn of the eighteenth century was a remarkable period in the linen trade to Africa, especially concerning Silesian linens. Of course, the total piece-numbers of Indian cottons equaled a large volume of textiles in this selected time span. However, if estimates of individual piece-sizes are taken into consideration, the picture presents itself in a slightly different manner.

Kazuo Kobayashi, a Japanese historian, explains that African weavers used narrow looms which could easily have been taken indoors in case of rain. Each piece of woven fabric measured approximately two meters in length and just 15 to 18 centimeters in width. Therefore, these strips were by no means convenient for clothing material, since individual strips had to be sewn together to make a piece.[50] According to Irwin and Schwartz, one piece of Indian long cloth measured one yard in width and approximately 37 to 40 yards in length (0.9 meters x 33–36 meters) in 1724. Since the width of 'salempores' and 'baftes' was also just one yard, one can assume that all other Indian cottons were of similar width.[51] Yet the various Indian articles were considerably shorter in length than long cloths.[52]

Measurements provided by linen merchants from Hirschberg, offering their merchandise in 1731 to the merchant Jan Isaac de Neufville in Amsterdam, show that fabrics labeled as 'silesias' were at least 1½ meters wide, some even close to two meters, while their length could approach as much as 40 meters ($^6/_4$–$^8/_4$ Silesian ells x 60 Silesian ells).[53] Their advantage as articles of clothing

---

50   K. Kobayashi, 'Indian Textiles and Gum Arabic in the Lower Senegal River: Global Significance of Local Trade and Consumers in the Early Nineteenth Century', *African Economic History* 45/2 (2017), pp. 27–53, here pp. 30f. A similar statement can be found in R. Sieber, *African Textiles and Decorative Arts* (New Haven, 1972), pp. 155, 159.

51   'Salempores' were an Indian cotton cloth from Salem in India, whereas 'baftes' were an Indian coarse cotton cloth: Irwin and Schwartz, *Studies*, pp. 24, 39.

52   Both assumptions regarding the length and width of Indian cotton cloths are supported by the textile database established by the research project 'Europe's Asian Centuries: Trading Eurasia 1600–1830' at the Global History and Culture Center of the University of Warwick. Accordingly, salempores measured from 12 to 18 yards in length and 1 yard or 1$^1/_{16}$ yards in width (11–16.5 meters x 0.9–1 meter). Baftes, in turn, varied from 7½ to 18 yards in length, and measured around 1 yard in width (6.4–16.5 meters x 0.9–1 meter).

53   Gemeente Amsterdam Stadsarchief, 88/1306A–1306D: letter from Gottfried Glafeys Witwe & Söhne (Hirschberg) to [Jan Isaac] de Neufville & Comp. (Amsterdam), dated 3 October 1731; letter from Johann Heinrich Martens (Hirschberg) to Jan Isaac de Neufville & Comp. (Amsterdam), dated 25 September 1740; and letter from David Knebel (Hirschberg) to Jan Isaac de Neufville (Amsterdam), dated 11 December 1757.

is obvious: wider pieces were more comfortably wrapped around one's body. Additionally, the comparatively large size of a piece of sletias factors in heavily when trying to understand the volume of the Silesian linen trade compared to other fabrics. Even if the plain piece-numbers of sletias in the invoices were initially smaller than those of some Indian cottons, there is reason to believe that the actual amount of linen fabrics on the African coast was greater, because of their larger proportions per piece. De Marees' statement that 'Sleser Lywaet' was 'the most popular cloth' worn seems much more plausible when viewed from this perspective.

A more differentiated picture emerges if the attributed purchase values paid by the RAC are taken into consideration (Figure 3.2). A clear price hierarchy becomes visible, showing that different types of textiles were available at considerably varying prices, enabling a broad section of the population to purchase overseas fabrics, as Colleen E. Kriger has already pointed out.[54] Some fabrics, however, could only have been bought by the elites with corresponding financial resources. Customarily, English woollens belonged to the most expensive textiles. Their piece-sizes were usually somewhat smaller than those of the linen fabrics, and the prices for its finer kind towered on top. In the medium price range, the long-pieced cotton cloth and the blue or red striped or flowered allejars from India figured together with the finer quality of Silesian linen. But since the Silesian cloth offered for sale was presumably larger in size, customers enjoyed an advantageous price-per-piece ratio when acquiring this kind of fabric in comparison to cottons (or even woollens!). The lower price range was occupied by coarser types of fabrics made from cotton or linen. Heavy price fluctuations aside, average African consumers could mostly choose whether they preferred linens or cottons. English woollens – especially the finer sort – were more or less limited to persons with greater purchasing power.

In the case of sletias, we can see that their prices decreased during the 1680s and 1690s. This drop may have been responsible for the remarkable increase of sletias shipped to Western Africa by the RAC during that very time and 30 years after. It is notable that the account books cease to distinguish between finer and coarser qualities at that time. The price-per-piece ratio could imply that, from around 1690 onwards, only coarser linens were acquired. It seems reasonable to assume that a shift occurred, turning Silesian linens from a commonplace clothing material into a sole slave commodity, as historians have repeatedly pointed out. However, the price never fell below the prices paid for the cheapest Indian cottons, which were exchanged for various African commodities and slaves,[55] with only the unsold leftovers having been used to dress them at the plantations.[56] Hence, it is much safer to assume that the competition on the

54 Kriger, 'Guinea Cloth', p. 123.
55 Ibid., p. 105.
56 Irwin and Schwartz, *Studies*, p. 12.

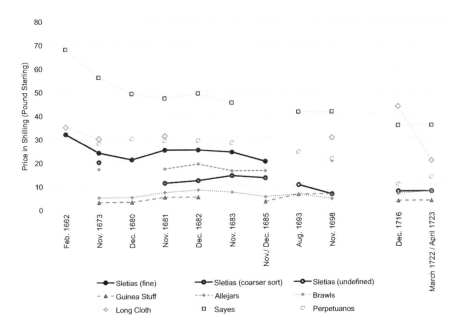

Figure 3.2. Piece-prices of textiles traded by the English Royal African
Company (1662–1722)

Source: TNA, T 70/910–923. The prices for single pieces of individual types of textiles
were taken from specific invoice entries in which nearly all selected types of textiles could
always be found listed: T 70/909 Marmaduke (February 1662), T 70/910 William Henery
(15 November 1673), T 70/911 Alexander (16 December 1680), T 70/911 Areana Merchant
(18 November 1681), T 70/912 Lisbon Merchant (9 December 1682), T 70/913 Pineapple
(7 November 1683), T 70/914 Goodhope and Sarah (20 November 1685, 26 December
1685), T 70/917 Mediteranian and Haniball (August 1693), T 70/918 Summers Friggatt
(30 November 1698), T 70/921 St George (20 December 1716), T 70/923 Advice Brigantine
and Royal African Packett (1 March 1721, 3 April 1722).

African market led to a decrease in price for Silesian linens in general, in order
to secure its share. It is therefore possible that the finer qualities of Silesian linen
were exported instead of the coarser ones, because they were now available
for the same price formerly payable for the cruder ones. This hypothesis is
supported by the fact that the RAC urged their suppliers in the 1720s to send
only thin, well-bleached and solid goods, which corresponded to African
consumer demands.

   Last but not least, ignoring routine price fluctuations, a tendency of falling
prices for textiles in general can be observed, except for those whose prices
were already low from the beginning. The cost ratio of Silesian linens dropped,
as prices for textiles purchased by the RAC declined overall. This price drop

was correlated with the people spinning, weaving and trading the fabrics in Silesia and distributing them to hubs of trade situated on the coasts of Western Europe. Whether this development was for the better or the worse will be touched on in the final part of this chapter.

Wealth and poverty in Silesia

Even if Silesian commercial actors did not involve themselves directly in inter-continental trade, they welcomed the opportunity to establish themselves within the trade network through which Silesian linens were channeled as far as Africa and the Americas. In the case of Lower Silesia, new fields of commercial activity closely related to the Atlantic slave trade and the development of plantation economies in the Caribbean emerged, which stimulated the domestic pre-industrial processing of linen and transformed labor conditions in the region.[57]

The huge investments in new bleaching facilities in order to enhance the trade in whitened cloth desired by African buyers on the West African coast is one example of Silesian entrepreneurial activism directly linked to Atlantic business operations. The exceptionally beautiful manor house (Figure 3.3) of Johann Martin Gottfried (1685–1737) in Wernersdorf (Pakoszów) is an expression of the enormous wealth that the linen trade generated, and at the same time shows how the production of linen cloth was enhanced and improved. In 1725, the merchant from the nearby trading town of Hirschberg expanded the former simple bleaching house into a representative living domicile surrounded by vast meadows, where pieces of linen cloth could be spread out under the sun. On the ground floor was the 'manufactory', where the linen cloth was processed and the raw material stored.

The reception room on the upper floor was decorated in the later 1720s with a ceiling fresco that shows a combination of allegories referring mainly to the religious beliefs that Silesian linen merchants shared. Imagining the mural painting as a picture in front of the viewer, the depiction 'Pax and Justitia embrace each other'[58] appears almost in the center, most likely memorializing the Peace Treaty of Altranstädt (1707) which settled the rights of Protestants in Silesia. In the wake of the convention signed between Charles XII, King of Sweden, and Joseph I, Holy Roman Emperor, one of the permitted six Lutheran 'mercy churches' was erected in Hirschberg and the linen merchants were permitted to

---

57   A. Steffen and K. Weber, 'Spinning and Weaving for the Slave Trade: Proto-Industry in Eighteenth-Century Silesia', *Slavery Hinterland: Transatlantic Slavery and Continental Europe, 1680–1850*, ed. F. Brahm and E. Rosenhaft (Suffolk, 2016), pp. 87–107.
58   'Justitia et Pax osculat', *Anthropometria, Sive Statura Hominis a Nativitate ad consum-matum aetatis incrementum ad dimensionum & proportionum Regulas discriminata, Oder: Statur des Menschen, Von der Geburt an, nach seinem Wachsthum und verschiedenen Alter*, ed. J. G. Bergmüller (Augsburg, 1723).

Figure 3.3. Wernersdorf Palace (Pałac Pakoszów), restored between 2008 and 2012

freely exercise their religious beliefs. The painting is a 'copy' of a copperplate print published in 1723 by Johann Georg Bergmüller from Augsburg, and was likely designed after the peace treaties of Rastatt and Baden (1714).[59] However, the ceiling decoration was expertly refined by rearranging or modifying some elements to highlight certain aspects of the original composition and to bestow additional significance on them. In the initial copperplate engraving, a distant naval vessel, barely visible to the eye, appears in the background. In the painting, though, the figure of Neptune, whose lower body is covered with a linen blanket and who carries a sea-going ship on his back, is depicted prominently. Above him, also cloaked in neat white linens, holding the horn of plenty in her left hand and carrying a spindle in her right hand, Fortuna supports the image of a thriving Atlantic linen trade (Figure 3.4). The novel context charges the personifications of 'Peace' and 'Justice' with a supplementary meaning. Both hint at the vital role of stable political and secure legal conditions around the Atlantic basin that were instrumental for the success of trade operations and, therefore, for the wealth of Silesian merchants. A dark-skinned child with what seems to be a linen kerchief wrapped around its head alludes to the fact that the destination of Silesian linen was Africa (Figure 3.5).

In stark contrast to the riches of the merchants, the rural, cloth-producing part of the population was solely occupied with worries about how to secure

---

59   W. Augustyn, 'Friede und Gerechtigkeit – Wandlungen eines Bildmotivs', *Pax. Beiträge zu Idee und Darstellung des Friedens*, ed. W. Augustyn (Munich, 2003), pp. 243–300.

Figure 3.4. Detail of the fresco in Wernersdorf Palace (Pałac Pakoszów)

basic subsistence for their families. This was especially true when their situation worsened noticeably as the merchants' trade began to thrive.

The years following the Thirty Years' War (1618–1648) had been marked by the expansion of feudalism. Landlords were able to get a grip on estates, while the size of the serfs' plots started to diminish and were soon reduced to units of absolute subsistence.[60] With little arable land left to work, rural laborers (including women and children) had to supplement the family's income by spinning and weaving. The entanglements between favorable international trade conditions for yarn and linen cloth and the growing number of land-poor, low-income laborers in Silesia created an unprecedented opportunity for the Silesian linen merchants. They started to invest in landed property, became landlords themselves, and began to make use of the serfs living on the land they had acquired. The institutionalized serfdom in the region made it much

60   K. Witold, *An Economic Theory of the Feudal System: Towards a Model of the Polish Economy 1500–1800* (Bristol, 1976), pp. 48ff.

Figure 3.5. Detail of the fresco in Wernersdorf Palace (Pałac Pakoszów)

easier for the merchant elite to increase the labor duties and, as a result, the output of cheap linen wares ready for sale. They were further able to reduce costs once they were able to bypass Dutch bleaching services, while upgrading their own bleaching capacities.[61] No wonder that the prices for Silesian linens on Atlantic markets – even those of better quality! – could be pushed down to increase their competitiveness with Indian cottons intended for the same customer groups overseas.

Evidently, the shifting orientation of trade toward the Atlantic during the early modern period did not fail to penetrate the landlocked regions of East-Central Europe. The quantum leap of sletias exported to Western Africa around 1700 was certainly related to two intertwined phenomena. Both the increasing trade in African slaves outfitted with basic garments and the accompanying consumer behavior of free Africans boosted the demand for them. The specific shape of the pre-industrial low-income home-manufacturing within the Silesian textile industry enabled low sales prices of Silesian linens on international markets. There could hardly have been better circumstances for merchants and traders alike to invest in Silesian linens.

61   S. Kühn, *Der Hirschberger Leinwand- und Schleyerhandel von 1648 bis 1806* (Aalen, 1982) [Breslau, 1938], p. 11.

Conclusion: Silesian linen and Prussia's Atlantic dimension

The compilation of commodities shipped to Western Africa by the English Royal African Company from the 1660s until the 1720s corresponded to the demand of African trading partners, who showed a fondness for foreign cloth. Silesian linens came into daily use across the Atlantic and became an 'atlanticized' merchandise. They proved to be an article of good quality, depending on what purposes they were required for. Sletias were highly appreciated by English and other traders who needed them to dress enslaved Africans, but they also satisfied demanding African buyers, who had clear ideas about what they wanted to wear or use in their daily lives, based on their status and financial means.

At least during the early period, Indian cottons had to compete with linens in the mid-range and lower price spectrum of available textiles. It is true that the peak of the linen trade in Africa ended much earlier than the slave trade, which persisted, and Indian cottons (later English imitations) eventually took over the market completely. Still, it should be clear that one must look beyond the established view about the dominance of Indian cottons within the African trade, or the slave trade in particular, to gain a fuller picture of the early modern textile trade.

The financial vitality of Silesia derived from its export-oriented trade in linens and explains why King Frederick II strove to incorporate this Austrian province into his kingdom, and even declared war on the Habsburg Monarchy in 1740 to achieve his goal. This point illustrates that even before 1772, when Prussia expanded at the expense of Poland after the first partition of the country (which Bernhard Struck has described in the previous chapter as an act that benefited from developments overseas), the Prussian crown increased its revenues by incorporating most parts of the region into its domain. This act cannot be dissociated from global circumstances, either. A closer look reveals that the tides of the commercial activities in the Atlantic splashed up to the mountain slopes of the linen processing area located in Lower Silesia, and that pieces of a seemingly inconspicuous cloth worked to bind Africans (both free and enslaved) and Silesians (free and coerced) closely together.[62] The province was hardly a far-away periphery of the Atlantic World. Silesia's position within the commercial web at that time was not measured by its geographical distance to the ocean, but by the proprietary article of trade exchanged within its basin.

---

62   A. Steffen, 'A Cloth that Binds – New Perspectives on the 18th-Century Prussian Economy' (unpublished working paper: Boston, 18th World Economic History Congress, 29 July to 3 August 2018). Forthcoming in *Slavery & Abolition* (2021).

4

Prussia's New Gate to the World:
Stettin's Overseas Imports (1720–1770)
and Prussia's Rise to Power

JUTTA WIMMLER[1]

The year 1720 was a momentous one for Prussia, as far as King Frederick Wilhelm I was concerned. In that year, Sweden finally ceded the Pomeranian port of Stettin – Szczecin, today located in Poland – as well as Western Pomerania to his kingdom, for a sum of two million *Reichsthaler*. Frederick had wanted the port for his kingdom for quite some time: he had hoped that it would guarantee access to seaborne trade and free his landlocked kingdom from its dependence on Hamburg as an intermediary, once and for all. There were quite a few issues with this seeming victory, however. In order to enter Stettin's port, ships first had to pass either the Peene or the Swine River (now the Świna River in Poland), and the water depth of both was exceedingly low and thus entirely unsuited to larger ships. For this reason, the larger ships had to anchor in the roadstead and reload their cargo on to smaller ships (so-called *Leichter*), which was both time- and labor-consuming. In order to carry the cargo to Berlin and the rest of the kingdom, the smaller ships then had to travel up the Oder River, whose waters were also shallow at various points and – to make matters worse – even silted. Overall, merchants considered the Oder River to be unreliable and greatly dependent on the weather. None of this made for a particularly good trade route. The following decades saw intense water-engineering projects in Stettin and along the Oder River system, including the construction and repair of canals connecting the Oder to the Havel and Spree Rivers, and thus to the

1 Research for this article was funded by the German Research Foundation (WE 3613/2–1, 'The Globalized Periphery: Atlantic Commerce, Socioeconomic and Cultural Change in Central Europe, 1680–1850'). I thank Friederike Gehrmann, who has helped me to research Polish literature. Since I do not speak Polish, I very much relied on Friederike for translations and summaries.

capital, Berlin. Trade regulations were devised, to encourage merchants to use the new port instead of Hamburg and the Elbe River. Prussia was to profit from overseas trade.

Scholars have tended to point out that the state's investment in this infrastructure was not particularly successful – a point they especially made for Prussia's export trade. Silesian linen merchants, for example, continued to prefer Hamburg because of its superior international shipping capabilities, but also because the Silesians had functioning business connections to that port, while they were sceptical about the capacity of Stettin's merchants to distribute their product.[2] Matters are more complicated with regard to the import trade, however: in this case, as some scholars have noted, the various measures taken by the government actually proved successful to a certain extent.[3] This rather general remark has, however, not been investigated in detail so far – and the implications for our understanding of Prussian history are far from clear.

This chapter has three interconnected goals. First, I intend to show that Stettin became relevant for Prussia's access to overseas products in the course of the eighteenth century. This seems like a minor statement, but it has not been scrutinized systematically so far for the period under investigation here (1720 to 1770). Instead, most scholars have focused on the period after the Seven Years' War. Second, the chapter tackles some methodological issues. To assess the growth of Stettin's trade in overseas products, I will use the Sound Toll Registers as a source.[4] In doing so, I also evaluate the suitability of this source for the analysis of trade volumes, which scholars often question. I will argue not only that these sources can be used to this end, but also that one should differentiate between different products instead of grouping everything together under the heading of 'colonial products', or assuming that individual products

2   T. Schmidt, 'Beiträge zur Geschichte des Stettiner Handels: Der Handel unter Friedrich dem Großen', *Baltische Studien* 20 (1864), pp. 165–273, here p. 177. See also R. Straubel, 'Stettin als Handelsplatz und wirtschaftlicher Vorort Pommerns im spätabsolutistischen Preußen', *Jahrbuch für die Geschichte Mittel- und Ostdeutschlands* 50 (2004), pp. 131–89, here pp. 142f; H. Lesiński, 'Kształtowanie się Stosunków Rynkowych pod Wpływem Merkantylistycznej Polityki Państwa', *Historia Pomorza: Tom II: Do Roku 1815; Część 3: Pomorze Zachodnie w Latach 1648–1815*, ed. G. Labuda (Poznań, 2003), pp. 681–98, here pp. 691f; G. Labuda, *Dzieje Szczecina Wiek X–1805* (Warsaw, 1963), p. 440; L. Beutin, *Der deutsche Seehandel im Mittelmeergebiet bis zu den napoleonischen Kriegen* (Neumünster, 1933), p. 93.

3   Schmidt, 'Beiträge', pp. 178, 180; Beutin, *Der deutsche Seehandel*, p. 98; Vogel, Bürgermeister zu Wolgast, 'Inwiefern gehört die Provinz Pommern zu den wichtigsten Erwerbungen des Hauses Hohenzollern', *Archiv für Landeskunde der Preußischen Monarchie* 5 (1858), pp. 219–75, here p. 265; Lesiński, 'Kształtowanie si Stosunków Rynkowych', p. 694; R. Gaziński, *Handel Morski Szczecina w Latach 1720–1805* (Szczecin, 2000), p. 346. Other scholars maintain that Prussia had to accept Hamburg as the preferred port for both the import and the export trade. See e.g. Michael Zeuske and Jörg Ludwig, 'Amerikanische Kolonialwaren und Wirtschaftspolitik in Preußen und Sachsen: Prolegomena (17./18. und frühes 19. Jahrhundert)', *Jahrbuch für Geschichte von Staat, Wirtschaft und Gesellschaft Lateinamerikas* 32 (1995), pp. 257–301, here p. 272.

4   The Sound Toll Registers are available as an online database at http://dietrich.soundtoll.nl.

like coffee or sugar are representative of all overseas (at least, all American) goods. Third, I will ponder whether this kind of analysis can help us to investigate the consumption of overseas products in eighteenth-century Prussia. To this end, I consult additional sources for the distribution of Stettin's imports through Prussia's river system, and I integrate my findings into a larger Atlantic context. Overall, I propose that my findings confirm the conclusion reached in the two preceding chapters of this book: that Prussia's rise to power should be seen in a global context.[5]

The Sound Toll Registers as a source for Stettin's imports

Already in the fifteenth century, the Danish King Erik VII had introduced a toll for all ships passing the strait between Denmark and Sweden, also called the Sound. The ships had to lie at anchor in Danish Elsinore (Helsingør), where the customs officials calculated the toll for the cargo and noted it in the Sound Toll Registers, which have been preserved (almost) in their entirety. Until 1715, ships heading to Stettin were exempt from the Sound Toll, but after the Prussians had occupied the port in 1713, the Danish crown refused to renew this privilege.[6] Although Stettin's merchants – and the Prussian government – were understandably unhappy with this change in policy and lobbied to have it reversed, it is lucky for us because this means that we have at our disposal quantitative sources for Stettin's trade. In the case of this port, they are the only such sources left. According to Stettin archivist M. Knitter, most records about the port's overseas trade were lost in the Second World War, which led him to conclude that its reconstruction is impossible.[7] This is all the more so since, as Knitter further explains, the remaining quantitative sources are unreliable – as is the secondary literature from the nineteenth and early twentieth centuries that had worked with the sources that have been lost.

Against this background, the Sound Toll Registers may have something to offer. They are to be used with caution, however. The customs officers in Elsinore rarely looked at the actual cargos – this would have cost too much time. They had the right to search the ships and did so if they suspected fraud, but this was certainly an extraordinary measure. Usually, they requested the ship's papers, issued in the country of loading, and calculated the toll based on these papers. The papers were usually accurate (after all, they were the basis for maritime insurance, and the person who signed them would be held responsible for incorrect information), but since ships often carried several cargos that were

---

5   See Anka Steffen and Bernhard Struck in this volume.
6   Straubel, 'Stettin als Handelsplatz', p. 143.
7   M. Knitter, 'Verifizierung von Schifffahrtsstatistiken des Stettiner Hafens in der zweiten Hälfte des 18. und Anfang des 19. Jahrhunderts', *Studia Maritima* 25 (2012), pp. 23–50, here p. 49.

loaded in several ports, a ship's captain could carry several ship's papers and easily hide a few from the customs officers. This practice was common enough to occasion a policy change in Elsinore by the mid seventeenth century. From then on, the officers requested general certificates that detailed the entire cargo, which seems to have contained the problem somewhat.[8] While scholars have questioned the reliability of the Sound Toll Registers to assess trade volumes,[9] the problem is less pronounced for the eighteenth century. These shortcomings do not invalidate the source as a whole – especially when we consider that comparable quantitative sources come with their own problems (for example, the Admiralty Tolls of Hamburg or the French port statistics).[10] None of these quantitative sources are completely reliable, yet we still use them for lack of better material.

After Stettin had become Prussian, the Prussian state immediately took steps to increase the attractiveness of the Oder River trade, but the project faced several problems. Besides the poor infrastructure, the cities along the Oder River (notably Stettin and Frankfurt an der Oder) insisted on the privilege of collecting tolls from ships passing through. Consequently, the regulations of 1723 and 1727 introducing (somewhat) free trade were short-lived, and the so-called *Oderhandelsrezess* of 1733/34, which exempted the merchants of Stettin and Berlin from any tolls on the route between the two cities, was also met with scepticism.[11] Based on the available sources, scholars usually assume that Stettin's import trade took off after the regulation of 1752 that freed the Oder River trade from Stettin to Frankfurt from all tolls.[12] By then, however, numerous construction projects had already been completed: in 1739, a port of trans-shipment had been created in Swinemünde (today Świnoujście) that simplified the reloading process from the larger ships to the *Leichter*.[13] In 1746, a project to deepen the Swine River was initiated and proved successful.[14] By

8   E. Gobel, 'The Sound Toll Registers Online Project, 1497–1857', *International Journal of Maritime History* 22/2 (2010), pp. 305–24, here p. 319; A. E. Christensen, 'Der handelsgeschicht-liche Wert der Sundzollregister: Ein Beitrag zu seiner Beurteilung', *Hansische Geschichtsblätter* 59 (1934), pp. 28–142, here pp. 111ff.

9   Gobel, 'The Sound Toll Registers', pp. 320f.

10   L. Charles and G. Daudin, 'Eighteenth-Century International Trade Statistics: Sources and Methods', *Revue de l'OFCE* 140/4 (2015), pp. 7–36. See also the chapter by Torsten dos Santos Arnold in this volume.

11   For example, G. Schmoller, 'Studien über die wirtschaftliche Politik Friedrichs des Großen und Preußens überhaupt von 1680–1786: Die Erwerbung Pommerns und der Handel auf der Oder und in Stettin bis 1740', *Jahrbuch für Gesetzgebung, Verwaltung und Volkswirtschaft im Deutschen Reich* 8/2 (1884), pp. 69–78.

12   Schmidt, 'Beiträge', p. 191.

13   On this point see also H. v. Beguelin, ed., *Historisch-kritische Darstellung der Accise- und Zollverfassung in den Preußischen Staaten* (Berlin, 1797), pp. 301f.

14   Gaziński, *Handel Morski Szczecina*, pp. 144ff; Labuda, *Dzieje Szczecina*, p. 446; H. Rachel, ed., *Die Handels-, Zoll- und Akzisepolitik Preußens 1740–1786: Dritter Band, Zweite Hälfte, Acta Borussica*, Abteilung C (Berlin/Frankfurt, 1928/1986–87), pp. 90ff; Schmoller, 'Studien', p. 59.

1755, larger ships could finally enter the port of Stettin without reloading.[15] The reconstruction of the Finow Canal, connecting Stettin and Berlin (and circumventing Frankfurt an der Oder) was completed in 1746.[16] The Plauer Canal was to connect Magdeburg (west of Berlin) to this route, and in 1749 trade between Stettin and Magdeburg also became free of tolls.[17] Simultaneously, tolls on the Elbe River (connecting Prussia to Hamburg) were raised, attacking the interests of several towns along the Elbe.

The primary goal of all these measures was to direct the export trade away from Hamburg and towards Stettin, which did not work. But as we will see, the measures proved successful for the import trade. Most of Stettin's imports will have traveled west to the Prussian heartland, especially to Berlin, Potsdam and Magdeburg. The newly annexed Silesia with its capital Breslau (now Wrocław) had a different legal framework and does not seem to have been a prime destination, at least for products from overseas. In their entirety, all the measures detailed above (the legal framework and the investment in infrastructure) had an impact on Stettin's trade, on the one hand, and on consumption in the Prussian heartland (primarily the so-called *Kurmark* Brandenburg) on the other. A closer look at individual products, however, reveals that one cannot generalize: the measures did not have the same impact on all of them.

The classics: 'plantation products' in Prussia

Analyses concerned with Atlantic trade tend to focus on the so-called 'plantation products', or what German-speaking historiography likes to call *Kolonialwaren* (colonial wares) – a nineteenth-century term that was not common in the early modern period.[18] To most people, it is immediately clear what this means: sugar, cotton, coffee, chocolate, and maybe tobacco. It is glaringly obvious that these 'big five' of early modern Atlantic trade are products constitutive of modernity; this may be one of the reasons why scholarship has tended to focus on these products rather than on others.[19] The other reason is the related issue that the

---

15   W. Buchholz, *Pommern* (Berlin, 1999), p. 351.

16   Vogel, 'Inwiefern', p. 261.

17   See Lesiński, 'Kształtowanie się Stosunków Rynkowych', pp. 691f; Gaziński, *Handel Morski Szczecina*, p. 113; G. Schmoller, W. Naudé and A. Skalweit, eds, *Die Getreidehandelspolitik und Kriegsmagazinverwaltung Preußens 1740–1756*, *Acta Borussica*, Reihe 2, Abteilung A, Band 3 (Frankfurt, 1986/87), p. 151; Schmidt, 'Beiträge', p. 176; Labuda, *Dzieje Szczecina*, p. 443.

18   Examples of the usage of the term are e.g. Zeuske and Ludwig, 'Amerikanische Kolonialwaren'; A. Radeff, 'Gewürzhandel en détail am Ende des Ancien Régime: Handeln und Wandern', *Gewürze: Produktion, Handel und Konsum in der Frühen Neuzeit*, ed. M. A. Denzel (St Katharinen, 1999), pp. 187–204.

19   See also J. Wimmler, 'Incidental Things in Historiography', *Cambridge Archaeological Journal* 30/1 (2020), pp. 153–6.

term *Kolonialwaren* was widely used in the nineteenth century, when it came to denote exactly these types of products. This chapter will propose that the usage of this term confuses our understanding of the broad variety of goods produced in the Americas for European consumption. Before I turn to these 'others', I will offer an analysis of Stettin's imports of these classic 'plantation products'. The goal is to see whether we can investigate the consumption of these products in Prussia with the help of the Sound Toll Registers – but also to illustrate that we need to look at these products more closely than is usually done.

There is no denying that sugar was one of the most heavily traded overseas products in the eighteenth-century Baltic, so it is not surprising to find that, according to the Sound Toll Registers, roughly 2,000 metric tons of sugar a year were officially headed for Stettin in the 1760s. No other overseas product was traded in higher quantities. Sugar imports ceased almost completely during the Seven Years' War, especially between 1758 and 1760. The complete lack of registered imports is unique: no other import of a certain product suffered from the war to this extent. Bordeaux was by far the most important port of origin for this product – for the most part, the French port dominated this trade. Again, this is hardly surprising: the French Caribbean island of Saint-Domingue (Haiti) was at the time the world's 'sugar basket', and Bordeaux was its most important trans-shipment center. This development dates back to the early eighteenth century, when a group of French colonial officers (headed by Jean-Baptiste du Casse) quite consciously started a sugar revolution on the island that started to pay off by 1720.[20]

More interesting about the Stettin data are the years before the Seven Years' War, and especially before 1753 when infrastructure measures and favorable trade conditions led to a considerable rise in sugar imports (Figure 4.1). Before Bordeaux began to dominate the European sugar trade in the late 1740s, Amsterdam was the point of origin of most sugar passing the Sound on its way to Stettin. It is possible that the sugar distributed via Amsterdam was still of French Caribbean origin, considering the important role of Dutch Curaçao as a trans-shipment center in the Caribbean.[21] It is curious, however, that Stettin seems to have experienced a few years of increased sugar imports in the early 1720s that even reached the level of the early 1750s, with c. 200 metric tons a year. From 1727 until 1748, on the other hand, a mere 5.5 tons a year were headed for Stettin. This may suggest favorable trade conditions in the early 1720s; however, to my knowledge, the time period does not correspond to specific trade regulations that improved trade on the Oder River. On the

20   K. Voss, *Sklaven als Ware und Kapital: Die Plantagenökonomie von Saint-Domingue als Entwicklungsprojekt* (Munich, 2016).

21   W. Klooster, 'Curaçao and the Caribbean Transit Trade', *Riches from Atlantic Commerce: Dutch Transatlantic Trade and Shipping, 1585–1817*, ed. J. Postma and V. Enthoven (Leiden/ Boston, 2003), pp. 203–18, here p. 214; V. Enthoven, 'An Assessment of Dutch Transatlantic Commerce, 1585–1817', ibid., pp. 385–445, here p. 439.

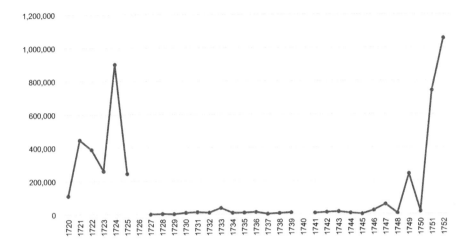

Figure 4.1. Sugar headed for Stettin before the increase of 1753, according to STRO (in *pund*). The *pund* is the Danish pound and amounted to 0.5 kilograms.

contrary: corresponding regulations were introduced in 1723 and 1727, and the 1723 regulation is usually assumed to have had little impact on trade (certainly less than the 1727 regulation). One could speculate that the sugar did not travel along the Oder at all, but either remained in Stettin and its surroundings or was re-exported from there to other Baltic ports.

If so, this certainly changed in the 1750s, once sugar from Stettin was meant to be forwarded to the Prussian heartland. Since 1749, the Berlin firm Splitgerber had started to establish several sugar refineries in the capital, and the king had decided to privilege this firm – once again with the intention of decreasing reliance on refined sugar arriving from Hamburg.[22] In 1751, he doubled the tax payable on imported refined sugar, while at the same time exempting Splitgerber's product from all taxes.[23] A year later, importing refined sugar became illegal in several Prussian provinces, as the king judged Splitgerber's refineries to be sufficient to supply these provinces with the desired product. In the following years, he extended the prohibition to other provinces, including Silesia.[24] However, several complaints about the high prices of Splitgerber sugar, as well as the firm's inability to provide it in sufficient quantities, illustrate that these regulations were not entirely successful. Refined sugar from Hamburg

22   H. Rachel, ed., *Die Handels-, Zoll- und Akzisepolitik Preußens 1740–1786: Dritter Band, Erste Hälfte, Acta Borussica*, Reihe 2, Abteilung C (Berlin, 1928), pp. 754ff.
23   Ibid., p. 756.
24   Ibid., pp. 757ff.

and elsewhere continued to be smuggled into the country.[25] In 1771, a new
regulation that all raw sugar had to enter the kingdom via Stettin and the
Oder River created more complaints.[26] In the 1770s, a sugar refinery opened
in Breslau (Silesia) and by the end of the century, Stettin had its own refineries
as well.[27] However, at least from the 1750s to 1770, sugar that entered the port
of Stettin was raw sugar to be transported to Splitgerber's refineries in Berlin
– officially, at least.[28]

Other types of sugar also appear regularly in the sources, however: 'top
sucker' and candied sugar (sucker candy/candis). 'Top sucker' is probably
identical to *sucre tête de forme* – a variety of sugar produced on French
Caribbean islands, amongst others. *Sucre tête de forme* was a cheap variety of
sugar compared to 'white' (refined) sugar or cassonade (*sucre terré*), but still
more expensive than raw sugar (*moscovade/sucre brut*).[29] It arrived in Stettin
primarily from Amsterdam, curiously enough on a more regular basis during
the 1730s and 1740s than thereafter (c. 5 metric tons a year in the 1730s, and 2.5
tons in the 1740s). In the last years of the 1760s, 'top sucker' again appears more
frequently, and begins to arrive in higher volumes than before. Even smaller
are the amounts of candied sugar brought to Stettin, again primarily from
Amsterdam: traded regularly since the 1720s at a moderate 50 to 200 pounds a
year, the amount of candied sugar headed for Stettin increased to 0.75 metric
tons in the 1730s and 2.25 tons a year in the 1740s. By the end of the 1740s,
c. 4.5 tons of candied sugar a year appear in the records. 'Candis' is a type of
crystallized sugar that was used primarily in medicine in the early modern
period (one can find many references to candied sugar in pharmacological
works of the time). It was thus not a product for daily consumption – but
certainly one that was available in the apothecary's shop. It is noteworthy that
the trade tendencies for this product differ from those of 'regular' sugar: since
it was traded in smaller quantities and was more expensive than the latter, it
was probably easier to transport it to Berlin (or elsewhere).[30]

While the Sound Toll Registers confirm what everyone suspects – that
sugar was an important trade item in the eighteenth century – it may come
as a surprise to some that the other members of the 'big five' are minor to

25   Ibid., p. 760.
26   Ibid., p. 760.
27   See H. Lesiński, 'Degredacja Feudalnej Produkcji Cechowej i Rozwój Przemysłu
Manufakturowego', *Historia Pomorza: Tom II: Do Roku 1815; Część 3: Pomorze Zachodnie w
Latach 1648–1815*, ed. G. Labuda (Poznań, 2003), pp. 657–98, here p. 674; Rachel, *Die Handels-,
Zoll- und Akzisepolitik Preußens 1740–1786: Dritter Band, Erste Hälfte*, p. 761.
28   In the Sound Toll Registers, 'raw sugar' occasionally appears as a distinct category, but it is
more than likely that the category 'sugar' also referred to unrefined/raw sugar.
29   J. Wimmler, *The Sun King's Atlantic: Drugs, Demons and Dyestuffs in the Atlantic World,
1640–1730* (Leiden/Boston, 2017), pp. 24f.
30   Considering its purpose, the numbers seem too high to assume that all the imported candied
sugar remained in Stettin for local use.

completely irrelevant trade items. Chocolate/cocoa appears merely seven times in the entire period of investigation, arriving from Málaga (Spain), Gallipoli (Italy) and Bordeaux in very small quantities. Cotton is all but absent until the 1750s and is then characterized by extremely erratic volumes (between 250 pounds and 44 metric tons a year).[31] The amount increases in the 1760s but remains variable (between one and 90 metric tons a year). Amsterdam appears as the most regular supplier of cotton, although Livorno and Smyrna (Izmir) in the Mediterranean furnish significantly higher quantities. This suggests that cotton from the Americas hardly reached Stettin. This is not entirely surprising, considering that cotton production for export was a rather late phenomenon in the Americas. France, for example, still bought most of its cotton in the Mediterranean until well into the eighteenth century.[32] As Giorgio Riello details, the 'second cotton revolution' that took place in the New World happened in the second half of the eighteenth century.[33] Since cotton is often considered a 'classic' plantation product of the early modern Atlantic World, this point should be stressed.

We could make a similar argument for coffee, which also began to reach Stettin more regularly from the middle of the eighteenth century onwards, but whose importance should not be overestimated. In the Sound, the toll for coffee was calculated according to value instead of weight – something that was usually done for high-value products that were not traded extensively. The Sound Toll Registers clearly illustrate the important role of Bordeaux – and to a lesser extent Nantes – as a point of origin for Stettin's coffee imports. This resulted from the rise of coffee cultivation in the French Caribbean, specifically on the island of Martinique. Coffee had been introduced to the French islands in the 1720s. It had begun to replace Levantine coffee in France by the 1730s and had managed to push the latter aside in Western and Northern Europe by the 1740s.[34] The Seven Years' War created opportunities for Amsterdam, Hamburg and London to act as distributors of coffee for Stettin, but Stettin's imports did not cease completely, as was the case with sugar.

While coffee hardly reached Stettin on the sea route, it is doubtful whether these numbers reflect coffee consumption in Prussia as a whole.[35] Frederick the Great was not an admirer of the beverage and tried to limit its consumption in

---

31   There are four categories of cotton in the sources: *Cattun, Cattun* Yarn, Cotton (*Bomuld*), Cotton Yarn. The first two are hardly worth mentioning – *Cattun* appears only sporadically and is counted in pieces (usually only 1–12 pieces per year; in individual years about 100 pieces may appear).

32   See Wimmler, *The Sun King's Atlantic*, p. 20. My analysis ended in 1734, but everything points to French Caribbean cotton being exported only in the very late eighteenth century.

33   G. Riello, *Cotton: The Fabric that Made the Modern World* (Cambridge, 2013), pp. 187ff.

34   Wimmler, *The Sun King's Atlantic*, pp. 18–19.

35   This subject is discussed at length by Zeuske and Ludwig, 'Amerikanische Kolonialwaren', pp. 278ff.

his kingdom by, for example, taxing it extensively. In a memoir, financial adviser Faesch was quite frank about the success of such measures: 'The high tax does not prevent people from drinking coffee, it just prevents honest merchants from having a chance against dishonest ones.'[36] According to Faesch, coffee was smuggled into the kingdom from foreign trade fairs, notably in Saxony. Silesians seem to have imported coffee from Austria, Bohemia, Saxony and Poland.[37] Merchants also tried to smuggle coffee into the kingdom by claiming that it was only passing through Prussia in transit. In 1781, the government issued a response to a merchant's request that illuminates this practice:

> The merchants have to prove that the coffee they claim to send out of the country is actually sold to foreigners and thus remains outside of the kingdom, and that they do not deposit it in a town at the border to establish a depot, from where they secretly carry the coffee – or whatever else it is – back into the country.[38]

Frederick II saw coffee as being in competition with beer and beer-soup (which was widely produced in Prussia), and he was upset that so much money left the country because of the increasing taste for coffee.[39] Besides merchants, monasteries were also accused of conducting contraband trade in coffee – as was the nobility, who were allowed to import small amounts tax-free for their own consumption.[40] An assessment of Stettin's imports thus hardly helps us to estimate coffee consumption in Prussia. We have seen that things are different with sugar; the same is true for dyestuffs, at least in part.

A little bit of color? The trade in dyestuffs

For the growth of Prussian textile industries, dyestuffs were key. In the early eighteenth century, Prussia did not produce a single dyestuff on its own territory, which meant that all of them (no matter their origin) had to be imported. The Prussian state perceived this as a great problem and encouraged the establishment of madder (reds), woad (blues) and weld (yellows) plantations in the kingdom, though with little success.[41] Although Prussia acquired

---

36 'Immediatsbericht des Geh. Fin.-Rats Faesch, Berlin 30. Juli 1750', Rachel, *Die Handels-, Zoll- und Akzisepolitik Preußens 1740–1786: Dritter Band, Erste Hälfte*, p. 743.
37 Ibid., p. 745.
38 'Königliche Ordres an die Deputierten der Kaufleute von der Frankfurter Messe, Potsdam 10. März 1781, auf deren Gesuch den außer Landes zu versendenden Caffee betreffend', ibid., pp. 748ff.
39 Ibid., pp. 271f.
40 Ibid., p. 272.
41 Geheimes Staatsarchiv Preußischer Kulturbesitz, I. HA Rep. 181, No. 49.

a madder-producing region with the gradual annexation of Silesia, and also began to cultivate the yellow dyestuff saw-wort as a local alternative to weld, this hardly proved sufficient to provision the growing textile industry with the required dyestuffs. For Prussia, this industry continued to depend entirely upon imports – and thus on Hamburg as a mediator. This can be illustrated by looking at Prussia's largest textile manufacturer, the Königliches Lagerhaus Berlin, which (amongst other things) produced uniforms for the Prussian army.[42] In the 1720s, the enterprise had tremendous problems acquiring high-quality dyestuffs: commission agents settled in Hamburg and Amsterdam sent the products directly via Hamburg and the Elbe River to Berlin. Since the commission agents had little expertise in dealing with dyestuffs, the Lagerhaus dyers were entirely unhappy with this practice; as it was impossible to purchase dyestuffs in Berlin, however, they had to contend with it.

By the 1750s, however, the situation had changed: Berlin was now full of so-called *Materialwarenhändler*, merchants who dealt in dyestuffs, medicinals and spices. The Lagerhaus could now buy its dyestuffs directly in Berlin. According to its director, this was cheaper than using commission agents in Amsterdam and Hamburg; it also took care of the quality issues, because the quality of the products could now be assessed directly in Berlin before purchase. One wonders, however, how Berlin's *Materialwarenhändler* were able to offer cheaper prices than a commission agent in Hamburg or Amsterdam. The Lagerhaus's director offers an explanation for this, as well: the transportation costs. By the 1750s, transportation up the Elbe River had become expensive. Even if the products were initially cheaper in Amsterdam or Hamburg, the costs of getting them to Berlin would have been too high. Where, then, did Berlin's *Materialwarenhändler* buy their dyestuffs and how could they circumvent this problem? It seems reasonable to assume that they received their dyestuffs via Stettin, and were able to profit from the cheaper Oder River trade. The increasing presence of *Materialwarenhändler* in Berlin and the growth of Stettin's import trade may very well be connected.

The Sound Toll Registers support the assumption that Stettin's imports of dyestuffs grew considerably around 1750, particularly where American dyewoods were concerned. Figure 4.2 illustrates the import of the two most important dyestuffs: the red dyestuff brazilwood and the multifaceted logwood that was mostly used to dye black.[43] We witness a first increase in the 1750s that is somewhat halted due to the Seven Years' War. In 1764, logwood imports

---

42 For the following see J. Wimmler, 'Dyeing Woollens in Eighteenth-Century Berlin: The *Königliches Lagerhaus* and the Globalization of Prussia through Colouring Materials', *Cotton in Context: Manufacturing, Marketing and Consuming Textiles in the German-Speaking World (1500–1900)*, ed. K. Siebenhüner, J. Jordan and G. Schopf (Vienna/Cologne/Weimar, 2019), pp. 195–221.
43 Brazilwood was cultivated in Brazil, Central America and the Caribbean (as well as parts of Asia), while logwood was native to the Yucatan peninsula, but also cultivated in the Caribbean.

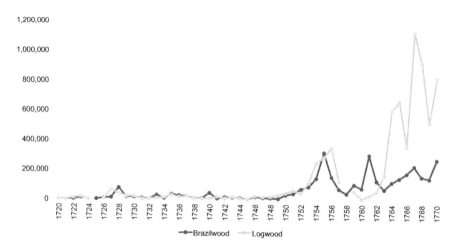

Figure 4.2. Brazilwood and logwood headed for Stettin, according to STRO (in *pund*)

increase significantly while brazilwood remains roughly stable. This may point either to an increasing use of the 'logwood method' for dyeing black, or a growing fashion for blacks in general. Brazilwood and logwood should not be considered as luxury items, nor as products producing luxury items. Brazilwood was a low-quality dyestuff that produced unstable colors. It either entered the production of low-quality dyes or it was used as part of a clever sales strategy: adding a thin layer of brazilwood could give a piece of cloth a beautiful luster that made it more attractive. The luster would quickly disappear after a few washings, however. In contrast, logwood produced high-quality blacks. Its major achievement was that it greatly reduced the cost of producing black textiles, which had previously required an elaborate process of dyeing and re-dyeing with woad, indigo, madder and gallnut. Logwood made the process much simpler and the end products cheaper. Both dyewoods thus enhanced access to colorful textiles (or in the case of logwood, to beautiful and lasting blacks) on Prussian territory.

Curiously, the most famous overseas dyestuff – indigo – followed an entirely different trend, as illustrated in Figure 4.3. Imports increased in the 1740s, and the growth after the Seven Years' War was less impressive than that of logwood. The absolute numbers are also much lower, but this is due to indigo's low weight compared to the heavy dyewoods. A small amount of indigo would certainly have produced a larger amount of dye than the same amount of logwood or brazilwood. Indigo's weight may also explain why its trade along the Oder River increased in the 1740s. To recapitulate: in 1739, a trans-shipment port in Swinemünde was constructed to facilitate the movement of goods from larger

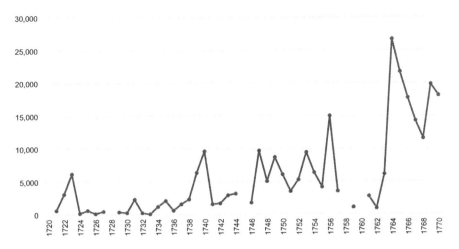

Figure 4.3. Indigo headed for Stettin, according to STRO (in *pund*)

ships to the smaller *Leichter*, since the large ships were unable to enter the port through the small Peene and Swine Rivers. Since such handling of cargo proved too time-consuming, the dredging of the Swine River and the construction of a mole were again attempted in 1746, but it took a few years to complete this project. By 1755, the infrastructure was finally at a point that allowed regular traffic of larger ships.

In order to allow trade in heavy and bulky dyewoods to increase, the larger ships needed to be able to enter the port. But what about indigo? Transported in barrels, comparatively light and at the same time of high value, reloading to the *Leichter* may not have been much of an operation in comparison. Two other factors may account for the different trends of indigo and dyewoods: first, the 1733 adjustment of the tolls along the Oder River to match those on the Elbe River benefited the indigo trade more than the trade in dyewoods. Before 1733, the toll for indigo was calculated according to value on the Oder, while the Elbe toll was calculated according to barrels.[44] This made indigo imported via Hamburg much cheaper. With the *Oderhandelsrezess* of 1733/34, calculation according to barrels was also introduced on the Oder River – which seems to have impacted Stettin's indigo imports. Second, the reconstruction of the Finow Canal (it had been destroyed in the Thirty Years' War) was concluded in 1746. This made it possible to transport goods from Stettin on the Oder River and via the new short cut directly to Berlin, without passing Frankfurt an der Oder, which still insisted on its right to collect tolls from ships passing through. If

44   Rachel, *Die Handels-, Zoll- und Akzisepolitik Preußens 1740–1786: Dritter Band, Zweite Hälfte*, p. 115.

we group all types of dyestuffs together into one category (or indeed all types of 'colonial wares'), as is often done, these specifics are invisible. It is exactly through these specifics, however, that the nexus between legal framework, infrastructure, and the practical dimensions of shipping becomes tangible.

Another case in point is cochineal, whose intriguing story illuminates other aspects of eighteenth-century Prussian trade. Cochineal is the name of a scale insect originating from Central America, which produced the most valuable red dye of the eighteenth century. The product was extremely light, and adding a very small amount of it to a dye could improve its quality considerably. Yet the Sound Toll Registers suggest that it was only traded to Stettin regularly from the 1760s onwards, and then in comparatively small quantities. Once again, the records of the Königliches Lagerhaus can help us to put the numbers in context: Prussia's biggest manufacturer of textiles imported on average 850 pounds of cochineal a year in the 1750s and 1760s.[45] During those years, only an average of 150 pounds a year was recorded at the Sound Toll as headed for Stettin. Unless the Sound Toll Registers are inaccurate, this would mean that cochineal could not have reached Berlin from Stettin. Where, then, did the remaining 700 pounds a year come from? The answer is not Hamburg. On the contrary: in the 1750s, the Lagerhaus bought 60 to 70 per cent of its cochineal from a merchant called Eckhardt – a man who resided in the Pomeranian port of Kolberg (Kołobrzeg), east of Stettin.[46]

This seems strange at first glance, but actually makes a lot of sense: Kolberg's merchants were partially exempt from the Sound Toll. Although they increasingly complained of being 'harassed' in the Sound, their privileges continued until 1857, when the Sound Toll was abolished altogether. However, the Danish government took the Seven Years' War as an opportunity to restrict this exemption to ships owned by Kolberg merchants (which means that a Kolberg merchant using a ship not owned by him or by another Kolberg merchant also had to pay the Sound Toll from then on).[47] This seems to have dealt a severe blow to the city's traders.

Scholars usually assume that Kolberg was a minor port that only distributed overseas products to its own hinterland and did not act as a re-exporter. Straubel has convincingly argued that this was the case in the 1780s, but the first part of the century has simply not been investigated closely enough to rule out Kolberg as a source of dyestuffs brought to Berlin.[48] Indeed, the fact that merchandise owned by Kolberg merchants was generally exempt from the Sound Toll until the Seven Years' War would suggest that this was the case. Lesiński noted that

---

45   Wimmler, 'Dyeing Woollens', p. 200.
46   Compiled from Geheimes Staatsarchiv Preußischer Kulturbesitz, I. HA Rep. 181, Nos. 94–9.
47   See H. Riemann, *Geschichte der Stadt Colberg: Aus den Quellen dargestellt* (Kolberg, 1873), pp. 170ff.
48   Straubel, 'Stettin als Handelsplatz', p. 178; H. Lesiński, 'Rozwój Handlu Morskiego Miast Zachodniopomorskich', *Historia Pomorza: Tom II: Do Roku 1815; Część 3: Pomorze Zachodnie w Latach 1648–1815*, ed. G. Labuda (Poznań, 2003), pp. 699–728, here p. 722.

Kolberg merchants had imported dyestuffs (including indigo and brazilwood) since the second half of the seventeenth century. According to Lesiński, the volume of dyeing materials had increased from three metric tons in 1653 to 25 metric tons annually in the early 1660s.[49] The trade in dyestuffs was thus certainly not a new branch of commerce. Since cochineal was highly taxed in the Sound, Kolberg merchants could easily have exploited this opportunity, as Eckhardt apparently did. He became the most important supplier of cochineal for Prussia's biggest manufacturer of textiles. During the Seven Years' War, however, he disappears in the records of the Lagerhaus, which suggests that he had relied on 'foreign' ships for his trade and that the new Danish policy hurt his business. This may help explain why cochineal starts to appear as a product traded to Stettin on a regular basis during and especially after the war.

The evidence presented in this section illustrates how we can combine the Sound Toll Registers with other sources – like that of the Lagerhaus – in order to assess the use and distribution of overseas products in eighteenth-century Prussia. It also illustrates how this can help us to re-evaluate some statements made in the literature – for example, concerning the minor role of Kolberg in the eighteenth century. While it is often pointed out that Kolberg's trade diminished as Stettin's grew,[50] the case of Eckhardt suggests that Kolberg's merchants could still find ways to establish themselves as suppliers for the Prussian capital – at least until the beginning of the war.

Ginger, pepper and 'luxury spices'

Among all of the Levantine spices that we have tried to grow in America, none has thrived like ginger, which arrives from there in abundance & in its perfection.[51]

… the largest consumption of ginger takes place in the North & Germany.[52]

The spice trade is traditionally associated with Asia, while its Atlantic dimensions are often overlooked. Its Central European dimensions are not much better explored: the distribution and consumption of spices in this region remain little investigated, except for the role of Upper German merchants in the early pepper trade.[53] Indeed, while much has been written about the medieval spice

49   H. Lesiński, *Handel Morski Kołobrzegu w XVII i XVIII Wieku* (Szczecin, 1982), p. 196.
50   E.g. ibid., pp. 202f.
51   C. de Rochefort, *Histoire Naturelle et Morale des Iles Antilles de l'Amérique* (Rotterdam, 1658), p. 99.
52   Chambon, *Le Commerce de l'Amérique par Marseille* (Avignon, 1764), p. 462.
53   For example, M. Kalus, *Pfeffer – Kupfer – Nachrichten: Kaufmannsnetzwerke und Handelsstrukturen im europäisch-asiatischen Handel am Ende des 16. Jahrhunderts* (Augsburg,

trade in the Mediterranean and the role of spices as a motivator for European expansion to Asia,[54] little is known about this trade in the eighteenth and even significant parts of the seventeenth century. The reason for this is simple: the new 'colonial staples' from the Americas – namely sugar, chocolate, tobacco, coffee and cotton – began their success stories. Meanwhile, spices lost their novelty character and seemed of declining importance in comparison. The focus on 'colonial staples' has, interestingly enough, not helped the discovery of the story of ginger; although of Asian origin, it was also one of the earliest American plantation products produced by servants and slaves, especially in the Caribbean. In the eighteenth century, Jamaica became the center of ginger production, with up to 1,000 metric tons a year exported in the 1740s – according to the official records, which most likely did not include all exports.[55] England thus emerged as the largest ginger-trading nation, distributing the Caribbean slave product all over Europe. As the French author Chambon noted in the 1760s (see quotation above), ginger was especially popular in German lands.

A comparison of Stettin's imports of ginger and pepper in the eighteenth century confirms that both spices were popular in Prussia: in terms of weight, the two were almost on a par (Figure 4.4). In 1753, roughly 28 metric tons of each traveled to Stettin; by 1764, this quantity had almost doubled. Even in the 1730s and 1740s, a few tons of ginger and pepper regularly reached the Pomeranian port each year. Weight does not tell us everything, of course; one pound of pepper would have had a higher potency than one pound of ginger. Nevertheless, there was a constant supply of both. Pepper and ginger were also often grouped together when they passed the Sound; one reason for this was that the toll rate for ginger and pepper was very similar. Stettin received most of its ginger from London, but Bordeaux, Amsterdam and Hamburg also acted as distributors. Of these four ports, Amsterdam was probably the only one that still furnished ginger from the Indian Ocean to some extent – the numbers remain low throughout. London's ginger most likely arrived primarily from the Caribbean islands, especially from Jamaica, while Bordeaux could distribute ginger produced on French islands (mainly Martinique, Guadeloupe and Saint-Domingue). We can also note that the Sound Toll Registers list three

2010); see also F. Braudel, *Das Mittelmeer und die mediterrane Welt in der Epoche Philipps II*, Vol. 2 (Frankfurt, 1992), p. 283; E. Schmitt, 'Europäischer Pfefferhandel und Pfefferkonsum im Ersten Kolonialzeitalter', *Gewürze: Produktion, Handel und Konsum in der Frühen Neuzeit*, ed. Denzel, here p. 18.

54   For example, E. Ashtor, 'The Volume of Mediaeval Spice Trade', *Journal of European Economic History* 9/3 (1980), pp. 753–63; C. H. H. Wake, 'The Changing Pattern of Europe's Pepper and Spice Imports, c. 1400–1700', *Spices in the Indian Ocean World*, ed. M. N. Pearson (Aldershot, 1996), pp. 141–84.

55   This is based on P. Browne, *The Civil and Natural History of Jamaica* (London, 1789), p. 14. He assumed that the official records in Jamaica only include roughly one third of the actual exports. The book was first published in 1752, but the data in the 1789 version is identical.

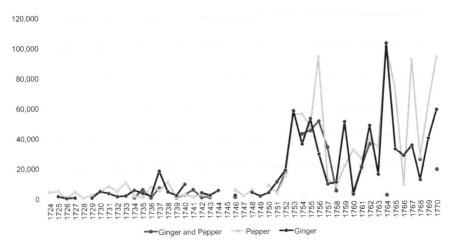

Figure 4.4. Ginger and pepper headed for Stettin, according to STRO (in *pund*)

types of ginger: ginger, dried ginger, and confected ginger. Sources on the production of ginger in the Caribbean suggest that dried ginger was the most common product, while confected ginger was a labor-intensive luxury that was traded in smaller numbers.[56] Against this background, 'ginger' is most likely a generic term that referred to the dried variety. While most of the dried ginger arrived from London (at least after 1750), confected ginger rarely came from England; Amsterdam and Hamburg were the most common suppliers of this more expensive variety, followed by Bordeaux.

Ginger and pepper had served culinary as well as medicinal purposes since the late Middle Ages. However, several scholars have argued that they lost ground in both areas after the seventeenth century. Wolfgang Schivelbusch proposed that the use of spices in the kitchen had been adopted by the 'bourgeoisie' by the end of the Middle Ages, and the demand for spices then peaked in the fifteenth century, which led to serious supply problems and what he calls a 'crisis situation'. According to Schivelbusch, this strong demand that could not be met was a major driving force for European expansion.[57] The narrative that Schivelbusch puts forth for the following centuries is not entirely convincing. He states that spices lost their attraction in Europe in the seventeenth century,

56   For example, Rochefort, *Histoire Naturelle et Morale*, pp. 315f; C. de Rochefort, *Histoire Naturelle et Morale des Iles Antilles de l'Amérique* (Rotterdam, 1681), pp. 335f.

57   W. Schivelbusch, 'Spices: Tastes of Paradise', *The Taste Culture Reader: Experiencing Food and Drink*, ed. C. Korsmeyer (Oxford, 2007), pp. 123–30, here p. 128. Mauruschat contests this, stating that even in the Middle Ages, spices continued to be an elite phenomenon: H. H. Mauruschat, *Gewürze, Zucker und Salz im vorindustriellen Europa: Eine preisgeschichtliche Untersuchung* (Göttingen, 1975), p. 110.

as well as their leading role in world trade. The market, he continues, was 'saturated, if not glutted', and European cooking largely rid itself of spices following the success of the French *nouvelle cuisine*.[58] Pearson follows the same line of argument about changing cooking styles, adding that new 'stimulants' from the Americas (notably cocoa, chocolate, coffee and tobacco) 'competed with or even replaced spices'[59] in the course of the seventeenth century.

It is doubtful that chocolate, coffee or tobacco would have been able to 'replace' spices, considering their very different usage. In addition, the *nouvelle cuisine* did not embrace chocolate, cocoa or coffee (let alone tobacco!).[60] The only 'American' product readily adopted in the new style of cooking was sugar – still a luxury product at that point. The argument that new European cooking styles reduced interest in spices is certainly correct. However, the *nouvelle cuisine* was the prerogative of a small elite in France itself and remained confined to this elite for quite some time. The new, more 'delicate' style of cooking aimed at highlighting the original flavor of meat and fish, and was based on butter, parsley and other local herbs. With the *nouvelle cuisine*, this elite turned away from spices precisely because they had become so widely distributed and had lost their role as a status symbol. Those who were not part of this elite culture, however, continued to use pepper and ginger in their everyday cooking. In contrast, the so-called 'luxury spices' (nutmeg, cinnamon and cloves – cardamom could also be added to the list) were never widely distributed, as the Stettin records confirm. Of these four, cinnamon was the most common, followed by cloves. They arrived from the Netherlands exclusively, primarily from Amsterdam.

Indeed, the *nouvelle cuisine* was slow to be adopted in countries other than France. Veronika Hyden-Hanscho has found compelling evidence that the early-eighteenth-century Viennese court despised the new French style of cooking, for example.[61] Anne Radeff notes that strong seasonings regularly shocked visitors to Poland and the northern parts of the Holy Roman Empire well into the eighteenth century.[62] The population of those regions likely had more use for ginger and pepper than the French elites. Stettin's records suggest that this was also the case in Prussia, and that pepper and especially ginger were hardly luxury products.

Moreover, if spices lost their leading role in world trade, this does not mean that their trade diminished. Instead, world trade grew and other products that had not previously been major items of trade (like sugar or coffee) now took center stage, especially in discourse. The relative importance of spices on the world market may have declined, but the absolute quantities reaching Europe

58   Schivelbusch, 'Spices', p. 130.
59   M. N. Pearson, 'Introduction', *Spices in the Indian Ocean World*, ed. M. N. Pearson (Aldershot, 1996), pp. xv–xxxvii, here p. xxxiii.
60   Wimmler, *The Sun King's Atlantic*, pp. 85f. .
61   V. Hyden-Hanscho, *Reisende, Migranten, Kulturmanager: Mittlerpersönlichkeiten zwischen Frankreich und dem Wiener Hof 1630–1730* (Stuttgart, 2013), pp. 204ff.
62   Radeff, 'Gewürzhandel', p. 197.

did not. Kristof Glamann also pointed this out in his analysis of the Dutch pepper trade: imports of pepper may have declined relatively in the second half of the seventeenth century, but the absolute numbers imported were in fact higher than they had been in the first half of the century.[63]

The ginger and pepper trades are particularly well suited to assess the accuracy of the Sound Toll Registers as a source, because we can compare the numbers to other data collected in the *Acta Borussica* on the basis of archival material that has since been lost.[64] According to this compilation, Stettin imported 34,500 pounds of ginger in 1754; the Sound Toll Registers suggest almost the same number for this year (34,869 pounds). While this seems to support the accuracy of both sources, the numbers provided for pepper differ: the *Acta Borussica* suggest 24,200 pounds, while the number calculated from the Sound Toll Registers is more than twice as high (54,900 pounds). Nevertheless, the dimensions are similar enough to support the conclusion that the Sound Toll Registers can be used to assess general trade tendencies. Another product that can be compared in this manner is also the last one I will detail in this chapter: according to the *Acta Borussica*, Stettin imported 219 metric tons of rice in 1754, while the Sound Toll Registers suggest 300 tons for that year. Both numbers are quite impressive – indeed, rice was easily the most important overseas product after sugar to end up in Stettin.

The forgotten consumer product: rice

One of the most heavily imported overseas products was a foodstuff not usually included in the category of traditional plantation products or *Kolonialwaren*: rice. In early modern Europe, rice was considered a crop for poor people: although it had to be imported, it was cheap and rich in nutrients and was often imported in times of famine. The general conclusion that *Kolonialwaren* were initially luxuries that benefited a small elite, especially in the cities,[65] does not ring true for rice, which certainly qualifies as a plantation and a colonial product. While rice was produced in some Mediterranean regions (especially in Italy), large-scale cultivation in the Americas (especially in South Carolina) made this crop more available by the middle of the eighteenth century. In North America, rice was produced by slaves, who may even have played a role in introducing technical knowledge for rice cultivation from Western Africa.[66]

---

63 K. Glamann, *Dutch-Asiatic Trade 1620–1740* (s'Gravenhage, 1981), p. 73.

64 Rachel, *Die Handels-, Zoll- und Akzisepolitik Preußens 1740–1786: Dritter Band, Erste Hälfte*, p. 497.

65 Zeuske and Ludwig, 'Amerikanische Kolonialwaren', pp. 276f, 299.

66 This theory, strongly discussed in scholarship after the publication of Judith Carney's *Black Rice* (Cambridge, 2001), is highly controversial: some scholars have pointed out that slaves from rice-growing regions in West Africa were hardly present in the rice-producing regions of North

Stettin's rice imports clearly connect to the growth of rice production in North America, especially in South Carolina. As H. R. Smith details, Europeans had experimented with rice cultivation in that region since the late seventeenth century, but they only succeeded in producing rice for export several decades later. By 1730, European demand for rice 'exploded' (according to Smith), which led to the establishment of further plantations in the region. South Carolina eventually depended entirely on profits from its rice plantations.[67] The Sound Toll records show that Stettin started to import rice at exactly that moment (Figure 4.5). This suggests that Stettin's trade responded quite quickly to broader developments in the Atlantic economy. The trends in the following decades support this conclusion: imports remained high throughout the 1740s and 1750s, when the price of rice was particularly low. The increase in the 1760s likely connects to a more general tendency, as a series of bad harvests in Europe made rice even more attractive as an alternative to other types of grain.[68]

In Stettin, rice arrived primarily from Britain, especially from London and Cowes. In 1762, 300 metric tons were registered in the Sound as destined for Stettin; in 1764 this quantity had almost doubled, and in 1766 almost 1,000 metric tons appear in the records. This makes rice the only overseas product able to compete with sugar in absolute numbers, although the numbers for rice are still clearly lower than those for sugar. If rice has nevertheless often been neglected in discussions of 'colonial wares', this may have several reasons. First, most analyses compare the value of products rather than their weight. Since rice was a low-value product, it would seem less important in such an analysis. Second, and probably more importantly, nobody associates rice with European modernity, as is the case with the 'big five'. It was a cheap product, which (much like the potato) moved up the social ladder instead of down: the integration of rice into the new style of cooking – as a somewhat decorative side dish instead of a full meal – was a rather late phenomenon.[69]

America. Walter Hawthorne has tried to find a middle ground between the two opposing positions: see e.g. W. Hawthorne, 'The Cultural Meaning of Work: The "Black Rice Debate" Reconsidered', *Rice: A Global History*, ed. R. Marton (London, 2014), pp. 279–90, here pp. 279ff; J. Carney, *Black Rice: The African Origins of Rice Cultivation in the Americas* (Cambridge, 2001). What Carney's book nevertheless highlights is that certain West African regions also produced rice. Europeans in fact imported West African rice as well – a subject that has received little attention in scholarship. See Wimmler, *The Sun King's Atlantic*, pp. 84ff.

67   H. R. Smith, 'Reserving Water: Environmental and Technological Relationships with Colonial South Carolina Inland Rice Plantations', *Rice: A Global History*, ed. Marton, pp. 189–211, here pp. 189ff.

68   Ibid., p. 191.

69   The foundational works of the *nouvelle cuisine* hardly mention rice – in Pinkard's analysis, rice appears once as an alternative to egg yolk to provide texture, and once in the form of rice pudding: see S. Pinkard, *A Revolution in Taste: The Rise of French Cuisine 1650–1800* (Cambridge, 2010), pp. 106, 175. See also Wimmler, *The Sun King's Atlantic*.

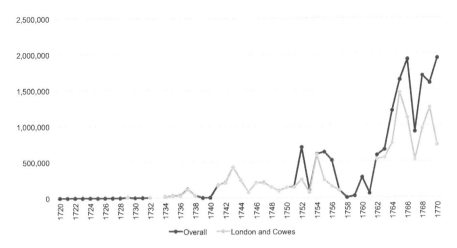

Figure 4.5. Rice headed for Stettin, according to STRO (in *pund*), with an emphasis on the market share of London and Cowes. Other points of origin registered in STRO include Amsterdam, Hamburg, South Carolina, Smyrna (Izmir in Turkey), Bordeaux, Dunbar (Edinburgh) and Bremen.

While the fact that rice imports were already at quite a high level in the 1740s (on average, 100 metric tons a year) certainly connects to broader tendencies, these high numbers also raise some questions about the Oder River trade and the provisioning of Pomerania with grain. There are two options: either Stettin's rice imports remained in Pomerania, or they were carried further into Prussian territory via the Oder River.[70] The grain trade – and the provisioning of Prussia with grain as a whole – was a complicated issue. For example, in 1740 Prussia exported so much grain that not enough was available for the kingdom's population. Throughout the first half of the century, merchants and the government also heavily debated allowing the import of Polish grain to guarantee the provisioning of the kingdom. Against this background, importing rice may have been an alternative – especially if rice was classified as a grain, which would have guaranteed extremely low tolls.[71]

The 1740s were years of war in Prussia, and harvests in Pomerania seem to have suffered.[72] However, the 1750s were years of good harvest,[73] and yet rice imports continued to increase. Considering that these were also years of war for Prussia, this may indicate that rice was needed for the provisioning of the

70   Theoretically, they could also have been re-exported, either via the Baltic or through the Oder River system to Poland – but this seems unlikely.

71   See Schmoller et al., *Die Getreidehandelspolitik*, pp. 128ff.

72   Ibid., p. 137.

73   Ibid., p. 254.

army.[74] Kolberg's rice imports also increased in the second half of the century (although the absolute numbers are much lower than Stettin's).[75] In addition, Kolberg began to import a few tons of rice annually from Stettin after the Seven Years' War.[76] Detailed information about the rice trade is not available in the *Acta Borussica* (which do not include rice in the volumes on Prussia's grain policies, for example) – but this should not come as a surprise, since rice consumption in Europe is altogether not a very thoroughly researched subject. This also stems from the fact that rice was not widely discussed at that time – unlike coffee, which was the subject of many controversies. The data presented in this chapter suggests that we should rethink this, considering the significant position of rice in Stettin's import of so-called 'colonial wares', amongst which we certainly need to place this grain.

Conclusion

This analysis has illustrated that the Sound Toll Registers can be used to investigate trade volumes, if used responsibly. Overall, the numbers are surprisingly accurate and – when I have been able to compare them to other sources – roughly correspond with the numbers found in other, no longer accessible, sources. However, as the example of coffee has shown, they do not necessarily reflect consumption in Prussia as a whole. They offer one piece of the puzzle; other pieces would be Hamburg's imports and the Elbe River trade (which, as we have seen, suffered from Prussian policies), as well as trade with other non-Prussian regions (especially Saxony), which also furnished the kingdom with products like coffee. In addition, we need to consult evidence from enterprises that employed or re-sold these products (such as the Königliches Lagerhaus or the Splitgerber firm, but also apothecary's shops), as well as the receipts or recipe books of individual households, where available. By collecting all of these sources, we may be able to paint a fuller picture of how access to overseas products impacted everyday life in Prussia.

Moreover, I propose that we need to integrate such investigations into the existing narrative of Prussia's growing importance in early modern Europe. One example is the army, which came to characterize Prussia in this century. Amongst other things, soldiers needed uniforms, and uniforms required dyestuffs – many of them imported from the Americas. The army also needed provisions, and rice may have been a sensible choice at certain times. The state's investment in infrastructure for trade and in changing a long-established legal framework (against much opposition from several Prussian towns) illustrates

---

74 I thank Neal Polhemus for pointing this out to me.
75 Lesiński, *Handel Morski Kolobrzegu*, p. 211.
76 Ibid., p. 229.

that the policy makers believed that trade and direct access to the sea were instrumental in increasing Prussia's power and strengthening its position in Europe. The fact that the measures were only partially successful (and in fact failed colossally concerning the export trade, which was the prime target of the measures) should not keep us from investigating the largely unintended side effect this had for imports and for patterns of consumption in the kingdom.

Lastly, the chapter suggests that the use of the term *Kolonialwaren*, or even 'plantation products', may not be ideal. First, both terms are somewhat exclusive, referring either to products produced in colonies or to products produced on plantations. This disregards the fact that some of these products were simultaneously produced and traded elsewhere, e.g. cotton or ginger. So even if some (or most) cotton or ginger was produced on plantations, this was not exclusively the case. At the same time, the terms exclude Asian and African products that entered European production processes and consumption simultaneously, suggesting that this was not part of the same general process. Second, the terms have become quite loaded and most people will have an image of certain products in their minds when hearing the term. As illustrated in this chapter, the 'big three' of Stettin's overseas imports in the 1720s to 1770s were sugar, rice and logwood – followed by brazilwood, pepper, ginger, and (by the 1760s) cotton. The alternative term 'overseas products' is probably not much better than the existing one, except that it seems a little more inclusive and less loaded.

We might think about using different types of categorization altogether. Contemporaries, for example, hardly categorized products on the basis of their region of origin. Instead, the merchants who distributed these products considered them to be part of the *Materialwaren* (an English translation as 'material goods' does not quite catch the word's meaning) – a term that included all kinds of products from all over the world (including Europe) and did not privilege certain merchandise over others. As we saw with the spices as well as the dyestuffs, high value but light products tended to follow a different logic than cheaper and heavier ones. Grouping together different types of products and assuming that a few of them are representative of all the others can obscure our view of the trading tendencies connected to individual products – and thus our understanding of the role they played for the people who handled them.

5

Luxuries from the Periphery:
The Global Dimensions of the
Eighteenth-Century Russian Rhubarb Trade

FRIEDERIKE GEHRMANN

According to Immanuel Wallerstein, Russia was for a long time a so-called 'external area' of the 'World-System', because it allegedly had no interest in importing European goods.[1] Wallerstein did not even consider the country to be part of Eastern Europe, which (as he explained in more detail in the introduction to that book) should be categorized as a 'periphery'.[2] This idea of Russia as a 'backward' country, needing and eventually failing to 'catch up' to Western Europe, has long been a popular theme – especially in English and German historiography of the twentieth century. Soviet historians, who were dealing with the restrictions of a limited ideological framework, did not challenge this narrative either. Only in recent years have scholars started to analyze this image more critically and to put Russian economic strategies in the wider global context of the time.[3] While it is true that Russian reliance on foreign goods was often small to non-existent, foreign trade and especially the levies on it were nevertheless an important source of income for the Russian state.[4] It is therefore unsurprising that the Russian government had actively promoted foreign trade since the Middle Ages, using tools and strategies common at the time. The three most important ones were the aforementioned tax revenues, the establishment of merchants' organizations, and the imposition of monopolies on certain (usually very valuable) trade goods. In the past historiography, these

1   I. Wallerstein, *The Modern World-System, Vol. 3: The Second Era of Great Expansion of the Capitalist World-Economy, 1730–1840s* (San Diego/London, 1989), p. 137.
2   Ibid., p. 131.
3   Examples include E. Monahan, *The Merchants of Siberia: Trade in Early Modern Russia* (Ithaca/London, 2016) and J. T. Kotilaine, *Russia's Foreign Trade and Economic Expansion in the Seventeenth Century: Windows on the World* (Leiden, 2005).
4   Monahan, *Merchants*, pp. 52f; Kotilaine, *Russia's Foreign Trade*, p. 8.

measures have been heavily criticized as prohibiting free trade and keeping the country in its 'backward' position.[5] However, duties on trade were in no way a characteristic unique to Russia. In fact, they were a common mercantilist measure in many Western and Central European economies.[6]

In this chapter, I will analyze the Russian rhubarb trade in the eighteenth century, to illustrate how the Russian government was able to become an important player in supplying Europe with a Chinese luxury product, by meticulously monitoring and supervising the trade of this plant. In exporting medicinal rhubarb to Western Europe, the often-criticized government measures turned out to be critical advantages. The chapter begins by outlining the fur trade as a prerequisite for the Russian rhubarb trade, as it laid the groundwork for the Russian expansion to Siberia and the establishment of relations with the Chinese government. I will then explore why the Russian government insisted on regulating the rhubarb trade and how this policy increased the value of this type of rhubarb for the European consumer. Finally, an analysis of the rhubarb trade through the lens of the Sound Toll Registers will confirm that increases and declines seen in the Sound Toll data can indeed be linked to developments in Siberia. The chapter thus argues not only that the Russian rhubarb trade connected Europe and Asia, but also that it helped to establish Russia as an important trading partner and intermediary for both China and several European countries, especially England and the Netherlands. It also suggests that the eighteenth century was a time of far-reaching change and upheaval in Russia, when even remote Siberia became a driver of global trade.

The Russian fur trade as a prerequisite for the rhubarb trade

In terms of volume, rhubarb made up only a small percentage of Russian exports. In the eighteenth and early nineteenth centuries, European merchants – many of them from England or Holland – made their way to the newly founded port city of St Petersburg, primarily to buy agricultural goods like hemp and flax, or to purchase iron from the Ural Mountains, a semi-finished product on

---

5 Examples of this position include C. M. Foust, *Rhubarb: The Wondrous Drug* (Princeton, 1992); W. L. Blackwell, ed., *Russian Economic Development from Peter the Great to Stalin: New Viewpoints* (New York, 1974); A. B. Kamenskij, *The Russian Empire in the Eighteenth Century: Searching for a Place in the World* (Armonk, 1997); K. Heller, 'Der russisch-chinesische Handel in Kjachta: Eine Besonderheit in den außenwirtschaftlichen Beziehungen Rußlands im 18. und 19. Jahrhundert', *Jahrbücher für Geschichte Osteuropas* 47/29 (1981), pp. 515–36.
6 See e.g. M. Isenmann, *Merkantilismus: Wiederaufnahme einer Debatte* (Stuttgart, 2014); S. R. Epstein, *Freedom and Growth: The Rise of States and Markets in Europe, 1300–1750* (London/ New York, 2000). See also the chapters by Torsten dos Santos Arnold and Jutta Wimmler in this volume.

which Britain had become dependent by the end of the eighteenth century.[7] The significant Russian export surplus at the time attests to the growing importance of Russian wares in Western and Central Europe. However, despite its small volume, the rhubarb trade was highly profitable. The rhubarb variety *Rheum palmatum* was a medicinal drug of Chinese origin, whose dried roots became a sought-after luxury drug in eighteenth-century Europe, where it was used mainly as a laxative.[8] Clifford M. Foust even speaks of a 'rhubarb mania' that swept the continent, and from there extended to the colonies.[9]

Historically, there were not many ways to obtain what Foust in his book title calls 'the wondrous drug', which was also due to the fact that only the dried roots of the plant were sold by the Chinese, making it impossible to plant medicinal rhubarb in Europe. In the Middle Ages, it was Arab merchants who carried the dried plant from Suzhou, in the north-west of China, to Aleppo, from where it was shipped to Italy. By 1536, another way of importing rhubarb to Europe had emerged, via ship, carried across the Indian Ocean, first by the Portuguese and later increasingly by the English. Because of these two different routes, the two kinds of rhubarb came to be called 'Turkish rhubarb' (transported by Arab merchants through the Levant) and 'Indian rhubarb' (transported via the Indian Ocean), though they both originally came from China. But from the seventeenth century onward a third variety emerged that came to be known as 'Crown rhubarb'.[10] This was the kind that was purchased from Russian intermediaries, and it seems that it had the highest quality of the three, which piqued the interest of European merchants, especially those from London and Amsterdam.

In order to understand the emergence of 'Crown rhubarb' on to the market, we have to investigate how it was obtained – an issue that connects directly to one of early modern Russia's more prominent trade goods: fur. The fur trade had played a significant role in Russia's medieval trade with Europe, but had declined significantly in early modern times.[11] In the early modern period, the Russian fur trade shifted from the European market to the Asian one, which made it the most important prerequisite of the Russian rhubarb trade. Amongst other things, valuable furs became the currency used by Russian merchants to purchase rhubarb.

7   C. Evans and G. Rydén, *Baltic Iron in the Atlantic World in the Eighteenth Century* (Boston, 2007), p. 37.
8   For the importance of purgatives in early modern medicine, see J. Wimmler, *The Sun King's Atlantic: Drugs, Demons and Dyestuffs in the Atlantic World, 1640–1730* (Leiden/Boston, 2017), pp. 78–9.
9   Foust, *Rhubarb*, p. xvi.
10   C. Che-Chia, 'Origins of a Misunderstanding: The Qianlong Emperor's Embargo on Rhubarb Exports to Russia, the Scenario and its Consequences', *Asian Medicine* 1/2 (2005), pp. 335–54, here pp. 340–1.
11   Kotilaine, *Russia's Foreign Trade*, pp. 250f.

While Immanuel Wallerstein may have been right to point out that the Russian economy did not depend on European commodities in early modern times, the fur trade illustrates that Russian merchants were nevertheless highly engaged in foreign trade. The export of furs to other European countries and to China was, in fact, so profitable – not only for the merchants, but also for the hunters – that they were willing to take significant risks in their search for the quickly declining populations of fur-bearing animals. Scholars agree that it was the fur trade that had led Russians to venture further and further east since the Middle Ages, eventually crossing the Ural Mountains and conquering Siberia.[12]

Even the quest to 'find' America with the prestigious Bering expeditions that Peter the Great initiated were mostly motivated by the fur trade and the desire for new, unexplored hunting grounds.[13] When the survivors of the second expedition returned to Siberia in 1743 and brought with them around 900 furs, which fetched previously unknown prices in the China trade, it caused a 'fur rush' that inspired many more adventurers to explore the North Pacific. The most sought-after type of fur at the time was that of the sea otter, an animal that had previously been unknown to Europeans[14] and whose pelts were sold for 90 to 100 rubles each to Chinese merchants.[15] It was the sea otter that led small private entrepreneurs to come together, to invest in ship-building and to send small expeditions out into the Pacific to hunt. Temporary hunting companies were established by lower-class hunters, private investors and sometimes government officials. After a successful hunting trip, 10 per cent of the profit had to be paid to the government as taxes; the rest was distributed among the investors in relation to their investment. Then the company was disbanded.[16]

Eventually, the first permanent hunting company was founded in 1781 by the Siberian merchants Grigori Shelikhov and Ivan Golikov, with the goal not only to trade but also to establish a permanent settlement on the American continent.[17] At the same time, other European powers started paying attention to the North Pacific, which led the Russian government to establish the Russian

12 D. Dahlmann, *Sibirien: Vom 16. Jahrhundert bis zur Gegenwart* (Paderborn, 2009), p. 48.
13 R. H. Fisher, 'Finding America', *Russian America: The Forgotten Frontier*, ed. B. Smith-Sweetland (Tacoma, 1990), pp. 17–31, here p. 18.
14 While there are several varieties of otters, the sea otter is a marine mammal native only to the coasts of the North Pacific, an area first explored by Europeans in the eighteenth century. Its valuable pelts very quickly led to an extensive hunt which made the otters almost extinct by the beginning of the nineteenth century. For more information see R. Ravalli, *Sea Otters: A History* (Lincoln/London, 2018).
15 M. E. Wheeler, 'The Origins of the Russian American Company', *Jahrbücher für Geschichte Osteuropas* 32/14 (1966), pp. 485–94, here p. 485.
16 Fisher, 'Finding America', p. 29.
17 Ibid., p. 30.

America Company (RAC) in 1799 and to equip it with a monopoly for the fur trade in the region. Considering the value and importance of the Russian fur trade, it is no surprise that Russia's first shared stock company dealt in furs and was additionally tasked with establishing Russian settlements in North America, which had become an important hunting ground.[18] It was, however, not the only one. John R. Bockstoce identified four ways in which Russian fur traders acquired their goods: through the RAC from America; hunting in Siberia; trade from Canada; and finally via a fair in Ostrovnoe in Siberia, where Russian merchants purchased the furs from native Siberians, who in turn acquired them from native Americans across the Bering Strait.[19]

While Wallerstein's assessment that Russia had no part in the World-System might lead scholars to the conclusion that international trade was of no importance in the country, the Russian fur trade can easily prove that the opposite was true. Whereas European countries had been the primary customer in the Middle Ages, in early modern times both the fur hunt and the fur trade shifted eastwards. There are many speculations as to why the Russian fur trade with Europe declined – the most likely reason being competition from North American furs, which decreased the demand for Russian furs in Europe. However, the decline of fur-bearing animals in Europe and the subsequent relocation of the hunt to Asia, in combination with the opening of the Chinese market, may have decreased the interest of Russian merchants in selling to European customers. Why transport the Asian and American furs through Siberia to Europe, when you could sell them to the Chinese? Especially in the eighteenth century, it made more sense to exchange furs and pelts for Chinese goods, which could be sold for a higher profit, either on the Russian domestic market or – in the case of rhubarb – in Western Europe.

Rather than being part of his global order, Wallerstein considered medieval and early modern Russia as its own 'World-System', with Moscow as the center and Siberia as a periphery. However, the fur trade illustrates that, from a Russian perspective, Europe may very well be considered peripheral as well, namely as a secondary output market compared to China.

The Russo-Chinese rhubarb trade in Asia

It was in the second half of the eighteenth century that a mass market for rhubarb emerged in Europe, with various countries – especially England – trying to satisfy the demand for the exotic medicinal plant. Matthew P. Romaniello argues that it was peace with Russia and therefore access to the high-quality

18   Dahlmann, *Sibirien*, p. 102.
19   J. R. Bockstoce, *Furs and Frontiers in the Far North: The Contest among Native and Foreign Nations for the Bering Strait Fur Trade* (New Haven, 2009), p. 103.

Crown rhubarb that led to the peak of the 'rhubarb mania' between 1760 and 1825.[20] Russian rhubarb was expensive; nevertheless, contemporary buyers seem to have deemed it worth the price.

As has been established, Russian merchants needed two things to acquire rhubarb: furs to trade with, as well as access to the Chinese market. The latter proved difficult, since the Chinese government was reluctant to initiate contact with any Europeans. From the beginning, the Russians were much more interested in establishing economic relations than their Chinese counterparts, who viewed the Russian advance in Siberia with concern and suspicion. But even before official contacts between the two governments were made, small amounts of rhubarb already reached Russia. It was Central Asian merchants who carried Chinese goods – including rhubarb – to the Russian trading place Tobolsk in Western Siberia.[21] Rhubarb is first mentioned in Russian sources as an import in 1568 but seems to have become a regular trade good by the seventeenth century.[22] It was exported to Western Europe mainly from Arkhangelsk, the Russian White Sea port in the far north.[23] However, already in the seventeenth century, small amounts of rhubarb can be found in the Sound Toll Registers. In 1655, 2,040 *pund*[24] of rhubarb were being shipped through the Sound, as well as another 100 *pund* in 1658.[25]

At this time, economic interest on the Russian side and geopolitical concerns on the Chinese side led to the establishment of continuous diplomatic relations, which lasted from the seventeenth century until the end of both empires in the early twentieth century. Two contracts regulating the relations and the trade between the two countries were signed.[26] The first of these contracts was the Treaty of Nerchinsk in 1689. It was the first modern, international contract signed by a Chinese government, and (at least in theory) it recognized the Russians as equals.[27] Most important for the Russians was an article allowing certain merchants to enter China, provided they carried official papers from the Russian government allowing them to do so.[28] This treaty made

20   M. P. Romaniello, 'True Rhubarb? Trading Eurasian Botanical and Medical Knowledge in the Eighteenth Century', *Journal of Global History* 11 (2016), pp. 3–23, here p. 4.

21   Foust, *Rhubarb*, p. 46.

22   Romaniello, 'True Rhubarb?', p. 12.

23   Foust, *Rhubarb*, p. 46.

24   In the Sound Toll Registers, rhubarb is usually declared in *pund* (the Danish pound). Very occasionally the units *skippund* or *lispund* are used, in which cases I have converted them into *pund* using the conversion rates by J. Kanstrup, 'Svigagtig angivelse: resundstolden i 1700–tallet', *Tolden i Sundet: Toldopkrævning, politik og skibsfart i Øresund 1429–1857*, ed. O. Degn (Copenhagen, 2010), pp. 371–454, here p. 444.

25   Sound Toll Registers Online (STRO), ship numbers 779,416; 782,346; 760,788.

26   Che-Chia, 'Origins of a Misunderstanding', p. 341.

27   Ibid., pp. 341f.

28   Akademiia Nauk SSSR, ed., *Russko-Kitaiskie Otnosheniia 1689–1916: Ofitsialnye Dokumenty* (Moscow, 1958), No. 1, pp. 9ff.

Russia the first – and at the time only – European country to have official trade relations with China.

In order to maximize the profits from the China trade, the Russian government excluded the most valuable commodities – including rhubarb – from private trade. Additionally, in 1693 Peter I restricted the fur trade by declaring black foxes and sables worth more than 40 rubles a state monopoly,[29] while rhubarb had already been monopolized in 1657.[30] Only certain merchants, who had signed contracts with the Russian government, were permitted to trade these items. It seems, however, that these restrictions could not actually be enforced. Siberia in the seventeenth and early eighteenth centuries was a remote colony and there was hardly any state supervision. While an estimated 14 government-sanctioned caravans were sent to do business in Beijing between 1689 and 1722, many private merchants traveled illegally to various towns in northern China where they traded with the locals. They did this with such success that the state caravans often found it difficult to dispose of their furs, which they were obligated to sell at a predetermined and therefore much higher price.[31]

Unfortunately, sources for this time period are rare and therefore it is impossible to determine the extent of this business, especially considering that much of it was illegal. The Sound Toll Registers can nevertheless offer some insights into the overall tendencies of the Russian rhubarb trade.[32] It is important to keep in mind that these registers are a very limited source, since they only let us trace rhubarb leaving the Baltic via the Sound. It is not possible to keep track of any other points of export, such as the Arctic sea port of Arkhangelsk (which still played an important role, at least in the seventeenth century), overland trade (especially to the fairs in Leipzig), and additional shipments of rhubarb to other Baltic sea ports like Lübeck (which Foust identified as one of the most important customers, next to London and Amsterdam). According to Foust, merchants from the Hanse city purchased almost 75 per cent of the amount London bought.[33] However, despite these flaws, the Sound Toll Registers are useful when it comes to outlining certain trends in the Russian rhubarb trade, such as increases and decreases at certain points in time.

Between 1700 and 1727, the Sound Toll recorded only five ships carrying rhubarb from Russia into the Atlantic: in 1716, 400 *pund* went from Riga to Amsterdam; in 1722, 1,600 *pund* were sold in St Petersburg and transported to London; and in 1723 three ships carried a total of 5,434 *pund* of the dried

29   C. M. Foust, *Muscovite and Mandarin: Russia's Trade with China and its Setting, 1727–1805* (Chapel Hill, 2012), p. 11.

30   Foust, *Rhubarb*, p. 25.

31   Ibid., p. 54; K. Heller, *Der russisch-chinesische Handel von seinen Anfängen bis zum Ausgang des 19. Jahrhunderts* (Erlangen, 1980), p. 27.

32   For more information on the Sound Toll Registers and their use as a source, see Jutta Wimmler's chapter in this volume.

33   Foust, *Rhubarb*, p. 75.

medicinal plant from Riga and St Petersburg to Amsterdam.[34] So, there was certainly some commerce going on in those years, illegal or otherwise.

Eventually though, in 1719, the Chinese – tired of the illegal border crossings of Russian merchants – put an end to Russo-Chinese trade by banning all official Russian caravans from entering the country, which in turn caused an uproar in Moscow. The Qing government had never been happy to allow foreigners into their country in the first place, and their interest in doing business with them was limited, so the constant breaches of the Nerchinsk Treaty by private Russian merchants led them to disband trade altogether. After several unsuccessful Russian attempts at regaining access to the Chinese market, both countries finally signed the Treaty of Kiakhta in 1727, which determined the border between Russia and China precisely, assuring the Chinese that there would be no further Russian advances, especially in the Amur region. The treaty further allowed for the establishment of two Russo-Chinese trading posts, one of which (the newly founded town of Kiakhta) would become the central place for acquiring rhubarb.[35] In a way, the trading conditions granted to the Russians in this treaty were much more favorable than those that other Europeans would later enjoy at Kanton, because it gave them direct access to the Chinese market – though not to the extent many had hoped for.[36] Nevertheless, the geographical location of Kiakhta at what is now the Russo-Mongolian border in Central Asia proved to be challenging, due to the enormous distances that goods and people had to travel. These distances (which for the most part consisted of overland routes, though sometimes connected by rivers) played a significant role in the pricing of Russian rhubarb.

The development of Kiakhta – initially nothing but a trading outpost on the most distant fringes of the Russian Empire – illustrates just how profitable the Russo-Chinese border trade was, despite all the difficulties. What started out as barely more than a military outpost, part of the Selenginsk administrative district, soon started to grow. Merchants built houses with ornamented balconies; a stone church replaced the wooden one; new inhabitants developed a suburb outside the town's gates; and from 1774 Kiakhta received its own administration and town hall, headed by one of the merchants who was elected as *starosta*, meaning 'town elder' – a title similar to that of a mayor.[37] Yet there were no trading companies in Kiakhta – unless you count families operating as enterprises. Most merchants took care of their own business, and sometimes rich European entrepreneurs sent their agents – in some cases, their serfs – to conduct trade in their name.[38] In the beginning, most Kiakhta merchants were

34   STRO, ship numbers 583,669; 1,749,598; 586,267; 594,760; 592,289.
35   Akademiia Nauk SSSR, ed., *Russko-Kitaiskie Otnosheniia*, No. 5, pp. 17ff.
36   Foust, *Muscovite*, p. 47.
37   Ibid., p. 81.
38   R. A. Pierce, 'Russian America and China', *Russian America*, ed. Smith-Sweetland, pp. 73–9, here p. 74; Foust, *Muscovite*, p. 208.

from Siberia – often ethnic Siberians, sometimes immigrants from Europe, who were experienced in the fur trade and even in hunting. However, this started to change in the second half of the eighteenth century, when many of the merchants came from Europe – not just ethnic Russians but also Russian subjects of Baltic, Finnish or German backgrounds, who then started to drive out the usually less wealthy Siberian merchants.[39] This change in the demographic of the town and therefore in the trade with China illustrates just how profitable it had become, attracting a growing number of wealthy merchants.

Nonetheless, despite its profitability, trade in Kiakhta was still heavily restricted. The most valuable furs in particular, which were needed to purchase rhubarb, could only be traded by government agents, which strongly encouraged smuggling. John R. Bockstoce estimates that up to 75 per cent of the furs in Kiakhta were traded illegally, which is one of the reasons why, in 1762, Catherine II lifted almost all monopolies and granted freedom in the fur trade (including trade in the most profitable kinds, like sea otter, lynx, squirrel, fox and sable). The monopoly on the rhubarb trade, however, remained intact.[40] Freeing the fur trade did not solve other problems, like the challenge of transporting the furs to Kiakhta. Especially in the case of American furs, the trading routes were long and arduous. So, while in many ways sharing a border with China and having this trading post was a big advantage, many would have additionally preferred access to the port in Kanton. Without it, American furs first had to be shipped to Okhotsk. From there they were carried overland to the Lena River, from where they were shipped to Iakutsk, where they were collected and sorted through and then finally sent to Kiakhta, along with the other American furs that were bought from the natives in Ostrovnoe.[41] It is thus understandable that many involved in the American fur trade would have preferred to trade in Kanton directly, but all attempts at this failed.[42]

Despite these various difficulties, the Kiakhta trade continued to blossom. While the few written sources and the great volume of illegal trade make it very difficult to establish figures, Chang Che-Chia estimates that in an average year in the eighteenth century profits and customs revenue from the monopolized trade made up about 15 to 20 per cent of Russia's national exchequer.[43] As has been thoroughly established, furs and pelts were the most important Russian export in the eighteenth century, even if their market share in Western Europe decreased due to imports from Canada. At Kiakhta alone, they amounted to up to 85 per cent of the total export volume between 1768 and 1785. The other 15 per cent of wares sold to the Chinese were leather goods, European textiles, glass

39   Ibid., p. 210.
40   Bockstoce, *Furs and Frontiers*, pp. 104f.
41   Ibid., p. 105.
42   Pierce, 'Russian America', p. 76.
43   Che-Chia, 'Origins of a Misunderstanding', p. 342.

and iron wares, as well as animals like horses, cattle, hunting dogs and camels.[44] Import goods were largely textiles made from cotton and silk,[45] but especially in the nineteenth century, tea gained importance and eventually made up 95 per cent of Russian imports at Kiakhta.[46] Apart from that, the Chinese exported various manufactured goods (like porcelain, earthenware and enamelware), spices (like anise and pepper) and various other products to Russia.[47]

Quantitatively, rhubarb was not one of the most important trade goods, but it was certainly considered one of the most valuable. As it was a highly sought-after luxury item, the Chinese made sure to control its trade thoroughly – not just with Russia but (for example) also with countries like Japan, Taiwan, Annam (today Vietnam), Siam (today Thailand), the Ryukyu Islands, and Hainan. All of them were only permitted to buy a small amount of rhubarb for a price prede-termined by the government in Beijing.[48] Chang Che-Chia strikingly illustrates the importance ascribed to the dried medicinal plant through an episode he calls the 'rhubarb embargo'. As previously mentioned, Russo-Chinese relations were often complicated, and since trade was more important to the Russians than to their Chinese counterparts, it was often used as a means of exerting political pressure. A Chinese source quoted by Chang Che-Chia even called rhubarb 'a weapon to control the foreign barbarians'.[49] When the Russians refused to extradite refugees fleeing from the Qing authorities in 1785, the Chinese government decided to cease all rhubarb trade until Russia complied with their requests. Four years later, when the Chinese discovered extensive smuggling of the plant, this confirmed their belief that the embargo was working and that the Russians were desperate for more rhubarb.[50] In the end, it turned out that it was not just the rhubarb but rather concern about the China trade in general that led the Russian government to make concessions. The Chinese had severely overestimated the European demand for rhubarb. Nevertheless, this small anecdote illustrates the significant role rhubarb played, not just in the commercial but also in the diplomatic relations between the two countries.

From St Petersburg to Europe

Chinese sources may have exaggerated the importance of rhubarb for the European market, but Peter I and his successors still took it very seriously. Already in the early eighteenth century, Peter made sure to keep a close eye on the plant,

---

44   Ibid., p. 74.
45   Foust, *Muscovite*, p. 232.
46   Heller, 'Der russisch-chinesische Handel', pp. 526f.
47   For the whole list of Chinese exports, see Bockstoce, *Furs and Frontiers*, p. 111.
48   Che-Chia, 'Origins of a Misunderstanding', pp. 335f.
49   Ibid., p. 345.
50   Ibid., p. 343.

monitoring its purchase, quality control and redistribution. Since 1657, when the Russian government had first sent a delegation to China, the rhubarb trade had been a monopoly of the state.[51] In 1681, the Dutch merchant Adolf Alferevich Gutman received a five-year contract from the Russian government that allowed him to buy a yearly amount of 5,400 pounds of rhubarb.[52] All rhubarb imported by other merchants had to be sold to Gutman, who in turn was to pay the Russian merchants with foreign coin – so-called *efimki* – which was an important source of precious metals for the Russian treasury. After Gutman's contract ran out, a merchant by the name of Isaev took over for another five years, followed by the Hamburg merchant Matthias Poppe (*Matvei Lavrentevich Poppe*).[53]

In 1736, after the Treaty of Kiakhta, an apothecary was appointed with the task of examining all purchased rhubarb to ensure that only pieces of the highest quality were transported to Europe. The first person to hold this position was Peter Rosing (Petr Rozing), presumably of Dutch origin, who until 1748 oversaw quality control, packaging, storage and transport of the rhubarb in Siberia.[54] In the same year – 1736 – Simon Svinin, a merchant from Vielkij Ustiug, was put in charge of all inner Russian rhubarb trade. Svinin and his two employees were dubbed the 'Kiakhta Rhubarb Commission' and tasked with ensuring that no private rhubarb trade was taking place anywhere in the country. They were to take stock of all rhubarb in Siberian store houses, track the ways by which rhubarb was brought to Moscow, buy up all rhubarb from private merchants for a price of no more than 12 rubles per *pud*, and ensure that only the highest quality rhubarb would find its way to European markets.[55]

It is important to note that for a brief period before the Treaty of Kiakhta was signed in the summer of 1727, the monopoly on rhubarb was lifted. It was reinstalled in 1731, after not even four years of free rhubarb trade, which means that these developments took place shortly thereafter.[56] It is evident in the Sound Toll Registers that during these few years the export volume of the dried plant to Western Europe increased significantly. The last time before 1728 that Russian rhubarb was recorded passing through the Sound had been 5,434 *pund* on three ships in 1723; so when a total of 9,671 *pund* transported on 22 different ships left Russia for the Atlantic in 1728, this was a dramatic increase. Only a year later, in 1729, it was almost six times the amount of the previous year, with 54,818 *pund* of rhubarb.[57] In the following years, the amounts of rhubarb then started to decline again and sank to zero *pund* in 1732.

51   Ibid., p. 346.
52   In his book, Foust converted the Russian units of measurement *pud* and *funty* into American pounds avoir. See Foust, *Rhubarb*, p. 47.
53   Ibid., pp. 49f.
54   Ibid., pp. 59f.
55   Ibid., p. 60.
56   Ibid., p. 56.
57   STRO, ship numbers 586,267; 594,760; 592,289.

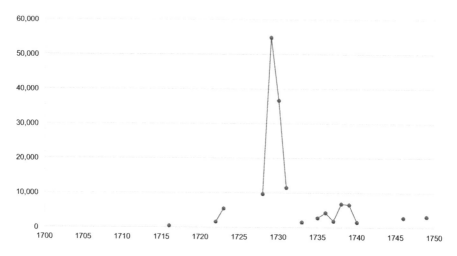

Figure 5.1. Rhubarb exports from Russian Baltic ports in the first half of the eighteenth century (in *pund*)

Source: STRO.

At first glance, these developments seem to prove Clifford M. Foust's conclusion that the government was unable to understand that a monopoly like theirs was harming business, blocking the development of a free market and keeping the country in a 'backward' position, unable to compete with Western European counterparts.[58] Yet the rise and fall of the figures raises the question why the Russian government reinstalled the monopoly. They obviously tried free trade, significantly increased their export volume in the process, and yet came to the conclusion that they preferred the restrictive monopoly. What was the reasoning behind this? The installment of a state-licensed apothecary and of a 'rhubarb commission' that completely controlled the trade show an attempt to gain full governmental control over the rhubarb trade. However, it was also an effort to ensure the product's quality. Svinin was even tasked with burning all the rhubarb of inferior quality to ensure it would never be traded.[59]

These developments indicate that during the period of free rhubarb trade, the quality of the exported rhubarb must have been significantly lower than before. Additionally, the prices at which the plant was sold apparently also declined during this episode.[60] Therefore, it seems that the government's strategy was to export only the highest quality rhubarb at the highest possible price, while accepting that this meant selling less of the plant than would otherwise have

58 Foust, *Rhubarb*, p. 69.
59 Ibid., p. 60.
60 Foust, *Muscovite*, p. 166.

been possible. And this apparently worked. Even Foust admitted this, despite
his strong opposition to the monopoly.

It must be stressed at this point that many Western scholars during the
twentieth century were looking at Russian economic history through the lens
of the Cold War. They were looking for weaknesses in Russia's early modern
economy that would explain why the Communists eventually came into power
in 1917. Or, as Erika Monahan puts it: 'Cold War Western scholars were writing
the history of the failure of capitalism' in Russia, believing that it was the
inherent Russian backwardness that prohibited the establishment of a free
market strong enough to withstand the revolution.[61] Among other factors,[62] the
existence of monopolies was used to substantiate these claims, even though they
completely served their purpose of guaranteeing the highest possible profits –
and even though monopolies were common all over Europe at the time. Despite
his prejudices, Foust admitted that the rhubarb monopoly was profitable: 'The
hefty money profits returned to St Petersburg … mesmerized the Collegium
bureaucracy and the senators into believing in this state monopoly.'[63] This
quotation illustrates that, while the rhubarb monopoly achieved exactly what
it was meant to do, it was still depicted as a symptom of backwardness that
tricked the naïve and gullible Russians into upholding it by making them a lot
of money.

In addition to generating profits for the Russian government, the monopoly
ensured Russia's competitiveness in the rhubarb trade. Even if the Russians
had exported all the rhubarb they had, including that of lower quality, they
would still have had to ask for a higher price than (for example) the English,
who imported rhubarb from China via the Indian Ocean. The long overland
routes through Siberia made the rhubarb transport more expensive, which is
why exporting less at a higher price made sense. Russia would never have been
able to compete with English rhubarb prices. Consequently, they found their
niche by ensuring that Crown rhubarb gained a faultless reputation as the most
luxurious variety of *Rheum palmatum*, which justified the high price. So, while
Foust correctly points out that the rhubarb monopoly did not help to establish
a free trade economy in the Russian Empire, we should note that it was never
meant to. Instead, the monopoly was very successful at what it set out to do:
increasing the European demand for Crown rhubarb, establishing its good
reputation and, first and foremost, making money for the state treasury. Karsten
Voss made a very similar point regarding the French companies established in
the early eighteenth century for the Caribbean trade.[64] Where previous scholars

61   Monahan, *Merchants*, p. 14.
62   For example: absolutism, serfdom, lack of a merchant fleet, etc.
63   Foust, *Rhubarb*, p. 69.
64   K. Voss, *Sklaven als Ware und Kapital: Die Plantagenökonomie von Saint Domingue als
Entwicklungsprojekt* (Munich, 2016).

had pointed out their apparent economic 'failure', Voss highlighted that they achieved the goal for which they were designed: initiating a sugar revolution on Saint-Domingue (Haiti). A failure to understand the motives of the actors has thus impeded our assessment of trade monopolies.

Jan Willem Veluwenkamp and Werner Scheltjens have proposed another reason for the sudden increase in Russian rhubarb exports in the late 1720s that has nothing to do with Russian economic policy. They argue that political unrest in the Middle East caused almost the entire rhubarb export from the Levant to come to a halt, which might be the reason why English merchants purchased more from St Petersburg.[65] However, the most convincing reason for the surge of rhubarb exports might once again be the ever-complicated Russo-Chinese relations. It can hardly be a coincidence that the amount of Russian rhubarb passing through the Sound saw such a remarkable increase only one year after the Treaty of Kiakhta between Russia and China was signed in 1727. The treaty significantly improved diplomatic relations as well as trade; therefore, more rhubarb was imported into Russia. Since almost all of these imports were intended for the European market, it makes sense that, after the time it took to transport the goods to the Baltic, exports would also increase.

Nevertheless, the Sound Toll Registers suggest significant droughts in the rhubarb exports from Russian Baltic ports in the first half of the eighteenth century, with or without the rhubarb monopoly. No rhubarb was declared in the Sound between 1724 and 1727, nor in 1732 or in 1734, and none from 1741 to 1745 and from 1747 to 1748. The 1740s are especially noticeable, because the only rhubarb passing through the Sound was 1,500 *pund* shipped to Schellingen in 1740; 1,568 and 1,200 *pund* going to London and Amsterdam respectively in 1746; and three ships with 2,215 *pund*, 900 *pund* and an unknown amount of rhubarb heading for Amsterdam in 1749.[66] Other than that, there is no rhubarb to be found in the Sound Toll Registers in the entire decade, which raises the question why. Interestingly, without using the Sound Toll Registers in his research, Clifford M. Foust mentions problems in Kiakhta during precisely this period. In 1742, the contract with a Central Asian merchant family who supplied the Russians with rhubarb in Kiakhta had run out, and a merchant called Murat (apparently the head of this family) wanted to renegotiate, demanding more money.[67] According to Foust, the rhubarb imports came to a halt during the 1740s as a consequence. With this story in mind, the Sound Toll data can not only be explained, but it illustrates how dependent the European market was on events taking place far away on the Russian frontier in Siberia.

---

65   J. W. Veluwenkamp and W. Scheltjens, 'Baltic Drugs Traffic 1650–1850: Sound Toll Registers Online as a Source for the Import of Medicines in the Baltic Sea Area', *Social History of Medicine* 31/1 (2017), pp. 140–76, here p. 143.

66   STRO, ship numbers 514,828; 534,959; 566,760; 572,897; 572,919; 496,841.

67   Foust, *Rhubarb*, p. 65.

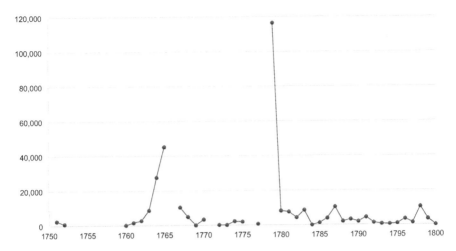

Figure 5.2. Rhubarb exports from Russian Baltic ports in the second half of the eighteenth century (in *pund*)

Source: STRO.

Little rhubarb passed the Sound in the 1750s. This changed in the 1760s, however, when rhubarb exports suddenly reached new heights. Foust, who did not work with the Sound Toll Registers when writing his book, seems largely unaware of this increase. He mentions only that the price was lowered in 1762, which, he concludes, did not have much effect.[68] Matthew P. Romaniello provides a simpler explanation for the sudden increase. He cites several trade treaties (1761 with England; 1763 with France, Sweden and the Netherlands) and the Seven Years' War as causes for the sudden boost in rhubarb exports in the 1760s.[69] It is certainly true that the war was a massive hindrance to all trade in Europe, and it seems plausible that a lot of rhubarb that would otherwise have been sold would start piling up in St Petersburg's store houses until the war was over. This explains why there was a sudden surge in the mid 1760s (when the piled-up rhubarb could finally be sold), followed by a quick drop to 'normal' levels.

The second peak in 1779 (Figure 5.2) cannot be explained so easily; in fact, it may result from a clerical error. According to the Sound Toll Registers, only one ship on its way to London carried 115,200 *pund* of rhubarb, which seems highly unlikely when compared to all other cargos over the entire eighteenth and nineteenth centuries. Without this one ship with its unrealistically large load, the graph in fact looks much more plausible, as can be seen in Figure 5.3.

68 Ibid., p. 73.
69 Romaniello, 'True Rhubarb?', pp. 14f.

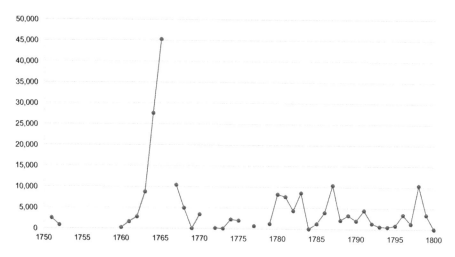

Figure 5.3. Rhubarb exports from Russian Baltic ports in the second half of the eighteenth century, without the one large load in 1779 (in *pund*)
Source: STRO.

The Sound Toll Registers also suggest that the abolition of the rhubarb monopoly by Catherine II in 1781 had no real effect – at least, none that is visible in the data. This contradicts Foust's critical assessment of the monopoly and underlines the point made in this chapter: that the monopoly was in fact useful in ensuring Russia's competitiveness in the hotly contested rhubarb market of the eighteenth century, and did not hinder trade as much as Foust claims. Only when looking at the numbers for the nineteenth century as well does it appear that the abolition of the monopoly led to more regular and steadier rhubarb exports compared to the years before, when exports would sometimes drop to zero for several years in a row. However, this apparent improvement was not necessarily caused by free trade. While permitting more merchants to enter the rhubarb business may certainly have had a stabilizing effect, the situation in Siberia once again had a large impact on these developments.

In the early days of Russo-Chinese relations in the seventeenth century, Siberia was hardly more than an unexplored frontier to the Russian government, then located in Moscow. In the course of the eighteenth century, infrastructure was improved and settlements turned into cities, which lowered the transportation costs of rhubarb. While for a long time the government in Beijing was able to dictate the terms between the two countries, by the nineteenth century they found themselves in a seriously weakened position and realized that the Russian Empire posed a real geopolitical threat on the Asian continent. When a long-expected Russian advance into the Amur region and a growing Russian military presence coincided with increasingly aggressive British trade tactics

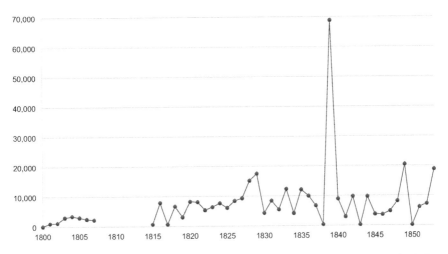

Figure 5.4. Rhubarb exports from Russian Baltic ports in the first half of the nineteenth century (in *pund*)

Source: STRO.

that eventually culminated in the Opium Wars, the Chinese appeared more willing to accommodate Russian economic interests.[70] As previously discussed, one of the main reasons for the difficulties in the Russo-Chinese rhubarb trade in the eighteenth century was that the Chinese government was not nearly as invested in the relationship as the Russians, and often used trade embargos as political weapons to enforce their own interests. With the changing geopolitical situation and the increased Russian strength and presence in Asia, they were likely unable to continue this policy, which explains the regularity in the Russian rhubarb exports in the nineteenth century.

Conclusion

The state's significant involvement in seemingly all economic matters is often cited as a reason for Russia's alleged 'backwardness', and rhubarb appears to be the perfect example.[71] It was a highly valuable and much sought-after commodity, but instead of maximizing its export and trying to make the highest possible profits, the Russian emperors and empresses restricted the trade by various means. And yet, Crown rhubarb became a highly sought-after commodity that European merchants were willing to pay higher prices for than for other

70   Bockstoce, *Furs and Frontiers*, p. 112.
71   Kamenskij, *The Russian Empire*, p. 102.

kinds of the same plant. It also illustrates how Russia was able to combat the competition from North American furs on the European market by shifting their business towards Asia, while simultaneously responding to the fluctuating demand in Europe by exporting what was essentially one of the eighteenth century's most fashionable drugs. The rhubarb monopoly, which remained in place over almost the entire course of the eighteenth century, was vital in ensuring the high quality of Crown rhubarb. Its superior quality safeguarded its good reputation in Europe and thereby made it possible to demand high prices, without which Russia would not have been able to compete with the cheap but low-quality Indian rhubarb, imported in great quantities by the English. The example of the Central Asian merchant Murat (who demanded more money for his services, causing rhubarb exports from St Petersburg to come to a halt), as well as the changing power dynamics in Asia in the nineteenth century illustrate how events in Siberia influenced the European market. They show Europe's dependence on the so-called 'periphery', and how closely connected these two regions were in the eighteenth and early nineteenth centuries.

This case study also illustrates that we need to include regions like Russia in the Atlantic perspective: the story of the rhubarb trade is not only linked to Asia and Western Europe, but also to America and the Pacific. As this chapter has shown, American furs were vital in order to access the Chinese market, where they served as valuable trade goods. The Russian case also helps us to contextualize and further explore the function of monopolies for early modern states as well as for private entrepreneurs, and to assess the historiography on the subject critically. The 'backwardness narrative' is usually written from the perspective that free trade amounts to economic growth and that states who prohibited free trade made a critical error. Hence Russia, Spain or even France are often described as economically handicapped by mercantilist policies, while England or the Netherlands are seen as havens of free trade. Aside from the fact that mercantilist policies existed in these two countries as well, this chapter has suggested that the rationale behind monopolies needs to be taken into account when assessing their 'success' or 'failure'.

6

Atlantic Sugar and Central Europe: Sugar Importers in Hamburg and their Trade with Bordeaux and Lisbon, 1733–1798

TORSTEN DOS SANTOS ARNOLD[1]

Early modern Central Europe was a major market for colonial goods, particularly plantation crops such as sugar, coffee, cotton, tobacco and dyestuffs, imported from France, Britain, Portugal and Spain. Until the disintegration of the *anciens régimes*, mercantilist restrictions issued by the Western European Atlantic empires impeded direct trade between their colonies and Central European ports. Consequently, colonial goods were first imported into Western European ports such as Bordeaux, Nantes, London, Lisbon, Seville and Cádiz, and reshipped to ports like Amsterdam and Hamburg. These two cities were important hubs for the processing of colonial goods and for transportation to the Central European hinterlands.

This chapter illuminates the long-term development of Hamburg's sugar market and the market portfolio of a sample of major sugar importers in Hamburg in the course of the eighteenth century. The primary sources for the following quantitative data analysis are the Admiralitäts- und Convoygeld-Einnahmebücher (the Admiralty and Convoy Duty records), hereafter referred to as ACEB. Sugar was one of the – if not *the* – major colonial commodity traded throughout the eighteenth century. It was cultivated on plantations in several regions within the Americas, and is well suited as a case study to explore Western European colonial trade and Central European markets in a long-term perspective. Of all taxable products imported into Hamburg and listed in the ACEB database, sugar made up a total value of 247 million *Mark Banco* (36.75 per cent), followed by coffee (131 million *Mark Banco*, 19.6 per

1   Research for this article was funded by the German Research Foundation (WE 3613/2–1, 'The Globalized Periphery: Atlantic Commerce, Socioeconomic and Cultural Change in Central Europe, 1680–1850').

cent) and woollens (30.2 million *Mark Banco*, 4.5 per cent).[2] Who were the merchants that imported sugar into Hamburg? How many merchants dealt with sugar and what were their market shares? What were their business strategies and how did they adapt to changing market conditions in times of warfare and during the Atlantic Revolutions?

To answer these questions, the first part of the chapter analyzes Hamburg's sugar market by quantities, types and origins, between 1733 and 1798. The second part deals with the sugar importers in Hamburg. The figures used in this chapter are taken directly from the ACEB database and not from the figures published by Jürgen Schneider, Otto-Ernst Krawehl and Markus A. Denzel.[3] The chapter argues that Hamburg played a vital role within the Atlantic sugar economies throughout the entire eighteenth century, and that merchants in Hamburg benefited from the political economies of the seaborne Western European empires, due to the combined factors of the neutrality of the Hanseatic city[4] and the merchants' commercial networks abroad. Although Central European merchants did not have direct access to trade with the Americas, they were able to profit from this trade at the far end of the commodity chain, especially by securing their role in intra-European distribution. The chapter further argues that the Seven Years' War (1756–1763) and the structural reforms in Portugal, introduced by the Marquis de Pombal following the Lisbon earthquake in 1755, actually worked in favor of these merchants by offering a set of new opportunities for trading in colonial products channeled through Bordeaux and Lisbon.

The Admiralty and Convoy Duty records as a historic source

In 1623, the Council of the Free and Hanseatic City of Hamburg (Rat der Freien und Hansestadt Hamburg) assigned maritime commercial jurisdiction to the newly created admiralty. The admiralty collected two types of duties: the first type (the admiralty duties) were *ad valorem* duties levied on both imports and exports. They were used to finance the admiralty's administration. The second type was the convoy fee, to be paid for the maintenance of a few convoy vessels which accompanied Hamburg ships as far as the Mediterranean Sea, to protect

2   M. A. Denzel, 'Der seewärtige Einfuhrhandel Hamburgs nach den Admiralitäts- und Convoygeld-Einnahmebüchern (1733–1798)', *Vierteljahresschrift für Sozial- und Wirtschaftsgeschichte* 102/2 (2015), pp. 131–60, here p. 140.
3   J. Schneider, O.-E. Krawehl and M. A. Denzel, *Statistiken des Hamburger seewärtigen Einfuhrhandels im 18. Jahrhundert: Nach den Admiralitäts- und Convoygeld-Einnahmebüchern* (St Katharinen, 2001). I want to thank Prof. Dr. M. A. Denzel, Department of Economic History, Leipzig University for providing the ACEB database.
4   F. Hatje, 'Libertät, Neutralität und Commercium: Zu den politischen Voraussetzungen für Hamburgs Handel', *Hamburger Wirtschafts-Chronik* 7 (2007/08), pp. 213–47.

them against North African corsairs. The annual books were mere records of payments of these duties, and they should not be confused with official trade statistics. For one thing, all merchandise arriving from the North Sea region (including Amsterdam) was exempt, as was the active transit trade.[5] This means that products that were not intended for Hamburg's own market – or to be stocked in the Hanseatic city for more than six months – do not appear in these records. In addition, the measurement units were not standardized in the books, which makes it difficult to assess the actual volume of imported merchandise beyond its monetary value. Finally, dutiable commodities were commonly registered without a detailed classification. For example, apart from a few exceptions in the late 1780s, all types of sugar were registered simply as 'sugar', regardless of their different origins and qualities. The case of sugar imports from Portugal demonstrates that the same general procedure of taxation was maintained throughout the entire eighteenth century: the admiralty duty for a box of sugar was always 140 *Mark Banco*,[6] regardless of the actual quantity of sugar contained in the box and of its monetary market value. Merchants declared their sugar imports to a clerk of the admiralty, a procedure based primarily on trust rather than on official verification by the admiralty itself.[7]

Since 1713, direct imports from the following regions were subject to the duties: Arkhangelsk, Brabant, Flanders, England, Scotland, Ireland, France, Spain, Portugal and the Mediterranean Sea. Direct imports from the northern Netherlands, the Baltic Sea, Swedish and Norwegian Atlantic ports, and Greenland were exempt from the admiralty duty. Goods in transit and a range of commodities such as beer, cereals or coal were not dutiable.[8] The customs books contain the following information:

- Dates of declaration
- Names of consigners or commissioners
- Types of commodities
- Amount of commodities in packaging units (barrels, boxes, pieces, et cetera)
- Values of commodities in *Mark Banco*
- Names of captains and ports of origins of the commodities.

---

5   E. Pitz, *Die Zolltarife der Stadt Hamburg* (Wiesbaden, 1961), pp. 500ff.
6   The earliest registration of the value of 140 *Mark Banco* for a box of sugar dates back to 1671: J. Poettering, *Handel, Nation und Religion: Kaufleute zwischen Portugal und Hamburg im 17. Jahrhundert* (Göttingen, 2013), p. 351.
7   J. Poettering, 'Hamburger Sefarden im atlantischen Zuckerhandel des 17. Jahrhunderts' (MA thesis, University of Hamburg, 2003), pp. 91ff; Ernst Baasch, *Quellen zur Geschichte von Hamburgs Handel und Schiffahrt im 17., 18., und 19. Jahrhundert* (Hamburg, 1910), pp. 219ff.
8   K. Weber, 'Die Admiralitätszoll- und Convoygeld Einnahmebücher: Eine wichtige Quelle für Hamburgs Wirtschaftsgeschichte im 18. Jahrhundert', *Hamburger Wirtschafts-Chronik* 1 (2000), pp. 83–112, here pp. 91ff.

The main difficulty in using the ACEB for comparative quantitative analyses is that the same commodity could be registered in a variety of packaging units. Two examples illustrate this problem: on 14 August 1776, Johannes Schuback declared the import of 209.5 boxes of sugar worth 29,330 *Mark Banco*, shipped from Lisbon by Robertson. On 14 May of the same year, Poppe & de Chapeaurouge declared the import of 68 hogsheads (German: *oxhoft*; a type of barrel) of sugar worth 12,000 *Mark Banco*, shipped from Bordeaux by Behrens.[9] Since it is impossible to ascertain the actual quantities in the boxes and the hogsheads, the ACEB is only appropriate for trend analyses, but not for the extraction of reliable quantitative data. Although the ACEB records do not cover the total of Hamburg's imports, the registration of the consigners and commissioner merchants and their commodities allows for the analysis of the market and commodity portfolios of individual merchants.[10]

Sugar imports into Hamburg, 1733–1798

At the beginning of the eighteenth century, Hamburg's sugar imports mainly came from Portuguese and British colonies – a situation that soon changed in favor of 'French' sugar from Saint-Domingue, Martinique and Guadeloupe.[11] The dominance of French sugar was caused by several factors: namely French colonial policies, the higher productivity and efficiency of the French plantations, and ultimately the superior quality of Saint Domingue's sugar compared to Brazilian sugar. As French sugar production in the Caribbean increased, prices fell in the European hubs of processing and redistribution.[12] The French leading position on the world's sugar market was only interrupted by the Seven Years' War (1756–1763) and ended with the disintegration of the *ancien régime* after 1789. This is clearly visible in Figure 6.1, which illustrates the major trends in Hamburg's sugar imports and confirms the overall dominance of France throughout the century.

9   State Archives of the Free and Hanseatic City of Hamburg, 3712, F6, Band 29, ACEB 1776, fols 113f.

10   Denzel, 'Der seewärtige Einfuhrhandel', pp. 134ff; K. Weber, 'Hamburg, 1728–1811', *Revue de l'OFCE* 140 (2015), pp. 265–8; Weber, 'Die Admiralitätszoll- und Convoygeld Einnahmebücher'; O.-E. Krawehl, 'Quellen zur Hamburger Handelsstatistik im 18. Jahrhundert', *Grundlagen der Historischen Statistik von Deutschland: Quellen, Methoden, Forschungsziele*, ed. W. Fischer and A. Kunz (Opladen, 1991), pp. 47–69, here pp. 56f. Poettering, 'Hamburger Sefarden', pp. 91ff.

11   Ibid.; J. Wimmler, *The Sun King's Atlantic: Drugs, Demons and Dyestuffs in the Atlantic World, 1640–1730* (Leiden/Boston, 2017), pp. 23ff.

12   K. Voss, *Sklaven als Ware und Kapital: Die Plantagenökonomie von Saint-Domingue als Entwicklungsprojekt 1697–1715* (Munich, 2016) pp. 31ff; D. W. Tomich, *Slavery in the Circuit of Sugar* (Albany, 2016), pp. 69ff; R. S. Dunn, *Sugar and Slaves: The Rise of the Planter Class in the British West Indies, 1624–1713* (Williamsburg, 2000), pp. 200ff.

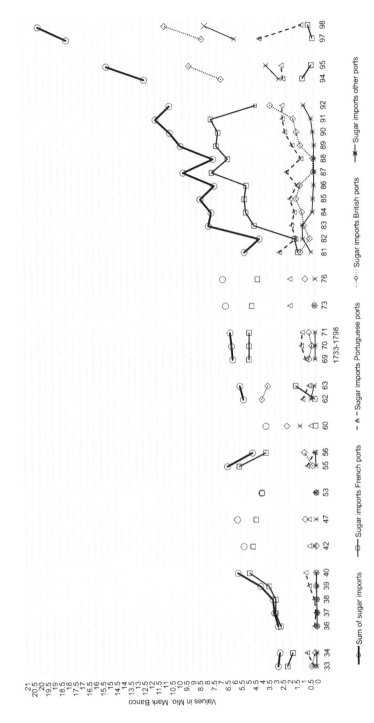

Figure 6.1. Declared sugar imports into Hamburg between 1733 and 1798, according to the ACEB database (values in millions of *Mark Banco*)

Table 6.1. Sugar entering Hamburg from Bordeaux (1733–1798)

Years	ACEB database	Compared to Denzel	Compared to Tamaki
1753	1,757,221	−170,100	−170,100
1756	2,100,906	−3,800	−3,800
1762	40,200	−6,500	−6,500
1769	2,451,800		+24,000
1770	2,991,515		+8,800
1771	3,004,685		+6,000
1782	1,273,688		+5,000
1783	2,646,730	−7,200	+4,000
1784	2,603,678		+5,750
1785	3,287,335		+5,500
1787	5,282,345	−90	+1,825,495
1788	4,745,880	+73,600	+1,580,455
1789	5,026,485	+900	+68,400
1790	4,541,550		+409,600
1791	4,954,085	−1,590	
1792	2,607,930		+10,100
1794	375,850		+4,500
1797	10,200		+5,800

Table 6.2. Sugar entering Hamburg from Lisbon (1733–1798)

Years	ACEB database	Compared to Denzel	Compared to Tamaki
1771	672,625	−2,170	−2,170
1786	404,250		+2,940
1787	973,855	−202,680	+29,960
1788	450,775	−147,320	+16,240
1789	847,380	−450	−450
1790	1,094,690	−23,100	−13,750
1795	1,159,530	+12,000	+12,000
1797	2,669,521	−9,980	−9,980
1798	779,855	−7,000	−7,000

Table 6.3. Sugar entering Hamburg from London (1733–1798)

Years	ACEB database	Compared to Denzel	Compared to Tamaki
1733	412,575	−4,500	−4,500
1739	51,980	−1,000	
1740	34,100	+2,268	+2,500
1747	678,505	−550	
1753	6,300	−850	
1755	121,000	−75	
1756	771,700	−1,650	
1760	1,564,490	−1,800	
1762	2,908,290	−8,700	+155,050
1763	2,572,696	−175	+241,400
1769	307,250		+119,050
1770	213,200		+40,200
1771	448,800	−700	+182,000
1776	688,955	−1,900	+392,350
1781	294,400		+40,550
1782	236,970	+1,100	+107,000
1783	489,400	−700	+245,800
1784	845,900	−4,450	+490,925
1785	1,304,165	−10,220	+827,615
1786	1,027,425	−5,785	+580,850
1787	70,575	−3,020	+61,125
1788	74,550	−30,720	+35,100
1789	941,790	+1,700	+511,415
1790	1,239,730	−2,700	+909,905
1791	1,384,665	−2,550	+842,590
1792	2,459,980	+2,180	+1,435,520
1794	5,590,821	+43,445	+3,134,180
1795	7,191,735	+37,650	+3,637,810
1797	5,482,045	+58,770	+1,489,010
1798	7,710,832	+34,550	+804,525

Tables 6.1 to 6.3 detail the overall development of sugar imports into Hamburg by value, according to the ACEB database. In general, Hamburg's customs authorities barely differentiated between different qualities or types of sugar at the time of registration, and generally used the broad umbrella term 'sugar' instead. However, more than 25 different types of sugar were traded in Hamburg, such as the French *sucre brut*, *sucre blanc*, *sucre terré* and *sucre tête*, British lump sugar (*Lumpenzucker*), and the Portuguese *açúcar branco* and *açúcar mascavado*. In order to generate an overview of all sugar imports into Hamburg, researchers need to be aware of the few exceptional cases when Hamburg's customs authorities actually differentiated between the qualities of sugar.

These now published numbers differ from those earlier generated and published by Markus Denzel and Toshiaki Tamaki.[13] Although the figures generated by Denzel are based on the ACEB records as well, the commodities are listed in alphabetical order without an aggregation, using umbrella terms such as 'sugar', among others. When using the figures published by Denzel, researchers need to be aware of the types of commodities and compute total figures. A comparison of the figures indicates that Tamaki's data was based on Denzel's data on sugar (the umbrella term), excluding the remaining types of sugar, such as lump sugar.

The figures provided in this chapter are higher than those published by Denzel and Tamaki, because they include all types of sugar listed in the ACEB database (including lump sugar imported from Great Britain). However, this does not change the picture of an overall French market dominance.

It should also be noted that direct sugar imports from the French Caribbean islands of Saint-Domingue, Guadeloupe and Martinique are registered in the ACEB for the years 1747, 1756, 1781 to 1784, and 1795. This became possible due to changes made to the so-called *L'Exclusif* policy of the French *ancien régime* in certain years. In general, the letters patent from 1717 and 1727 had laid out the framework for foreign trade with French colonial markets. The new colonies were properties of the French kingdom and were subject to their policies and jurisdiction.[14] Ships bound for the colonies (and the ports of Western Africa) were required to re-enter the French port of departure on their return. This guaranteed increased tax revenues for the respective port cities and led to the individual ports' specialization in specific colonial markets: Bordeaux

---

13   Schneider, Krawehl and Denzel, *Statistiken*; T. Tamaki, 'Hamburg as a Gateway: The Economic Connections between the Atlantic and the Baltic in the Long Eighteenth-Century with Special Reference to French Colonial Goods', *The Rise of the Atlantic Economy and the North Sea/Baltic Trade, 1500–1800*, ed. L. Müller, P. R. Rössner and T. Tamaki (Stuttgart, 2011), pp. 61–80, here p. 66.

14   J. Tarrade, *Le Commerce Colonial de la France à la Fin de l'Ancien Régime*, Vol. 1 (Paris, 1972), p. 86.

became France's major port for the Caribbean trade, whereas Nantes became its main port for the slave trade.[15]

This policy was nothing new: the Portuguese and Spanish had introduced similar regulations in the early days of Western European engagement with the Atlantic basin. In the case of Portugal, the structural reforms of the Marquis de Pombal and the creation of monopolistic shareholder companies (such as the Companhia Geral do Comércio de Grão-Pará e Maranhão and the Companhia Geral do Comércio de Pernambuco e Paraíba) transformed the hitherto exclusive private trade of subjects of the Portuguese crown with Brazil (and Western Africa) into a henceforth state-regulated and state-organized trade. These reforms of Portugal's colonial trade in the Atlantic World not only allowed the Portuguese crown to control private trade and the direct taxation of imported and exported commodities. The fact that Portuguese and foreign merchants participated in the companies as shareholders increased national and foreign investment. This made a restructuring of the plantation system possible, which improved the quality and quantity of plantation crops, in turn increasing profits from Portuguese colonial trade.[16]

As in the case of Portugal and France, British navigation acts prohibited direct foreign trade with their colonies, especially in the Americas. Until the Seven Years' War, London was the only hub for 'British' sugar exports to Hamburg. After the outbreak of the war in 1756, sugar was also imported from Bristol, Hull, Liverpool and Plymouth. Hamburg's first registered sugar imports via North America came in 1760. The importance of Baltimore, New York, Philadelphia and Salem as transit ports for Caribbean sugar rose from 1786, with the independence of the United States, and increased with the outbreak of the French Revolution (1789) and of the slave revolt in Saint-Domingue, which triggered the Haitian Revolution (1791–1804). The Atlantic Revolutions obviously had a huge impact on Hanseatic networks of trade.

Direct sugar imports from Caribbean ports (particularly from Cuba and the Danish West Indies) occurred only occasionally, especially during the Seven Years' War. Hamburg merchants declared direct sugar imports from this region more frequently after the 1780s, which suggests that they had managed to establish contacts in these regions by then.

As described above, a broad variety of types and qualities of sugar entered Hamburg from French, Portuguese and British ports. For example, the *Preis-Courant der Waaren in Partheyen* of 14 March 1777 listed 28 different types of

---

15 Voss, *Sklaven*, pp. 45ff.
16 S. B. Schwartz, 'The Economy of the Portuguese Empire', *Portuguese Oceanic Expansion, 1400–1800*, ed. F. Bethencourt and D. Ramada Curto (Cambridge, 2007), pp. 19–48, here esp. pp. 38ff; A. C. Jucá de Sampaio, 'A Economia do Império Português no Período Pombalino', *A 'Época Pombalina' no Mundo Luso-Brasileiro*, ed. F. Falcon and C. Rodrigues (Rio de Janeiro, 2015), pp. 31–58, here esp. pp. 38ff.

Table 6.4. French sugar exports to the North (quantities in millions of *livre de poids*, c. 480g).*

Bordeaux	Total exports	*Sucre brut*	*Sucre blanc*	*Sucre terre, sucre tête*, others
1730–39	51.32	26.27	0.01	25
1740–49	108.6	49.28	54.7	4.58
1750–59	112.1	48.71	63.30	0
1760–69	85.47	35.19	50.30	0
1770–76	135	83.09	51.90	0
Sum	492.3	242.5	220	29.6

Nantes	Total exports	*Sucre brut*	*Sucre blanc*	*Sucre terre, sucre tête*, others
1730–39	61.45	35.47	1.69	24.3
1740–49	46.93	3.36	0.43	15.1
1750–59	47.03	29.74	0	17.3
1760–69	30.22	11.22	0	19
1770–76	39.8	16.6	0	23.2
Sum	225.4	124.4	2.12	9.9

* H. Doursther, *Dictionnaire Universel des Poids et Mesures Anciens et Modernes, Contenant des Tables de Monnaies de tous les Pays* (Brussels, 1840), p. 367.

sugar.[17] Astrid Petersson and Pierrick Pourchasse probably over-emphasized the importance of raw sugar on Hamburg's sugar market.[18] Semi-refined and refined sugar were imported in substantial quantities, besides raw sugar that was processed in Hamburg's sugar refineries throughout the eighteenth and nineteenth centuries. Data extracted from the local *Ferme Générale* offices of

17 The Commerz-Deputation (Chamber of Commerce) published wholesale market prices for all sorts of sugar traded in Hamburg since 1736: *Preis-Courant der Waaren in Partheyen* 14.03.1777, Wirtschaftsarchiv, Commerzbibliothek Hamburg Safebestand S/49; the annual prices for refined sugar (*Zucker Raffinade*), brown candy sugar (*Zucker Candis braun*), refined sugar lumps (*Zucker raffiniert Lumpen*) and raw white Brazil sugar (*Zucker roh weiß Brasilien*) are published in *Preise im Vor- und Frühindustriellen Deutschland: Nahrungsmittel – Getränke – Gewürze – Rohstoffe und Gewerbeprodukte*, ed. H.-J. Gerhard and K. H. Kaufhold (Stuttgart, 2001), pp. 102–11.
18 A. Petersson, *Zuckersiedergewerbe und Zuckerhandel in Hamburg im Zeitraum von 1814 bis 1834* (Stuttgart 1998), pp. 31–8, 75–103; P. Pourchasse, 'The French Atlantic Economy and Northern Europe', *The Rise of the Atlantic Economy and the North Sea/Baltic Trade, 1500–1800*, ed. L. Müller, P. R. Rössner and T. Tamaki (Stuttgart, 2011), pp. 92–3.

Bordeaux and Nantes (Table 6.4) shows that *sucre blanc* exports to the 'North' were mainly dispatched from Bordeaux, whereas *sucre brut, sucre terré* and *sucre tête* exports to the 'North' were mainly dispatched from Nantes.[19] The 'North' was a general geographic term used by the French *Ferme Générale* for the Hanseatic ports, but initially also included Denmark, Sweden and even Russia. After several redefinitions of the geo-economic areas in the 1730s and 1740s, the term came to denote solely the Hanseatic ports.[20]

The Portuguese trade balances for the years 1776, 1777, 1783, 1787, and 1796 to 1830 show a similar pattern of a slightly higher quantity of exports of semi-refined (*açúcar branco*) than raw (*açúcar mascavado*) sugar exports to Hamburg. In 1776, Lisbon exported 136,227 *arrobas* of *açúcar branco* and only 60,936 *arrobas* of *açúcar mascavado* to Hamburg. In 1787, Lisbon's sugar exports to Hamburg amounted to 104,685 *arrobas* of *açúcar branco* and only 48,600 *arrobas* of *açúcar mascavado*.[21]

Although the available French and Portuguese source material does not allow for a direct comparison of the volume of sugar exports to Hamburg, data from 1776 is available for both countries and allows us to make a tentative comparison. That year, Bordeaux dispatched a total of 35,801,620 *livre de poids* of sugar (c. 17,184 metric tons) to the North, while Lisbon only dispatched 195,966 *arrobas* of sugar (c. 2,887 metric tons) to Hamburg. The data thus confirms that Portuguese/Brazilian sugar held a significant share of the Hamburg market, even if it was far lower than that of French Caribbean sugar.

Hamburg's merchants and their trade with Bordeaux

Eighteenth-century intra-European trade in either colonial or European goods was a commission business, mainly carried out by Dutch and Central European merchants who had either a family member or an entrusted commissioner located in a foreign port city. The favorable policy of France, Portugal and Britain towards foreign merchants in their own port cities provided the basis for the successful continuation and growth of the 'German' merchant colonies in

---

19   Archives départementales de la Gironde, Bordeaux, Chambre de Commerce, C4386–8; Archives départementales de la Loire Atlantique, Nantes, Chambre de Commerce, C706, C716–17. I thank Loïc Charles and Guillaume Daudin for privileged access to the data within the framework of the database project, 'TOFLIT18: Transformations of the French Economy through the Lens of International Trade, 1716–1821'.
20   L. Charles and G. Daudin, 'France, c. 1713 – c. 1821', *Revue de l'OFCE* 140 (2015), pp. 237–48.
21   *Arrobas* were a measurement unit equivalent to 32 *libras* (pounds): *Negócios Coloniais: Uma correspondência comercial do século XVIII*, Vol. 1, ed. L. Lisanti (Rio de Janeiro, 1971), p. lxxxiv. I thank Maria Cristina Moreira, EEG-UMinho Braga, for privileged access to the data extracted from a work-in-progress database of the Portuguese trade balances.

these places during the eighteenth century.[22] Networks based on kinship played
an important role in the success of sugar importers in Hamburg and their trade
with Bordeaux and Lisbon. Sons of merchants – in this case, sons of Hamburg
merchants – commonly started their education in their father's firm and spent
their apprenticeship years abroad. The choice of the port city depended on a
variety of factors, including the apprentice merchant's financial situation, his
father's existing networks abroad, and the prospects of increasing profits in the
future. Upon arrival, the young men found themselves in an already existing
'German' colony and started their careers as apprentices. They then became
associates of the same firm, founded their own company, or started a temporary
joint business with one or several associates.[23] The number of 'German' merchants
who traded in Bordeaux and Lisbon increased significantly in the second half
of the eighteenth century: in Bordeaux after the Seven Years' War (1756–1763)
and in Lisbon after the earthquake (1755).[24] Kinship was not the only factor
for a successful import and export business of Hamburg merchants. They also
depended on a network of entrusted agents abroad who were not family members.

The cluster of sugar importers in Hamburg between 1733 and 1798 was
tripartite. Most firms were small (up to 200 *Mark Banco* in admiralty duties per
annum), followed by a small group of mid-sized businessmen and firms (200 to
500 *Mark Banco* in admiralty duties per annum). The ACEB shows that women
played no small role in this business world, although it was mainly controlled
by men. Women became *Kauffrauen* (the German term for a businesswoman)
when their businessmen husbands died. The sugar imports of the widow of
H. J. Möller in 1763, amounting to 225,000 *Mark Banco* in total, is only one
example of a remarkable number of successful businesswomen registered in
the ACEB.[25] Of all the businesses dealing in sugar, however, only a handful of
merchants – like Boué and His (both of Huguenot descent), Rücker & Wortmann,
or Schuback – can be identified as large-scale sugar importers. In addition,
we witness a shift in the course of the eighteenth century, away from family

22   K. Weber, *Deutsche Kaufleute im Atlantikhandel 1680–1850: Unternehmerkräfte und
Familien in Hamburg, Cádiz und Bordeaux* (Munich, 2004); M. Schulte Beerbühl, *Deutsche
Kaufleute in London: Welthandel und Einbürgerung, 1660–1818* (London, 2007); T. dos Santos
Arnold, 'Central Europe and the Portuguese, Spanish and French Atlantic: 15th to 19th Centuries',
European Review 26/3 (2018), pp. 421–9.
23   Weber, *Deutsche Kaufleute*, pp. 179ff; J. Poettering, 'Kein Banghase sein: Hamburger
Kaufmannslehrlinge im katholischen Lissabon des 17. Jahrhunderts', *Portugal und das Heilige
Römische Reich (16.–18. Jahrhundert) – Portugal e o Sacro Império (Séculos XVI–XVIII)*, ed.
A. Curvelo and M. Simões (Münster, 2011), pp. 207–16.
24   Weber, *Deutsche Kaufleute*, pp. 154ff, 369ff; Poettering, *Handel, Nation und Religion*;
H. Kellenbenz, 'Der Lutherische Gottesdienst und die Niederlassung Hamburger Kaufleute in
Lissabon im Anfang des Achtzehnten Jahrhunderts', *Hamburger Wirtschafts-Chronik* 1 (1950),
pp. 31–40.
25   See also N. Dufournaud and B. Michon, 'Les Femmes et le Commerce Maritime à Nantes
(1660–1740): Un Role Largement Méconnu', *Clio: Femmes, Genre, Histoire* 23 (2005), pp. 1–16.

businesses towards joint business firms and limited business partnerships, such as Rücker & Wortmann, Rücker & Westphalen, or Henckel & Eimbcke.

The prominence of Huguenots in the Hamburg sugar sector is not a coincidence. Many French Protestants were among the protagonists of French expansion into the Caribbean: plantation owners, ship owners, financiers, et cetera.[26] The Revocation of the Edict of Nantes (1685) and the subsequent emigration of the Huguenots to Central and Northern Europe worked in favor of Hamburg's trade with France and with French colonial produce. Even though the orthodox Lutheran clergy and parts of the citizenry discriminated against Huguenot merchants who migrated to Hamburg, the few Huguenots who established their businesses there became very successful. This was only possible because they kept their close ties with French business partners. They held a leading position in the Hamburg import and export trade with France during the first half of the eighteenth century.[27] At the same time, Hamburg merchants who wanted to establish themselves in a French port city enjoyed tolerance, and almost the same rights as French citizens, regardless of whether they were Lutherans or Catholics.

Yet in Hamburg, only Lutheran merchants were privileged with full citizenship. As citizens, they had to pay duties only on sugar they handled as commission agents, not on sugar they owned themselves. Calvinists (alongside Catholics and Jews) were not admitted to full citizenship, and therefore had to pay commission on goods where they acted as agents and on their own goods. Even having considered this bias, the ACEB database reveals the strong position of the Huguenot firms in Hamburg's imports of French products around the mid eighteenth century – not only of sugar, but also of coffee and indigo.[28] The firms of Pierre His and Pierre Boué enjoyed the highest market share during the earlier decades. Other Huguenot merchants (such as Boisierre, Bosanquet, and Michel & Grou) also held prominent places. During this particular period, the lion's share of all declared sugar imports from Bordeaux to Hamburg was handled by these merchants.[29] These firms mainly imported sugar from Bordeaux and Nantes, but they also received smaller quantities from Le Havre and La Rochelle. Both the Boué and the His firms additionally imported sugar from British ports during the Seven Years' War, when the British occupied Martinique and Guadeloupe. It can reasonably be assumed that both firms

---

26 B. van Ruymbeke, 'Minority Survival: The Huguenot Paradigm in France and the Diaspora', *Memory and Identity: The Huguenots and the Atlantic Diaspora*, ed. B. van Ruymbeke and R. J. Sparks (Columbia, 2003), pp. 1–25.

27 K. Weber, 'Zwischen Religion und Ökonomie: Sepharden und Hugenotten in Hamburg, 1580–1800', *Religion und Mobilität: Zum Verhältnis von raumbezogener Mobilität und religiöser Identitätsbildung im frühneuzeitlichen Europa*, ed. H. P. Jürgen and T. Weller (Göttingen, 2010), pp. 148–64; Weber, *Deutsche Kaufleute*, pp. 165ff.

28 Ibid., pp. 249ff; Weber, 'Zwischen Religion und Ökonomie', pp. 137ff, 158f.

29 See Weber, 'Zwischen Religion und Ökonomie', pp. 158ff.

channeled 'French' Caribbean sugar through British ports.[30] Although both firms also imported Brazilian sugar via Portuguese ports, this segment was only a rather small branch of their portfolio. After 1763, and until the French Revolution and the outbreak of the Slave Revolt in Saint-Domingue, Bordeaux remained the major port of transit for Hamburg's sugar imports.

The ACEB database supports Klaus Weber's conclusion that the overall cluster of sugar importers in Hamburg changed after the Seven Years' War.[31] From this point forward, firms like Rücker & Wortmann, Reiners, Peterssen and Hinrichsen dominated the sugar market. This shift away from the hitherto Huguenot supremacy in Hamburg's trade with France towards a henceforth 'German' controlled trade was caused by a rising number of 'German' merchants in Bordeaux. It also seems that Hamburg merchants who imported sugar from Bordeaux managed to adapt quite rapidly to the changing commodity flows during the Seven Years' War. This was made possible by a widespread network, based on kinship and trusted agents throughout Europe. At a minimum, the following Hamburg merchants had a family member in Bordeaux, who represented their business interests abroad: Westphalen (c. 1730), Boutin (c. 1734), Lienau (c. 1735), von Döhren (c. 1753), Brauer (c. 1768) and Rücker (c. 1777).[32]

This adaptability becomes evident when looking at the market portfolio of the sugar importers in Hamburg. In 1753, Hinrich C. Lienau exclusively imported sugar from Nantes and Bordeaux (declared value of imports c. 75,300 *Mark Banco*). Already in 1756, Lienau's imports (worth 273,450 *Mark Banco*) were mainly dispatched from London (171,800 *Mark Banco*), and only a smaller share was dispatched from Bordeaux and Nantes. At the peak of the Seven Years' War, in 1760, Lienau imported sugar only from British ports (worth 55,520 *Mark Banco*); there were no sugar imports from France in that year. After the end of the war, the pattern slowly changed back to the French dominance of the pre-war period. In 1763, sugar imports from London accounted for some 143,000 *Mark Banco* of a total volume worth 191,500 *Mark Banco*, whereas sugar imports from Bordeaux were worth about 38,900 *Mark Banco*. In 1769, Lienau declared sugar imports into Hamburg worth a total of 102,360 *Mark Banco*, of which 94,800 *Mark Banco* were declared as imports dispatched from the French ports of Bordeaux, La Rochelle and Nantes.

A similar change in the market portfolio can be found for the Lütkens & Engelhardt company. In 1753, Lütkens & Engelhardt almost exclusively imported sugar from French ports, worth 367,500 *Mark Banco*. In 1756, c. 24 per cent (142,700 *Mark Banco*) of their sugar imports were dispatched from

30   P. E. Schramm, 'His, Pierre', *Neue Deutsche Biographie* 9 (Berlin, 1972), p. 248; K. Weber, 'Boué, Pierre', *Hamburgische Biografie* 5 (Göttingen, 2010), pp. 59f.
31   Weber, 'Die Admiralitätszoll- und Convoygeld Einnahmebücher', pp. 97ff, 103.
32   Weber, *Deutsche Kaufleute*, pp. 371, 373, 374, 376. The year indicates the date the individuals' presence in Bordeaux is first mentioned in sources or secondary literature.

a British port, namely London, whereas 76 per cent of their sugar imports (worth 452,300 *Mark Banco*) were still dispatched from French ports, namely Bordeaux and Nantes. As in the case of H. C. Lienau, Lütkens & Engelhardt adapted their business strategies to the macro-economic and macro-political circumstances during the Seven Years' War. In 1760, they declared the import of sugar worth 91,200 *Mark Banco* from British ports, but also that of Brazilian sugar worth 13,300 *Mark Banco* from Lisbon (c. 13 per cent of their total sugar imports in 1760). When the British occupation of Guadeloupe and Martinique ended, Lütkens again redirected his sugar imports to the French redistribution hubs of Bordeaux, Nantes and Le Havre. In 1763, N. G. Lütkens declared Brazilian sugar worth 40,040 *Mark Banco* and sugar from British ports worth 71,700 *Mark Banco* – but 55 per cent of his sugar imports for that year (worth 139,600 *Mark Banco*) once again arrived from French ports.[33]

The case of the firm Rücker & Wortmann further illustrates the adaptability of sugar importers in Hamburg in times of warfare and the Atlantic Revolutions. Rücker & Wortmann had a network of business partners, particularly members of the Rücker family, who resided in Bordeaux, London and New York.[34] In addition, Rücker & Wortmann established a network of trusted agents in Cádiz and Lisbon.[35] In the 1770s and early 1780s, this Hamburg firm mainly imported sugar from Bordeaux, Nantes and other French Atlantic ports. In the late 1780s, this supply orientation shifted towards British, Portuguese and Spanish ports. Rücker & Wortmann were one of the first merchant houses who channeled their flow of goods through US-American ports, namely Baltimore, Charleston and Boston. During the era of the Atlantic Revolutions, these ports became the new hubs for Caribbean sugar imports into Hamburg.

The scope of the businesses of the Rücker family (including the Wortmanns) with the Americas becomes even more evident when looking at their trading partners outside Europe. In the early 1780s, the Baltimore house of Samuel and John Smith had a correspondent at Aux Cayes (Saint-Domingue) named Edward Hall Jr. In 1788, Hall spent some time in France and 'stayed with Matthew (Matthias) Rücker while on a trip to Bordeaux'.[36] This particular business relationship between Hall and Rücker became quite profitable for Rücker & Wortmann during the following years. Whereas 'French' sugar had made up some 98 per cent of their total declared sugar imports into Hamburg in 1788 (317,400 *Mark Banco* out of a total value of 322,720 *Mark Banco*), sugar dispatched from US-American ports made up 78 per cent of their declared sugar imports into Hamburg in 1798 (1,092,660 out of a total value of 1,403,540 *Mark Banco*).

33   These figures are taken from the ACEB database.
34   Weber, *Deutsche Kaufleute*, p. 376; Schulte Beerbühl, *Deutsche Kaufleute*, pp. 174ff.
35   D. A. Rabuzzi, 'Cutting out the Middlemen? American Trade in Northern Europe, 1783–1815', *Merchant Organization and Maritime Trade with the North Atlantic, 1660–1815*, ed. O. U. Janzen (St Johns, 1998), pp. 175–99, here pp. 186f.
36   Ibid.

Trade with Lisbon

The situation was quite different for Hamburg's sugar imports from Portugal. During the seventeenth century, Hamburg's trade with Portugal was conducted by three major parties: first, the 'German' merchants of Hamburg, followed by the Dutch merchants who operated in Hamburg and lastly, the Portuguese merchants who had immigrated to Hamburg. In 1713, the 'German' merchant community in Lisbon consisted of some 61 members only, similar to the number of 'German' merchants (65) residing in Lisbon at the time of the earthquake on 1 November 1755.[37] As in the case of Bordeaux, kinship and a network of agents provided the basis for the successful business of Hamburg merchants in Lisbon. A cross-referencing of the sugar importers listed in the ACEB and the Hamburg merchants residing in Lisbon in 1713 and 1755 indicates that at least the following merchants had a family member who resided in Lisbon and represented their business interests abroad: Jenquel [Jenckel] (1713), Burmester (1713), Borchers (1713), Borchers (1713, 1755), Klefecker (1755), Petersen (1755), Schuback (1755) and Süverkrub (1755).[38]

When the Marquis de Pombal created the monopolistic companies of Grão-Pará e Maranhão and Pernambuco é Paraíba, this created new opportunities for foreign merchants to participate in the Portuguese colonial trade. Although they were still excluded from direct trade with the colonial markets, particularly within the Atlantic World, Hamburg merchants could now sell their products destined for overseas markets and buy colonial products destined for intra-European reshipment within a state-controlled framework. The shift away from a privately organized colonial trade towards a monopolistic state-controlled form of organization had several benefits for the merchants. The companies established a system of regular shipping between Portugal, the Americas and West African ports, as well as a bureaucracy that controlled imports and exports. As stated above, the two companies invested the newly gained profits into improving the plantation economies in the Americas, which ultimately led to an increase in the annual crop yields, particularly of sugar and tobacco.

German merchants benefited from this monopolistic system as shareholders of these companies, and as either suppliers of European manufactured goods destined for export to the Atlantic basin or as clients of colonial products destined for European markets. A list of individuals who traded with the Grão-Pará e Maranhão company indicates that at least 25 German merchants (among them Schuback, Meyer, Metzener, and Lang & Hasenclever) had

---

37 Kellenbenz, 'Der Lutherische Gottesdienst', p. 34; U. Löffler, *Lissabons Fall – Europas Schrecken: Die Deutung des Erdbebens von Lissabon im deutschsprachigen Protestantismus des 18. Jahrhunderts* (Berlin/New York, 1999), pp. 142ff.
38 Kellenbenz, 'Der Lutherische Gottesdienst', p. 34; Löffler, *Lissabons Fall*, pp. 142ff.

direct business relations with the company between 1755 and 1785.[39] One of these, Johannes Schuback, was a noteworthy Hamburg merchant who mainly imported sugar from Lisbon, but also from Porto. As son of a merchant and mayor of Hamburg, Schuback spent his apprenticeship years in Lisbon and was one of the 'German' survivors of the Lisbon earthquake (1755). He returned to Hamburg shortly after the earthquake and founded his own company. In 1761, he was appointed as the general agent (*feitor*) of the company Grão-Pará e Maranhão in Hamburg, a fact that explains his strong business ties with Portugal and the profits he made.[40] His knowledge and personal experience of Portuguese policies and business mechanisms, together with his commercial network in Lisbon, formed the basis for his success during the years 1760 to 1790.[41] After 1790, Schuback gradually shifted his imports away from Portuguese ports towards direct imports from the Caribbean and US-American ports, namely Cuba, St Thomas and Baltimore (MD).

Conclusion

As this case study of sugar importers in Hamburg between 1733 and 1798 shows, Hamburg's importers not only adapted to circumstances during wartime, especially the Seven Years' War, but also to the new possibilities of direct imports from the West Indies, which opened up in the era of the Atlantic Revolutions. Kinship and a network of trusted agents in ports like Bordeaux and Lisbon played an important role for the successful business of Hamburg merchants in times of commissioned trade with foreign marketplaces. Most of the 'French' sugar came via Bordeaux, but Hamburg merchants also imported large quantities of sugar via Nantes, Le Havre and La Rochelle. 'French' sugar imports in Hamburg were first dominated by the Huguenot families of Boué and His, among others. During and after the Seven Years' War, their dominant position was taken over by Lutheran Hamburg merchants, who managed to adapt their businesses according to the change of commodity flows. During the British occupation of Martinique and Guadeloupe, sugar from these two islands was shipped to Hamburg via British ports, as the case of Lienau showed.

In comparison, Lisbon and Porto were significantly less important hubs for sugar imports until the late 1760s, since 'French' sugar was cheaper, available in larger quantities, and of better quality than the Brazilian sugar. The structural reforms of the Marquis de Pombal and the creation of two monopolistic

39   A. Carreira, *A Companhia Geral do Grão-Pará e Maranhão*, Vol. 2 (São Paulo, 1988), pp. 296ff.
40   M. Nunes Dias, 'Fomento Ultramarino e Mercantilismo: A Companhia do Grão-Pará e Maranhão, 1775–1778', *Revista de História* 32 (1966), pp. 367–415, here p. 395.
41   D. Brietzke, 'Schuback, Johannes', *Neue Deutsche Biographie* 23 (Berlin, 2007), pp. 601–2.

companies for Portugal's Atlantic trade enabled Portugal to increase its sugar output and to compete with other sugar suppliers on Hamburg's market. These reforms also created profitable opportunities for Hamburg merchants in the Portugal trade, and in the sugar trade in particular.

The figures of the ACEB show that North American ports took over the leading position as ports of origin only after 1789, but especially after 1792 – more than a decade after the Declaration of Independence by the former British colonies in North America. The second half of the eighteenth century also saw a change in business strategies and the concept of merchant firms. Traditionally family-held businesses were now in competition with joint business firms and limited business partnerships, such as Rücker & Wortmann, Rücker & Westphalen, or Henckel & Eimbcke. This chapter has also illustrated the value of the ACEB as a source for the quantitative analysis of markets and merchants, especially when combined with additional source material from other European port cities.

7

A Gateway to the Spanish Atlantic?
The Habsburg Port City of Trieste as Intermediary in Commodity Flows between the Habsburg Monarchy and Spain in the Eighteenth Century

KLEMENS KAPS[1]

The Habsburg Monarchy in early modern globalization
– a periphery of the world economy?

The term 'periphery' is usually used in historical scholarship in two ways: first, as a postcolonial concept pointing to perceptual patterns that perpetuate an asymmetrical power relationship; and second, as a structural category of economic geography, mainly coined by world-systems analysis, designating economically underdeveloped territories that depend on the centers of the world economy. Ideally, peripheries deliver those raw materials that are turned into finished goods in the core regions and are eventually sold on the peripheries' consumer markets.[2] While this second meaning of 'periphery' has been critiqued substantially over the course of recent decades, it is still a highly coherent and useful tool for analyzing spatial disparities and uneven development. This involves a critical revision of both the conceptual tools and the historical narrative of world-systems analysis, as Andrea Komlosy and I have argued.[3]

Immanuel Wallerstein classified the Habsburg Monarchy between the sixteenth and the early nineteenth centuries as a 'semi-periphery'.[4] In this, he

1 This article is based on the preliminary results of the ongoing research project, 'Connectors between a Polycentric Empire and Global Markets, 1713–1815', funded by the Austrian Science Fund (FWF), P 28612–G28.

2 I. Wallerstein, *Der historische Kapitalismus* (Berlin, 1984).

3 K. Kaps and A. Komlosy, 'Centers and Peripheries Revisited: Polycentric Connections or Entangled Hierarchies', *Review Fernand Braudel Center* 36, 3/4 (2013), pp. 237–65.

4 I. Wallerstein, *The Modern World-System, Vol. 1: Capitalist Agriculture and the Origins of the European World-Economy in the Sixteenth Century* (New York/San Francisco/London, 1974),

followed the standard historical scholarship that framed the Central European Habsburg space as economically 'backward' compared to Western Europe, and at the same time as relatively marginalized from world markets. Numerous works since the 1970s and 1980s have challenged this traditional perception: on the one hand, studies pointed to developmental processes within the Habsburg Monarchy, without leaving aside the internal disparities or the differences from the centers of the world economy.[5] On the other hand, research highlighted the Habsburg dominion's international and even global connections in commerce and cultural exchange, mainly focusing on the early-modern Spanish Empire.[6] While the metanarrative has not changed much, the current chapter builds on this research to revisit the relevance of Habsburg foreign trade in the eighteenth century, focusing on commercial exchange with Spain in the Mediterranean and the Atlantic as a paradigmatic example.

Habsburg maritime: Trieste as the Habsburg Monarchy's foreign sea trade hub, 1717–1815

The Habsburg Monarchy is usually regarded as a landlocked empire. True as this characterization may be in comparison to the maritime colonial empires of Western Europe, the integration of Habsburg Central Europe into maritime trade should not be overlooked. Although the trade connections via Venice, Hamburg and Trieste are basically known, they have not yet been comprehensively and profoundly studied, and often their significance is called into question. The latter applies in particular to Trieste, which, although under Habsburg rule since 1382, only became an international trading hub during the eighteenth century.[7] The transformation from a local and regional harbor into a center of long-distance trade is usually linked to measures imposed by

pp. 81, 85, 97, 171, 307f; I. Wallerstein, *The Modern World-System, Vol. 2: Mercantilism and the Consolidation of the European World-Economy, 1600–1750* (New York, 1980), pp. 34, 77, 232.
5   D. Good, *Der wirtschaftliche Aufstieg des Habsburgerreichs 1750–1918* (Vienna/Cologne/Graz, 1986); J. Komlos, *Die Habsburgermonarchie als Zollunion: Die wirtschaftliche Entwicklung Österreich-Ungarns im 19. Jahrhundert* (Vienna, 1986); A. Komlosy, *Grenze und ungleiche regionale Entwicklung: Binnenmarkt und Migration in der Habsburgermonarchie* (Vienna, 2003).
6   R. Pieper, 'Zur Anbindung Innerösterreichs an die atlantischen Märkte in der Frühen Neuzeit (1670–1758)', *Kuppeln – Korn – Kanonen: Unerkannte und unbekannte Spuren in Südosteuropa von der Aufklärung bis in die Gegenwart*, ed. U. Tischler-Hofer and R. Zedinger (Innsbruck/Vienna/Bozen, 2010), pp. 175–86; K. Weber, *Deutsche Kaufleute im Atlantikhandel 1680–1830: Unternehmen und Familien in Hamburg, Cádiz und Bordeaux* (Munich, 2004).
7   See e.g. H. Rumpler, 'Economia e Potere Politico: Il Ruolo di Trieste nella Politica di Sviluppo Economico di Vienna', *Storia Economica e Sociale di Trieste*, ed. R. Finzi, L. Panariti and G. Panjek (Trieste, 2003), pp. 55–124, here pp. 63ff, 67; M. Hochedlinger, *Austria's Wars of Emergence: War, State and Society in the Habsburg Monarchy 1683–1797* (London, 2003), pp. 196f.

Emperor Charles VI, such as the proclamation of free shipping in the Adriatic (1717) and the declaration of Trieste as a free port (first in 1717, renewed in 1719 and 1725). These measures need to be contextualized within the complex relations extending from the regional to the global level, however. Only after Dutch and English merchant fleets and warships had penetrated the Adriatic, undermining the maritime monopoly claimed by the Republic of Venice, could the Habsburg court pursue its own maritime policy. The War of the Spanish Succession played a key role in creating an environment favorable to this plan: the fact that imperial ships sailed across Venetian waters in order to supply imperial troops in Mantua, Milan and Naples created the conditions that allowed Trieste to be declared a free port.[8]

The much-vaunted decline of *La Serenissima* (Venice) was an important prerequisite for Trieste's rise. This was a lengthy process that had set in with Venice's loss of control over trade routes and the lucrative cabotage trade in its remote possessions in the Adriatic, as well as demographic stagnation.[9] These changes were related to the erosion of Venice's geopolitical power and its dependence on the Viennese court, whose rule was tremendously strengthened by the Treaty of Rastatt (1714), even though it had failed to achieve its original goals in the War of the Spanish Succession. The territorial acquisitions of Lombardy (Mantua in 1707 and Milan in 1714), the southern Netherlands (1714), Naples (1707–1714), and Sicily (1720) for a short period, as well as the dynastically-based control over Tuscany (1737), also strengthened the Viennese court's orientation towards maritime trade. The cameralist idea of 'universal commerce' between all Habsburg possessions was extended to include commercial exchange in the Mediterranean and the Atlantic.[10]

However, these moves were not simply implemented 'from above', but were always negotiated with local actors and representatives of mercantile interests. Thus, Trieste's transformation into an international long-distance mercantile center relied on numerous institutions and regulations, most importantly the foundation of a commercial court (Mercantil- und Wechselgericht, 1722), the granting of religious tolerance to non-Catholic individuals and groups, as well as the recognition of the wholesale merchant guild (Borsa dei Mercanti, 1755).[11]

---

8   D. Frigo, 'Le "Disavventure della Navigazione": Neutralità Veneziana e Conflitti Europei nel primo Settecento', *Attraverso i Conflitti: Neutralità e Commercio fra età Moderna ed età Contemporanea*, ed. D. Andreozzi (Trieste, 2017), pp. 53–74, here pp. 55ff.

9   D. Andreozzi, 'Tra Trieste, Ancona, Venezia e Bologna: La Canapa e il Commercio nell'Adriatico del '700', *Trieste e l'Adriatico: Uomini, Merci, Conflitti*, ed. D. Andreozzi and C. Gatti (Trieste, 2005), pp. 153–201.

10   E. Faber, *Litorale Austriaco: Das österreichische und kroatische Küstenland* (Trondheim/Graz, 1995), pp. 39ff, 52ff.

11   M. Cattaruzza, 'Cittadinanza e Ceto Mercantile a Trieste (1749–1850)', *Österreichisches Italien – Italienisches Österreich: Interkulturelle Gemeinsamkeiten und nationale Differenzen vom 18. Jahrhundert bis zum Ende des Ersten Weltkrieges*, ed. B. Mazohl-Wallnig and M. Meriggi (Vienna, 1999), pp. 113–37, here p. 121; U. Tucci, 'Die Triestiner Kaufmannschaft im 18.

These measures – in particular, the granting of religious freedoms – facilitated the immigration of wholesale merchants to Trieste. Its location between Italian-Romance, Slavic and German language regions made Trieste something of a 'multicultural' hub in the region, which was decisively increased by immigrants from the Habsburg territories, the Holy Roman Empire, states on the Italian Peninsula (such as Lombardy, Genoa and Venice), and the Ottoman Empire. German Protestants, Orthodox Greeks and Serbs, Catholic Germans from the other Habsburg regions, Jews and Armenians started to live in the city, especially after 1750, although some migrants already arrived in the early 1730s.[12]

Due to this immigration, Trieste's population increased: moderately at first, from 3,865 (1735) to 6,433 (1758), and then rising rapidly to 10,664 inhabitants (1775); by 1798, there were 30,000 residents in the city, before a significant demographic decline set in during the third Napoleonic occupation (1809–1813).[13] Thus, at the end of the eighteenth century, Trieste was no longer much smaller than other leading Mediterranean commercial centers such as Livorno, which was home to 40,000 people in 1787.[14]

The expansion of the volume of goods traded through Trieste was just as marked as the increase in its population, growing sevenfold between 1746 and 1784 (from 3.2 to 22.2 million *florins*), measured in official monetary value.[15] In spite of the customs privileges for maritime transit trade (for which only 0.5 per cent of consular tax had to be paid), trade between the Habsburg regions and international markets channeled via Trieste represented the overwhelming majority of the trade volume. Transit trade at sea and between the Adriatic port and inland economies beyond the Habsburg regions amounted to an average of only 14.7 per cent between 1753 and 1766. This clearly underlines the fact that, from the middle of the century onwards, Trieste acted primarily as a gateway for the Habsburg regions' external trade in the Mediterranean and beyond. This disproves one of the many conventional wisdoms regarding the development of Trieste's foreign trade, and brings with it further important corrections. For

Jahrhundert: Ihre Ausrichtung, ihre Gutachten', *Beiträge zur Handels- und Verkehrsgeschichte*, ed. P. W. Roth (Graz, 1978), pp. 121–33, here pp. 123f.

12   A. Millo, 'The Creation of a New Bourgeoisie in Trieste', *Social Change in the Habsburg Monarchy / Les transformations de la société dans la monarchie des Habsbourg: l'époque des Lumières*, Das achtzehnte Jahrhundert und Österreich (Internationale Beihefte), Vol. 3, ed. H. Heppner, P. Urbanitsch and R. Zedinger (Bochum, 2011), pp. 215–28.

13   Faber, *Litorale Austriaco*, p. 13; G. Panjek, 'Una "Commercial Officina" fra Vie di Mare e di Terra', *La Cittá dei Traffici 1719–1918: Storia Economica e Sociale di Trieste*, ed. R. Finzi, L. Panariti and G. Panjek (Trieste, 2003), pp. 235–348, here p. 281.

14   F. Trivellato, *The Familiarity of Strangers: The Sephardic Diaspora, Livorno, and Cross-Cultural Trade in the Early Modern Period* (New Haven/London, 2009), p. 57.

15   Data according to: Panjek, 'Una "Commercial Officina"', pp. 260f, 273; E. Bruckmüller, 'Triest und Österreich im 18. Jahrhundert', *Österreichische Osthefte* 3 (1985), pp. 300–30, here p. 316. Haus-, Hof- und Staatsarchiv (hereafter: HHStA), KA, Nachlass Zinzendorf, Handschriften, Vol. 118, pp. 4ff, 22f, 32, 38f, 395, 596.

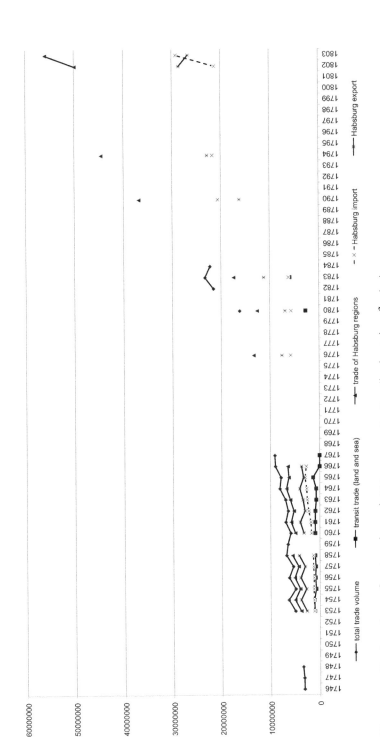

Figure 7.1. Trade volume flowing through Trieste, 1746–1803 (in Austrian *florins*)

Source: ASTS, CRS Intendenza Commerciale No. 587, fols 70–72, 74, 78; 589, fols 70–72, 79–80; 588, fols 70–71, 79–80; 589, fols 110, 112–113, 155; 590, fols 49, 53, 119–121, 181, 185–186; 867, fols 1–21. HHStA, KA, Nachlass Zinzendorf, Handschriften, Vol. 118, pp. 4–6, 22–3, 32, 38–9, 395, 596. ÖStA, FHA, NHK, Kommerz Litorale Akten No. 856, fols 464, 526, 648, 653. Panjek, 'Commercial Officina', pp. 260–1, 273; Bruckmüller, *Triest*, p. 316.

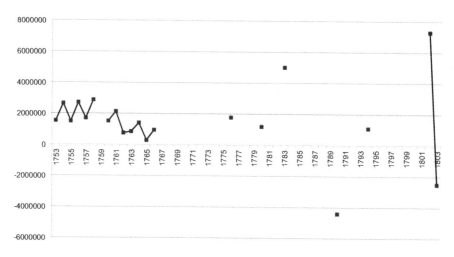

Figure 7.2. Trade balance of the Habsburg dominions through Trieste, 1753–1803 (in Austrian *florins*). Own calculation according to Figure 7.1.

example, the volume of the Habsburg regions' foreign trade channeled through Trieste increased almost 15-fold between 1753 and 1803. This is strong evidence that prevalent assumptions regarding Habsburg 'isolation from world markets' are hardly tenable (see Figure 7.1).

At the same time, it becomes clear that, contrary to widespread claims in the literature, the balance of trade was mostly positive for the Habsburg Monarchy: in only two years (1780 and 1803) did the Habsburg lands import more through Trieste than they exported (see Figure 7.2). The extent of involvement with Trieste's external trade also differed from region to region. Between 1758/61 and 1766, Carniola, followed by Hungary and Carinthia, was the region most heavily involved in export via Trieste's customs enclave. These three regions delivered almost three-quarters (72.5 per cent) of all goods exported through Trieste. However, the pull of Trieste's export mediation stretched far into the east and north of the Monarchy – as the shares of Upper and Lower Austria (6.6 per cent), Transylvania (3.9 per cent) and Bohemia (3 per cent) prove. The northern Austrian and Bohemian countries also played a larger role in the import trade during this period. Upper and Lower Austria even occupied the leading position (31.7 per cent), ahead of Hungary (15.2 per cent), Styria (13.2 per cent), Carinthia (11.5 per cent) and Bohemia (9.2 per cent), while Carniola (4.8 per cent) was just ahead of Moravia (4.7 per cent) at the bottom of the scale.[16]

16   Own calculations according to the data provided by Archivio di Stato di Trieste (hereafter: ASTS), Cesarea Regia Suprema (hereafter: CRS) Intendenza Commerciale, No. 587, fols 93ff; No. 588, fols 73, 78; No. 589, fol. 112; No. 590, fols 121, 186.

This already illustrates that the geographical location alone was not decisive for the extent of trade links through Trieste, but that – promoted by the newly-built road connection from Trieste via Ljubljana and Graz to Vienna and further on to Brno – different production structures and purchasing powers strongly influenced the spatial orientation of the trade. This is illustrated by the commodity structure of this trade: Trieste's exports between 1761 and 1763 were led by hardware (25 per cent), followed by linen and ticking (11.1 per cent), wax (11 per cent), brass and brassware (4.6 per cent), wheat (2.2 per cent), glassware (1.6 per cent), and cloth, woollen goods and loden (1.2 per cent). In turn, imports in 1765 were made up of olive oil (28.1 per cent), followed by medicinal products, spices, and colonial goods (7.3 per cent), raw cotton (5.6 per cent), sugar (3.7 per cent), almonds (3.5 per cent) and fruits (3.1 per cent).[17]

This trade pattern suggests that the Habsburg Monarchy was a core economy rather than a peripheral one, in Wallerstein's terms: the Monarchy exported finished goods and imported raw materials. For the western Habsburg regions – where proto-industry had already gained a foothold by 1700 and continued to spread over the course of the eighteenth century – this is even more evident. In 1783, more than half of the exports from the so-called Bohemian-Austrian Customs Area[18] through Trieste consisted of finished goods, with mining products taking the lead, followed by textiles, glassware and leather.[19] This means that the proto-industries of the western regions of Habsburg Central Europe were able to compete on international export markets in the late eighteenth century. Textile exports came mainly from the Bohemian lands and from Upper and Lower Austria, but also from Carinthia, Styria and Carniola. Carinthia and Styria were ahead of Carniola as well as Upper and Lower Austria in the export of iron and metals, while Bohemia and Styria furnished glass. The Hungarian lands, Transylvania and Croatia supplied most of the grain, wax and potash.[20]

In this light, Trieste clearly emerges as a hub for the Habsburg dominions' access to the world market after 1750. By 1783/84, Trieste's share of the foreign trade of the Bohemian-Austrian Customs Area was about one quarter of these

17   Own calculations according to: W. Kaltenstadler, 'Der österreichische Seehandel über Triest im 18. Jahrhundert, Teil 2', *Vierteljahresschrift für Sozial- und Wirtschaftsgeschichte* 56 (1969), pp. 1–104, here pp. 33f.
18   This area encompassed the western regions of the Habsburg Monarchy, excluding only Trieste, the Tyrol and Galicia, where all internal customs tariffs, excluding tolls and payments for the use of bridges and roads, were abolished in 1775. From 1785, Galicia was part of this customs area; Tyrol joined in 1826, Trieste only in 1880.
19   Own calculations according to: Österreichisches Staatsarchiv (hereafter: ÖStA), Finanz- und Hofkammerarchiv (hereafter: FHKA), Neue Hofkammer (hereafter: NHK), Kommerz Oberösterreich und Niederösterreich Akten 144, fol. 706.
20   ASTS, CRS Intendenza Commerciale, Nos. 587–90, fol. 867.

regions' entire exchange of goods with foreign countries.[21] Of course, this aggregated value has to be differentiated for individual product groups: a considerable portion of Bohemia's linen exports destined for England was still handled by Hamburg.[22] In fact, between 1782 and 1791, 55 per cent of Bohemian linen was exported to Prussian Silesia, where the fabrics were finalized and then sold as Silesian linen to various international markets around the Atlantic Ocean.[23] Still, at least 24 per cent of Bohemian linen was exported to Spain and Portugal, and another 11 per cent to Italy, which points to a remarkable orientation of more than a third of Bohemian linen exports to Mediterranean and Iberian markets.[24] Thus, while Trieste was neither the dominant nor the sole intermediary gateway between the Habsburg regions and global markets, it nevertheless constituted an important hub, especially for access to the Spanish and Ottoman markets.

Commodity flows between Habsburg Central Europe and Spain

The spatial orientation of Trieste's foreign trade can be difficult to pinpoint, because the statistics of the years 1761 to 1766, which include trading partners for the first time, frequently mention several countries or places of origin and destination at once. It has already become clear that a number of trading partners were reached through Trieste: in addition to a number of Italian states, they were located in the Ottoman Empire, Great Britain, the Netherlands, France, the North African 'Barbary' states and Morocco. Hamburg, Ragusa and Malta are also mentioned. Spain mainly appears together with other countries. It is unclear which of these trading partners were marketplaces serving as a commercial outlet for production sites in their vicinity, and which indicated transit nodes.[25]

A rough calculation of the proportions of trading partners for the 1760s therefore comes with some reservations. It was not until 1775, 1776 and 1783 that detailed trade accounts were compiled that clearly distinguished commodity exchange according to trading partners.[26] All three statistics show

21 Trieste's share in overall imports was 23.3 per cent (1783) and 24 per cent (1784); figures for exports were 24.5 per cent and 27.3 per cent respectively. Own calculation according to: HHStA, KA, Nachlass Zinzendorf, Vol. 118, pp. 315, 317, 527.
22 HHStA, KA, Nachlass Zinzendorf, Vol. 118, p. 32.
23 Concerning the export of Silesian linen to Atlantic markets, see Anka Steffen's contribution in this volume.
24 H. Hassinger, 'Der Außenhandel der Habsburgermonarchie in der zweiten Hälfte des 18. Jahrhunderts', *Die wirtschaftliche Situation in Deutschland und Österreich an der Wende vom 18. zum 19. Jahrhundert*, ed. F. Lütge (Stuttgart, 1964), pp. 61–98, here p. 68.
25 See: ÖStA, FHKA, NHK, Kommerz Litorale Akten 856; ASTS, CRS Intendenza Commerciale, Nos. 587–90.
26 Kaltenstadler, 'Der österreichische Seehandel, Teil 2', pp. 97f; F. Cusin, 'Precedenti di Concorrenza fra i Porti del Mare del Nord ed i Porti dell'Adriatico: Saggio sul Commercio del

that the main trading partners were certainly situated in the Adriatic – namely the Republic of Venice, the Papal State and Naples-Sicily, which in 1783 alone accounted for at least 45 per cent of the total volume of Trieste's foreign trade. Direct trade with destinations further afield lagged far behind.[27]

I should emphasize that this does not necessarily mean that Trieste's trade was mainly geared to regional markets on the Apennine Peninsula. On the contrary: statistics point to a high level of transit points through which the flow of goods passed on their way from Trieste to the Levant, but mainly to the western Mediterranean and the Atlantic. The case of Spain is particularly striking in this respect: the statistically proven direct trade might give the impression that these flows of goods were at best of limited importance for the foreign trade of the Habsburg regions channeled via Trieste.

According to the statistic of 1776, direct trade with Spain amounted to just 16,000 *florins* in exports and imports,[28] although it had increased rapidly to 176,587 *florins* (17-fold) by 1783, while imports were then specified as 39,373 *florins* (which also included Malta).[29] However, a closer look at exports in 1783 quickly reveals that they consisted to a large extent of copper (70.6 per cent or 195,402 *florins*). This was due to a contract concluded in 1782 between the imperial consul in Cádiz and his Swedish counterpart, to supply the Spanish navy with copper from Upper Hungary. Without this exceptional business, the increase in direct exports from the Habsburg territories via Trieste to Spain would have been more moderate (to 81,185 *florins*, or fivefold).[30] Even without copper, the majority of these exports consisted of raw materials, mostly timber (59.8 per cent of the remaining export value). Proto-industrial goods still occupied a strong position with an overall share of 40 per cent: steel (22 per cent) took the lead, ahead of glass (9.1 per cent) and linen (4.9 per cent), followed by leather goods (1.2 per cent), wooden products (1.1 per cent), hardware (0.6 per cent) and hats (0.4 per cent).[31]

This export trade was far more extensive than meets the eye, and went back much farther. The trading company Rocci e Balletti had already exported socks to the Canary Islands in 1746,[32] before one of the two partners, Giacomo Balletti, as director of a company founded specifically for the Spanish trade (Compagna del Commercio di Spagna), consigned a large shipment of 38,105 *florins* to Cádiz two decades later. The exported products consisted almost

---

Porto di Trieste nel Secolo XVIII (1760–1776)', *Annali della R. Università degli Studi Economici e Commerciali di Trieste* 3 (1931), pp. 3–68, here p. 64. ÖStA, FHKA, NHK, Kommerz Litorale Akten 850. I am very thankful to Jonathan Singerton, Innsbruck, for sharing this statistic with me.

27 Own calculation: HHStA, KA, Nachlass Zinzendorf, Handschriften, Vol. 118, p. 395.
28 Cusin, 'Precedenti di Concorrenza', p. 64.
29 ÖStA, FHKA, NHK, Kommerz Litorale Akten 850.
30 Own calculations according to: ibid.
31 Own calculations according to: ibid.
32 ASTS, CRS Intendenza Commerciale, No. 479, fol. 25.

exclusively of proto-industrial goods, led by textiles (47.2 per cent, mainly linen), followed by metal goods (15.6 per cent), shipbuilding materials (12 per cent), glass (7.3 per cent), food (especially alcohol, 6.5 per cent in total), household goods (4.9 per cent), chemical products (2.7 per cent), wax (1.9 per cent), jewelry (1.6 per cent) and furniture (0.3 per cent). The geographical origin of the goods, which can be determined for 90 per cent of the goods (by value), turns the trade geography outlined so far on its head: the exported goods mainly came from Bohemia (32.1 per cent), Trieste (19.6 per cent) and Lower Austria (15.7 per cent). This example emphasizes the intertwining of the Central European proto-industrial regions and Spain's Atlantic markets, here represented by the colonial port of Cádiz.[33]

In 1778 the 'free trade' decree entitled Barcelona (like Alicante and Málaga) to trade directly with Spanish America. In practice, however, the vast majority of the Spanish colonial trade continued to be channeled through Cádiz (76.4 per cent of exports and 84.3 per cent of imports between 1782 and 1796).[34] In addition to the aforementioned copper from Upper Hungary, mercury from Idrija (a mine in Carniola) was supplied to Cádiz between 1785 and 1791. These deliveries were managed in both cases by the imperial consul in the Andalusian port, Paolo Greppi.[35] In the shipping lists sent to Vienna by the imperial consuls in Cádiz and Alicante (Paolo Greppi and Jean-Pierre Arabet) for the years 1784 and 1785, there are further references to exports of grain, beans, steel and linen from Trieste to the trading house Ponte e Villavecchia in Barcelona being transported on imperial ships. Liquor and a number of unspecified goods were consigned to Cádiz.[36] In late autumn 1783, the Trieste trader Ambrosio (Ambrogio) di Strohlendorf consigned shipbuilding timber to Greppi in Cádiz, but the ship *Carinthia* that carried the cargo sank near Sicily.[37]

These examples at the micro level reveal that proto-industrial products played a prominent role, even though agricultural products were in high demand as well, especially on the Spanish Mediterranean coast (for instance, in Catalonia). However, these examples do not address the question of transit trade. Only the

33   Own calculations and compilations according to: ÖStA, FHKA, NHK Kommerz Litorale Akten 856, fol. 491. For Balletti and the Compagna di Commercio di Spagna, see ASTS, Notai, 322, fol. 158.
34   C. Martínez Shaw, 'Bourbon Reformism and Spanish Colonial Trade, 1717–1778', *Atlantic History: History of the Atlantic System 1580–1830*, ed. H. Pietschmann (Göttingen, 2002), pp. 375–86; J. R. Fisher, *Commercial Relations between Spain and Spanish America in the Era of Free Trade, 1778–1796* (Liverpool, 1985), pp. 149, 165.
35   K. Kaps, 'Entre Servicio Estatal y los Negocios Transnacionales: El Caso de Paolo Greppi, Cónsul Imperial en Cádiz (1774–1791)', *Los Consules Extranjeros en la Edad Moderna y a Principios de la Edad Contemporánea (Siglos XV–XIX)*, ed. M. Aglietti, M. Herrero Sánchez and F. Zamora Rodríguez (Madrid, 2013), pp. 225–35.
36   ÖStA, HHStA, Diplomatische Korrespondenz Staatenabteilung (hereafter: DK StAbt) 117/42, fols 7, 9–10.
37   Archivo Histórico Provincial de Cádiz (hereafter: AHPC), Protocolos Notariales 21/5115, fols 7–10.

shipping lists of 1784/85 include references to the intertwined trade route from Trieste through Malta and Genoa to Barcelona and Cádiz.

A quantitative evaluation on the basis of the customs books for Genoa's import and transit trade in 1779 reveals that a considerable amount of Habsburg goods such as steel, iron, linen, glass, and also grain arrived in Genoa (by sea) from Trieste. The sources also show that Genoese agents were instrumental in re-exporting these products to Spain. A substantial part of the commodity flows between Trieste and Genoa recorded by Trieste's export statistics of 1783 was thus actually destined for Spain.[38] Besides Genoa, other transit centers also mediated Habsburg-Spanish trade. In addition to Livorno and the kingdom of Naples-Sicily, Malta mediated linen, cloth, potash, vitriol and steel from Trieste to Barcelona as late as the 1790s. While Maltese merchants maintained close ties with Spanish trading ports in the eighteenth century, Habsburg merchants were also able to establish themselves in this exchange.[39]

The same applies to imports, where direct trade was less pronounced, according to the 1783 sources. Significant imports of colonial goods such as cocoa, coffee, tobacco, sugar, dyes (such as indigo, cochineal or logwood of Campeche), as well as medicinal substances, usually passed through Genoa. Products native to the Iberian Peninsula were also dispatched to Trieste, led by olives, dried fruit, the sought-after Spanish merino wool, silk from Valencia, wine from Málaga and Alicante, and sherry from Andalusia. Giacomo Balletti had already ordered these goods from several Spanish ports for Trieste in 1764, and the shipping lists of 1784/85 listed logwood from Campeche and coffee as being delivered to Trieste from Cádiz.

The statistics of 1783 make it possible to compare the significance of the Mediterranean route for the mediation of these Iberian and Spanish-American goods to the Habsburg dominions with that of other gateways such as Hamburg. Accordingly, Trieste was the dominant reference market of the Bohemian-Austrian Customs Area for some commodities, such as cocoa (including cocoa shells), jalapa root and sugar (including molasses). For vanilla, the difference from other delivery channels was not large; otherwise, particularly with dyestuffs, other gateways dominated. Tobacco, in turn, reached Trieste mostly from the Ottoman Empire rather than from Atlantic markets.[40] This illustrates even more clearly than the case of exports that Trieste in the late eighteenth century was a rising marketplace – even though it was by no means the only gateway to global markets for the Habsburg Monarchy.

38   Archivio di Stato di Genova, Casa di San Giorgio 184,01529; 183,00093.
39   E. M. Corrales, 'Comerciantes Malteses e Importaciones Catalanas de Algodón, 1728–1804', *Actas del Primer Coloquio Internacional Hispano Maltés de Historia* (Madrid, 1991), pp. 119–61, here pp. 134ff; C. Vassallo, *Corsairing to Commerce: Maltese Merchants in XVIII Century Spain* (Malta, 1997).
40   Own calculations according to: HHStA, KA, Nachlass Zinzendorf, Handschriften, Vol. 118, pp. 287–310.

The intermediaries: organizing the trading business

Several studies have shown that merchant communities usually settled in port cities, in order to control trade routes and markets through family and intracultural networks. This was only rarely the case for merchants from the Habsburg Monarchy. As has become clear from the examples given above, Spanish-Habsburg trade was mostly carried out through intercultural or interstate co-operation between merchants based in Trieste and their trading partners in Barcelona or Cádiz. These were mostly Spanish merchants, but various non-Habsburg foreign traders (such as Ponte e Villavecchia in Barcelona) also appeared as business partners.

It was rather rare that Habsburg merchants (such as the Milanese Paolo Greppi in Cádiz) were involved in this mediation. Only two groups of merchants – the Bohemian and Tyrolean traders – followed the typical pattern and settled in a number of Spanish ports, such as Barcelona, Alicante and Cádiz. However, both groups mostly traded in products from their regions of origin. The Bohemians commercialized above all glass, while the Tyrolean traders specialized in devotional items such as crucifixes, but also distributed textiles, metal goods and white lead in Barcelona and Cádiz.[41] In addition to connections from Trieste to Barcelona and Cádiz, and from there to Peru, their networks also involved Genoa.[42] The group of Milanese merchants based in Cádiz also has to be taken into consideration, but their connection with the Habsburg core countries – with the exception of Paolo Greppi – was negligible.[43]

This highlights the weak domestic commercial capital of the Habsburg regions, which is why only selected groups emigrated to port cities. Also, they did so for different reasons: the Bohemian glass traders – it is unclear to what degree they alternatively used the North Sea route through Hamburg and Altona – followed a traditional commercialization strategy in the wholesale trade with ties to the retail trade, and were also heavily involved in colonial trade with direct branches in Mexico and Peru.[44] In contrast, the Tyrolean traders not only seem to have operated on a more modest, almost marginal, economic level.

41   Weber, *Deutsche Kaufleute*, pp. 133ff; K. Weber and M. Schulte Beerbühl, 'From Westphalia to the Caribbean: Networks of German Textile Merchants in the Eighteenth Century', *Cosmopolitan Networks in Commerce and Society 1660–1914*, ed. A. Gestrich and M. Schulte Beerbühl (London, 2011), pp. 53–98, here pp. 70ff; Archivo de la Corona de Aragón, Real Audiencia, Tribunal Real del Consulado de Comercio de Cataluña, C, 11247, fol. 1; Archivo Histórico Nacional, Consejos 20246, Exp. 6.
42   AHPC, Protocolos Notariales Cádiz 1/52, fols 751–2. ASTS, Testamenti 10, 1141/2.
43   K. Kaps, 'Zwischen Zentraleuropa und iberischem Atlantik: Mailänder Kaufleute in Cádiz im 18. Jahrhundert', *Annales Mercaturae* 3 (2017), pp. 85–105.
44   Weber, *Deutsche Kaufleute*, pp. 133ff; A. Klíma, 'Glassmaking Industry and Trade in Bohemia in the 17th and 18th Centuries', *Journal of European Economic History* 13/3 (1984), pp. 499–520.

Their emigration was also motivated by the lack of employment in the region itself, especially in Gardena and Teferegg in the Puster Valley, even though they also had direct networks across the Atlantic and even to the Pacific.[45]

Triestinian merchants' attempts to control the mediation channels themselves are first documented for the 1760s, when at least three Triestinian firms established branch offices in Cádiz. Among them was the aforementioned Compagna del Commercio di Spagna, which was headed by Giacomo Balletti, one of the leading merchants of Trieste.[46] All these companies attempted to establish a direct link between the Habsburg possessions in Central Europe and the Spanish Atlantic, and were successful for a decade at maximum before they failed.

Although these failures may have been related to the international financial crisis of 1772, the bankruptcies were a major setback for the Trieste merchants' attempt to organize the Spanish-Central European distribution channels themselves. This perception is also reflected in government files, which record that the Court Chamber (Hofkanzlei) in Vienna and the Supreme Commercial Intendency (Hauptkommerzialintendenz, Suprema Intendenza Commerciale) in Trieste discussed how to respond to this situation with the leading merchants (Balletti, Languidir, Antonio Rossetti, Joachim Hierschl and Marco Levi). It is clear from the minutes of these deliberations in Trieste that in the early 1770s, these leading Trieste merchants did not believe they would be able to compete with the Genoese and Livonian merchants.[47] In fact, it took individual Trieste merchants until the late eighteenth century to settle in Spain once more.[48]

However, this is not to say that Trieste's trade in Spain had been at a standstill in the meantime. On the contrary: through close collaboration – possibly even a formal society – between Antonio Rossetti of Trieste and Paolo Greppi's potent trading company in Cádiz, they were able to conduct the most lucrative export transactions from Trieste to Cádiz and from there on to Cuba and Guatemala with their own ships, which sailed under the imperial flag between 1780 and about 1785. In addition to the exports of copper already mentioned, Rossetti and Greppi also exported nails and Bohemian glass.[49] Although this

45   G. Zwanowetz, 'Zur wirtschaftlichen Lage Tirols und Vorarlbergs gegen Ende der Regierungszeit Kaiser Josephs II', *Erzeugung, Verkehr und Handel in der Geschichte der Alpenländer*, ed. F. Huter, F. Mathis and G. Zwanowetz (Innsbruck, 1977), pp. 417–77, here pp. 425ff.
46   ASTS, Notai, 322, fols 158, 160; 684, fol. 7; CRS Intendenza Commerciale, No. 253, fols 355, 357f, 360, 362, 504f, fol. 467. Faber, *Litorale Austriaco*, p. 152. P. Gasser, 'Triests Handelsversuche mit Spanien und die Probleme der Österreichischen Schiffahrt in den Jahren 1750–1800, Teil 1', *Mitteilungen des Österreichischen Staatsarchivs* 36 (1983), pp. 150–87, here pp. 166, 170ff.
47   Ibid., pp. 176f.
48   AHPC, Protocolos Notariales Cádiz 2/432, fols 264f.
49   AHPC, Protocolos Notariales Cádiz 31/5935, fols 88ff; 21/5113, fols 754ff. Giovanni Liva, 'L'Archivio Greppi e l'attività della filiale di P. G. a Cadice nella corrispondenza commerciale (1769–1799)', *Archivio Storico Lombardo* 122 (1995), pp. 431–87, here pp. 464ff; Gasser, 'Triests Handelsversuche', p. 86.

co-operation came to an end, presumably because Rossetti was bankrupted in the financial crisis of 1785, the Trieste firm Frapp e Rokert stepped in as mediator for the even more lucrative mercury business between 1785 and 1791.[50] These deals have to be seen in the context of the American War of Independence. These years saw an increase in the demand for grain and potash, which were supplied from the Hungarian regions. In addition, opportunities arose for Trieste's merchants to engage directly in Habsburg-Spanish trade alongside other maritime trade connections in the Atlantic and Pacific. This was a real opportunity for Trieste's merchants to expand the scope of their direct trade, and with it their control of trade routes and gateways, thus overcoming their status as 'segmental merchants'.[51]

And from this point of view, this phase – despite setbacks – was an important basis for Trieste's direct trade with Spain that evolved later: notarial records and customs data prove that during the Revolutionary and Napoleonic Wars, direct merchant networks channeled the commodity flows between Trieste and Barcelona as well as Málaga.[52] Between 1804 and 1806, there was significant direct shipping traffic between Trieste and Barcelona (31, 14 and 28 incoming ships in 1804, 1805 and 1806 respectively).[53] However, transit trade did not disappear completely: as late as 1820, Habsburg steel of a value of 37,880 Genoese *Lire* was traded from Trieste via Genoa to Barcelona.[54]

This increasing direct trade also points to two important aspects: on the one hand, Habsburg and Trieste merchants were now increasingly able to organize shipping, meaning the transport of commodities. While the companies of the 1760s had mainly relied on Genoese, English and Ragusan ships and crews, by 1784/85 a considerable number of imperial ships were active in the Spanish trade, in particular between Trieste on the one hand, and Barcelona and Cádiz on the other.[55] The second aspect concerns the ownership of capital and the funding of this trade. While co-operation between Trieste's merchants and partners on the Iberian Peninsula and the Canary Islands, at least since 1746, always resulted in forms of profit-sharing in exchange for limiting risks, the 1760s companies in Cádiz attempted to provide their own capital in a bid

50   Liva, 'L'Archivio Greppi', pp. 467ff. Archivio di Stato di Milano, Dono Greppi, Carteggio 343, Milano, 5 October 1785: Antonio Greppi a Paolo Greppi Marliano e Compagna. AHPC, Protocolos Notariales Cádiz 21/5117, fol. 63.
51   D. Andreozzi, 'From the Black Sea to the Americas: The Trading Companies of Trieste and the Global Commercial Network (18th Century)', *Mediterranean Doubts: Trading Companies, Conflicts and Strategies in the Global Spaces (XV–XIX Centuries)*, ed. D. Andreozzi (Palermo, 2017), pp. 65–87, here p. 84.
52   ASTS, Notai, 286, fols 45f; 289, fols 97f, 349ff, 354ff; 456, fol. 16.
53   P. Vilar, *La Catalogne dans l'Espagne Moderne: Recherches sur les Fondements Économiques des Structures Nationales*, Vol. 3 (Paris, 1962), p. 135.
54   J. M. Fradera, *Indústria i Mercat: Les Bases Comercials de la Indústria Catalana Moderna (1814–1845)* (Barcelona, 1987), p. 90.
55   ÖStA, HHStA, DK StAbt 117/42, fols 7, 9f.

to control the lion's share of this trade. The capital apparently came from merchants residing in Trieste, although for the most part they had to rely on additional financial resources from abroad and from other Habsburg regions.[56]

With the increasing self-financing of these companies with capital based in the Habsburg Monarchy, the possibility of direct trade increased, transaction costs shrank, and profits for the Habsburg service sector rose.

Conclusion

There were extensive trade relations between the Habsburg Monarchy and Spain in the eighteenth century. Apart from various gateways such as Hamburg, Amsterdam or Ostend, which were much harder to reach by land, Trieste's steady and rapid growth after 1750 led to a significant expansion of Spanish-Habsburg commercial contacts, as well as to a shift from Venice to Trieste. Although direct trade between Trieste and Spanish port cities grew significantly in the second half of the century, transit trade through Naples, Sicily, Malta, Livorno and Genoa remained strong. Only by taking into account this overall trade can we properly assess the importance of the Spanish markets for Habsburg foreign trade. A certain continuity in the flow of goods is also visible, compared to earlier centuries when Styrian iron and steel as well as mercury from Idrija were exported. However, exports not only expanded quantitatively. The product range also diversified notably. In addition to new goods in the metal industry, this is especially true for textile production. Linen was exported via Trieste to Barcelona and above all to Cádiz, from where it was dispatched further to Spanish American colonial markets. Conversely, the intensification of plantation economies in the colonies allowed the expansion of imports, so that in addition to Iberian commodities such as merino wool, dried fruit, wine or ashes, now coffee, tobacco, sugar, cocoa, dyes and medicinal plants were imported.

The turnaround in Habsburg-Spanish trade was not only the material dimension of the exchange of goods, but also its organization: the migrations of merchants to Trieste and Vienna made direct mercantile networks between Trieste and the hinterland possible, and encouraged similar connections between Trieste and Barcelona, Cádiz, Alicante and Málaga. These networks subsequently extended across the Atlantic and even to the Pacific. This process was by no means linear and uninterrupted; it was accompanied by various setbacks, as the bankruptcies of the Trieste trading companies in Cádiz at the turn of the 1760s to the 1770s indicate. In the long run, however, Trieste's

---

56 I. Mittenzwei, *Zwischen Gestern und Morgen: Wiens frühe Bourgeoisie an der Wende vom 18. zum 19. Jahrhundert* (Vienna/Cologne/Weimar, 1998), pp. 206–15.

merchants were able to assert themselves by attempting to control these trade routes and the operations associated with trade, from financing to shipping.

With the cutback of transit trade, the transaction costs for the Habsburg economy's access to global markets in the Mediterranean and Atlantic regions declined. This not only increased the chances for Habsburg trading companies and banks to expand their wealth, but also opened up sales markets for the Habsburg economy in Spain. At the same time, it became possible to purchase new and/or more raw materials and consumer items. On the whole, contrary to the claims in the older literature, the Habsburg economy was intertwined with Spanish markets to a considerable degree. The interaction with the Atlantic peripheries of the Spanish colonial empire, as well as with the semi-peripheral economy of the Spanish motherland, contributed to economic development in the Habsburg Monarchy.

8

A Cartel on the Periphery:
Wupper Valley Merchants and their Strategies
in Atlantic Trade (1790s–1820s)

ANNE SOPHIE OVERKAMP

The title of this chapter seems to contain a contradiction in terms: one of them is associated with strength (cartel), the other with weakness (periphery); nonetheless, they are used in conjunction. The aim of this chapter is to resolve this contradiction, to explain its particularities, and by so doing to highlight certain structural features of the early modern Atlantic economy. To do so, I will first discuss the two terms – cartel and periphery – and then secondly present findings from a case study of the seemingly peripheral Atlantic World, before thirdly drawing some conclusions about the incorporation of ostensibly peripheral regions into Atlantic trade and into the Atlantic World in general.

The terms: (1) cartel

A cartel is commonly defined as a group of independent producers who strike an agreement, either in writing (a contractual cartel) or orally (a 'gentleman's agreement'), to increase their collective profits by means of price-fixing, limiting supply, or other restrictive measures. Cartels usually occur in oligopolies, where there is a small number of suppliers offering a homogenous product. The effects of cartels are commonly described as the following: cartels change the relations between supply and demand in the economy by providing the supply side with greater market power. Competition is curtailed as suppliers harmonize their production and investment policies, as well as their course of action against intruders or newcomers; prices are determined by the supply side, which means they are flexible upwards but are seldom or never cut; consumer choice is limited and the guiding principle of prices is suspended.[1]

In the early modern economy, price-fixing was a well established practice, most famously (or infamously) used by privileged trading companies such as the Dutch and English East India companies.[2] Adam Smith, the father of modern economics, was one of the first to deliver a fundamental critique of such merchants' conspiracies against the public, in his major work *The Wealth of Nations*. Systematic theorizing about cartels and their economic effects emerged only towards the end of the nineteenth century. Contrary to Smith's critique and to current notions, at that point in time members of the legal and economic professions rather advocated the regulating and rationalizing possibilities of cartels, highlighting their stabilizing effects. By controlling the outlet and/or production of goods, and thus maintaining regular employment as well as avoiding crises, cartels were thought to be economically beneficial for employers and workers, and for the community as a whole. Stipulations in cartel contracts were enforced by law and there generally existed a high internal pressure within the different industries towards forming a cartel.[3] Even though Germany was something of a forerunner, similar trends existed in most countries – the United States of America being a notable exception. Consequently, between the 1870s and the 1930s, cartelization increased both quantitatively and qualitatively, nationally as well as internationally. It was only after World War II that, under the auspices of the United States government, Germany and other European countries seriously started to decartelize their economies and to introduce restrictive anti-trust legislation, championing competition over putative stability. Only Switzerland maintained the older kind of 'co-operative capitalism' (as Alfred Chandler put it) to a notable degree, refusing to participate in the paradigm change that was spreading across the world.[4]

What becomes clear from this short historical outline is that cartels have a long history and that their assessment has changed over time. Economic historians who are interested in price effects, institutional arrangements, and economic development in general, have tended to concentrate on larger conglomerations that have left easily recognizable traces in the archives and consequently in the historiography. So far, research into cartelization in

1   See for example U. Taenzer, *Kernprobleme der Marktwirtschaft, Unternehmenskonzentration: Ein Lehr- und Arbeitsbuch* (Stuttgart, 1981).
2   S. Ogilvie, *Institutions and European Trade: Merchants' Guilds, 1000–1800* (Cambridge, 2011).
3   C. E. Fischer, 'Die Geschichte der deutschen Versuche zur Lösung des Kartell- und Monopol-Problems', *Zeitschrift für die gesamte Staatswissenschaft/Journal of Institutional and Theoretical Economics* 110 (1954), pp. 425–56; H. G. Schröter, 'Kartellierung und Dekartellierung 1890–1990', *Vierteljahrschrift für Sozial- und Wirtschaftsgeschichte* 81 (1994), pp. 457–93.
4   Schröter, 'Kartellierung', pp. 490f; A. D. Chandler, with the assistance of Takashi Hikino, *Scale and Scope: The Dynamics of Industrial Capitalism* (Cambridge, MA, 1990).

Germany really only considers the developments of the German Empire and later, even though earlier consortia such as the Neckarsalinen-Verein (founded in 1828) or the Alaun-Syndikat (founded in 1836) have received some attention.[5]

As the following case study of the Wupper Valley merchants' attempts at organization and cartelization shows, economic history ought also to take into account these earlier developments, which might have operated on a different scale than those in an industrialized economy, but which nevertheless fulfilled all the qualifications of a cartel. They offer important insights into the degree of collective organization achievable within the early modern economy, even outside large institutionalized bodies such as chartered companies or guilds. Studying these seemingly peripheral attempts therefore answers more comprehensive questions about the early modern economy's structure, on the one hand, and about long-running features of the economy in general, on the other hand.

The terms: (2) periphery

'Periphery' is a relational term; so much so, in fact, that the urban sociologist Walter Prigge took on the task of editing a thought-provoking volume titled *Peripherie ist überall (Periphery is Everywhere)*, transcending the dichotomy of a clearly defined center and the outskirts of such a center.[6] Instead, according to several contributors to that volume, the attribution of center and periphery is created in a performative act by agents who move between these two poles and award the implied hierarchy according to their own needs and customs, turning (for example) what is commonly called the periphery of a city, namely suburbia, into the center of their daily life. Periphery is therefore not so much a given place as a status or a situation within a certain order, highlighting the fact that what is regarded as center and what is regarded as periphery depends on the hierarchy imposed by the beholder.

Recent scholarship in the field of Atlantic history has extensively discussed the notion of periphery, hinterland and back-country with regard to the Atlantic World, trying to extend the field beyond the maritime littoral. Scholars have not only traced how regions beyond the rim of the Atlantic basin were integrated into the Atlantic World, but have also found that to some of them, the Atlantic was in fact peripheral. Thus, they support the view that peripheries are relational.[7]

---

5   See for example M. Müller, H. R. Schmidt and L. Tissot, eds, *Regulierte Märkte: Zünfte und Kartelle – Marchés Régulés: Corporations et Cartels* (Zurich, 2011).

6   W. Prigge, ed., *Peripherie ist überall* (Frankfurt, 1998).

7   See for example C. Daniels and M. V. Kennedy, eds, *Negotiated Empires: Centers and Peripheries in the Americas, 1500–1820* (New York, 2002). For an overview of the discussion,

Despite this relativity, it is nevertheless pertinent to remember that there were certain hierarchies inscribed into the Atlantic World, and in particular into its economy. A classic attempt to trace and analyze these hierarchies – not only of the Atlantic, but rather of the entire world – is Immanuel Wallerstein's masterful four-volume study, *The Modern World-System*.[8] In Wallerstein's analysis, relations within the World-System are shaped by economic factors, in particular by the hierarchical and spatially distributed division of labor. Even though this Marxist interpretation of worldwide relations has severe limitations and has accordingly been heavily criticized, Wallerstein's zoning of the world into cores, peripheries and semi-peripheries nevertheless helps to raise awareness of the particular opportunities and limitations of a given locality, and of how it was part of a complex interchange within the early modern economy.[9]

Taking up Wallerstein's integrated outlook as a starting point is a means of moving beyond the most commonly favored approach in the field of Atlantic history – namely, following goods or people across the Atlantic in order to write Atlantic history. As the renowned scholar Philip D. Morgan recently put it, the tendency of Atlantic history as a field to 'follow what moves – whether people, ships, products, microbes, ideas, or cultural practices' favors what is easily visible and blanks out quite a few dimensions of the Atlantic World. Accordingly, Morgan prompts 'historians of the Atlantic World' to 'pay more attention to what stays still, the sedentary, bounded, fixed locations, stable territories, local rootedness'.[10] Studying a landlocked locality, its sedentary merchants and their stake in Atlantic trade seems to be one way of doing that.

see S. Lachenicht, 'Europeans Engaging the Atlantic: Knowledge and Trade, c. 1500–1800: An Introduction', *Europeans Engaging the Atlantic: Knowledge and Trade, 1500–1800*, ed. S. Lachenicht (Frankfurt, 2014), pp. 7–21; F. Brahm and E. Rosenhaft, 'Introduction: Towards a Comprehensive European History of Slavery and Abolition', *Slavery Hinterland: Transatlantic Slavery and Continental Europe, 1680–1850*, ed. F. Brahm and E. Rosenhaft (Woodbridge, 2016), pp. 1–23. On Atlantic history as a field, see B. Bailyn and P. L. Denault, eds, *Soundings in Atlantic History: Latent Structures and Intellectual Currents, 1500–1830* (Cambridge, 2009); J. P. Greene and P. D. Morgan, eds, *Atlantic History: A Critical Appraisal* (Oxford, 2009); N. Canny and P. D. Morgan, eds, *The Oxford Handbook of the Atlantic World 1450–1850* (Oxford, 2013).

8 I. Wallerstein, *The Modern World-System*, 4 vols (New York, 1974–2011).

9 One of Wallerstein's most prominent critics is A. G. Frank, *ReORIENT: Global Economy in the Asian Age* (Berkeley, 1998). For an overview see also L. Zündorf, *Zur Aktualität von Immanuel Wallerstein: Einleitung in sein Werk* (Wiesbaden, 2010), pp. 103f. An assessment is furthermore given by D. Rothermund, *Geschichte als Prozess und Aussage: Eine Einführung in Theorien des historischen Wandels und der Geschichtsschreibung* (Munich, 1995), pp. 117f. The heuristic value of Wallerstein's and other Marxist-inspired scholars' approaches to widen the somewhat self-contained field of Atlantic history is lauded by P. A. Coclanis, 'Atlantic World or Atlantic/World?', *William and Mary Quarterly* 63 (2006), pp. 725–42, particularly pp. 737ff.

10 P. D. Morgan, 'A Comment', *Europeans Engaging the Atlantic*, ed. Lachenicht, pp. 151–60, here p. 156.

Specialization on the edge:
the tape manufacturers of the Wupper Valley

The Wupper Valley, the location in question, was part of the Duchy of Berg, one of the smaller territories of the Holy Roman Empire, situated in the border region between Westphalia and the Rhineland. The reigning Wittelsbach dynasty perceived the territory, however, as a *Nebenland* (subsidiary territory) and was more interested in realigning its territories in southern Germany. In 1806, their long-held plans came to fruition with a little help from Napoleon. The Duchy of Berg was ceded by the Bavarians and in 1806 was made part of the Grand Duchy of Berg, which existed until the fall of Napoleon's empire. At the Congress of Vienna, Prussia secured these territories and incorporated them into its subsequently established Rhine Province, which immediately became the backbone of Prussia's industrial development.[11]

Despite (or perhaps because of) the peripheral political treatment just sketched, the Duchy of Berg thrived economically and became one of the forerunners of industrialization and mechanization on the continent. Centers in this were the two adjacent towns of Elberfeld and Barmen, as well as the two towns of Solingen and Remscheid located nearby, all of which formed the so-called Wupper Rectangle. Since the Middle Ages, merchant-manufacturers in Solingen and Remscheid had focused on ironmongery products – especially all kinds of blades – while their counterparts in the Wupper Valley concentrated on textile production, turning the region into a proto-industrial 'hotspot' in the seventeenth and eighteenth centuries.[12]

At the very core of the Wupper Valley's economic success story lay a political concession. In 1527, the Duke of Berg granted the merchants from Elberfeld and Barmen the so-called *Garnnahrungsprivileg* (yarn privilege). The privilege consisted of a monopoly for the commercial bleaching of linen in the Duchy of Berg, and it became the starting point for a success story lasting well into the twentieth century.[13] Throughout the early modern period, linen yarn was bleached on the banks of the Wupper in a lengthy process taking several

---

11   S. Gorißen, H. Sassin and K. Wesoly, eds, *Geschichte des Bergischen Landes*, 2 vols (Bielefeld, 2014–2016).

12   S. Gorißen, 'Gewerbe im Herzogtum Berg vom Spätmittelalter bis 1806', *Geschichte des Bergischen Landes, Vol. 1: Bis zum Ende des Alten Herzogtums 1806*, ed. S. Gorißen, H. Sassin and K. Wesoly (Bielefeld, 2014), pp. 407–67.

13   W. Dietz, *Die Wuppertaler Garnnahrung* (Neustadt an der Aisch, 1957); H. Kisch, 'From Monopoly to Laissez-faire: The Early Growth of the Wupper Valley Textile Trades', *Journal of European Economic History* 1 (1972), pp. 298–407; S. Gorißen, 'Interessen und ökonomische Funktionen merkantilistischer Privilegienpolitik: Das Herzogtum Berg und seine Textilgewerbe zwischen 16. und 18. Jahrhundert', *Die Ökonomie des Privilegs, Westeuropa 16.–19. Jahrhundert/ L'Économie du Privilège, Europe Occidentale XVIe–XIX Siècles*, ed. G. Garner (Frankfurt, 2016), pp. 279–329.

months, before being either sold to customers in the Netherlands or France, or put through local processing. During earlier times, processing simply involved turning the yarn into twine; but from the early seventeenth century onward, the production of linen tape and further finishing steps such as dyeing were added.

Unlike many long-established mercantile centers such as Cologne, Frankfurt am Main or Nuremberg, there was no resistance in the Wupper Valley's tape industry to the early introduction of the engine loom (*Bandmühle*) that increased output dramatically.[14] Thanks to the putting-out system, which laid some of the production costs at the laborer's door, the merchant-manufacturers could also maintain reasonably low wages. By combining high rates of production with low labor costs, the Wupper Valley merchants thus gained a competitive edge. The yarn bleached and the smallwares produced in the Wupper Valley came to dominate German fairs, as well as French and Dutch markets, during the course of the seventeenth century. Their prices also made them competitive on more distant markets, securing them customers in Spain, Portugal and, by the turn of the nineteenth century, also in the Americas.

In some instances, the Wupper Valley merchants were able to place the goods directly with their final customers. This was mostly the case with German and French buyers. Concerning the important Atlantic trade, however, they mostly relied on intermediaries in port towns such as Amsterdam, London, Bordeaux and Cádiz.[15] Here, they experienced most sharply their position once-removed in geographic terms, which also led to a less acute involvement in terms of knowledge, speed of information and interaction. Traveling surprisingly little, the Wupper Valley merchants always had to rely on intermediaries for transferring money, goods and information. It puts quite a spotlight on the high degree of the Atlantic economy's integration when we understand that, despite their disadvantaged position, the Wupper Valley merchants engaged in this branch of their trade successfully for most of the eighteenth century.

All in all, the Barmen and Elberfeld merchant-manufacturers were in fact so effective that by the 1790s there was hardly any other place in the Holy Roman Empire where linen tape was produced.[16] All the other textile-producing regions

14   On the adaptation of the engine loom in England and on the continent, see J. de Lacy Mann and A. Powell Wadsworth, *The Cotton Trade and Industrial Lancashire, 1600–1780* (Bristol, 1999).
15   I have detailed the outreach of the Wupper Valley merchant-manufacturers in A. S. Overkamp, 'Of Tape and Ties: Abraham Frowein from Elberfeld and Atlantic Trade', *Europeans Engaging the Atlantic*, ed. Lachenicht, pp. 127–50; A. S. Overkamp, 'A Hinterland to the Slave Trade? Atlantic Connections of the Wupper Valley in the Early Nineteenth Century', *Slavery Hinterland*, ed. Brahm and Rosenhaft, pp. 161–85. On German merchants and their transatlantic connections in general, see K. Weber, *Deutsche Kaufleute im Atlantikhandel, 1680–1830: Unternehmen und Familien in Hamburg, Cádiz und Bordeaux* (Munich, 2004); M. Schulte Beerbühl, *The Forgotten Majority: German Merchants in London, Naturalization, and Global Trade, 1660–1815* (New York, 2015).
16   J. C. Gädicke, *Fabriken- und Manufacturen Addreß-Lexicon von Teutschland und einigen angränzenden Ländern*, Part 1 (Weimar, 1798), pp. 10f.

within the Holy Roman Empire seemed to have given way to the Wupper Valley merchants, allowing them to capitalize on a monopoly created over time by a technological lead. In fact, it seems that most of Europe bought its tape in the Wupper Valley.[17] The scale of the area's industry might be demonstrated by the fact that on each of the 2,000 engine looms overseen by the Wupper Valley merchant-manufacturers, up to 40 ribbons could be woven simultaneously, turning almost 13,000 hundredweight of linen and woollen yarn per year into immeasurable amounts of tape.

But to what use were these large amounts of tape put? The little snippets that are attached to the correspondence preserved in the archives, as well as the one set of sample cards that survives, show a variety of linen and woollen tape, some of it plain, some of it in fancier patterns. The names of the different tapes give an indication of their usage: there is hatband (for the inside of hats, not as decoration for the outside), boot tape, gimp cord, straps and laces. But then there are also a great number of ribbon types whose material meaning has become lost in time: *Lothband* (very thin ribbon), another called *bigarré* which might have been used to tie bundles, various patterned ribbons made out of wool and linen called *carreaux*, *flammés*, *espagnolettes*, et cetera. By looking at material objects, some of the tape's usages can be discerned. Linen tape obviously found its way into the making of clothing, but often in hidden places: it was used to form the casings for the boning in hoopskirts or to stiffen the interior of men's vests. Curtains were bound with tape. Bookbinders needed tape and twine, and so did furniture makers who used tape for the webbing in their seating furniture. Carriage upholstery depended on webbing as well. Tape went into the making of sails and other furnishings of ships. In general, shopkeepers used tape to tie wares into bundles, sacks and bags that needed to be fastened. All these crafts depended to some extent on the inexpensive heavy-duty goods produced in the Wupper Valley.

The raw materials used for the massive textile production in the Wupper Valley came from eastern Westphalia, Lower Saxony and Hesse (linen yarn), as well as from Saxony (woollen yarn). Cotton was usually imported from Britain, either as raw material or already spun. In 1783, the first cotton mill on the continent was founded by a member of the Elberfeld merchant community. The mill's output, however, could not satisfy the demand of the Wupper Valley industry.[18] After all, by the 1770s Wupper Valley merchants imported annually around 25,000 hundredweight of textile fibres, to say nothing about dyestuffs,

17   The British Isles seem to have been a notable exception. The Dutch engine loom was also introduced at a relatively early date in Lancashire, where a competitive smallwares industry emerged. Interestingly, the yarn was also imported (until the mid eighteenth century mostly from the continent) and then bleached locally before it was processed, very much like in the Wupper Valley. Mann and Wadsworth, *Cotton Trade*, pp. 284ff.

18   Landesverband Rheinland Industriemuseum and C. Gottfried, eds, *Cromford Ratingen: Lebenswelten zwischen erster Fabrik und Herrenhaus um 1800* (Ratingen, 2010).

soap, lime, and other raw materials used in the industry.[19] The magnitude of the industry also becomes apparent in the export values, which were estimated at 3.2 million *Reichstaler* per year and which made the Wupper Valley one of the – if not *the* – most important of the manufacturing centers in Germany at that time.[20]

The economic growth was mirrored and fueled by a dramatic increase in population. At the beginning of the eighteenth century, about 5,000 people lived in Elberfeld and Barmen; only Elberfeld had the character of a town at this point in time, however, while Barmen was rather a conglomeration of several smaller dwellings. A good hundred years later, the two towns counted more than 35,000 inhabitants, making the valley one of the largest urban centers in Prussia.[21] The halcyon days of the Wupper Valley textile industry came to an abrupt end in the 1790s, however, directing the tape merchants to seek new ways of dealing with their location on the rim.

Cartelization on the periphery

'Soon we won't be able to draw on Holland [for bills of exchange] anymore.' 'The trade in Elberfeld has great difficulties because of the war.' 'We make none of our friends [i.e. customers] any offers.' 'In view of the falling exchange rates, we have retained the second barrel of tape we were to send you.'[22]

These extracts from letters sent by an Elberfeld merchant-manufacturer in 1794 to business associates present an industry in crisis. Ever since the beginning of the French Revolution, trade for the Wupper Valley merchants had lost its stable footing. Increased tariffs on the French border, as well as the introduction of paper money and its unstable rate of exchange, had made trade with France – one of the main customers for the output of inexpensive textiles produced in the Wupper Valley – uncertain and volatile. The outbreak of war intensified the problems as trade routes were cut off or endangered, and it became increasingly

---

19   The total is calculated according to the tables in the contemporary statistics given in W. Gebhard, ed., 'Bericht des Hof-Kammerrats Friedrich Heinrich Jacobi über die Industrie der Herzogtümer Jülich und Berg aus den Jahren 1773 und 1774', *Zeitschrift des Bergischen Geschichtsvereins* 18 (1882), pp. 1–148.

20   Ibid. The textile production of the Wupper Valley also surpassed that of the most productive Prussian district, Hirschberg in Silesia, which exported linen for about two million *Reichstaler* per annum. M. Boldorf, *Europäische Leinenregionen im Wandel: Institutionelle Weichenstellungen in Schlesien und Irland (1750–1850)* (Cologne, 2006), p. 56, Ill. 4.

21   V. Wittmütz, *Kleine Wuppertaler Stadtgeschichte* (Regensburg, 2013).

22   The quotations are from the copy letter book by Abraham & Bros. Frowein, held by the Frowein Company Archive (hereafter: FCA), No. 1341. In order of the quotes: letter to Lud. Joh. Kumme Albs. Sohn, Hanover, 12 February 1794; letter to Christ. H. Denckla, Philadelphia, 25 February 1794; letter to Chalon, Rouen, 4 March 1794.

difficult for the Wupper Valley merchants to satisfy their customers – not only in France, but also in Holland, Spain and the Americas. Acquiring dyestuffs and other necessities of trade also became more difficult and costly. As the merchants expressed in their letters, they feared the 'standstill of trade'.[23]

The attempt to establish a cartel, documented in the so-called Convention of June 1795, formed by 11 tape merchant-manufacturers, appears to have been a direct outcome of this crisis.[24] The 11 merchants who joined were among the largest tape manufacturers in the Wupper Valley, and most of them were involved in long-distance trade.[25] Although 48 companies dealt in linen and woollen tape in the valley in 1794, those 11 merchants covered a significant share of the market. This was also due to the fact that several of the remaining companies supplied the larger export merchants, rather than dealing with customers outside the valley themselves.[26]

In the recorded document, the merchants agreed on fixed prices for French customers, which they extended a year later to customers in Spain, Portugal and the Americas. The prices listed were very exact, detailing rates for about 20 different types of tape in up to 29 widths, cut in four different lengths. Furthermore, the modalities concerning discounts and payment terms were also fixed, accepting payment no later than six months after delivery or offering a four per cent discount, which were still rather reasonable terms.[27] Before the convention, these terms had been open to negotiation between each merchant and his or her customers, usually exceeding the terms here mentioned. The convention thus forestalled a price war among its members. The agreement also regulated competition at home: merchant-manufacturers who had not joined the convention were to receive no more than eight per cent discount or a 12-month payment period. Payment with other than the local money (*Reichstaler*) was not to be accepted, thus protecting the merchants from currency speculation.

23   See the copy letter books of the Wupper Valley merchants Abraham Frowein (FCA No. 1341); Johann Peter von Eynern (Historisches Zentrum Wuppertal (hereafter: HZW), Coll. von Eynern, No. 132); and Johann Friedrich Bredt (Landesarchiv Rheinland, 2011–35).

24   The convention from 1795 has not been conserved, but the supplement from 1796 which did survive allows us to infer the content of the earlier convention. FCA No. 1484. Interestingly, two large tape-manufacturing firms from Lancashire also struck a secret pricing agreement in the mid eighteenth century. The standardization of the article seems to have lent itself to such. Mann and Wadsworth, *Cotton Trade*, pp. 298f.

25   Among them were the three companies (Wülfing & Comp., Caspar & Abr. Rübel, and Joh. Gottfr. Rübel) which bleached the largest amounts of yarn on the banks of the Wupper in 1793 (807, 892 and 935 hundredweight respectively). Wuppertal Municipal Archive, J I 6. Most of the other signatories to the convention also bleached considerable amounts, hinting at the quantity of raw material they processed in manufacturing tape. There are no tax lists or comparable statistical material available to provide an insight into the economic structure of the valley.

26   All the companies are listed in J. A. Mannes, *Gülich und bergischer gnädigst privilegirter Kaufmannskalender für das Jahr 1794* (Elberfeld, 1794).

27   At least when compared with Lancashire customs. See Mann and Wadsworth, *Cotton Trade*, p. 297.

The convention also contained a contractual penalty and certain provisions for maintaining the power to compete with other suppliers.

The agreement turned out to be binding, even beyond the inner circle. Johann Peter von Eynern, who had not participated in the convention, wrote to a French business partner in 1797: 'In answer to your letter of November 9, I have to say that I am not allowed to accord you an extended term [of payment]. The merchants of here have struck an accord among themselves by which it is agreed to not grant credit to anyone from your country. Those who do it all the same are condemned to pay a certain sum.' If the business partner, Vauquelin, Poisson & Roeoux in Rouen, were not to agree to these terms (immediate payment with a six per cent discount), Eynern would not carry out the order.[28] But as the ensuing events show, Eynern could not enforce these terms, which went even further than the 1795 convention. Rather, he delivered the goods and agreed to receive payment in six months' time. As Eynern had to discover, cutting off all credit to customers was a measure that could not be enforced. After all, it went against all early modern trading conventions that simply operated on extended terms of payment, especially because of the distances covered.

What is striking about the cartel, and about the dealings of the Wupper Valley tape merchants in general, is the fact that they were not at all concerned with questions of quality and quality control, issues that were a standard concern in most mercantile situations.[29] In contrast to the very detailed regulations on lengths and pricing arrangements, the maintenance of standards in terms of raw material or of finished products did not enter the record at all. Rather, the convenors simply agreed to increase the prices of tapes that contained the more expensive red dyestuff. It might be that the long-lasting relationships with customers, who had in some instances been ordering the same kind of tape from the Wupper Valley for decades, yielded a binding effect.[30] But, as will be discussed below, the Wupper Valley merchants were also bound to each other by their practice of supplementing each other's orders. That was only possible if they adhered to the same standards, which seem to have been upheld without any institutionalized control. Practice therefore substituted institution in this instance.

A formal institution was also lacking concerning the merchant-manufacturers' relations with their workers. The tape weavers did not belong to a guild and their craft was not carried out in the time-honored positions of apprentice or master craftsmen, but rather 'on the side', often during the slack periods in agriculture.

---

28   HZW, Coll. von Eynern, No. 132, Joh. Pet. von Eynern to Vauquelin, Poisson & Roeoux, Rouen, 19 November 1797. The ensuing letter is dated 23 January 1798.
29   A. Stanziani, ed., *La Qualité des Produits en France, XVIIIe–XXe siècles* (Paris, 2003); C. Jeggle, 'Pre-Industrial Worlds of Production: Conventions, Institutions and Organizations', *Historical Social Research* 36 (2011), pp. 125–49.
30   The standard of quality must have been very enduring. During the 30 years of recorded correspondence, the tape merchant-manufacturer Abraham Frowein hardly ever received a complaint regarding quality.

Lacking this kind of institution, the tape weavers could not organize themselves or call on legal assistance (as the linen weavers were able to do), but they seem to have found a middle ground with their employers. In the few instances when tape weavers are mentioned in the merchant-manufacturers' records, a somewhat patriarchal relationship between the two groups is revealed. Johann Peter von Eynern, for example, passed on 'his' weavers' complaints about badly spun wool to a supplier in several instances, and expressed his concerns to another business friend about having to shut down production and the results this would have on his workers' livelihood.[31]

It is not documented whether the merchant-manufacturers' cartel extended to fixing the workers' wages, but there is ample evidence that the merchants stood together in the face of workers' demands. In the confrontation with the weavers' guild in the 1780s, the merchants even admitted to this.[32] Even if the merchants did not strike official agreements, competition and mutual monitoring kept wages down. The company Abr. & Bros. Frowein, for example, received a letter of complaint from a fellow merchant, asking them whether they had really offered the weavers in Langenfeld a certain wage for colored ribbons: 'If that is true then you are spoiling the workers who are always talking about more money anyway.'[33] Nevertheless, wages rose between 1787 and 1799 for the tape weavers, indicating that despite all complaints, the merchants still had some margin for a raise – which, by the way, the workers desperately needed in times of disrupted and meager harvests.[34]

By 1807, however, the merchants felt themselves in dire straits, due to the commercial war waging between France and Britain.[35] They reacted by developing plans to form a syndicate:

> In Barmen there are plans to fuse all companies into a single one whereby all competition will be inhibited and the existence of the business secured for every stockholder's children and grandchildren. I have declared to be willing to join any commendable outfit, insofar as the feasibility, reliability, and proper objectives of selfsame can be quite clearly discerned.[36]

31   HZW, Coll. von Eynern, No. 132, letters to Adolph Bültermann, 2 February 1798, Joh. Georg Eichel, 30 June 1789, Melchior Gau, 22 June 1799.

32   M. Henkel, *Zunftmissbräuche: 'Arbeiterbewegung' im Merkantilismus* (Frankfurt, 1989), p. 226.

33   FCA No. 1, Wuppermann & Cramer, Barmen, to Abr. & Bros. Frowein, 14 March 1815.

34   FCA No. 1528 contains two wage lists from 1787 and 1799, detailing the weavers' wages for the different kinds and widths of tapes. The lists are contained in the same folder as the convention contracts, but it is not indicated whether the wage lists were part of the conventions or not.

35   Considering the date, the ensuing actions can hardly be considered to be an effect of the continental blockade. For a general reassessment of the blockade see K. Aaslestad and J. Joor, eds, *Revisiting Napoleon's Continental System: Local, Regional and European Experiences* (Basingstoke, 2015).

36   FCA No. 34, Bros. Bockmühl, Barmen, to Abr. & Bros. Frowein, 26 August 1807.

Apparently, the Barmen merchants viewed internal competition as a threat to their livelihood, thereby revealing how closely the local industry was intertwined and how it hinged on co-operation. The 'fusing of all companies' did not come about, but regulating prices remained an important activity within the Wupper Valley merchant community:

> On Monday evening Peter Keuchen told us that he made an arrangement with you and Bros. Bockmühl to regulate the prices for America, and that he would inform us about it. As there are already enquiries about prices, everyone very much desires that you will make public your agreement once it is effective.[37]

Wuppermann & Cramer, the sender of the letter, suggested another timely meeting to which all the parties concerned ought to be invited, to strike a speedy regulation of the prices. In 1813, the Duchy of Berg had become part of the general government (*Generalgouvernement*) headed by Prussian government officials, and trade had livened up again.[38] Old trade routes reopened and the important outlet on the Iberian Peninsula became accessible again. Fears in the valley ran high that competitors would try to take over their established markets:

> Others are tracing the trade to Lisbon for there is presently a travelling salesman from Hamburg in town whom you will know as well. He asked us for a sample card for Lisbon. As we know that he has done business with others but none with us, we presume that one wants to elicit our patterns. He said that one of their travelling salesmen will set out for Lisbon soon and strike up important business in linen tape. But we played dumb and said that we did not know this article. ... We must take good care otherwise we will have many rivals. We know that there are also salesmen from Creveld in Lisbon which in time is going to turn out disadvantageously.[39]

This competition from Creveld (another proto-industrial center for textiles in Westphalia, famous for its inexpensive silks and silk ribbons) seems to have been particularly dangerous to the Wupper Valley merchants. After all, the Creveld merchant-manufacturers stood in the same tradition of producing cheap textiles and placing them on distant markets.[40] Co-operation in the valley seemed to be the answer to these threats:

---

37 FCA No. 1, Wuppermann & Cramer, Barmen, to Abr. & Bros. Frowein, 12 January 1814.
38 W. Treue, *Wirtschaftszustände und Wirtschaftspolitik in Preußen 1815–1825* (Stuttgart, 1937), p. 101.
39 FCA No. 1, Wuppermann & Cramer, Barmen, to Abr. & Bros. Frowein, 14 May 1815.
40 On Creveld and its industries, see P. Kriedte, *Taufgesinnte und grosses Kapital: Die niederrheinisch-bergischen Mennoniten und der Aufstieg des Krefelder Seidengewerbes (Mitte des 17. Jahrhunderts–1815)* (Göttingen, 2007).

The day before yesterday Mr Hoeninghaus from de Greiff in Creveld was
here and asked about prices for Harlem superfin. We have offered 12 per
cent so far but need to write in more detail on Friday. What do you think,
how much discount should we give? With these gentlemen it seems to be
particularly relevant to stay united. Could you find out approximately what
Mr. Bockmühl offered.[41]

Apart from these bilateral agreements, continuing the cartel seemed to be the
mutually accepted response to these challenges in the valley. The next formal
agreement preserved in the archives is dated 1821. Among those who struck
the accord in that year, six firms were from the group of those who had already
participated in the 1795 cartel, testifying to a high continuity of action.[42]
        The 1821 agreement closely resembled that of 1795, including detailed lists
of prices, an agreement on the lengths of the pieces of tape, as well as terms
and conditions of payment and delivery. The conditions for trade with Spain
were made to follow the conventions for the French market, so as not to hurt the
middling tradesmen in Perpignan and Bayonne. If anyone still had goods in stock
that were reeled in the older lengths, these might still be sold as is, but in line
with the new price list. The merchants also voted positively to ask the Prussian
government to give its stamp of approval for the units of lengths fixed in the
price convention, heightening the binding character of the agreement and giving
it a semi-official air.[43] The costs for printing the price list were shared among the
companies involved, presenting another cost benefit of the cartel. The merchants
also agreed to meet monthly to discuss trade and to adapt terms if necessary.[44]
        Besides these formal cartels regulating prices, units and terms, the Wupper
Valley merchants also continued to co-operate closely to fulfill orders and to
keep ahead of their customers. As was already mentioned, the Wupper Valley
merchants supplied an amazing variety of tape in different widths and lengths
– more, in fact, than any single supplier could keep in stock.[45] So, in order to

---

41 FCA No. 1, Wuppermann & Cramer, Barmen, to Abr. & Bros. Frowein, 20 April 1814.
42 Two of them still traded under the same name (Abr. & Bros. Frowein; Bros. Bockmühl). Four
others had passed into the hands of successors and changed the name somewhat. Eight of them
were listed among the most important industrialists in their sector in 1820. See *General-Tabelle der
vorzüglichsten Fabricken und Manufakturen in den Königlich Preußischen Provinzen Niederrhein,
Cleve, Jülich u. Berg, Westphalen und Sachsen* (Cologne, 1820), pp. 84f.
43 FCA No. 1528. That the price lists actually went into action is shown by a surviving example
of the eventually printed list, whose prices correspond with those in the written agreement. The
printed price list was found by chance within the unrelated documents of another Wupper Valley
firm. HZW, Coll. von Eynern, No. 133.
44 However, the three large manufacturers of woollen tape that were also invited to join the
convention had declined to participate. They seem to have opted for greater flexibility in responding
to customers' orders. The cartel agreement stated clearly that the woollen tape manufacturers
were not bound to cut their tape in the lengths stipulated in the contract. See FCA No. 1528.
45 The repeated inventories done by Abr. & Bros. Frowein show, for example, that their stock
does not contain all the articles found on price lists sent out to customers.

satisfy customers' orders without great delay, merchants within the valley relied on each other to complement their assortments. Letters like the following were part of the daily flurry of correspondence exchanged within the valley:

> Attached you will find the six dozen espagnolettes 6 aunes. ... You would do us a great favour if you could let us have 3 to 400 pieces No. 28 as well as just as much No. 34 Serge. No. 28 we could use up to 600. ... If you would rather sell us the serge in dozens [i.e. cut and wrapped] we will let you have the ell measures that we need.[46]

The close co-operation within the valley also meant that the merchants had more influence over their customers. For example, when a partner from the newly established trading house Sperry & Kintzing in Philadelphia toured Germany to identify trading partners and obtain favorable conditions, he tried to pit the different merchant-manufacturers against each other. But he did not stand a chance among the tight business community of the Wupper Valley: 'Please let us know whether you are in agreement with us [about the conditions offered to Sperry & Kintzing]. ... His claim that he has got [more favorable] conditions from others cannot be true and he only wants to entice us.'[47] And indeed, Sperry & Kintzing grumblingly had to accept the payment conditions and prices fixed among the Wupper Valley merchants, as none of them would budge.

The end of cartelization

Despite a continuity of firms, goods and market relations, the particular profile of 'co-operative capitalism' found in the Wupper Valley waned in the 1820s. The last formal pricing agreement that can be found in the archives dates from 1830 and was struck between just three companies, two of them furnishers of woollen tape who had declined to join the convention nine years earlier.[48] After that, these kinds of arrangements ceased, as did the frank exchange about orders, customers and the mutual supply of goods. Why did this form of co-operation end?

The demand for the Wupper Valley linen tape and its by-products started to change when the British began to flood the world with similar products made from cotton, which were considerably cheaper – albeit less durable. The Wupper

---

46 FCA No. 1, Wuppermann, Springmann & Cramer, Barmen, to Abr. & Bros. Frowein, 4 May 1813.
47 FCA No. 1, Wuppermann & Cramer, Barmen, to Abr. & Bros. Frowein, Elberfeld, 10 August 1815.
48 FCA No. 1528. The agreement concerned the companies Abr. & Bros. Frowein, Joh. Pet. von Eynern & Sons, and Peter Wolff.

Valley merchants started to feel the change in demand in earnest by the mid 1820s, heightened by the economic crisis of 1825. Suddenly the American outlets, which had become an alternative to the tariff-protected markets within Europe, were uninterested and the Wupper Valley tape merchants found it hard to place their staples. Even after the moment of extreme crisis had passed, their long-held trading expertise and knowledge of customers' desires could no longer compete with the superior distribution of British goods and their cheaper prices, which had come with mechanized production.[49]

From those years onwards, the Wupper Valley textile industry underwent a period of realignment, affirming François Crouzet's assessment of a general realignment of the continental industries.[50] From the 1820s, mechanization really started to take hold, particularly when it came to the establishment of cotton and silk mills.[51] In the ribbon and tape industries that are our main concern here, the merchant-manufacturers recognized the signs of the time and gave up on the old and time-honored products made from linen and traditional patterns, which they could no longer place in larger numbers on either the European or the Atlantic markets. Even though they maintained some of their old staples, such as seam binding, stay tape, laces and hatbands, they turned much of their production over to fashion items that changed annually or even seasonally, and focused on national outlets. Usually, they copied French patterns and models in cheaper materials, spreading and popularizing high fashion.[52] The reliance on fashion items meant that the practice of co-operation detailed above had to come to an end. Rather, competition between the manufacturers ran high, as each of them sought to produce unique items that pleased in the fickle world of fashion. After the realignment, they were far removed from producing the sort of standardized, homogenous product that is the prerequisite for the successful operation of a cartel. Informal accords between the manufacturers now focused on low wages for their workers, or government support, rather than high prices for

49 M. Zeuske, 'Preußen und Westindien: Die vergessenen Anfänge der Handels- und Konsularbeziehungen Deutschlands mit der Karibik und Lateinamerika 1800–1870', *Preußen und Lateinamerika*, ed. S. Carreras and G. Maihold (Münster, 2004), pp. 145–215; Overkamp, 'A Hinterland'.

50 F. Crouzet, 'Wars, Blockade, and Economic Change in Europe, 1792–1815', *The Journal of Economic History* 24 (1964), pp. 567–88.

51 J. Kermann, *Die Manufakturen im Rheinland 1750–1833* (Bonn, 1972); W. Hoth, *Die Industrialisierung einer rheinischen Gewerbestadt – dargestellt am Beispiel Wuppertal* (Cologne, 1975).

52 A. Thun, *Die Industrie am Niederrhein und ihre Arbeiter* (Leipzig, 1879), Vol. 2, p. 201. Ironically, it was the quick turnover demanded by fashion which helped to prolong the old means of production: the manually operated ribbon mill was far more quickly adapted to a different pattern than the complicated machinery of the mechanized looms. These were reserved for staples. Ibid., pp. 202f.

customers abroad. Institutions such as the chamber of commerce, established in 1831, now provided powerful means to exercise influence.[53] The 'period of the linen tape cartel' had come to an end.

Conclusion

Modern economic theory assumes that the economy thrives on competition and that cartelization is harmful, not only because it hurts consumer interests, but also because it damages the economy as a whole. Older notions highlighted the stabilizing effects of cartels. In the Wupper Valley, neither assessment seems to be entirely correct. The profit margins achievable in the smallwares sector were so low that the cartel might have hurt the interests of the middling tradesmen to some extent, but hardly those of the final consumer. The Wupper Valley merchants achieved their outstanding position in their international outlets only because their prices were low. The cartel was rather an attempt to prevent a race to the bottom. Yet in the later 1810s, the warehouses were still full of stock, so the cartel was not successful in hedging against over-production. Neither assessment really captures the Wupper Valley attempts at cartelization, because they were mostly informed by the Wupper Valley merchants' peripheral position relating to the driving force of early modern trade – that is, the Atlantic economy – which I want to discuss in terms of conclusion.

   This chapter set out to explore certain structural features of the early modern economy, particularly the relational position of a landlocked locality within the Atlantic economy of that time, and the particular strengths and weaknesses that were associated with that position. By highlighting the attempts at cartelization, lasting about 30 years, as well as the bilateral arrangements between merchant-manufacturers in the Wupper Valley, this chapter demonstrated that, even on the geographical periphery of the Atlantic World, agents knew how to muster strength and how to improve their disadvantaged position. The frank conversations about prices, conditions and customers' orders within the valley allowed the merchants to engage successfully with distant markets, and to maintain a share of the market even in challenging times. This demonstrates that, on the one hand, people living on the edge of the Atlantic World were able to exercise control and to defend their interests. They were in a position to negotiate, and they used it to their advantage.

   On the other hand, the Wupper Valley merchants remained in a geographically and structurally difficult position, heightened by the particularities of their

---

53   H. Herberts, *Alles ist Kirche und Handel: Wirtschaft und Gesellschaft des Wuppertals im Vormärz und in der Revolution 1848/49* (Neustadt an der Aisch, 1980); Industrie- u. Handelskammer Wuppertal in Verb. mit W. Köllmann, eds, *Industrie- und Handelskammer Wuppertal, 1831–1956: Festschrift zum 125 jährigen Jubiläum am 17. Jan. 1956* (Wuppertal, 1956).

industry. Firstly, they had to rely on a number of intermediaries to participate in Atlantic trade. Secondly, their goods were mundane and, from a technical point of view, rather simple products where competition could develop quickly. It was mostly the wide range of articles and the swift satisfaction of customers that set the valley's merchants apart. Thirdly, the Wupper Valley's competitive participation in the early modern Atlantic economy depended on low production costs – a classic feature of a periphery. It is these structural features that explain why collaboration was in fact a dire necessity. Only through co-operation could the merchant-manufacturers offer the comprehensive selection of merchandise and the swift fulfilment of orders, and maintain the valley's reputation as the foremost supplier of smallwares for a wide circle of customers. Because of this, the actively negotiated strength of the cartel did not accrue to a real competitive edge on which the Wupper Valley merchants could capitalize in terms of increased prices. It simply kept them in business.[54]

At the beginning of this chapter, I cited a book putting forward the idea that the rating of a location as peripheral is in the eye of the beholder – a notion that has also been explored in the introduction to this volume by Jutta Wimmler and Klaus Weber. This leads to the question of how the Wupper Valley merchants perceived themselves and their position within the wider world. Surprisingly, they did not talk about it at all – at least, not in the records consulted for this chapter. There are no complaints about structural disadvantages or about difficulties due to their geographic location. Rather, they perceived themselves as well-integrated into markets – markets that they actively sought to protect against competition from elsewhere. If they lamented the 'difficult times' at all, their concern was rather the (changing) political situation, not the (unchanging) geographical one. They exhibited just as vigorous a spirit of enterprise as any other merchant community in the Atlantic World. They certainly did not feel peripheral.

The Wupper Valley merchant-manufacturers' willingness to co-operate went far beyond that of other business associates in the Atlantic World, and their often jointly pursued trading ventures.[55] It also surpassed that of other merchant-manufacturers who maintained a far more competitive stance.[56] It

---

54   To understand more fully the limitations of the Wupper Valley industries, it would in fact be necessary to do a comparative study with firms from e.g. Lancashire.
55   Take, for example, the trading communities of Bordeaux, Philadelphia and London, detailed by P. Butel, *Les Négociants Bordelais, l'Europe et les Iles au XVIIe Siècle* (Paris, 1974); T. M. Doerflinger, *A Vigorous Spirit of Enterprise: Merchants and Economic Developments in Revolutionary Philadelphia* (Williamsburg, 1986); D. Hancock, *Citizens of the World: London Merchants and the Integration of the British Atlantic Community, 1735–1785* (Cambridge, 2005).
56   The dealings of merchant-manufacturers from other textile regions are among many others exemplified in A. Flügel, *Kaufleute und Manufakturen in Bielefeld: Soziale und wirtschaftliche Entwicklung im proto-industriellen Leinengewerbe von 1680 bis 1850* (Bielefeld, 1993); Kriedte, *Taufgesinnte*.

seems reasonable to conclude that they developed a particular kind of business culture.[57] The particularity of their business culture – that is, the favoring of co-operation over competition – can be attributed to their somewhat marginal position. Studying this cartel on the periphery therefore invites us to reconsider the local preconditions for Atlantic and also global trade, and to think carefully about the local requirements that enabled the flow of goods and people across the Atlantic Ocean.

Considering a seemingly peripheral region in terms of Atlantic history and studying how its merchants were affected by the structural pressures of Atlantic trade has also demonstrated how much regions far removed from the Atlantic littoral were influenced by the complex interchange that formed the Atlantic World, thereby trying to answer the query for a 'broader, richer, amplified view of Atlantic dynamics'.[58] The efforts undertaken by the merchant-manufacturers from the Wupper Valley certainly tell us a lot about what it took for a remote region to become and to stay incorporated not only in the Atlantic but also in the world economy.

57 On early modern business culture see S. Gorißen, 'Der Preis des Vertrauens: Unsicherheit, Institutionen und Rationalität im vorindustriellen Fernhandel', *Vertrauen: Historische Annäherungen*, ed. U. Frevert (Göttingen, 2003), pp. 90–118; F. Trivellato, *The Familiarity of Strangers: The Sephardic Diaspora, Livorno, and Cross-Cultural Trade in the Early Modern Period* (New Haven, 2009); S. Haggerty, *'Merely for Money'? Business Culture in the British Atlantic, 1750–1815* (Liverpool, 2012).
58 P. A. Coclanis, 'Beyond Atlantic History', *Atlantic History: A Critical Appraisal*, ed. J. P. Greene and P. D. Morgan (Oxford, 2009), pp. 337–56, here p. 349.

9

Linen and Merchants from the Duchy of Berg, Lower Saxony and Westphalia, and their Global Trade in Eighteenth-Century London

MARGRIT SCHULTE BEERBÜHL

German linen fabrics enjoyed an enduring popularity from the sixteenth century onwards, not only in England but also in the New World. The linen goods, which were in such demand on domestic English and colonial markets, mainly came from three regions: the north-west of Germany, Saxony, and Silesia. These regions produced a variety of products of middling and lower quality, though the range of qualities was considerable. This chapter will analyze the causes of the lasting success of linen fabrics and show how German traders contributed to the expansion of the early modern global trade by their migration and settlement pattern, despite the fact that Germany did not have colonies of any significance, and despite the mercantilist trade restrictions of the late seventeenth and eighteenth centuries.

This chapter focuses on linen produced in the north-western parts of Germany.[1] Today, this region comprises the eastern part of Westphalia, the southern parts of Lower Saxony, and the Wupper Valley. In the late seventeenth and eighteenth centuries this region was a patchwork of small independent states, of principalities, duchies, et cetera, including some parts of the electorate of Hanover. The entire region was known for its linen industries. In the Duchy of Berg, the towns of Elberfeld and Barmen (today Wuppertal) were known for their white linen and linen yarn, while some towns of the duchy such as Solingen and Remscheid were centers of metal production.[2]

According to Beverly Lemire, 'European linens ... burst into the English market' in the seventeenth century.[3] Certainly, the quantities imported exploded,

---

1   For Silesian linen, see Anka Steffen's chapter in this volume.
2   See Anne Sophie Overkamp's chapter in this volume.
3   B. Lemire, 'Transforming Consumer Custom: Linen, Cotton, and the English Market,

but German linen was already widely consumed in England at the time of the Hanseatic League. The question is rather, what changes caused the spectacular growth in demand for German linens in the seventeenth century? The end of the Hanseatic League in 1598, the civil wars, as well as the colonial wars and mercantilistic policies caused major reorganizations of trade routes and the expansion of self-organized merchant networks after 1660. These changes, as will be discussed, not only led to a new linen boom but also affected trade routes and restructured trade.

As London emerged as the world's leading commercial and financial center from the late seventeenth century onwards, the capital attracted merchants and entrepreneurs from all over Germany and Europe. Large numbers came from the Hanseatic cities of Hamburg and Bremen, but a surprisingly large proportion also arrived from the north-western parts of Germany – that is, Westphalia, other nearby principalities and bishoprics, the Duchy of Berg, and to a smaller extent from Saxony and Silesia.

Linen exports from the north-west of Germany to Britain

From at least late medieval times, linen was not exclusively produced for home consumption in Germany, but was exported to England, the Netherlands and Italy, as well as the Habsburg Monarchy.[4] England was an important market for German linen, as the country did not yet have an established linen industry.[5] Originally, German linens were named in the London customs records after the regions they came from, like *Westfale* or *Prucie*.[6] In the course of the fifteenth century, German linens came to be known by their urban origins. Linens from Westphalia were named *Ozenbrugh/Ozenbrigh* or *Herford* in the customs records.[7] These two fabrics alone accounted for 34 per cent and 27 per cent of the London linen imports in the sixteenth century.[8] Linens from Brunswick and Saxony, which had previously been popular, had disappeared by that time. This was caused not only by the conflicts between the Hanseatic League and England, but also by internal disputes between Hamburg (the main export port for Saxon linen) and the Saxon merchants.[9]

1660–1800', *The European Linen Industry in Historical Perspective*, ed. B. Collins and P. Ollerenshaw (Oxford, 2003), pp. 187–207, here p. 187.
4 E. Schmitz, *Leinengewerbe und Leinenhandel in Nordwestdeutschland, 1650–1850* (Cologne, 1967), pp. 22f.
5 A. Huang, *Die Textilien des Hanseraums: Produktion und Distribution einer spätmittelalterlichen Fernhandelsware* (Cologne, 2015), p. 114.
6 See more explicitly, Huang, *Die Textilien*, pp. 96ff.
7 The spelling of *Ozenbrigh* varied very much in the contemporary writings.
8 Imports from Münsterland amounted to only 4 per cent: see Huang, *Die Textilien*, pp. 97f.
9 Ibid.

An important factor that contributed to the new popularity of Westphalian linen in England was the introduction of the *Legge*, an urban institution which inspected the linen and stamped all the bales that met the requirements. Such a control of quality did not yet exist in the Saxon towns, nor in Hanover or Brunswick. The introduction of the *Legge* meant that production became standardized, with a uniform and guaranteed quality. This triggered a growing demand for linen, and in turn changed the cultivation methods of flax in the county of Ravensberg. Flax, which used to be cultivated in gardens and small plots, became a cash crop that was grown in large fields and replaced the regional cultivation of grain.[10]

Standardized production directives and institutionalized quality controls not only improved the quality, but also established the necessary preconditions for mass production. Angela Huang states that the *Legge* generated economies of scale, not by mechanization, as is usually associated with the concept of economies of scale, but by organizational innovations, which allowed for mass production at low cost.[11]

The political events of the seventeenth century mark a turning point in the export history of German linen. During the time of the Hanseatic League, competition on the English market had been interregional between several linen-producing regions in Germany. After 1660, competition that had been interregional became international. Besides calicos from India, a variety of new linen sorts from the Netherlands, France, Silesia and other German regions appeared on the English and colonial markets.[12] As German linens were cheaper and standardized, they dominated the markets – not only in the New World, but also in Africa. Beverly Lemire suggests that linens of a middling and lower quality, such as the Westphalian textiles, were of greater economic importance than the high-quality textiles.[13]

In the late seventeenth and eighteenth centuries, linen exported from the north-west of Germany comprised two different linen sorts of at least 12 different qualities.[14] The two different linen sorts were flax linen and hemp linen, each of which comprised at least six different quality levels. These depended on the quality of the yarn, the bleaching process, and whether the yarn was bleached before or after weaving. Different qualities of bleaching depended on the place (e.g. because of water quality) and whether it was fully bleached, half

---

10   Schmitz, *Leinengewerbe*, p. 76.
11   Huang, *Die Textilien*, pp. 115f. See also C. Jeggle, 'Pre-industrial Worlds of Production: Conventions, Institutions and Organizations', *Historical Social Research* 36/4 (2011), pp. 125–49, here p. 135.
12   M. Boldorf, *Europäische Leinenregionen im Wandel: Institutionelle Weichenstellung in Schlesien und Irland, 1750–1850* (Cologne, 2006), esp. Chapter 2 on Ireland; C. Gill, *The Rise of the Irish Linen Industry* (Oxford, 1925).
13   Lemire, 'Transforming Consumer Custom', p. 190.
14   For Silesian linen in Africa, see Anka Steffen's contribution in this volume.

Table 9.1. Main linen sorts from the north-west of Germany

Flax linen (six different qualities)	
1st sort Ozenbrighs	
England/North America	*True-born Ozenbrighs*
Spain and Colonies	*Coletas or Creguelas de Lino*
Portugal	*Aniagems con 5 pingos*
3rd sort	
England	*Stout Weser Flaxen*
Spain	*Creguelas de Westphalia*
Portugal	*Aniagems con 2 y 3 pingos*
West Indies	*Ozenbrighs*
Hemp linen	
1st and 2nd sort	
England/North America	*Tecklenburghs*
Spain	*Creguelas de Canamo*

bleached or unbleached.[15] The width of the various linen sorts also differed. Here only the most popular linen sorts are listed, including their quality levels and the names used in markets abroad (Table 9.1).

The most popular sorts were Ozenbrighs, Tecklenburghs and Stout Weser Flaxen. The 'true-born Ozenbrighs', as they were called in England (*Löwendlinnen* in German), were made of flax linen and were of the first sort, or highest quality. They were above all in demand in the West Indies, even after the end of the Napoleonic Wars.[16] The enslaved in the West Indies were clothed in a lower quality of flax linen, which was of the fourth quality sort, called *Bodenwerder* in German and 'brown Ozenbrighs' in England and the New World. Similarly, a hemp linen of the second quality sort (called Tecklenburghs), which was described abroad as 'half bleached and brown hemp linen', was the most widely consumed hemp linen across the Atlantic. It was used for making sails, canvas and tents, as well as trousers for the British army and navy, because it could resist rain and dampness for a long time.[17]

The popularity of German linens, especially those from Osnabrück, caused the English government to promote the domestic as well as Scottish and Irish linen industry by passing a law to attract foreign linen workers in 1663.

15   The following description of the several linen qualities is based on the study of F. W. Freiherr von Reden, *Der Leinwand- und Garnhandel Norddeutschlands* (Hanover, 1838), pp. 3ff.
16   Ibid.
17   Ibid., p. 19; Schmitz, *Leinengewerbe*, p. 15.

However, competition between the German, Irish and Scottish linens remained limited, due to the rapidly expanding New World markets. The frequent wars of that period, nevertheless, caused volatility and sharp short-term fluctuations. The Anglo-Dutch wars and the ban on French products in the early 1680s and after the beginning of the Nine Years' War in 1689 contributed to the buoyancy of German linen imports. The German linen and yarn trades seem to have experienced the most important expansion in the second half of the seventeenth and the early eighteenth centuries.

The Irish and Scottish linen industries primarily aimed at imitating Ozenbrighs. Merchants from Ireland and Scotland who were interrogated before the Parliamentary Committee on linens maintained that they could produce linens of the widths and fabric of narrow German linen and Ozenbrighs, but they complained about the reductions on export duties on foreign linens that prevented their competitiveness with the German linens. Around 1740, they saw these drawbacks as the main cause of the fact that German linens to the value of two million pounds sterling were still sent to plantations.[18] Throughout the century, they continued to lament the drawbacks. It is doubtful whether the duties and drawbacks actually disadvantaged the Irish and Scottish linen trade, as they secured bounties and other forms of government aid to undersell the continental linens.[19] A statement before the 1773 Parliamentary Committee on linens reveals that German producers had responded to the British challenge by producing finer qualities at lower prices.[20]

Quantitative data are very limited for the early modern period and can only be regarded as rough indicators. Nevertheless, they provide valuable insights. According to Ralph Davis' calculations, England's re-exports trebled during the period 1660 to 1700.[21] He attributed the astonishing rise mainly to three items: linen, sugar and tobacco. Corresponding imports from Germany rose from £185,000 to £732,000 between 1662/63 and 1699/1701.[22] In 1696, Bremen alone exported linen worth a million *thaler* to England.[23] Imports from Hamburg were even higher. According to Elizabeth Karen Newman, linens and linen yarn accounted for about 80 per cent of Hamburg's exports to England in 1701 to

18   British Parliamentary Papers (hereafter: BPP), Report from the Committee to whom the Petitions of the Merchants and Others of Great Britain and Ireland … was referred, 1744, p. 5.

19   R. S. DuPlessis, *The Material Atlantic: Clothing, Commerce, and Colonization in the Atlantic World, 1650–1800* (Cambridge, 2016), p. 239.

20   BPP, Committee appointed to enquire into the present state of the linen industry in Great Britain and Ireland, 1773, p. 103.

21   R. Davis, 'English Foreign Trade, 1660–1700', reprinted in *The Growth of English Overseas Trade in the Seventeenth and Eighteenth Century*, ed. W. E. Minchinton (London, 1969), pp. 78–98.

22   E. K. Newman, 'Anglo-Hamburg Trade in the Late Seventeenth and Early Eighteenth Centuries' (unpublished Ph.D., London, 1979), pp. 84, 86.

23   Von Reden, *Leinwand- und Garnhandel*, p. 55.

Table 9.2. Imports from Germany to London

Linen, hessian canvas	3,895	Ells
Canvas sail cloth	2,555	Pieces
German linen, broad and narrow	nearly 10,000	Ells
Hambro linen, broad and narrow	458	Ells
Holland linen	241	Ells
Lawns sletia	29,092	Pieces
Ozenbruggs	657,826	Ells
Damask, napkin of sletia	12,928	Yards
Damask, tabling of sletia	5,319	Yards
Diaper, tabling of sletia	9,906	Yards
Hinterlands brown	1,464	Ells
Linen yarn raw	727,462	Pounds
Mohair yarn	398	Pounds
Spruce yarn	92	Hundredweight

Source: House of Lords Record Office, HL/PO/JO/10/5/32.

1713. About 90 per cent of the imported linen was re-exported to the British colonies in North America and the West Indies.[24]

London's exportation books for the year 1692/93 provide an interesting insight into the imports and re-exports of German linen. They not only distinguish between different linen sorts, but also mention their destinations. This source comprises many volumes; therefore, only a sample of some selected linens imported from Germany to London (Table 9.2) and linens of various origins re-exported from London to Barbados (Table 9.3) can be given in this chapter. As to the reliability of this source, Ralph Davis judges the data for London to be more reliable than those for the outports.[25]

Measuring the total volume of British imports of German linen is difficult. German textiles were not shipped exclusively via Bremen and Hamburg but also via the Dutch and Flemish ports, and they may have been called Dutch linens, although they were of German origin. This may account for the fact that the re-export figures from London to Barbados are higher than from German ports alone for that year.

The great popularity of certain textiles and the need to remain competitive contributed to a rapid diversification and expansion of linen fabrics. For

24 Newman, 'Anglo-Hamburg Trade', pp. 29, 199.
25 Davis, 'English Foreign Trade', pp. 78ff.

Table 9.3. London's exports to Barbados

Scots linen	4,065	Ells
Holland linen	15,852	Ells
Holland duck	70,700	Ells
Sletia lawns	661	Pieces
Broad German linen	100,000	Ells
Ozenbrighs	22,692	Ells
Narrow German linen	800,990	Ells

Source: House of Lords Record Office, HL/PO/JO/10/5/31; see also London Importations for 1694/95, which mention 43,644 ells Ozensbrugs coming from Holland to London, and 410,846 ells Ozenbrugs from Germany (ibid., HL/PO/JO/10/5/40).

Britain, Lemire refers to more than a hundred different sorts of linens and mixtures of linens with silk, wool or cotton by the middle of the eighteenth century. The new variety of fabrics was accompanied by a new variety of colors, color retention, weight and feel.[26] Furthermore, the popularity of fabrics like Ozenbrighs induced competitors to imitate them. As indicated above, researchers face the difficulty of tracing the actual place of production. An Ozenbrigh or Sletia lawn could be produced somewhere else – for example, in Ireland or in the Netherlands. Moreover, from the mid eighteenth century onwards, a new competitor appeared on the global textile market: Russia. Cheap linens produced in Russia were sent across the Atlantic in rapidly growing quantities.

The extent to which the increasing competition from cotton caused a decline in the German linen industry is an open question. The decline was certainly more gradual than generally assumed. German linens continued to be popular in the Spanish and French colonies. Continuing complaints from British merchants about their own declining competitiveness on the Atlantic linen market hint at the continuing demand for German linen in the Americas. In 1806, British merchants petitioned Parliament for a reduction of duties on foreign linens, because they could not sell them as cheaply as the Americans and other nations. In the British trade with the West Indies, they argued, 'foreign linen appears to be indispensably necessary', referring especially to chequered and striped German and Russian linen wares, which were imported by foreign vessels.[27] Demands to reduce the duties on foreign (especially German) linen continued to be heard before Parliament, even after the end of the Napoleonic

26   Lemire, 'Transforming Consumer Custom', p. 199.
27   BPP, Minutes of Committee of Council for Trade on Duty on Foreign Linens exported to West India Islands, 1805, p. 623.

Wars. New fears had arisen by that time; British merchants complained that the direct trade organized by Americans and Europeans would undersell the British and destroy their (re-)export markets in their Caribbean colonies.[28]

The reorganization of trade routes and supply networks after 1660

With the rise of international and transatlantic markets for German linens from the middle of the seventeenth century onwards, trade routes and supply networks changed. In the time of the Hanseatic League, linen exports had been organized along corporate lines. In the second half of the seventeenth century, trade between England, the New World and the German states was restructured along private lines. Self-organized private enterprises shaped the Atlantic trade. This led to the decline of Cologne's trade with England, while Bremen emerged as an important new export harbor for Britain.[29]

A direct trade between the linen-producing regions in the European hinterland and the New World – that is, a direct link between the two peripheries – was prevented by the mercantilist policy of the age and by the Navigation Acts.[30] England was not the only country that restricted its colonial trade to its own subjects; more or less all imperial powers had similar restrictions. The restrictive policy severely affected those countries that did not have colonies of any significance. Trade from the German hinterlands to the New World was thus forced to take a detour via London (or via French, Dutch and Spanish ports).[31] Given the fact that a modern financial market that was able to finance a risky and long-distance trade was only in its infancy, a detour via London was to some extent advantageous. Goods shipped in British vessels across the Atlantic were often protected by the navy, which reduced the risk of loss through piracy and privateering.

The mercantilist trade restrictions, which aimed to bar foreigners from participation, were on the other hand impaired by English immigration policy. According to the mercantilist doctrine, people (meaning an 'employed people') increased the wealth of a nation.[32] At that time, a common view prevailed that

---

28   BPP, Memorial of Merchants of City of London respecting Transit Duties on Foreign Linens, May 1817, p. 2.

29   See M. Schulte Beerbühl, *The Forgotten Majority: German Merchants in London, Naturalization, and Global Trade, 1660–1815* (New York, 2015), p. 36.

30   'An Act for Increase of Shipping, and Encouragement of the Navigation of this Nation', 9 October 1651; the later Acts strengthened the restrictions.

31   See K. Weber, *Deutsche Kaufleute im Atlantikhandel, 1680–1830: Unternehmen und Familien in Hamburg, Cádiz und Bordeaux* (Munich, 2004).

32   See D. Statt, *Foreigners and Englishmen: The Controversy over Immigration and Population, 1660–1760* (London, 1995).

England was underpopulated.[33] Therefore, the immigration of craftsmen and other skilled groups was advocated. In view of these policies, foreign merchants could gain access to the colonial markets, provided they settled in the country (at least nominally) and obtained naturalization in England.[34]

Besides the reasons mentioned above, several domestic factors induced merchants from Westphalia, Lower Saxony and the Duchy of Berg to leave their birthplace and try their luck in London. Economic as well as demographic aspects and familial business strategies influenced their decision. The Thirty Years' War had devastating economic effects on many regions in Germany, from which they recovered only slowly. After the war, birth rates rose conspicuously. The towns in Westphalia and Berg were small, each counting a few thousand inhabitants and offering few economic opportunities. Merchant families with many children feared an unwanted competition within the next generation, and possible loss of social and economic status. In order to keep competition within families low, the younger generation was encouraged to leave home and to seek their fortune elsewhere.[35] This strategy was not new, dating back to at least the time of the Hanseatic League. Young members were sent to foreign places, not only for education but also to explore new markets which could become profitable for the family businesses. A temporary stay in a distant or foreign place could, if prospects were bright, turn into a permanent settlement.

Naturalization records have survived and are fairly complete from the second half of the seventeenth century until the French and Napoleonic Wars.[36] They reveal that a substantial number of Germans from the linen regions of the hinterlands moved to England, predominantly to London. Although the number of merchants from Bremen and Hamburg taken together was higher than of those from the north-western regions, the number of the latter was not negligible. Between 1715 and 1800, 79 migrants from Hamburg, 69 from Bremen and 81 from the north-west can be traced in the naturalization records. To these numbers need to be added those who did not apply for British citizenship. Usually, either the younger or minor partner in a business avoided the cost of naturalization. According to a modest estimate, roughly a third more merchants who did not apply have to be added to these figures.[37]

Migration from the German hinterlands to London was part of a more complex migration pattern; that is, of step-and-chain migration. One of the first imperatives for merchants from the hinterlands was to gain access to the sea, in Bremen or Hamburg, for example, in order to organize the maritime trade. A settlement in the leading port cities of the imperial powers, which were

33 Schulte Beerbühl, *Forgotten Majority*, pp. 13ff.
34 The English naturalization law did not have any residential requirements at that time.
35 Schulte Beerbühl, *Forgotten Majority*, p. 37.
36 Ibid., p. 15. Naturalization was granted only to Protestants until 1829.
37 For numbers see Schulte Beerbühl, *Forgotten Majority*, pp. 17ff.

gateways to the colonies and had a corresponding infrastructure, was the next stepping-stone to access the non-European world. In the case of merchants from the north-west of Germany, the preferred port of departure on the continent was Bremen, followed by Hamburg. At the same time, other family members settled in London. Migration to the British capital was then continued by the succeeding generations in the form of a chain migration.[38]

Two long-term emigration clusters can be identified from Westphalia and Berg. One started from Herford and the surrounding towns in Westphalia, and the other from Elberfeld (today part of Wuppertal) in the Duchy of Berg. The move to London began in the 1660s and continued until the 1770s. Thereafter, they increasingly moved to the new industrial regions in the north of England and became entrepreneurs. Between about the 1660s until about 1770, at least 14 merchants from Elberfeld left for London, 10 from Herford, and nine from towns adjacent to Herford.[39]

The following examples illustrate this pattern. The Teschemacher family of Elberfeld had 10 children (six sons and four daughters); of the sons, four left their hometown between the 1660s and 1680s, one to settle in Bremen and three in London. Similarly, one of the Dorrien family from Hildesheim moved to Bremen, another to London, thus creating a triangular network. Their aim to interconnect the linen-producing regions with London via Bremen can be gleaned from the fact that they were among the founders of the English Company in the Hansetown in 1686. The company aimed at monopolizing trade with England, but never achieved its goal.[40] Some of these merchant families also expanded their commercial networks beyond the triangular network, to places like Amsterdam, Cádiz or Livorno. The commercial networks of the linen merchants mentioned above did not only encompass their hometowns and the port cities of the imperial powers, but also interconnected the several linen regions in the German hinterlands. Members of the same families expanded their networks to the Saxon and Silesian textile regions. Of the Herford cluster of emigrants, one (Christopher Pritzler) moved via London on to Zittau in Saxony to open a textile business; another (Henry Klausing) moved via London to Russia. Peter Hasenclever of Remscheid moved via Lisbon and Cádiz to London, while his brother opened a business in Hirschberg in Silesia.[41]

---

38   Ibid., pp. 107–13; M. Schulte Beerbühl, 'Internationale Handelsnetze Westfälischer Kaufleute in London (c. 1660–1815)', *Kultur, Strategien und Netzwerke: Familienunternehmen in Westfalen im 19. und 20. Jahrhundert*, ed. K.-P. Ellerbrock et al. (Dortmund, 2014), pp. 153–74.

39   M. Schulte Beerbühl and K. Weber, 'From Westphalia to the Caribbean: Networks of German Textile Merchants in the Eighteenth Century', *Cosmopolitan Networks in Commerce and Society 1660–1914*, ed. A. Gestrich and M. Schulte Beerbühl, Bulletin Supplement No. 2 (London, 2011), pp. 53–98, here pp. 59–74.

40   Staatsarchiv Bremen 2-R.10.aa.13.a.2; Schulte Beerbühl, *Forgotten Majority*, p. 36.

41   P. Hasenclever, *Neue Deutsche Biographie*; see also Tanja Junggeburth's article on Hasenclever in Rheinisches Portal (http://www.rheinische-geschichte.lvr.de/Persoenlichkeiten/

Thus, they interlinked seemingly peripheral German regions into a dense commercial network that reached across Europe to the leading port cities of the colonial powers, gaining access to their colonial trade. Those who moved to London turned the city into an essentially global entrepôt. Via the capital, they sent linens and other goods across the Atlantic and re-exported colonial goods to Germany.

German merchants in London and their trade

Business records of the immigrant merchants from Westphalia, Hanover or the Duchy of Berg are scarce. Those that still exist cover only a few years. For the late seventeenth century, the London port books (that is, the customs records) allow a limited insight into the trade, but they no longer exist for the eighteenth century. Due to the volume and the sometimes poor condition of the port books, samples were taken only for selected years. They reveal that German merchants traded in a variety of goods besides linen.

John Kaus, the first immigrant merchant from Elberfeld, who probably arrived in London in the late 1650s, imported above all sword blades and other metal wares. Information on the import of linen could not be found in the selected port books, but it cannot be ruled out. Besides metal wares, Kaus also imported Rhenish as well as Spanish wines.[42] Information on John Kaus and his two brothers in London is unfortunately rather limited. The next generation of immigrants from Elberfeld, the Teshmakers (Teschemachers), allow more insights into the structure of the trade.

The three Teshmaker brothers arrived in London in the 1680s at the latest. According to D. Jones' compilation of the 500 largest importers and exporters in the 1690s, two immigrant merchants from the north-western part of Germany were among the largest London importers: John William Teshmaker from Elberfeld and Frederick Hermann Dorrien from Hildesheim.[43] John William Teshmaker was the second largest exporter of textiles of all native and naturalized importers in the capital, exporting goods worth nearly £29,000. Besides Ozenbrighs, he exported and imported narrow and broad German linen, buckrams and kerseys, as well as Sletia damask tabling, Sletia napkins, and other linen textiles from Silesia. Among the non-textile goods he imported from Germany were wares like wrought iron pewter, weapons

---

peter-hasenclever/DE-2086/lido/57c827b7a0aa19.48080583, accessed 18 July 2018); for Klausing, see A. Cross, *By the Banks of the Neva: Chapters from the Lives and Careers of the British in Eighteenth-Century Russia* (Cambridge, 1997), p. 407, n. 114.

42   TNA port books E 190/154/1; E 190/114/4 (overseas wine imports).

43   D. W Jones, *London Overseas-Merchant Groups at the End of the Seventeenth Century and the Moves against the East India Company* (Oxford, 1970), App. B; see also D. W. Jones, *War and Economy in the Age of William III and Marlborough* (Oxford, 1988).

and tin plates; from the Caribbean, he imported muscovado sugar from Barbados, and scraped ginger, pepper, rice, cinnamon and other spices from Jamaica.[44] Furthermore, his will shows that he also traded with Vienna and Transylvania.

Anthony Teshmaker, his brother, also had an account with the East India Company; unfortunately, however, the account does not reveal the goods that he bought.[45] The involvement of the Teshmaker family with India was closer than the account book of the East India Company suggests, for the son of John William, who described himself as a 'mariner of Calcutta' in his will, died there in 1719 or 1720.[46] John Engelbert Teshmaker, the third brother, applied for a patent to introduce a new method of spinning yarn. For that purpose, he had already erected a 'bucking' house and had brought several workmen from Germany.[47]

John William Teshmaker left a huge fortune. He bequeathed several freeholds and copyholds in Edmonton to his wife and four children, as well as about a thousand Rixdollars to various family members and friends.[48] He was not the only immigrant who acquired a huge fortune during that period. Peter Vansittart from Danzig and Raymond de Smeth from Hamburg also left large fortunes.[49] The attractiveness of the English and overseas market at the end of the seventeenth century can also be deduced from the fact that textile merchants from Silesia and Saxony moved to London.

After the death of John William in 1713, John Engelbert Teshmaker took over his brother's business for a few years, before he handed it over to John Abraham Korten from Elberfeld. One of Korten's account books survives, covering the last few years of his business before his death in 1742. The account book covers only his business share in the company. Nevertheless, it provides an interesting insight into his business. He entertained geographically far-reaching trade relations that stretched across the Atlantic to the North American colonies and the West Indies, and in the east to Russia and even further to Persia. The account book gives an impressive insight into the range of partners, but provides little

---

44   TNA E 190/158/1, E 190/121/1; E 190/156/5.
45   British Library, L/AG/1/1/10.
46   For the will: TNA Prob 11/932.
47   Calendar of State Papers, Domestic Ser. 3, Vol. 2, 25 September and 28 November 1691.
48   TNA Prob 11/537. As mentioned above, the textile trade was a very volatile business during the wars and to mention only the successful would give a one-sided picture. John Bode of Bremen, for example, gave up the linen trade after the outbreak of the Nine Years' War because he thought that the trade was too expensive and profits were too low, and decided to deal exclusively in wooden wares (Staatsarchiv Bremen 7.2075, letter dated 20 February 1691); in the 1680s he had dealt extensively with a variety of linen sorts from Westphalia (see undated note fol. 14).
49   When Peter Vansittart died in 1706, he left a fortune of more than £100,000 which was unusually high at that time (City of London Record Office, Orphans' Inventories 2718, Box 40, fol. 150b; for Peter Vansittart see also Schulte Beerbühl, *Forgotten Majority*, pp. 51f).

information about the goods he traded in. Some of the few wares mentioned
are several linen sorts – for example, Holland linen belonging to John Rudger
Wupperman of Elberfeld that Korten shipped on board a vessel destined to
Barbados, or two bales of Lubeck Duck for Job Lewis in Boston, New England.
In the profit and loss account, Swiss linen as well as Russian linen bales are
mentioned. Most entries, however, do not mention the origin of the linen.
Among the colonial goods he traded in are clayed sugars, muscovado (which
he received from his partner in Barbados), and other colonial goods like dyes.[50]

For centuries, connections between the towns of Herford and Elberfeld had
been very close, for most of the raw yarn that was bleached and processed
in Elberfeld came from Herford.[51] The latter town had a sizeable number of
yarn merchants, but few linen merchants. The business community of Herford
lacked capital and they often turned to merchants in Elberfeld for credit. Yarn
from Herford and the surrounding rural district was also exported to Holland,
France, Switzerland and England, but the main customer was Elberfeld. With
the exception of Holland, Herford's yarn merchants did not trade directly with
customers abroad. Instead, the linen was exported via Elberfeld and some other
entrepôts. Contemporaries thought that Herford's merchants lacked entrepre-
neurship.[52] This did not, however, apply to those who went to London. Some
of them also acquired fortunes; for example, Henry Voguell of Herford, or his
nephews Godfrey and Frederick Molling.

We do not have any of Henry Voguell's business records, but the little information we have is that he also traded in Silesian and Saxon linen. He had settled
in London in 1707 and during his commercial career established close links
with Silesian and Saxon merchants. Many merchants from Zittau in Saxony
regarded his house in London as their 'best customer'.[53] Carl Christian Besser,
one of the wealthiest merchants in Zittau, was Voguell's main supplier of linen
from this region. Other Saxon merchants, like Johann Christoph Prenzel or
Elias Neumann, even worked in Voguell's London merchant house for some
years. The importance Voguell attributed to this textile region is obvious from
the decision of Christoph Frederick Pritzler, Voguell's cousin, who had worked
with him in London for some years, to return to Germany and open a business
in Zittau with Johann Friederich Mölling, another of Voguell's relatives from
Herford, and Christian Biedermann from Reichenau. By the time of his death,
Voguell was also partner in an Irish linen firm.[54] He bequeathed his share in the

50   Herfordshire Record Office 156/VI/2. For Korten see more explicitly Schulte Beerbühl,
Forgotten Majority, pp. 191ff.
51   E. Schönfeld, *Herford als Garn- und Leinemarkt in zwei Jahrhunderten, 1670–1870* (Bielefeld,
1929), pp. 50ff.
52   Ibid., p. 55.
53   A. Kunz, 'Der Zittauer Leinengroßhandel im 18. Jahrhundert', *Zittauer Geschichtsblätter*
6 (1930), pp. 43–8, here p. 44.
54   TNA Prob 11/751.

firm to Protestant schools to foster the Irish linen industry. He evidently also traded with Russia, for he joined the Russia Company in London in the 1720s, before the conclusion of the commercial treaty with Russia.[55]

From the 1720s onwards, Russia became the most important supplier for the raw materials that Britain needed for its navy and for its construction sector (like wood, bar iron, and so-called naval stores). Britain's dependence on imports from Russia induced the government in London to conclude a very favorable commercial treaty with the Tsar's empire in 1734. As the British merchants lacked language skills and knowledge about Russian customs, many British-born merchants co-operated with Germans and German-Russians.[56]

British trade with Russia was monopolized by the London Russia Company, and the records of the company reveal a conspicuously high percentage of Germans among its members. John Abraham Korten even sat on the Court of Assistants of the company. Naturalized British subjects were excluded from the highest offices – not only from gaining a seat in Parliament, but also from becoming governor of a trading or insurance company. However, throughout the century we find at least one naturalized Briton of German birth in the Court of Assistants, the governing body of the Russia Company.[57]

Voguell, who died without issue in 1746, had handed his business over to a group of partners. A balance sheet of 1771/72 by Amyand & Siebel, Voguell's successors in business, reveals that Zittau – as well as several towns in Silesia, like Schmiedeberg, Hirschberg and other places – were important suppliers of Silesian, Saxon and Russian linens.[58] Voguell's nephews, Frederick and Godfrey Molling, Theophilus Pritzler and his godson Henry Uhthoff, who had all worked with Voguell for some time, founded their own businesses after his death. Within a decade, the Mollings became substantial linen and tobacco traders and later even entered banking.[59]

Although German merchants were a visible group among the London merchants, they were a minority that had to cope with the social and economic reservations of the native merchants. Trading houses in London usually consisted of two or more partners. Most of the German merchant houses worked with other German immigrants and also intermarried with partners

55   The National Archives of Scotland (Edinburgh), Shairp Papers, GD 30/1583; see also A. B. Demkin, *Britanskoe Kupeestvo v Rossii XVIII Veka* (Moscow, 1998), p. 247. One of his partners, Anthony Fürstenau from Osnabrück, was a substantial Russia merchant. His ancestors came from Herford; see R. Pape, 'Anton Fürstenau: Ein Kaufmann und Diplomat der Reichsstadt Herford im 17. Jahrhundert', *Herforder Jahrbuch* 22/14 (1771/72), pp. 61–155.
56   Schulte Beerbühl, *Forgotten Majority*, pp. 139ff.
57   Ibid., p. 145.
58   George Amyand married Korten's daughter. Siebel was Korten's nephew from Elberfeld.
59   J. Price, ed., *Joshua Johnson's Letterbook, 1771–1774: Letters from a Merchant in London to his Partners in Maryland* (London, 1979), pp. xxvf. Johnson and his partners in America were substantial buyers of Ozenbrighs; Schulte Beerbühl, *Forgotten Majority*, p. 100.

from other German towns. Only a small number worked in partnership with other European merchants, and even fewer with British partners.

The Dorriens from Hildesheim are an interesting example. Commercial co-operation and intermarriage laid the foundation of their rise into the London elite. Frederick Hermann Dorrien, the first immigrant, worked in partnership with Georg Stehn (Stein) from Lübeck in the 1690s. Frederick had two sons; one of them married into the German-Russian Schiffner family in London (one of the leading Russia houses), and the other became one of the directors of the Bank of England. Their sons again intermarried with several immigrant families from Hamburg. Similarly, Herford immigrants co-operated in joint partnerships and intermarried with those from Elberfeld, Brunswick and other German towns. In London, Henry Voguell had traded in partnerships with German immigrants from Hamburg and Berlin, in addition to his cousins and nephews from Herford and nearby towns.[60]

Trade in sugar was extremely profitable. Sugar merchants were among the wealthiest income group in Britain. In sugar business, vertical integration (i.e. plantation ownership, trade and refining) was highly sophisticated. Unlike the British-born merchants, German immigrants did not generally own plantations, nor did they rank among the big slave traders. That trade was jealously defended by native merchants. Only a tiny minority of immigrants could overcome these difficulties and acquire plantations. However, some of them integrated sugar-refining into their business activities. Sugar-refining was carried out in Europe; in the eighteenth century, the East End of London was the leading sugar-refining center in Britain. A large part of this business was in the hands of Germans or people of German descent.[61] Family members of the aforementioned Pritzlers from Herford, for example, owned a sugar refinery in Wellclose Square in London. Such a vertical integration can also be perceived in the leather or fur trade.[62]

The advent of cotton and the first spinning machines increasingly caused migrants to move to the new industrial regions. One such example is John Roger Teshmaker, the last of the Teshmakers who applied for British citizenship. He settled as a hosier in Nottingham, the center of the knitting trade.[63] Besides importing linen cloth and yarn, German immigrants began to export cotton yarn and cotton textiles to the continent. By the time of the Napoleonic Wars, the firm Molling, Spitta, Molling & Co. exported large amounts of cotton

60 Schulte Beerbühl, 'Internationale Handelsnetze Westfälischer Kaufleute'.
61 H. Rössler, '"Die Zuckerbäcker waren vornehmlich Hannoveraner": Zur Geschichte der Wanderung aus dem Elbe-Weser-Dreieck in die britische Zuckerindustrie', *Jahrbuch der Männer vom Morgenstern* 81 (2002), pp. 137–236.
62 For example, the Paul brothers from Silesia, John Daniel and John William, imported hides and furs from North America, Russia and Turkey. They also owned a tannery (Schulte Beerbühl, *Forgotten Majority*, pp. 136f).
63 Bailey's Directory of Nottingham for 1783 and 1784.

yarns and textiles from one of the largest cotton firms of Manchester to the continent.[64]

A further shift of trade routes and a certain reorganization of foreign trade occurred after the independence of the United States and the French and Napoleonic Wars. The independence of the United States opened a new legal channel of direct trade between the German hinterlands and the New World. From the late 1780s onwards, textiles were shipped less via Britain but increasingly directly to the USA. Furthermore, secret loopholes existed in the Caribbean to circumvent the mercantilist restrictions between the colonial powers. The Danish free port of St Thomas in the Caribbean, for example, became a major entrepôt for European goods that were secretly distributed to the Spanish and Portuguese colonies.[65]

Growing competition from the Irish and Scottish linens also affected the German linen industry. Merchants responded to this competition by adapting the textiles to Irish processes. We know from the correspondence of the Delius family, among the leading linen merchants in Bielefeld, that they had adapted Silesian linens to Irish measures in order to sell them in America and in the British Caribbean colonies. Arnold Delius in Bremen, furthermore, advised his cousin Ernst August Delius in Bielefeld to introduce the Irish finishing process in order to compete with the Irish linens in the English colonies.[66] After the introduction of the Irish finishing process, demand for Bielefeld linen rose so considerably in America and the Caribbean that one of the Delius family settled in the United States. In the 1790s, customers in Baltimore and Philadelphia bought linens from the Delius family worth more than 2,000 dollars each per annum.[67]

Although it is not the aim of this chapter to deal with the advance of cotton in the north-western parts of Germany, it should be noted very briefly that German linen producers increasingly turned to manufacturing mixed fabrics of linen and cotton by the middle of the eighteenth century. The textile regions of the left bank of the Rhine, as well as the Duchy of Berg, were among the first to introduce cottons and to produce fabrics like the Siamoises.[68] In Ratingen, near Düsseldorf, Gottfried Brügelmann erected the first mechanized spinning manufactory in the early 1780s.[69] The transition to cotton and mechanization

64   TNA Bankruptcy Records B 3/4549.
65   Von Reden, *Leinwand- und Garnhandel*, pp. 302f.
66   Arnold Delius to Ernst August Delius, 7 February 1790. (From a private collection held by the Delius family in Bielefeld. I would like to thank Eberhard Delius for allowing me to consult the letters.)
67   H. Schmidt, *Die Entwicklung der Bielefelder Firmen E. A. Delius, E. A. Delius & Söhne und C. A. Delius & Söhne und die Betätigung ihrer Inhaber im Rahmen des Ravensberger Wirtschaftslebens, 1787–1925* (Lemgo, 1926), p. 47.
68   See Anne Sophie Overkamp's contribution in this volume.
69   G. Adelmann, 'Strukturwandlungen der rheinischen Leinen- und Baumwollgewerbe zu Beginn der Industrialisierung', *Vierteljahrschrift für Sozial- und Wirtschaftsgeschichte* 53 (1966), pp. 162–84.

Table 9.4. Flax yarn and linen exports from Münster

Year	Flax yarn	Linen	Year	Flax yarn	Linen
1832	8,702	1,774,727	1839	818,485	3,414,967
1833	72,006	2,167,024	1840	822,876	3,306,088
1834	136,312	2,443,346	1841	970,840	3,356,030
1835	216,635	2,992,143	1842	1,023,978	2,360,152
1836	318,772	3,326,325	1843	873,164	2,816,111
1837	479,307	2,127,445	1844	1,021,796	3,055,243
1838	746,162	2,820,272			

was rather uneven in the German textile regions: while the regions on the left bank of the Rhine and the Duchy of Berg were the first to industrialize, Westphalian merchants and entrepreneurs reacted much more slowly.

After the end of the Napoleonic Wars in 1815, English cottons glutted the markets on the continent. Nevertheless, handmade German linens and linen yarn continued to find their markets abroad, even in Britain. Figures are only available for the region around Münster in Westphalia (the Münsterland) for the years 1832 to 1844 (Table 9.4). The export figures show a small though uneven growth.[70] As the figures reveal, the export value of yarn rose more markedly than that of linen between 1830 and 1844. However, the late 1840s and 1850s finally saw the transition from handmade yarns and linens to mechanized production.

Conclusion

To sum up, the English market had been an important outlet for German linens from Westphalia, Lower Saxony and the Duchy of Berg already at the time of the Hanseatic League. The fabrics enjoyed a widespread popularity in England because they were quality-controlled and standardized products inspected and stamped by the *Legge*, an urban inspection institution. Organizational innovations as well as competition among the several linen-producing regions in Germany kept wages and prices low and contributed to the rise of economies of scale. German linen was therefore not an unknown fabric in seventeenth-century England, but enjoyed widespread popularity.

The 1660s marked a decisive turning point. While the Hanseatic League had interlinked peripheral regions within Europe (including England) during its five centuries of existence, new peripheral regions outside Europe were now

---

70 Schmitz, *Leinengewerbe*, p. 110.

accessed and turned the old transnational European linen trade into a global one. A huge market for cheap German linens for clothing slaves and poorer whites emerged in the colonies.

Furthermore, commercial restrictions imposed by the imperial states necessitated a shift of trade routes and a reorganization of trade structures. In order to successfully participate in the profitable new colonial markets, new supply networks had to be established and new trade routes developed. A direct trade between peripheral regions in Central Europe on the one hand and in the Americas on the other was prevented by the English Navigation Acts. German merchants had to make the detour via London until the independence of the United States. Then, for the first time, a direct legal trade without a detour opened up.

While the mercantilist policy aimed to reserve the profitable colonial trade for its inhabitants, the mercantilist population doctrine opened a hole in the wall by inviting qualified and prosperous foreigners to settle in the country. By settling in London, German merchants from the north-western linen regions interlinked the two peripheries by turning London into a place of transit.

Migration and settlement in Britain were part of a more comprehensive commercial networking strategy, which even included the other colonial empires. Expatriate communities in the leading European port cities maintained informal connections and thereby encouraged knowledge flows beyond the bilateral British-German connections, which allowed merchants to respond quickly to various challenges. Also, competitive challenges by the Irish and Scottish industries could be taken up quickly and new market niches could be exploited. Despite growing competition and the rise of cotton, German linens maintained considerable market shares for a longer time than is generally assumed. In all, although Germany did not become a colonial power until the second half of the nineteenth century, German merchants from the hinterlands contributed to the emergence of early modern global trade from the mid seventeenth century onwards.

10

Ambiguous Passages:
Non-Europeans Brought to Europe by the
Moravian Brethren during the Eighteenth Century

JOSEF KÖSTLBAUER[1]

Visitors to the Moravian meeting house in Zeist in the Netherlands find themselves in front of a remarkable painting: created in 1747 by the Moravian painter Johann Valentin Haidt, it became known as *The First Fruits*. At the center of the picture is Christ, sitting slightly elevated on a throne formed by clouds and framed by two adulating angels. Surrounding him are 21 individuals, adults as well as children, most of them of non-European origin. The composition, as well as the palm leaves in the figures' hands, signalize the eschatological theme of the painting, namely Revelation 7:9: 'after this I beheld, and, lo, a great multitude, which no man could number, of all nations, and kindreds, and people, and tongues, stood before the throne, and before the Lamb, clothed with white robes, and palms in their hands'.[2] The individuals depicted in Haidt's painting are not clad in white robes, however; some of them are wearing Moravian garb, while others are shown in their respective national attire – or at least, the artist's notion of it.[3] There is the Inuit Samuel Kajarnak in his fur and leather outfit; directly beside him, the Mingrelian Christian Thomas Mamucha is dressed in a generic Oriental costume featuring a turban and long frock coat. The Huron Thomas and the Mahican Johannes to the right and left of Christ are wearing nondescript leather robes, and Rachel and

1   This article is based on research produced during the research project, *The Holy Roman Empire of the German Nation and its Slaves* (2015–2020), which has received funding from the European Research Council (ERC) under the European Union's Horizon 2020 research and innovation program (grant agreement no. 641110).
2   Book of Revelation, Ch. 7, King James Bible.
3   For a thorough analysis, see R. Kröger, 'Die Erstlingsbilder in der Brüdergemeine', *Unitas Fratrum* 67/68 (2012), pp. 135–63.

Figure 10.1. Johann Valentin Haidt, *The First Fruits*, 1747

Anna Maria, two women from the Danish West Indies, are clothed in Moravian women's dresses.

This work is a prime example of Moravian eighteenth-century art. As such, it is also a product of the astonishing media system created by the Moravian Church during the eighteenth century, which encompassed handwritten and print media as well as pictorial media, and which served to foster a sense of connectedness and shared identity within a highly mobile community active around the globe.[4] The painting is also a source that clearly shows the Moravian community's global reach and the deep integration into the Atlantic World that Moravians had achieved by 1747. The fact that 12 of the depicted individuals were slaves, former slaves or captives is a clear indication of the Moravian Church's involvement in the early modern slave trade. Especially through their missionary activities in the West Indies and North America, Moravian towns in Europe became part of what Felix Brahm and Eve Rosenhaft have termed a 'slavery hinterland'.[5]

The Moravian Brethren, also known as *Unitas Fratrum* in Latin, or as *Herrnhuter* or *Evangelische Brüderunität* in German, were a pietistic community founded on 13 August 1727 in Upper Lusatia by the charismatic Count Nikolaus Ludwig von Zinzendorf, together with members of the old church of the Bohemian Brethren.[6] The latter had fled Habsburg Moravia to avoid religious persecution, and beginning in 1722 they found refuge on Zinzendorf's estates in the region of Upper Lusatia in south-eastern Saxony, where they began to establish a settlement.[7] The fledgling town's name was Herrnhut, and from this the community derived its German name. Starting from these unlikely beginnings, the Moravian community spawned numerous additional settlements (*Gemeinorte*) and smaller societies (*Sozietäten*) throughout Protestant Europe and North America – as well as missionary outposts in America, Africa and Asia – within a few decades. By the second half of the eighteenth century, the Moravian world reached from the Bay of Bengal to the Pennsylvanian back country. This global reach is also evidenced in the diverse geographic origins of the individuals depicted in the *First Fruits* painting.[8]

4   G. Mettele, *Weltbürgertum oder Gottesreich: Die Herrnhuter Brüdergemeine als globale Gemeinschaft 1727–1857* (Göttingen, 2009); G. Mettele, 'Identities across Borders: The Moravian Brethren as a Global Community', *Pietism and Community in Europe and North America, 1650–1850*, ed. J. Strom (Leiden/Boston, 2010) pp. 155–77.
5   F. Brahm and E. Rosenhaft, eds, *Slavery Hinterland: Transatlantic Slavery and Continental Europe, 1680–1850* (Woodbridge, 2016).
6   D. Meyer, *Zinzendorf und die Herrnhuter Brüdergemeine 1700–2000* (Göttingen, 2009), pp. 19ff; H.-J. Wollstadt, *Geordnetes Dienen in der christlichen Gemeinde* (Göttingen, 1966), pp. 24ff.
7   Emigration from Moravia to Herrnhut continued until 1732: U. Fischer, 'Die Entwicklung des Ortes Herrnhut bis 1760', *Graf ohne Grenzen: Leben und Werk von Nikolaus Ludwig Graf von Zinzendorf*, ed. P. Peucker and D. Meyer (Herrnhut, 2000), pp. 32ff.
8   For a list of settlements and mission stations, see Mettele, *Weltbürgertum*, pp. 277ff.

According to David Cranz's history of the Moravian Church, published in 1771, the occasion for the painting was the death of 'Johannes, the first fruit and teacher among the Mahicans'.[9] While all of the figures in the painting were representations of actual persons, only a scant few of them were personally known to Haidt or had been portrayed during their lifetimes.[10]

What is the meaning of the term 'first fruits'? The Moravians used it to designate the first converts of a people or place. Their missionary concept was not aimed at mass conversions; instead, Moravian missionaries were on the lookout for individual souls who had already been secretly prepared by Christ.[11] These converts occupied a special place in the Moravian culture of memory and remembrance. They were visible proof of the Moravian mission acting in accordance with Christ's plans, and they heralded the future redemption of all humanity. By means of paintings such as Haidt's, as well as through letters, diaries and journals read aloud during meetings, the names of the first fruits were made known throughout the Moravian world. Mediated communication brought these converts living in far-away peripheral places (from a European perspective) into the very center of the Moravian community. It established a virtual presence that helped to project visions of missionary success and communal identity.

But the Moravians did not leave it at that: from 1735 until the first half of the nineteenth century, they also brought individuals from mission areas to Europe. Of the 21 persons depicted in the *First Fruits* painting in Zeist, 14 had lived in Moravian towns in Europe or visited there for extended periods of time. And they were by no means the only ones: so far, in an ongoing research project, I have been able to identify 42 individuals who were sent to Moravian communities in Europe, traveled there of their own accord, or came into contact with them in other ways. It seems safe to assume that traces of several more such individuals can be found through further research in archives in the Netherlands, Denmark or England.[12]

The majority of these individuals – 24 men, women and children – were of African origin, with 17 of them coming to Europe from the Danish West

9   D. Cranz, *Alte und Neue Brüder-Historie oder kurz gefaßte Geschichte der Evangelischen Brüder-Unität in den älteren Zeiten insonderheit in dem gegenwärtigen Jahrhundert* (Barby, 1771), p. 454.
10   The Unity Archives in Herrnhut hold three versions of an explanation of the painting, one of them annotated by Zinzendorf: Unity Archives (hereafter: UA) R.15.A.2,1; UA R.15.A.2.2; UA R.15.A.2.3.
11   N. L. Zinzendorf, 'Die zwey und zwanzigste Rede, von denen Ursachen, warum die Ungläubigen vornehmen und gelehrten, noch ungerner mit dem Heilande zu thun haben wollen als andere', *Hauptschriften in sechs Bänden*, ed. E. Beyreuther and G. Meyer (Hildesheim, 1962/63), pp. 170–82, esp. pp. 172ff.
12   Paul Peucker published a pioneering article in 2007 in which he identified 31 non-Europeans living in Moravian communities in Germany. See P. Peucker, 'Aus allen Nationen: Nichteuropäer in den deutschen Brüdergemeinden des 18. Jahrhunderts', *Unitas Fratrum* 59/60 (2007), pp. 1–35.

Indies. There were also Native Americans from Suriname and Berbice, as well as Inuit from Greenland and Labrador. The influx of converts was not a purely Atlantic affair, however: a boy and a woman from the Malabar Coast, a Tatar from Kazan, a Persian, an Armenian and an Ottoman Turk are likewise documented.[13]

Although not all of the non-Europeans traveling in the Moravian orbit were slaves, many of them did have their roots in the maelstrom of the Atlantic slave trade. But no matter where they came from, or whether they were slaves or free individuals, men or women, adults or children, servants or laborers – as aliens in foreign surroundings, they found themselves deeply dependent on those who had brought them there, and their legal and social status remained ambiguous. One might object that there is nothing ambiguous about slavery, but it did not always take the form of chattel slavery as practiced in the early modern plantation economy. Especially for European societies that did not consider themselves slave-holding societies, it is often difficult to determine the status of enslaved people brought there.[14]

This chapter attempts to sketch the muddled borderlands inhabited by these individuals, as well as by their Moravian masters/brethren. They are border-lands not only in the sense of colonial and imperial peripheries, but also in the sense of vague and contested legal and social delineations between free and unfree, between slavery, serfdom and servitude, experienced by many (if not all) of them.

Furthermore, the Moravian case highlights a peculiar dimension of the metropolis-periphery dynamics at work in the Atlantic World, in that the Brethren were operating in the Atlantic World, but not necessarily along familiar spatial structures. While Moravian missionaries and colonists as well as Moravian servants and slaves moved along the trading routes and established nodes of early modern Atlantic space, they created their own Moravian space in which places in Lusatia, Saxony, could feel much closer to Greenland or the West Indies than to London, Paris or Vienna. The Moravian community's use of media and communication in particular served to reduce distance, drawing peripheral locations on either side of the Atlantic closer together.

During Zinzendorf's lifetime (1700–1760), the centers of the Moravian community were such disparate towns as Herrnhut in Upper Lusatia, Marienborn and Herrnhaag (1738–1753) in the Wetterau, a region in Hesse north-east of Frankfurt, Zeist in the Netherlands (1745), Lindsey Hall near London (1752) and Bethlehem in Pennsylvania (1741). While some of these

13   On Ernst Albert Christiani, formerly Mustafa, see G. Philipp, 'Integrationsprobleme im 18. Jahrhundert: Ein Türke am Weimarer Hofe und bei den Herrnhutern', *Pietismus und Neuzeit* 33 (2007), pp. 99–127.

14   R. v. Mallinckrodt, 'There are no Slaves in Prussia?', *Slavery Hinterland*, ed. Brahm and Rosenhaft, pp. 109–33, here pp. 109ff.

places definitely *were* centers of the Atlantic World, others were situated at its margins – but what was peripheral in a wider Atlantic context could be central to the Moravian community and the spiritual and communitarian space it occupied.

The Moravian Brethren and slavery

It was their missionary activity that brought the Moravians into contact with slavery: starting in 1732, their first missionary endeavor took them to the Danish Caribbean islands of St Thomas, St Croix and St Jan.[15] Within a few years, they transitioned from preaching to the slaves to being slaveholders themselves, and soon expanded their activities to further slave-holding regions like Suriname, Berbice, South Africa, Pennsylvania, North Carolina, Antigua and Jamaica. As early as 1738, the Moravians acquired their first plantation on St Thomas, later named Posaunenberg, which came with nine slaves.[16]

Moravians neither questioned slavery as an institution nor did they hesitate to partake in it.[17] Whatever feelings individual Moravians may have harbored regarding slavery, the community's leadership was well aware that a position of acquiescence was a prerequisite for missionary work in places like St Thomas or Suriname, where slave owners were initially violently opposed to missionary activities amongst their slaves. Upon leaving St Thomas after a short visit to the island in 1739, Count Zinzendorf gave a well-known farewell speech in which he defined the slaves' position as God-given and exhorted them to

15   P. Vogt, 'Die Mission der Herrnhuter Brüdergemeinde und ihre Bedeutung für den Neubeginn der protestantischen Missionen am Ende des 18. Jahrhunderts', *Pietismus und Neuzeit* 35 (2009), pp. 204–36.

16   For a Moravian account of how the missionaries acquired slaves and plantations, see C. G. A. Oldendorp, *Geschichte der Mission der evangelischen Brüder auf den caraibischen Inseln S. Thomas, S. Croix und S. Jan* (Barby, 1777), pp. 106f, 555ff. A near-contemporary Moravian account of events is UA R.15.B.a.3.31, *Historia wie die mährischen Brüder [...] zur Plantage mit Sclaven gekommen*, 1738 (copy of original dating to 1755).

17   For details on the Moravian discourse on slavery, see J. F. Sensbach, '"Don't Teach My Negroes to Be Pietists": Pietism and the Roots of the Black Protestant Church', *Pietism in Germany and North America 1680–1820*, ed. J. Strom, H. Lehmann and J. Van Horn Melton (Leyden, 2009), pp. 183–98; J. Hüsgen, *Mission und Sklaverei: Die Herrnhuter Brüdergemeine und die Sklavenemanzipation in Britisch- und Dänisch-Westindien* (Stuttgart, 2016); K. Gerbner, *Christian Slavery: Conversion and Race in the Protestant Atlantic World* (Philadelphia, 2018); J. Cronshagen, 'Owning the Body, Wooing the Soul: How Forced Labor Was Justified in the Moravian Correspondence Network in Eighteenth-Century Surinam', *Connecting Worlds and People: Early Modern Diasporas*, ed. D. Freist and S. Lachenicht (London/New York, 2016); C. Füllberg-Stolberg, 'Die Herrnhuter Mission: Sklaverei und Sklavenemanzipation in der Karibik', *Sklaverei und Zwangsarbeit zwischen Akzeptanz und Widerstand*, ed. E. Herrmann-Otto, M. Simonis and A. Trefz (Hildesheim, 2011) pp. 254–80; J. C. S. Mason, *The Moravian Church and the Missionary Awakening in England, 1760–1800* (Woodbridge/Rochester, 2001), pp. 100ff.

patiently submit to their lot.[18] Such statements did not result purely from political prudence: there is no evidence that the Moravian community as a whole (or individual members) ever contemplated a condemnation of slavery – on the contrary, numerous sources make it very clear that slavery continued to be accepted.[19]

The Moravian Brethren owned and bought slaves for various reasons: whether working on plantations, in the household or as craftsmen, slaves provided the economic support required for missionary activity. Sometimes enslaved members of a mission congregation were bought by missionaries to prevent them from being sold to a far-away place – essentially, this was a way of keeping a congregation intact. A number of such cases are documented; Zinzendorf, for example, initiated the purchase of two converts, Andreas and Johannes, who had been sold from St Thomas to the neighboring island of St Croix.[20] Andreas eventually accompanied Zinzendorf to Europe and traveled to Herrnhaag, Marienborn, Herrnhut, Zeist, London and Bethlehem as a member of the count's entourage.[21] Furthermore, enslaved individuals were acquired by missionaries or Moravian visitors because they regarded them as prospective converts or community members. In 1756, for instance, the Moravian ship captain Nicholas Garrison brought a nine-year-old boy named Fortune to Germany from Suriname, because he 'recognized his pleasant, cheerful, and honest character … and thought he might thrive for the Savior'.[22]

Despite its involvement with slavery, the Moravian mission is notable for the equality practiced within the community. Becoming a member of the community meant being integrated into a group that treated all members as brothers and sisters, regardless of race, class, legal status or gender.[23] Free and enslaved converts alike could become 'helpers' or 'elders', playing a role in the congregation's spiritual and material life. Some non-European members even achieved clerical positions: Maria Andresen and Rebecca Freundlich, for example, were both ordained as deaconesses in Germany in 1745 and 1746.[24]

18   UA R.15.B.a.3.64, Zinzendorf's farewell address, 15 February 1739, pp. 21f.
19   Hüsgen, *Mission*, pp. 119ff; A. G. Spangenberg, *Von der Arbeit der evangelischen Brüder unter den Heiden* (Barby, 1782), pp. 62ff.
20   Oldendorp, *Geschichte der Mission*, p. 590. Zinzendorf's own account in UA R.15.B.a.2.a.3, Diarium des sel. Jüngers von seiner Reise nach Thomas zu Ende 1738 u. anfangs 1739, p. 21.
21   Peucker, 'Aus allen Nationen', pp. 23f.
22   Gemeinarchiv Niesky, 27 March 1763, Lebenslauf Fortune.
23   This has recently been emphasized by H. Raphael-Hernandez, 'The Right to Freedom: Eighteenth-Century Slave Resistance and Early Moravian Missions in the Danish West Indies and Dutch Suriname', *Atlantic Studies* 14/4 (2017), pp. 457–75, here p. 459.
24   For Rebecca Freundlich's (later Protten) biography, see J. F. Sensbach, *Rebecca's Revival: Creating Black Christianity in the Atlantic World* (Cambridge, 2006); on Maria Andresen, see Peucker, 'Aus allen Nationen', pp. 1ff.

The result of the Moravian mission and the integration of enslaved individuals
into Moravian congregations was a remarkable situation: a convert could be a
respected sister or brother, and could even assume important functions while
living in close community with his or her European brothers and sisters. At the
same time, however, some of these black Moravians were also the legal property
of their white brothers and sisters.

Ambiguous journeys

Eighteenth-century Europeans were hardly sedentary, with their spatial mobility
depending on factors like profession, social status, age, gender and faith.[25] But
even in this context, the mobility of members of the Moravian community
was extraordinary: they were apt to change occupation, place of residence
and their role within the community multiple times during their lives. This
was especially true for the missionaries, both male and female, many of whom
were transferred from one mission area to another every few years. But other
members were likewise asked or directed to join different Moravian settlements
where their skills might be needed. Count Zinzendorf led such an itinerant life
as well, constantly traveling between locations in Germany, the Netherlands and
Britain. He even journeyed to the New World twice: to the Danish West Indies
in 1739 and to British North America in 1741 to 1743. The group consisting
of Zinzendorf's household, staff and collaborators was called the *Pilgerhaus*
(Pilgrim's House).

        With the commencement of the Moravian mission among slaves and the
Moravians' concomitant involvement in slavery, enslaved individuals were also
included in the constant transferrals within the ever-expanding spatial network
of Moravian communities. Insofar as they occurred in the context of their
communal mobility, it is difficult to ascertain whether the slaves' travels were
voluntary or involuntary, or the degree to which they had a say in them.

        An example is provided by Maria Andresen. In 1742, the church leadership
decided to send her from St Thomas to Bethlehem, where she was to marry the
aforementioned Andreas, who had become a part of the *Pilgerhaus* and was
once again crossing the Atlantic in the count's entourage, this time to North
America. Both as a member of the congregation and as a slave, Maria had to
follow decisions made by others. Already a vice-elder in the St Thomas slave
congregation, she had been bought from her original owner by the Moravian
missionaries in 1741 to facilitate her marriage to Andreas.[26] The fact that the

25 H. Gräf and R. Pröve, *Wege ins Ungewisse: Reisen in der Frühen Neuzeit 1500–1800*
(Frankfurt, 1997), pp. 37ff.
26 UA R.15.B.a.4.12, letter to Zinzendorf regarding the purchase of Maria, 12 September 1742.
For more information on Maria, see Peucker, 'Aus allen Nationen', pp. 1ff.

marriage was prearranged had nothing to do with the couple being enslaved, since marriages within the congregation were generally arranged by seniors in the church hierarchy.[27]

Such transatlantic relocations were usually triggered by the motivations and interests of the Moravian leadership. The available sources provide no indication of how Maria reacted to being told she would have to leave St Thomas, but it was likely not an easy situation for her – she left behind three children born into an earlier relationship, as well as her other relatives.[28] Then again, she may have considered it an honor and welcomed the prestige associated with marrying someone living close to Zinzendorf. Perhaps she was also excited at the prospect of visiting the spiritual center of the community in Marienborn and Herrnhaag. But what if she trembled at the thought of never seeing her children again? What if she secretly feared isolation and utter dependency, living among strangers in a strange country? This is speculation, of course, but certainly not far-fetched; given the bias of Moravian sources, I would go so far as to call it appropriate.

An interesting twist is added to Maria's story by a short document now kept in the Unity Archives in Herrnhut, in which Friedrich Martin, a missionary in St Thomas, states that Maria was able to marry because her former husband had passed away. In an almost passing remark, she is described as having been 'brought into freedom' ('in Freiheit gesetzt') by the Brethren, and a few lines later as 'completely free, single, and unwed'.[29] The document is unique: while a number of bills of sale documenting Moravians purchasing slaves have survived, Martin's attestation is the only one I know of that describes the transaction as setting the slave free. In the *Büdingische Sammlung* (of 1745), the document is reprinted under the title, 'Letter of Manumission of the Negro-Eldress'.[30] The receipt for the sale of Maria by her master Johan Uytendal, which has likewise survived in the Unity Archives, does not mention her freedom being bought.[31] Similarly, the sources describing the purchase and ownership of Maria's prospective husband, Andreas, who was bought to prevent his separation from the congregation (see above), never imply him being manumitted.[32] Nor

---

27   On Moravian ideas on marriage and sexuality, see P. Peucker, 'In the Blue Cabinet: Moravians, Marriage, and Sex', *Journal of Moravian History* 10 (2011), pp. 7–37; P. Vogt, 'Zinzendorf's "Seventeen Points of Matrimony": A Fundamental Document on the Moravian Understanding of Marriage and Sexuality', *Journal of Moravian History* 10 (2011), pp. 38–67.

28   UA R.22.10.37, Andresen Maria, undated.

29   UA R.15.B.a.11.232, attestation regarding Maria, 10 November 1742.

30   'Frey-Brief der Neger-Aeltestin', *Büdingische Sammlung einiger in die Kirchen-Historie einschlagender sonderlich neuerer Schriften*, ed. Nikolaus Ludwig Zinzendorf (Leipzig/Büdingen, 1744/45), pp. 480f.

31   UA R.15.B.a.4.12.

32   UA R.15.B.a.11.3, purchase of Bertel (Andreas) and Peter, 10 February 1739; UA R.15.b.a.3.82, Johan Lorentz Carsten's letter of purchase for Deknadel Plantation, 29 July 1739.

is Maria ever described as manumitted and free in later documents – not even in her brief *Lebenslauf* (she died in Herrnhaag in 1749).[33]

A look at the marriage laws of eighteenth-century Pennsylvania provides some clarification. In Pennsylvania, slaves were subject to laws prohibiting servants to marry without their masters' consent. According to a succession of Acts regulating marriages in the colony, proof of the prospective partners' freedom from any prior engagements had to be furnished by way of a certificate 'from credible persons where they have lived or do live'.[34] This was the purpose of the document signed by Friedrich Martin. The assertion that Maria had been freed does not seem to have been strictly necessary, but perhaps the Brethren wished to make sure no legal objection against the marriage could be raised. Unfortunately, no similar certificate concerning Andreas exists, which supports the assumption that he legally remained a slave.

The Moravians bought Maria for a specific reason, namely because they intended to marry her to Andreas in Bethlehem. There is no indication that guaranteeing her individual freedom or personal autonomy was part of the motivation for this transaction – but then again, such a concept of freedom was not a feature of early modern German society, and even less so in a tightly organized and close-knit religious community. Indeed, obedience to what was considered the Savior's plan and the decisions made accordingly by the Moravian leadership was a central element of becoming and being a Moravian. From a Moravian point of view, Maria's legal status was presumably irrelevant as long as she remained an obedient member of the community. Aside from the document mentioned above, there are no other sources describing Maria as free or mentioning her former slave status.

The question of how Maria defined and interpreted her obligations to the Brethren and what she thought about the marriage arranged for her will have to remain unanswered. It seems important to point out one thing, however: to her and her husband Andreas, it must have been glaringly obvious where they came from and that their experiences and former lives were quite distinct from those of the European-born sisters and brothers they lived with in Bethlehem and the Wetterau. And whatever Friedrich Martin's attestation of Maria's freedom meant to the different parties concerned, Maria and Andreas must have known that they were utterly dependent on their Moravian surroundings.

A rare glimpse of the perceptions of a slave brought into the Moravian community is provided by the *Lebenslauf* of Christian Gottfried, formerly known as London, a West African man who was born in Guinea around 1731 and died in Bethlehem in 1756. The *Lebensläufe* (memoirs) are short

---

33   UA R.22.10.37.
34   'An Act for the Preventing of Clandestine Marriages, 28 October 1701', *Statutes at Large of Pennsylvania* 2, pp. 161f; 'A Supplement to the Act Entitled "An Act for Preventing Clandestine Marriages"', 14 February 1729/30, *Statutes at Large of Pennsylvania* 4, pp. 152ff.

autobiographical accounts intended to be read at a person's funeral. Essentially intended for the edification of posterity, they are highly formalized and stereotypical. Such memoirs are rare for non-European members of the congregation, and those that do exist were usually written by others and kept very short. Christian Gottfried's *Lebenslauf* is slightly longer, however, covering four pages. We do not know how and when he was enslaved, but he was apparently transported to the West Indies and from there to London on an English slave ship. He was sold into the household of a Mr Jones, a member of the Fetter Lane Society, who eventually gave him to Zinzendorf in 1749. Whether the count expected such a 'present' remains unknown, but he seemingly had little use for the man, and in May 1750, London was sent to Bethlehem with a large group of Moravian emigrants.[35] Judging from a terse statement in the source, London did not relish being sent to the American back country. The author of the *Lebenslauf* describes what was probably a very understandable expression of opposition and resentment as London's 'wild and evil ways'. However, he eventually seems to have resigned himself to his fate, consisting of hard work in the tannery. On 23 December 1751 he was baptized Christian Gottfried, and in 1753 he was transferred to the tiny Moravian outpost of Christiansbrunn located a few miles north of Bethlehem. He eventually died of an illness in Bethlehem on 4 January 1756.[36]

Consigned to one of the peripheries of the Atlantic World, Christian Gottfried seems to have cultivated the notion of a special relationship to Zinzendorf, based on the fact that he was technically the count's slave. He referred to him as his master and even wrote letters to him, allegedly expressing the wish to meet him again. Zinzendorf reacted at least once, sending Christian Gottfried a present in 1755. The *Lebenslauf* dedicates only a few sentences to this aspect, creating the impression of quaint, childlike devotion that is typical of early modern representations of master-servant relationships. It is feasible, however, that Christian Gottfried used the fact that he had originally been given to Count Zinzendorf to create for himself an imaginary tie connecting him to the center of the Moravian community, or to the hurly-burly of the London metropolis. Ostensibly, this makes sense as a strategy to enhance his status, however futile such an attempt may have been. But it may also have been due to the memory of a better or more interesting place and life, held dear by a man relegated to a back-breaking job in an American back country region.[37]

Unlike Maria and Andreas or Rebecca Freundlich, all of whom attained a modestly privileged position within the Moravian community,

---

35   For a list of the colonists traveling with the 'Henry Jorde Company', including 'London (a negro from London)', see J. W. Jordan, 'Moravian Immigration to Pennsylvania, 1734–1767', *Transactions of the Moravian Historical Society* 5/2 (1896), pp. 51–90, here pp. 74f.
36   UA R.22.143.3, Christian Gottfried alias London, 4 January 1756.
37   Ibid.

London/Christian Gottfried seems to have remained a slave. That certainly also had to do with the fact that he wound up in a North American colony, where slavery was common within Moravian settlements. There is little ambiguity to be found in his case; all of Gottfried's transatlantic passages were forced travels. And if he hoped to be able to return to England one day, he did so in vain.

Native Americans and Inuit

The trafficking of enslaved Native Americans to Europe has received little attention so far.[38] This is remarkable, since there has been a lot of research on Native American slavery and the enslavement of Native Americans by Europeans in recent years. Native American slaves also entered the Moravian orbit. Stopping in St Eustatius during his voyage to St Thomas in 1739, Zinzendorf acquired two Native Americans. We do not know how he met them. One of the two young men, named Sam, is described as an 'Anakunkas Indian from Boston in New England'.[39] Native American captives were common enough in New England's port cities, since the New England colonies as well as the province of New York were tied into a transcontinental trading network through which horses, humans and European commodities were exchanged. For all we know, Sam may have hailed from the Great Plains or some other far-away place, with New England simply being his last stop before being transported to St Eustatius.[40] The other Native American slave boy is described by Zinzendorf simply as a 'little Indian from the island where bishop Gervaise was killed'.[41] Since Nicolas Gervais de Labrid was killed in the Orinoco area (and not on an island), the boy may have been of mainland Carib (Kalina) extraction.[42]

38 Exceptions are C. F. Feest, ed., *Indians and Europe: An Interdisciplinary Collection of Essays* (Lincoln/London, 1999); J. Weaver, *Red Atlantic: American Indigenes and the Making of the Modern World 1000–1927* (Chapel Hill, 2014); N. E. van Deusen, *Global Indios: The Indigenous Struggle for Justice in Sixteenth-Century Spain* (Durham/London, 2015).
39 UA R.15.B.a.11.19, copy of receipt for Indian Sam from Boston, 27 February 1739; a Native American nation known as Anakunkas could not be identified. In an unrelated source, Zinzendorf wrote of the Anakunkas in Canada, but no such nation is known there either; besides, the Moravians used the term 'Canada' very unspecifically. See Zinzendorf, *Ein und zwanzig Discurse über die Augspurgische Confession: Gehalten vom 15. December 1747 bis zum 3. Mart. 1748 denen Seminariis theologicis fratrum zum Besten aufgefaßt und bis zur nochmaligen Revision des Auctoris einstweilen mitgetheilet* (1748), p. 125.
40 C. G. Calloway, *One Vast Winter Count: The Native American West before Lewis and Clark* (Lincoln, 2003) pp. 316ff; R. E. Desrochers, 'Slave-for-Sale Advertisements and Slavery in Massachusetts, 1704–1781', *The William and Mary Quarterly* 59 (2002), pp. 623–64.
41 UA R.15.B.a.2.a.3, p. 39; UA R.15.B.a.11.19, receipt for the purchase of a 'garcon indien insulaire', 27 February 1739.
42 'H. Gelskerke to the Governor-General of Martinique, 2 March 1730', *Extracts from Archives*, United States Commission on Boundary between Venezuela and British Guiana (1897), pp. 251–3.

Contrary to initial plans, the two Native Americans were not taken to Europe but to St Thomas, where they remained for the rest of their short lives. Both died in 1739. According to a terse statement by Oldendorp, the nameless boy seems to have actively opposed his enslavement. Sam, the mysterious Anakunkas, was held in higher regard; he eventually made it into the *First Fruits* painting.[43]

The Moravians also brought at least two Arawak from Berbice to Europe. One of them, a boy named Janke, had a life that was short but typical for the Moravian transatlantic world, touching both Atlantic peripheries and metropolitan regions. There is mention of him being born to an Arawak mother and a European father.[44] He was 'gifted' to Moravian missionaries in 1741 or 1742 and, as a talented translator, became a valuable asset. Janke was brought to Bethlehem in 1748, allegedly of his own professed volition. There, he was baptized by Zinzendorf's son-in-law Johannes Watteville and christened Johannes Renatus. He joined Watteville and his company on their journey back to Europe in 1749 and was taken to London, Zeist and Herrnhaag before eventually being sent to the Moravian children's home in Hennersdorf in 1751, where he died of smallpox.[45]

His legal status remains unclear. The Moravian missionaries in Suriname and Berbice worked among sovereign Arawak communities. Arawak people were sometimes enslaved as captives, but since we know nothing about Janke's parents with certainty, it is impossible to determine whether only his mother or both his parents were captives. However, an Arawak child moving in the Moravian Atlantic was obviously in a position of comprehensive dependency.

Clearly *not* slaves were five Inuit from Greenland who did a circuit of Atlantic Moravian communities between 1747 and 1749, visiting Amsterdam, Zeist, Herrnhaag, Herrnhut, Ebersdorf, London, Philadelphia and Bethlehem before returning home to Greenland.[46] According to the Moravian chronicler David Cranz, these three men and two women traveled of their own volition, having 'expressed a desire to see Christianity'.[47] Indeed, there is a record from 1741 of Pussimek, later christened Sara, stating her wish to visit the congregation in Europe.[48] They seem to have had little influence on the itinerary, however.

---

43 UA R.15.A.2.1; both cases are discussed in Peucker, 'Aus allen Nationen', p. 8.

44 UA R.22.05.28, Johannes Renatus, 16 October 1751.

45 UA R.22.1.a.69, Ludwig Christoph Dähne, 1769; Moravian Archives Bethlehem, Diarium Bethlehem, Vol. 7, 1748, pp. 228, 778ff; UA GN.1749.2.XXXIX–LII, Gemeinnachrichten 1749, Diarien Reisegemeinde, pp. 306ff; UA GN.1750.Bd.1.I–XII, Gemeinnachrichten 1750, p. 318; UA R.22.05.28.

46 D. Cranz, *Historie von Grönland: Enthaltend die Beschreibung des Landes und der Einwohner &c. insbesondere die Geschichte der dortigen Mission der Evangelischen Brüder zu Neu-Herrnhut und Lichtenfels* (Barby, 1765), pp. 673ff. The Moravian mission to Greenland was their second missionary endeavor after the West Indian mission. It began in 1733. See ibid., pp. 409ff.

47 Ibid., p. 673.

48 J. Beck, 'Brief aus Grönland an den in Teutschland sich befindenden Boten an die Grönländer Matthäus Stachen (Schreiben vom 14 Juli 1741, aus Neu-Herrnhut in Grönland)', *Büdingische Sammlung*, pp. 215–19, esp. p. 217.

Apparently, they were meant to stay in Europe for only a few months and return before the onset of winter, because the missionaries – here assuming the role of 'experts' – were concerned that the warm climate and unaccustomed diet might harm them. Due to organizational difficulties, the Greenlanders' journey ended up lasting much longer than expected.[49]

While their freedom was never subject to debate, as recent converts the five Inuit were nevertheless perceived in ways similar to individuals from the West Indies or North America. The rhetoric of the mission turned all such individuals – free or unfree – into children, 'braune Herzeln' (brown darlings) to be lovingly guided and sometimes cajoled along on the path to Christ. And as children, they were obviously dependent on their elders, who were more experienced in the ways of the world and Christian religion. In addition, people like the five Inuit were naturally dependent on the Moravian Brethren for their survival in foreign lands, and it was Moravians who eventually decided where they went, what they did there, and when they could return home.

Children

Age is a further aspect to be considered. Of the 42 non-European persons identified so far, 17 were children or adolescents, and an additional four were offspring of non-European parents born in European settlements.[50] In some cases, the sources straightforwardly report children as having been bought, proving that they came into the Moravian community as slaves. In fact, the first person brought to Europe from the West Indies by the Moravians was a boy of about seven by the name of Carmel, who accompanied the missionary Leonhard Dober from St Thomas to Germany.[51] According to Oldendorp, he had been bought by the missionaries, but the author provides no further information on the circumstances.[52] Carmel is also depicted in the *First Fruits* painting; he is one of the two boys in white jackets in the lower mid-section of the painting.[53]

During the visit to St Thomas mentioned above, Zinzendorf himself acquired several children: in addition to the Native American boy discussed earlier, there were Andres (about two years old) and the four-year-old girl Anna Gratia, with

49   Cranz, *Historie von Grönland*, p. 674.
50   Concerning children, see also Peucker, 'Aus allen Nationen', p. 11.
51   For Carmel, originally named Oly and baptized Joshua, see ibid., pp. 29f. Leonhard Dober, a potter by profession, was one of the first two missionaries ever sent out by the Moravians. He served in St Thomas from 1732 to 1735. Carmel's story is also referred to in Gerbner, *Christian Slavery*.
52   Oldendorp, *Geschichte der Mission*, p. 492.
53   UA R.15.A.2.1, Erklärung des Gemäldes von den Heiden-Erstlingen, 1747.

the latter destined to be a companion to Zinzendorf's daughter Benigna.[54] Anna Gratia and Andres were transported to Amsterdam together in 1739 on a ship owned by Johann Lorentz Carstens; they arrived in Marienborn in August of the same year. Another girl or young woman named Cecilia was supposed to be acquired for Zinzendorf's wife, the Countess Erdmuthe Dorothea, but the deal was called off when Carstens and his wife decided to keep her in their own household in Copenhagen.[55]

Amongst the children in the *First Fruits* painting is a boy named Jupiter, an eight-year-old who was purchased by the Moravian bishop David Nitschmann in New York in 1736. Jupiter was baptized in Herrnhut on 11 January 1739 and henceforth known as Emanuel. In Zinzendorf's explanation of the painting, he is described as being from Carolina; but in one of the three versions of the document in the archives of Herrnhut, he is mentioned as hailing from New York.[56] On the one hand, it is entirely feasible that the boy was born in Carolina and later brought to New York: David Nitschmann had been traveling from Georgia to New York in 1736, and he may have bought Jupiter either in Carolina or in New York before leaving the colonies.[57] On the other hand, the discrepancy may be a simple mistake resulting from ignorance. Like other owners of slaves, the Moravians apparently were not overly concerned with the origins of trafficked people. The involuntary mobilization and 'commodification' of human beings inherent in the slave trade practically turned them into people without home or origin.

Not all cases are so straightforward, however. Particularly in connection with children, rather diffuse wording was often used. Children are frequently mentioned as being 'given' or 'gifted' to Moravians, either by their parents or by other responsible adults. In May 1742 in London, for instance, George Whitefield[58] gave a 12-year-old black boy named Andrew to the Brethren, 'to bring him up for the Lord and to dispose of him as they shall find fit'.[59] Whitefield had brought Andrew along from South Carolina, where he had received him from the boy's own mother. The only certain fact in this case is that Andrew was in a situation of absolute dependency. Decisions about his future were made by virtual strangers who may have had no title to him but were

---

54 For Andres and Anna Gratia, see UA R.15.B.a.2.a.3, p. 39; UA R.15.B.a.1.IV.2.b, Zinzendorf to Carstens, 1 March 1740.

55 There ensued a bitter quarrel between the Zinzendorfs and Carstens that caused Carstens' estrangement, thus depriving the Moravians of an influential and rich patron. For a brief overview, see Peucker, 'Aus allen Nationen', pp. 7f.

56 UA R.15.A.2.1.

57 Cranz, *Alte und Neue Brüder-Historie*, pp. 251, 254.

58 George Whitefield, famous preacher of the Great Awakening, friend of George and Thomas Wesley, and intimately connected to the Fetter Lane Society for some time. See C. Podmore, *The Moravian Church in England, 1728–1760* (Oxford/New York, 1998).

59 Cited according to ibid., p. 83. Podmore's sources are UA R.13.C.1.6 and Fetter Lane Daily Helpers' Conference, DHC 4, 26 May and 9 June 1742.

obviously considered to be his masters and to have the right and obligation to decide on his behalf. Whitefield himself may have had qualms about the entire affair, since he asked the Moravians to return the boy to him in December 1743, prior to another trip to America. But the Brethren declined, having already placed him in the *Kinderanstalt* in Marienborn.[60]

The 'giving' of a child may be considered a transfer of responsibility and was tied to certain expectations, like the provision of support and education. In the context of early modern society, this practice can be understood as a strategy of providing for a child – of giving it access to all-important social networks. Thus, a child like Andrew could find himself in a position not unlike that of European-born children sent away to learn a trade, receive an education or earn their own keep. In November 1742, it was decided that Andrew was to learn a trade; he was sent to a shoemaker.[61]

This was obviously a position of dependency, albeit a dependency that could be expected to end when the child had come of age or when training/schooling was considered complete. But what about a child of African descent from South Carolina? Would he or she be considered permanently bound to the Moravian community in some sort of serfdom? Or would he be considered a free man when his training was finished, able to go wherever he pleased? Such questions never arose in this case, however, as Andrew died in Marienborn in 1744.[62]

Conclusion

Whether free or unfree, the persons brought to Moravian communities in Europe and Bethlehem in North America were assigned a specific role in the enactment of Moravian (self-)representation. First of all, they were symbols of the success of the Moravians' missionary endeavors. The physical presence of such persons, their ability to speak of their conversion, and their relationship with the Savior clearly demonstrated the success of Count Zinzendorf's vision. Visitors to Herrnhaag or Zeist in the 1740s will have seen foreigners from different parts of the globe – some in plain but well-made Moravian dress, others in their national costumes. They may even have been able to observe the Inuit Simon demonstrating his kayaking skills in the ditch surrounding the palace in Zeist, or gape at the 'Moorish couple', Andreas and Maria.[63]

---

60   Ibid., p. 87; D. Bentham, *Memoirs of James Hutton: Comprising the Annals of his Life, and Connection with the United Brethren* (London, 1856), pp. 81f; UA R.8.33.b.3, 1742, Kurzes Diarium der Gemeine des Lammes in der Wetterau, vom Jahr 1742; UA R.8.33.b.2.b, Continuatio des Gemein Diarii zu Herrnhaag vom 14 May 1742 an.
61   UA R.8.33.b.2.c, Diarium Herrnhaag, 1 November 1742 to 31 January 1743.
62   UA R.8.33.d.5, Diarium Marienborn, 9 August 1744.
63   On kayaking, see UA R.10.A.b.2.a, Diarium Zeist, 12 August 1747.

The symbolic value of these non-Europeans was multiplied by the Moravians' media strategy, notably through the use of visual media. Their portraits hung beside those of other members of the congregation on the walls of meeting halls or the rooms used by Zinzendorf. The effect of their presence – both real and virtual – can hardly be overestimated in the context of a baroque culture that comprehended the world through allegories, parables and analogies. To underline the significance of the function of these living symbols, I will introduce the concept of 'representation labor'. The task of these Africans, West Indians, Native Americans and other 'exotic' foreigners in the Moravian communities in Europe was to increase the status of the community and to represent the ideal of worldwide community, both for outsiders and for Moravians themselves. There may have been a distinct spatial component to the way this worked: while a West Indian couple like Maria and Andreas probably did not cause much of a stir in places like eighteenth-century London or Amsterdam, their representative value may have been much higher in the European periphery, in places like Marienborn and Herrnhaag in the Wetterau, or in Herrnhut and Niesky in Saxony. This idea should not be overstated, however; after all, even in very cosmopolitan environments, the presence of non-European converts could effectively transport a message of missionary success. Nevertheless, the impression created was surely different and probably more intense in the 'newly globalized' peripheries.

Furthermore, it seems reasonable to assume that members of mission congregations in the West Indies were especially interested in learning about fellow black Moravians doing important work in Europe. This was something actively fostered and encouraged through the reading of diaries and letters from far-away congregations during community meetings. In this sense, non-European sisters and brothers presented a sort of imaginary link between colonial and European peripheral regions of the Moravian Atlantic World.

As far as the individual men, women and children themselves are concerned, their significance increased the ambivalence of their own positions. They were highly visible and highly regarded – though this regard was not necessarily for who they were but for the role they fulfilled, a role that they had little choice but to accept.

Moravian sources pose a methodological challenge, since they maintain a peculiar silence regarding the legal status of non-Europeans and the perception of slavery. In the cases of many brothers, sisters and children brought to Europe from the West Indies, Suriname, Berbice, or British North America by the Moravians, it hardly seems possible to say with any certainty who was a slave and who was free, where and when the latter may have gained that freedom, or what it meant. This veil of silence can be partly lifted by comparison with other contemporary cases, as well as through a close reading of texts and rhetorical analysis. As was often the case at the time, not everything was deemed worthy of being committed to paper, and matters of legal and social status may have been perfectly clear to the contemporaries concerned. Therefore, we must always ask ourselves what was left unsaid or remained outside the discourse represented in sources.

The presence of unfree persons within Moravian communities in Europe vividly demonstrates the existence of practices and routes of slavery and slave trafficking in early modern Europe, even in regions far removed from the Atlantic seaboard. In a very real sense, Moravian mobility across American and European (as well as Asian and African) spaces meant that Moravian communities and their *Gemeinorte* everywhere became slavery hinterlands.[64] Whether this extends the boundaries of the Atlantic World into regions like eastern Saxony or challenges the Atlantic paradigm in favor of a global one remains an open question, however.

64   F. Brahm and E. Rosenhaft, 'Introduction: Towards a Comprehensive European History of Slavery and Abolition', *Slavery Hinterland*, ed. Brahm and Rosenhaft, pp. 1–23, here pp. 3ff.

11

German Emigrants as a Commodity in the Eighteenth-Century Atlantic World

ALEXANDRA GITTERMANN

When analyzing the type of commodities that found their way from the peripheries into the Atlantic economy during the early modern period and how they did so, it is important to bear in mind that not only goods but also human beings were bought and sold. Whereas the African slave trade is obviously an essential and well explored subject in this respect, the economic structures underlying the trade in European – in this case, German – migrants are not exactly an entirely new research field.[1] However, they remain a lesser-known part of the story that should be borne in mind when answering the question of just how both goods and people from Central European regions were integrated into the transatlantic trading system.

Involving an estimated 100,000 people, German emigration to North America during the eighteenth century was not the mass phenomenon it became during the nineteenth and twentieth centuries.[2] In fact, in numbers it lagged behind emigration to Prussia and more or less equaled the number of German settlers recruited by Austria during the same period, although it is difficult to make

1   See above all M. S. Wokeck, *Trade in Strangers: The Beginnings of Mass Migration to North America* (University Park, 1999) and also A. Brinck, *Die deutsche Auswanderungswelle in die britischen Kolonien Nordamerikas um die Mitte des 18. Jahrhunderts* (Stuttgart, 1993).

2   In comparison: between 1847 and 1914 an estimated 4.5 million Germans emigrated to the United States (K. J. Bade, 'German Transatlantic Emigration in the Nineteenth and Twentieth Centuries', *European Expansion and Migration: Essays on the Intercontinental Migration from Africa, Asia and Europe*, ed. P. C. Emmer and M. Mörner (New York/Oxford, 1992), pp. 121–55, here p. 125). For the role German immigrants played in forming the North American colonies, see M. S. Wokeck, 'Expanding the Paths of Immigration: The Role of German Pioneers in Regional Settlements in North America', *Atlantic Migrations: Regions and Movements in Germany and North America/USA during the 18th and 19th Century*, ed. S. Heerwart and C. Schnurmann (Hamburg/Münster, 2007), pp. 83–109.

exact calculations. It is, however, remarkable that despite the costs, the difficulties and perils involved in crossing the Atlantic, so many migrants preferred this route over the much shorter and safer journey to, for example, Prussian, Austrian or Russian territories, whose monarchs issued invitations to potential settlers throughout the century.

While the prospect of religious tolerance and ownership of a piece of land were certainly powerful incentives for Germans to emigrate, these goals could also have been achieved in regions that were much closer to home. This chapter will argue that the reasons behind the irregular but increasing flow of German emigrants to North America until the eve of the Seven Years' War are in large part to be found in the economic interests and business structures which began to form with William Penn's efforts to attract settlers to Pennsylvania, and which developed further during the first waves of emigration in 1709 and later during the 1720s and 1750s. The following pages aim to examine the various stages of the migrants' journeys, insofar as they are related to these economic implications. The research period mainly covers the years between 1681 and 1755; that is, from William Penn's activities to the year before the outbreak of the Seven Years' War, when the insecurity caused by the growing tensions between France and England brought the flourishing trade in emigrants to a halt. Due to various European monarchs' successful recruitment measures in the years following the war, it would not reach the same numbers again until the beginning of the mass migration of the nineteenth century.

Pennsylvania and the redemptioner-system

The beginnings of German emigration to North America can be traced back to the founding of Pennsylvania in 1681. What was to be a 'holy experiment' necessarily also had a strong economic side. William Penn had to attract settlers, and from the beginning he relied heavily on promotional texts that praised the fertility of the land, the abundance of fish and wild animals, the temperate climate, and the possibilities for trading that his new province offered to newcomers.[3]

Penn went to the Rhineland several times and apparently used the contacts he established there to people his lands. In 1683, a company founded by Pietists from Frankfurt bought 15,000 acres of land in Pennsylvania. Its spokesman, Francis Daniel Pastorius, landed in Philadelphia that same year, bringing with him various Quaker and Mennonite families. Both Penn and Pastorius wrote profusely about the colony's virtues to attract more settlers, and at the same

---

3   W. Penn, 'Some Account of the Province of Pennsylvania (1681)', *Colonial North America and the Atlantic World: A History in Documents*, ed. B. Rushforth and P. W. Mapp (New Jersey, 2009), pp. 215–18.

time pointed out the 'profits' and 'revenues' that could be made by investors.[4] During the following years, both Penn's and Pastorius' works circulated in south-west Germany, where religious pressure and the devastations of war made emigration an increasingly tempting prospect. In addition, agents employed by Penn traveled the Rhineland to recruit even more immigrants, such that Knittle rightfully called Pennsylvania 'the best advertised province' in America.[5]

Some of the traits that were to characterize the future recruitment of German migrants throughout the century were already present at this early stage: the need to develop the land granted to individuals in the British colonies, and the use of 'advertising material' and agents to attract the settlers needed for the enterprise. Over the next 20 years, chartered ships transporting German emigrants occasionally crossed the Atlantic. During the first big wave of emigration, which took place in 1708/09, however, transportation became a central issue that was to be optimized during the following decades.

In spite of the fact that various German and Swiss entrepreneurs were traveling to South Carolina in search of profitable business ventures at this early stage of German migration to North America,[6] the reliability of religious networks apparently prevailed, and the vast majority of emigrants embarked for Philadelphia, whose population rose to 40,000 in 1726 and then to 150,000 in 1755. German immigration was estimated at 5,000 before 1727 but rose sharply afterwards until 1755, with an estimated 37,000 reaching Pennsylvania during the peak years of 1749 to 1755.[7]

The main port of embarkation was Rotterdam, and British merchants based there took the leading role in the business, because the British Navigation Act required all trade with the colonies to be carried out on British ships. The relationship between Benjamin Furly (an eminent Quaker and friend of William Penn, who supported him in his search for German settlers) and the brothers

4   In Penn's case, they were represented by the Free Society of Traders in London, while Pastorius reported to the Frankfurt company: see William Penn, 'A Letter from William Penn ... to the Committee of the Free Society of Traders ... (1683)', and Francis D. Pastorius, 'Positive Information from America (1684)', printed in *William Penn and the Founding of Pennsylvania, 1680–1684: A Documentary History*, ed. J. R. Soderlund (Philadelphia, 1983), pp. 309–22, 353–60.

5   W. A. Knittle, *Early Eighteenth Century Palatine Emigration: A British Government Redemptioner Project to Manufacture Naval Stores* (Baltimore, 1965), p. 20. Bernard Bailyn, among others, has stressed the importance of land speculation as a driving force for the recruitment of immigrants and the peopling of the North American colonies: B. Bailyn, *The Peopling of British North America: An Introduction* (London, 1987), pp. 67f.

6   See for example the letters written by Franz Ludwig Michel, printed in *Alles ist ganz anders hier: Auswandererschicksale in Briefen aus zwei Jahrhunderten*, eds. L. Schelbert and H. Rappolt (Olten/Freiburg, 1997), pp. 33–9.

7   All this according to R. W. Unger, 'Income Differentials, Institutions and Religion: Working in the Rhineland or Pennsylvania in the Eighteenth Century', *Working on Labor: Essays in Honor of Jan Lucassen*, ed. M. van der Linden and L. Lucassen (Leiden, 2012), pp. 269–95, here pp. 275f.

Isaac and Zachary Hope seems to have been influential in the structure that the transatlantic shipping of German emigrants was to take on.[8] It was not an entirely new business model, though, as it relied heavily on the transporting of indentured servants from England to the colonies throughout the seventeenth century, which Wareing states was characterized by 'the transformation of many servants into commodities'.[9]

While religious networks and charities initially helped finance the emigrants' journeys, as early as 1718[10] the Hopes seem to have played a major part in establishing a system designed to enable even people without sufficient means to cross the Atlantic – and thus to attract as many passengers as possible to the ships they had chartered for the occasion. This redemptioner-system was a variation of the indenture-system, according to which passengers could work off their fare after their arrival, and which had been in use since the seventeenth century to ship mainly English and Irish migrants across the Atlantic. While in the latter case the migrants negotiated a contract with the shipper, who sold them off to the highest bidder after their arrival in the colonies, the redemptioner-system left it to the emigrants to negotiate the terms of their servitude themselves after landing, which could have positive as well as negative effects for them.[11]

On arriving in the North American colonies, migrants who lacked the means to cover their travel expenses could (a) hope to find someone they knew who was willing to pay for them, but mostly (b) sign a contract establishing the terms and duration of their servitude. In 1769 Heinrich Melchior Mühlenberg, a German pastor who migrated to North America in 1742, described the proceedings as follows:

> Announcements are printed in the newspapers, stating how many of the new arrivals are to be sold. Those who have money are released. ... The ship becomes the market-place. The buyers make their choice among the arrivals and bargain with them for a certain number of years and days. They

8   See Unger, 'Income Differentials', pp. 291f. On the Hope family as members of the Dutch Quaker community, see W. H. Hull, *Benjamin Furly and Quakerism in Rotterdam* (Lancaster, 1941), pp. 247ff.
9   See J. Wareing, *Indentured Migration and the Servant Trade from London to America, 1618–1718: 'There is a Great Want of Servants'* (Oxford, 2016), pp. 95, 104.
10   See Wokeck, *Trade in Strangers*, p. 100.
11   For the basic structures of the system, see F. Grubb, 'The Auction of *Redemptioner Servants*, Philadelphia, 1771–1808: An Economic Analysis', *The Journal of Economic History* 48 (1988), pp. 583–603, here pp. 583ff; also G. Moltmann, 'The Migration of German *Redemptioners* to North America, 1720–1820', *Colonialism and Migration: Indentured Labour Before and After Slavery*, ed. P. C. Emmer (Dordrecht, 1986), pp. 105–22. Bade states that between 1727 and 1820, an estimated half or even two-thirds of the emigrants entered the North American ports as redemptioners: Bade, 'German Transatlantic Emigration', p. 123.

then take them to the merchant, pay their passage and their other debts and receive from the government authorities a written document, which makes the newcomers their property for a definite period.[12]

This system was often criticized, for example by the migrant Gottlieb Mittelberger, who called the redemptioner-system a 'traffic in human flesh' and pointed out that parents were often separated from their children in the process, among other aspects.[13] However, the system held many advantages for the migrants. First of all, it made emigration possible for many who otherwise could not have afforded it. Furthermore, while the sick and the aged – and, as one observer noted, also members of the military and the learned[14] – often lagged behind on the ships, young people could generally hope to sign a favorable contract; so much so, in fact, that by 'selling' a child or teenager, a family could pay the fares of other family members. Selling a child or oneself was apparently not necessarily regarded as a disgrace – in fact, in many cases it probably did not differ much from what the migrants would have had to expect in Germany. The Swedish traveler Peter Kalm observed that some people who could have afforded to pay for their passage sold themselves, because working in an established household offered the chance to learn about life in the colony before asking for a grant of land themselves.[15]

According to Kalm, prices for the redemptioners differed according to age, strength, and the size of debts contracted during the voyage, but buying a redemptioner was not only more affordable than buying an African slave (whose purchase required a larger sum to be paid immediately), but was also cheaper than paying annual wages to free servants.[16] Redemptioners were employed as household servants and also to prepare and cultivate the land. After they had been freed, their owners had to provide them with clothes and tools, and they were then at liberty to ask for grants of land of their own.

John Brownfield, the factor of an English trading firm, stressed the economic importance of bringing servants to Georgia when he wrote to the Trustees from Savannah in May 1737 on the possibilities of promoting the colony's trade:

---

12 Cited in R. B. Strassburger and W. J. Hinke, eds, *Pennsylvania German Pioneers: A Publication of the Lists of Arrivals in the Port of Philadelphia from 1727 to 1808*, Vol. 1 (Norristown/Pennsylvania, 1934), p. 37.

13 G. Mittelberger, *Journey to Pennsylvania in the Year 1750 and Return to Germany in the Year 1754*, ed. C. T. Eben (Philadelphia, 1898), pp. 25, 27.

14 F. Kapp, *Geschichte der Deutschen im Staate New York bis zum Anfang des neuzehnten Jahrhunderts* (New York, 1869), p. 298.

15 P. Kalm, *Des Herrn Peter Kalms Professors der Haushaltungskunst in Aobo und Mitglied der königlichen schwedischen Akademie der Wissenschaften Beschreibung der Reise die er nach dem nördlichen Amerika auf den Befehl gedachter Akademie und öffentlichen Kosten unternommen hat*, Vol. 2 (Göttingen, 1757), p. 535.

16 Ibid.

However, this is saying nothing unless we could supply the West Indies as cheap as our Neighbours can & that I believe we shall never do unless greater Numbers of servants are sent over ... It may also be said that the Indian Trade is fixed here, but the Province has received very little benefit from it; nor can receive more till we are able to furnish the Traders with Goods.[17]

The authorities also tried to consolidate their control over American soil in other colonies, and at the same time to contribute to the economic development of their provinces by intensifying commercial relations with Great Britain. This was the case in Nova Scotia, for example, where the importing of Protestants was promoted after the expulsion of the Catholic inhabitants of French origin in 1755.[18] It was also true for South Carolina, whose inhabitants lived in constant fear of an alliance between the French and some Amerindian societies, as well as of slave riots.[19]

In a letter written in 1735 by Benjamin Martyn, Secretary to the Trustees, to Charleston-based merchant Samuel Eveleigh, who planned to purchase land in Georgia, he strongly advised against purchasing slaves:

The Trustees Sr. recommend it to You to think rather of getting German Servants (Who can with ease be procured by several People here in London) than English Men; and if you consider it well, you will find much to Your Advantage to have German Servants rather than Negro Slaves. The Germans are a sober, strong, laborious People; and since the Expiration of their Service they will be fit to become Tenants, they will make your Lands of much more Value.[20]

When it came to attracting settlers, however, the American authorities faced great difficulties in comparison to private business ventures, which would prove to be much more successful. This helps explain why Pennsylvania, where the latter had been established at an early stage, attracted by far the highest numbers of immigrants throughout the period in question, in spite of efforts made by other colonies to do the same.[21]

---

17   *The Colonial Records of the State of Georgia*, Vol. 21 (New York, 1970), p. 414. See also G. F. Jones, *The Georgia Dutch: From the Rhine and Danube to the Savannah, 1733–1783* (Athens/London, 1992).
18   See C. Hodson, *The Acadian Diaspora: An Eighteenth-Century History* (Oxford, 2012).
19   See J. Kelly, *America's Longest Siege: Charleston, Slavery, and the Slow March toward Civil War* (New York, 2013), pp. 19ff.
20   *Colonial Records of the State of Georgia*, Vol. 21, p. 66. Martyn's identification with the government's principles can also be detected here: 'The Trustees are very much obliged to You for turning Your thoughts on Anything for the Good of the Colony; But they cannot approve of setting up any Manufactury, that will interfere with those of Great Britain.' Ibid., p. 37.
21   This has already been stressed by Brinck, *Auswanderungswelle*, pp. 72ff, and Wokeck, *Trade in Strangers*, p. 58.

Recruitment strategies

The recruitment of settlers naturally began in their countries of origin. A great deal has been written about the recruitment agents and their often dubious and fraudulent measures. However, the entrepreneurial side of their activities will be stressed in this context (as Mark Häberlein did in his analysis of their work), as part of the business ventures carried out between Germany and the American colonies during the eighteenth century.[22] Several types of agents have to be taken into account here. While some were interested in developing land in the colonies on behalf of the authorities, others worked on their own account; and last but not least, yet others were employed by the merchant firms based in Rotterdam.

One important way of attracting emigrants was by using pamphlets, which were distributed in the countries of origin and which usually contained a (not always adequate) description of the recruiting region, together with the conditions offered by authorities and the expected costs of the voyage. Adding credibility to the agents' promises was crucial, so Hans Jacob Riemensperger, for example, who was engaged in bringing settlers to South Carolina, added the testimony of 40 settlers he had already taken there to his pamphlet.[23] Letters written from the New World were another important element, so much so that considerable efforts were undertaken to forge letters from emigrants to families and friends in Germany.[24]

One aspect that has received little attention until now is the use the agents made of the press to influence the population. The fact that Joseph Crellius, agent for Massachusetts, enlisted four printers and one newspaper editor as collaborators in south-west Germany, who were to be paid per head, speaks for itself.[25] A real battle seems to have been fought via newspapers and pamphlets in those years, in which agents tried to denigrate their competitors and the regions they represented.[26]

After recruitment, the next stage for the emigrants was their journey to the port of embarkation, the part of the voyage about which least is known. Few contracts have survived, but it is clear that the Rhine shippers were an important

---

22 M. Häberlein, 'Migration and Business Ventures: German-Speaking Migrants and Commercial Networks in the Eighteenth-Century British-Atlantic World', *German Migrants in the British Empire*, ed. S. Manz (Leiden, 2011), pp. 19–57, here pp. 23f.

23 R. L. Meriwether, *The Expansion of South Carolina, 1729–1765* (Kingsport, 1940), p. 151.

24 For the discussion of this aspect, see Brinck, *Auswanderungswelle*, pp. 99ff.

25 See E. Risch, 'Joseph Crellius: Immigrant Broker', *The New England Quarterly* 12 (1939), pp. 241–67, here p. 249.

26 Ibid., p. 259. On the negative press on Nova Scotia obviously promoted by Rotterdam-based competitors, see W. P. Bell, *The Foreign Protestants and the Settlement of Nova Scotia: The History of a Piece of Arrested British Colonial Policy in the Eighteenth Century* (Toronto, 1961), p. 139.

part of the economic network that connected south-west Germany with the American colonies, either in agreement with the merchants who provided the transport overseas, or by transporting emigrants who negotiated their fares on their own.[27]

In both cases, many already saw their savings dwindle during this first stage of the route, due to delays in the onward journey. Mittelberger describes it as follows:

> the Rhine-boats from Heilbronn to Holland have to pass by 36 custom-houses, at all of which the ships are examined, which is done when it suits the convenience of the custom-house officials. In the meantime the ships with the people are detained long, so that the passengers have to spend much money. The trip down the Rhine lasts therefore, 4, 5 and even 6 weeks. When the ships with the people come to Holland, they are detained there likewise 5 or 6 weeks.[28]

Mittelberger suggests that all those who profited from transporting the emigrants deliberately tried to slow down the journey to draw as much money as possible out of their pockets. In fact, many emigrants had already had to indebt themselves to the agents to be able to pay for this first leg. Reports by John Dick, a Rotterdam-based merchant who acted as official agent for Nova Scotia, allow a glimpse of the machinations that emigrants had to endure on their way to Holland. Always keen on distancing himself from the tricks allegedly used by other Rotterdam merchants, Dick wrote that Ruhrort, a Prussian toll station close to the Dutch border, was a gathering point for agents, and it was here that many contracts were concluded. The emigrants needed passports, and the agents and shippers made sure to provide them for those who were willing to sign contracts.[29] John Dick reported that any delay in providing

27 For a more detailed description, see M. S. Wokeck, *A Tide of Alien Tongues: The Flow and Ebb of German Immigration to Pennsylvania, 1683–1776* (Ann Arbor, 1983), pp. 162ff.
28 Mittelberger, *Journey to Pennsylvania*, p. 18.
29 They had to provide them, in fact, as the Dutch authorities held them responsible for not attracting anyone to Rotterdam who would eventually be a burden on the community, something the city had experienced repeatedly since the first wave of mass emigration in 1709/10. From Schenkenschanz, the first station at the Dutch border, only people with valid passports were allowed to proceed to the port cities; see Wokeck, *Trade in Strangers*, pp. 63–7. The bigger players in the trade apparently applied for a high number of passports in advance. In January 1751 – that is, well ahead of the beginning of the season – Nicolas Oursel, for example, asked for permission to transport 2,000 persons in parties of 40, 50 or 60 through the lands, who were to be shipped 'to the English colonies' (Stadsarchief Rotterdam, Resolutiën van de Heeren Staaten van Holland en Westvriesland, in haar Edele Groot Mog, Vergadering, Vol. 1, 1751). On the other hand, the combined factors of possible conflicts with the German authorities regarding the recruitment of their subjects and the need to provide passports were certainly responsible for the efforts undertaken by agents and shippers alike to employ people who had ties to German officials and courts. So, among the persons involved in the activities of Joseph Crellius are two 'counsellors'

these documents ran the risk of losing the emigrants to other agents.[30] However, other less bureaucratic means were also apparently employed in the fight for emigrants in the border region between the German states and the Netherlands.

Along with the Hopes, another 'big fish' in the business was John Stedman, and although it has been shown that the two firms did not have a monopoly and that there were many newcomers to the business, especially during the emigration wave caused by the settlement projects of 1749 to 1755, he was still one of the main players. A former captain engaged in the Palatine trade[31] himself, he now regularly consigned redemptioners to his brothers, who had settled in Philadelphia for that reason.[32]

Stedman had been in the business since the 1720s and obviously maintained excellent relations with the toll officials (there are even accusations of bribery), having his own landing places and taverns at various places close to the border.[33] Dick complained that Stedman's agents pretended to be authorized to sign contracts for Nova Scotia and even threatened to throw new arrivals' baggage into the water if they refused to sign a contract with Stedman, which also implies an understanding between the latter and some of the Rhine shippers.[34]

A contract dating from 1751 suggests that Stedman, in this case working closely with the Hopes, indeed attracted emigrants who came to Rotterdam to embark for other regions. The contract was concluded with German agent Jacob Friedrich Kurtz and Captain Daniel Montpellier of *The Scarborough* in May 1751, and was obviously designed to give Kurtz a share in the emigrant trade by allowing him to load the ship with passengers he had recruited, while on the other hand consenting to concede:

> what Number of passengers above the four hundred for the said Ship the Scarborough said Mr. Curtius shall bring down this year, for to go from Germany to Philadelphia, New England, Carolina or any other Colonys, shall be divided between the appearors on the other part, vist by Mr. John Stedman for the one half part, and by Messrs. Isaac & Zachary Hope for the other half part, in Consideration of which, said Mr. Curtius shall have and

---

(Risch, 'Joseph Crellius', pp. 248f), while among the contracts the Rotterdam firm John Dunlop & Co. signed with recruitment agents during those years, the fact that one of them was 'Conseiller de la Cour de Son Excellence Mr. le Comte de Linage [sic] a Guntersblum' was also stressed (Stadsarchief Rotterdam, Oud Notarieel Archief 2698–210).

30   Bell, *Foreign Protestants*, p. 170.

31   The term 'Palatines' was generally used by contemporaries to denominate all the emigrants who crossed the Atlantic following the routes and procedures described in this chapter; hence also the term 'Palatine trade', although they came not only from different regions in south-west Germany, but also from other German regions, from Switzerland, Alsace, Lorraine, or Holland.

32   See F. Grubb, 'The Market Structure of Shipping German Immigrants to Colonial America', *The Pennsylvania Magazine of History and Biography* 111 (1987), pp. 27–48.

33   Bell, *Foreign Protestants*, p. 137.

34   Ibid.

enjoy one third part of the Commission in Philadelphia, of all such Numbers
as he above the said four hundred for the said ship Scarborough shall bring
down this year.[35]

This implies that wherever the emigrants who reached Rotterdam wanted
to go, they would in the end be 'convinced' to be shipped to Philadelphia,
regardless of the fact that prices there were rising and land was becoming more
expensive, which made it more difficult for newcomers to settle.[36]

Whether or not they applied unfair measures, private entrepreneurs like
John Stedman, Hope & Co., Daniel Harvart, John Dunlop, Nicholas Oursel
and others had one decisive advantage over government-launched recruitment
activities: by means of the redemptioner-system they could offer free passages.
This was an aspect that gave those involved in 'official' settlement projects quite
a headache, apart from the fact that Philadelphia was a place with an established German community, which was already quite well known in Germany.
When the Trustees of Georgia tried to recruit a number of settlers directly
in Rotterdam in 1737, their agent Johann Matthias Kramer tried in vain to
convince 'Mr Hope' to help him in his endeavors:

> by Reason that every One is enclined to go to Pensilvania, and is in Hopes,
> that the Captains of Ship will take them on Board, and carry them, without
> Paying for their Passage. But, since the Number of such Poor, as cannot pay
> for their Passage is very great, its doubtfull, whether they will be all carried
> over, consequently when they at last shall Know how to shift They might
> possibly be persuaded to go to Georgia. ... I shall remain here till All Ships
> for Pensylvania shall be gone. But it is not to be presumed, that any Persons
> of Substance shall be left behind by the Captains for Pensilvania, but only
> Such as cannot pay for their Passage; and as Messieurs Hope cannot send a
> Ship to Georgia with Sixty Persons. But require 140, to 150, at least, it will be
> necessary to have Orders, whether I might increase the First required Number
> of 60, to 140, or 150, Servants in Order to have a full Loading.[37]

This passage is very revealing with regard to the conditions that prevailed
in Rotterdam at the time. Obviously, despite the Dutch authorities' measures
to prevent people lacking sufficient means and/or a contract to be shipped to
America from coming to the city, there were so many people waiting to board

---

35   Stadsarchief Rotterdam, Oud Notarieel Archief 2779–108.
36   The diversion of skilled workers especially does not seem to have been a problem that existed
solely between the colonies and the shippers, but also between the colonies themselves. Oglethorpe
urged the Board of Trade in 1735 not to send 'any Passengers or Servants by Ships bound for
Charles Town, or who have any cargo for that Place' for fear of them being persuaded to stay
there, especially the 'Cooper and Smither' the colony was expecting (*Colonial Records of the
State of Georgia*, Vol. 21, pp. 51f).
37   *Colonial Records of the State of Georgia*, Vol. 21, p. 418.

a ship that the merchants could make a selection of those they agreed to carry. And these were beyond a doubt those individuals who disposed of sufficient means to pay for their passage, or who were most likely to be sold as servants for a good profit.[38]

Colonies like Georgia, with a fixed recruitment budget, had difficulties providing transport for their settlers, because there was not enough profit to be made in this endeavor. In Georgia, where life was still rudimentary and even food was sometimes scarce, hardly anyone could afford a servant, so the redemptioner-system could not be applied to the same degree.[39] John Dick pointed out the same difficulties for Nova Scotia. In the end, the authorities chose to employ redemptioners themselves in the public works being carried out in Halifax.[40]

The characteristics of the Palatine trade

Shipping emigrants to places where there was no profit to be made by merchants thus proved a difficult task. However, even private entrepreneurs encountered difficulties when they attempted to enter new markets. One such case is Liverpool merchant Foster Cunliffe's failure to sell a shipload of redemptioners in Charleston in 1751. As there were not enough buyers, the remaining immigrants had to be released on bonds; according to Charleston-based merchant Henry Laurens, who tried to collect the money over the following years, they had been unable to earn enough to pay their fares as late as 1757.[41]

This incident also points to another aspect of the business. Foster Cunliffe was one of several Liverpool merchants who were engaged in the tobacco trade in the Chesapeake area. By shipping servants to this region, they managed to get 'a foothold in the staple trade',[42] as these were among the few 'import merchandises' that were sought after by the planters. Like other Liverpool merchants who were interested in trading with Chesapeake, Foster Cunliffe also began trading slaves and became the second largest importer in the area, although he

38   This is confirmed in one of the letters published in Schelbert/Rappolt, *Alles ist ganz anders hier*, p. 103. See also Grubb, 'Market Structure', pp. 35f.
39   See, for example, *Colonial Records of the State of Georgia*, Vol. 21, pp. 116, 417. See also the case of land developer Daniel Dulany of Maryland, who was able to persuade his Dutch partners to accept payment in kind for their freights of redemptioners (Brinck, *Auswanderungswelle*, p. 80).
40   Bell, *Foreign Protestants*, pp. 147f.
41   See various letters from Henry Laurens to Foster Cunliffe and James Rocquette, *The Papers of Henry Laurens*, Vol. 2, ed. P. M. Hamer (Columbia, 1970).
42   L. S. Walsh, 'Liverpool's Slave Trade to the Colonial Chesapeake: Slaving on the Periphery', *Liverpool and Transatlantic Slavery*, ed. David Richardson et al. (Liverpool, 2007), pp. 98–117, here p. 100. J. W. Tyler, 'Foster Cunliffe and Sons: Liverpool Merchants in the Maryland Tobacco Trade, 1738–1765', *Maryland Historical Magazine* 73 (1978), pp. 246–79.

continued to ship indentured servants until the 1760s.[43] His contacts with Henry Laurens can be traced back to 1749, when the latter entered a partnership with George Austin, who had become rich in the slave trade. Laurens was in London the year the partnership was established, and before returning to Charleston he traveled to Bristol and Liverpool to convince the slave traders there to direct their ships to their newly established house; quite successfully, as it turned out, as the firm made a considerable profit in the slave trade during the following years and Henry Laurens, the future president of the Continental Congress, became one of the richest men in North America.

This partnership is symptomatic of the Palatine trade: first, none of the participants was a major player at the time; no one who was involved in this business in either Rotterdam, England or the colonies belonged to one of the big merchant houses. The rudimentary state of some of the provinces meant that not many people could afford to buy expensive manufactured goods or hire a servant. Henry Laurens' letters are telling in this respect, as he very often complains about the market being 'glutted with European goods' and is very cautious about letting his partners in Europe know which goods he was likely to sell at a profit.[44] For his part, in his study on the Philadelphia merchant community, Thomas Doerflinger gives a vivid description of the comparatively modest lifestyle of the economic elite of this major American port on the eve of independence.[45]

The same applies to merchant houses on the other side of the Atlantic. Neither John Stedman nor the Hope brothers seem to have accumulated considerable wealth in the Palatine trade, nor were they likely to do so.[46] The statistics compiled by Marianne Wokeck show that the trade in German emigrants was highly volatile; in some years, only one or two transportations are recorded, and none at all in 1726. Between 1720 and 1749, numbers vary between zero and 4,700 emigrants. Only during the peak years was the flow constantly high; it culminated in 62 transportations carrying 16,700 emigrants in 1752, before abruptly descending to three in 1755 during the run-up to the Seven Years' War.[47]

This means that no one could know for sure how many emigrants would apply to be shipped to America in any given year, which explains the efforts that went into recruitment measures. Assumptions only became possible in spring and early summer, when the emigrants reached the border, because the Palatine trade was a seasonal business. The migrants usually sold their belongings and

43 Walsh, 'Liverpool's Slave Trade', pp. 102f.
44 See, for example, his letter to Foster Cunliffe, 20 January 1749, *The Papers of Henry Laurens*, Vol. 1, ed. P. M. Hamer (Columbia, 1968), p. 202.
45 T. Doerflinger, *A Vigorous Spirit of Enterprise: Merchants and Economic Development in Revolutionary Philadelphia* (Chapel Hill/London, 2001), pp. 26f.
46 Although the Hope family was very well established in Amsterdam; see M. G. Buist, *Ad Spes non Fracta: Hope & Co. 1770–1815* (The Hague, 1974).
47 See Wokeck, *Trade in Strangers*, p. 45.

settled their affairs in winter and then left in spring, so that even including the delays mentioned above, they reached Rotterdam in early summer, in order to arrive in America before bad weather could further delay their journey or ice impede their landing.

Given the Hopes' and John Stedman's experience and connections, it must have been of little use to try and get a foothold in the trade most years. For the rest of the time, and on both sides of the Atlantic, the Palatine trade seems to have been in large part an occasional business with occasional partnerships. The same applies to the captains of the ships who transported the migrants, and also to the firms to whom the redemptioners were consigned in America.[48]

New competitors mainly entered the market on a more regular basis during the peak years, and one example is the firm of John Dunlop & Co. In August 1751 Dunlop and two other Rotterdam merchants went to a notary to reach an 'agreement for establishing together and in partnership a House at Philadelphia' with one Alexander Ray. The latter was to depart immediately, with the necessary recommendations, to a merchant firm in London, 'who are to introduce him to the Manufacturers, Shopkeepers and People who are accustomed to furnish the Stores necessary and required in America'. From these he was to order goods to send to Philadelphia in the future, which he was to sell 'to the best advantage of the said Partnership ... and furthermore they allow him to have a fourth part of all the Profit arriving from the business of the House, either on the sale of Goods, consignments of Palatines, or otherwise'.[49]

That Dunlop was serious about the Palatine trade being a part of the business is demonstrated by the fact that, on the following 4 December, he concluded two recruitment contracts with German agents for the following year, before including a fourth Rotterdam merchant into their partnership in January 1752, 'for Carrying on a Trade in Palatines, with Philadelphia, and Rice from Carolina and in any other branch of Trade with America as shall be agreed upon between the Partners', while 'all the Palatines sent to Philadelphia are to be addressed to Mr Alexander Ray'.[50] During the following years, this partnership seems to have been quite successful, with various charter parties concluded during the peak years and new recruitment contracts signed regularly.[51] So, in addition to being a business which many merchants exercised only temporarily, it was also only one part of any given firm's business ventures, and must be seen in the context of their further economic interests in North America.

48 See Grubb, 'Market Structure', pp. 43f. Unger states that of the 170 ships that made the 324 voyages carrying German emigrants to Philadelphia, only 12 made more than two or three voyages (Unger, 'Income Differentials', p. 283), which is not very surprising given the limited number of emigrants over many years.
49 Stadsarchief Rotterdam, Oud Notarieel Archief 2698–152.
50 Ibid., 2698–210, 2698–211, 2699–6.
51 See, for example, ibid., 2699–53, 2699–84, 2699–85, 2699–102, 2747–140, 2747–242, 2699–123/24/25, 2747–148.

A triangular trade

Recent research agrees that the decisive advantage of the Palatine trade was to fill freight space, which remained largely under-utilized on the passage from Europe to North America.[52] The freighters usually paid for the measures that had to be taken to fit out the ships so they could take on their human freight. When all was finished, one contract stated (and many others used similar clauses) that the captain should take on 'as many Passengers as the said Fraighters shall judge he can conveniently carry under the Deck, and so many of their goods and Bagage in her Hold as she above her Materials and Provisions safely will stow and carry'.[53]

The Palatines and their belongings were, therefore, likely to have been the only 'goods' on board. Of course, the fact that the more of these paying 'freights' the ship carried, the more profit was made could lead to rather crowded conditions, although Brinck has shown that Mittelberger's accusation that emigrants were loaded 'like herrings' was probably only true during the peak years.[54] Nevertheless, as roughly half the emigrants in the eighteenth century undertook the voyage across the Atlantic during those years, a fairly large proportion of them were involved, and Mittelberger was not the only one who witnessed deprivation, sickness and death during the passage.[55]

So, if the passengers and their belongings were the only goods that were being shipped, what could be earned in this business? Brinck calculated that a maximum of three or four pounds sterling per passenger could be gained.[56] This can hardly be considered an exceedingly high profit when compared with slave prices, for example, and also given the fact that the ships used in the Palatine trade were comparatively small. Those that appear in the charter parties mostly

---

52   See, for example, Grubb, 'Market Structure', p. 45, and Brinck, *Auswanderungswelle*, p. 86.

53   Stadsarchief Rotterdam, Oud Notarieel Archief 2332–143.

54   Mittelberger, *Journey to Pennsylvania*, p. 19.

55   Brinck, *Auswanderungswelle*, pp. 200ff. For a balanced description of the travel conditions and the risks involved, see also M. Häberlein, *Vom Oberrhein zum Susquehanna: Studien zur badischen Auswanderung nach Pennsylvania im 18. Jahrhundert* (Stuttgart, 1993), pp. 108ff.

56   Brinck, *Auswanderungswelle*, p. 77. The emigrants were usually divided into three categories: children under four years of age traveled free; up to 14 years of age they were considered 'half freights'; and adults were 'full freights'. Similar patterns seem to have applied to the journey on the Rhine. In John Dick's case, the price structure can be traced from the beginning, taking as a basis his recruitment pamphlet (Hauptstaatsarchiv Stuttgart, A 211 Bü. 673): for the journey on the river, the emigrants did not have to pay anything for children who were still being breastfed; children up to 12 years old were considered half freights; and full freights had to pay the shipper two ducats plus seven *Kreuzer* 'passage fee'. For the Atlantic passage, they would have to pay seven pistols for full freights, while children up to 14 were considered half freights, and children under four would travel free. Provision on board was also enumerated in detail.

averaged around 180 or 200 tons, or even less, and it was only occasionally that someone managed to fill a 400-ton ship with Palatines.[57]

As the transporting of emigrants could hardly be carried out as a business in itself, and rather served to fill under-utilized freight space on the westward passage, the picture has to be completed by taking into consideration the passage back to Europe. It has already been stated that the vast majority of voyages went to Philadelphia. In terms of a profitable back-freight, this was not necessarily an advantageous choice, as Philadelphia did not produce any attractive staple goods that could easily be sold in Europe at the time, instead relying heavily on the production of agricultural products like wheat or timber, which were mainly shipped along the coast of North America to pay for the import of manufactured goods from England.[58]

Given this precondition, the Palatine trade took on a triangular structure almost naturally. Although some voyages were designed simply to deliver their human freight to the respective American business partners and come straight back to Europe with goods chosen by the latter, most of the ships sailed on to other ports to take on more profitable back-freight.

Although it is difficult to follow the ships' routes after they delivered the emigrants to the factors or partners of the Rotterdam trading houses, Brinck has made a considerable effort for the peak years. His lists for the years from 1748 to 1754 show that almost all the ships destined for Philadelphia went on to one of the main export ports for American staple goods: Charleston, Virginia, Maryland, or the West Indies.[59] As detailed above, John Dunlop established a partnership mainly to convey Palatines to Philadelphia and to import rice from South Carolina, and in fact many of the ships chartered by his firm took this route, but one also went on to Virginia.[60] Having received their shipload of redemptioners, John Stedman's brothers in Philadelphia redirected the vessels to Charleston or the West Indies. *The Cunliffe*, which not surprisingly belonged to Foster Cunliffe, went from Charleston to Maryland in 1752 and from there to Liverpool, in accordance with the firm's role in the Maryland tobacco trade.[61]

Hope & Co., for their part, were heavily involved in trading logwood in the Bay of Honduras.[62] On 17 June 1752 they authorized Captain Charles

---

57 Whereas Unger states that an average cargo ship of the era was around 400 to 500 tons (Unger, 'Income Differentials', p. 284).

58 See J. J. McCusker and R. R. Menard, *The Economy of British America, 1607–1789* (Chapel Hill/London, 1985), pp. 191ff, 204f.

59 Brinck, *Auswanderungswelle*, pp. 260ff.

60 A charter party from the Stadsarchief Rotterdam (27/2/1751, 2698–36) shows that John Dunlop was also engaged in importing tobacco from Glasgow; given his interest in the tobacco trade, it is not surprising that he should take advantage of the opportunity provided by the Palatine trade to direct his ships to a tobacco-producing region.

61 Brinck, *Auswanderungswelle*, p. 264.

62 In 1744, the Baymen of Honduras, the British logwood cutters in the area, even decided to trade logwood to Europe exclusively via the Hope family. See R. A. Newton, '"Good and Kind

Kenneway of the *Ann*, whom they had just contracted to transport passengers to Philadelphia, to 'in their name and to their use to ask, demand, sue for … all and every such sum and sums of money, goods, wares and merchandizes' owed to the Hopes by people of the Bay area.[63] Only two weeks later, Captain Spurrier of *The Phoenix*, chartered to convey German passengers to Philadelphia on behalf of Nicolas Oursel on 23 June 1752, was also authorized by Hope & Co. to act on their behalf in the region.[64] Neither captain was new to the Palatine trade and they obviously enjoyed the Hopes' confidence, as both had carried Palatines for them to Pennsylvania and Charleston the year before.[65]

Ships destined for Charleston, on the other hand, were most likely to return directly to Europe.[66] It should be stressed that the Palatine trading season fit in perfectly with the harvest season, as the ships carrying emigrants arrived in late summer and could consequently take on board the colonies' agricultural products.[67] It is thus clear that the merchants did not necessarily carry out their trade in emigrants with only one given port, and obviously adjusted their charters to immediate economic prospects. This is underlined by the fact that various charter parties did not fix a port of destination in America.[68]

There is one last important aspect with regard to the Palatine trade and its role in linking the hinterland to the Atlantic commerce. It clearly brought financial benefits to a multitude of people, from recruitment agents, printers and Rhine shippers in south-west Germany – and other regions later on – to merchants based in Holland and England, as well as North American land speculators and settlers. One final group that needs to be mentioned are the merchants in the American ports where the Palatine ships landed, who profited by charging commission on the sale of the redemptioners. As Dunlop & Co. attached such importance to building a stable partnership with a trading house in Philadelphia, it was obviously considered an advantage to be able to have experienced and reliable partners. John Dick urged the Nova Scotia authorities to install an agent in Halifax who would receive the redemptioners and see to the necessary proceedings and financial transactions in the same way as in Philadelphia.[69] The slightly dominant role played by Hope & Co. and John Stedman's partners in Philadelphia – Benjamin Shoemaker and the Stedman

---

Benefactors": British Logwood Merchants and Boston's Christ Church', *Early American Studies* 11 (2013), pp. 15–36, here pp. 29ff.

63   Stadsarchief Rotterdam, Oud Notarieel Archief 2699–111.

64   Ibid., 2699–113, 2699–117.

65   See Brinck, *Auswanderungswelle*, p. 262.

66   See, for example, the charter party concluded between Rocquette & Van Teylingen with Captain John Robinson of *The John & Mary* (26 July 1752, Stadsarchief Rotterdam, Oud Notarieel Archief 2747–159).

67   See Brinck, *Auswanderungswelle*, p. 24.

68   See, for example, Stadsarchief Rotterdam, Oud Notarieel Archief 2747–82, 2747–123/124, 2699–99/100.

69   See Bell, *Foreign Protestants*, p. 147.

brothers, respectively – mirrored business patterns on the other side of the Atlantic. However, most other actors seem to have taken on 'occasional consignments', and there also seems to have been a certain competition to attract consignments from the European Palatine traders.[70]

That there was another advantage to be derived from the Palatine trade for American merchants is made clear by the multitude of complaints raised by Henry Laurens in 1755, when the threat of war interrupted the steady stream of ships carrying emigrants that the port had experienced during the previous years, for example:

> We have very few Ships as yet reach'd us to help off our Crops of Rice which are this Year Pretty good ... The present price of Rice 35/ per Ct. but the Shippers dont buy Cordially in expectation it must be lower very soon as we cant learn but of very few Vessells comeing this way. The Palatine Trade to America being Stopt will deprive us of many Ships that Constantly resorted here & have been the Chief means for Years past of keeping down our Freights.[71]

Later on, he complained that the declining number of ships had caused the price of rice to fall, and with it the possibilities of selling slaves.[72]

So, apart from enabling American merchants to earn money as factors for European firms, the fact that the Palatine trade made the westward passage more profitable obviously enabled European merchants to send more ships from Europe to the colonies. These, in turn, not only benefited from the number of settlers and servants they received, but also from rising exports and lower freight rates.

And so, although the volume of the trade in German emigrants may have been modest in comparison to the slave trade, it had a considerable influence on American economy and society. The influx of foreigners it caused, as well as the directions it took, were largely 'dictated by the needs of commerce and colonial enterprise – not by politicians', as William O'Reilly put it.[73] This statement would remain true throughout the nineteenth and twentieth centuries, when demographic growth, proletarization and/or political persecution would move a great number of Germans to leave their homelands; their movements would, in the end, also be mainly directed by the commercial interests of merchants and ship-owners alike.

---

70 See Grubb, 'Market Structure', pp. 42ff.
71 To Richard Meyler & Co., 8 December 1755, *The Papers of Henry Laurens*, Vol. 2, p. 30.
72 See Laurens' letter to Foster Cunliffe (24 February 1756: 'The low price of Rice has quite discourag'd our Planters from purchasing slaves', *The Papers of Henry Laurens*, Vol. 2, p. 100).
73 See W. O'Reilly, 'Working for the Crown: German Migrants and Britain's Commercial Success in the Early Eighteenth-Century American Colonies', *Journal of Modern European History* 15 (2017), pp. 130–52, here p. 150.

12

Reorienting Atlantic World Financial Capitalism: America and the German States

DAVID K. THOMSON

The story of transatlantic finance in the nineteenth century has often been one that fixates largely on a US-British binary. Capital flows between these two nations (increasingly centered around financial instruments pertaining to cotton) have been detailed at length in an array of monographs. While some historians have explored the power of Dutch financiers, especially as it pertained to American railroad stock, little attention has been paid to German financiers in the nineteenth century, specifically as it pertains to their increasing interest and interconnectedness with the United States. While this paucity of attention is partly down to a dearth of surviving primary source evidence, the importance of connections between German financiers and American counterparts helps to explain not only evolving notions of transatlantic finance, but also in part the respective rise of these two economies as they eclipsed the British by the early twentieth century. What began as two economies operating on the periphery of a dominant British financial network in the earlier part of the nineteenth century evolved by the century's end. Finance played but one part in this narrative of American and German ascension, but the financing of debt is one window into this critical story of the nineteenth century.[1]

American Civil War bonds in particular offer a window into domestic – but perhaps even more crucially – international ramifications of the conflict. While traditional Civil War diplomacy is a topic of much exploration, little has been said in regard to the financial dimensions of the war on the international stage.

---

1   Aside from numerous works by Rondo Cameron and Youssef Cassis, one other monograph worth noting that details the evolution of European financial houses and specifically caters to the rise of German banking as a function of various familial and social networks is D. S. Landes, *Bankers and Pashas: International Finance and Economic Imperialism in Egypt* (New York, 1958).

For Civil War bonds played a large role in reorienting transatlantic banking structures for United States' banks in the nineteenth century, paving the way for a new era of American finance. Crucial to all of this were the emerging financial ties between the United States and the German states – two relative financial peripheries compared to London, Paris and Amsterdam – as the Civil War drastically expanded their financial footprints globally. The financial connections between the German states and the United States that grew and developed from 1848 onwards play a vital role in understanding the development of financial networks between these two nations. The sale of bonds not only enabled the United States to pay for a war, but also helped to flip financial structures and reorient certain financial markets away from traditional markets, to expand financial offerings on a transatlantic level.[2]

To put this transformation in greater perspective, in June 1853, foreign countries held approximately 53 million dollars in American railroad securities and 27 million dollars in US government bonds. Largely owned by German, French, Swiss and British investors, this represented a modest investment by foreigners in American securities – both state debt and railways. By 1869, government bonds held by foreigners had spiraled upwards to one billion dollars and railroad securities had grown to approximately 250 million dollars. What accounted for such a stark transformation? On one level, the expansion of railways in the United States and their subsequent capitalization undoubtedly played a role. But this does not account for the exponential growth as it pertained to US securities. In order to understand this, one must look at the rapid financial transformation afforded by Union securities during the Civil War and in its immediate aftermath.[3]

2   For more information on the *antebellum* economy in the United States and the close relationship between North and South, see W. Johnson, *River of Dark Dreams: Slavery and Empire in the Cotton Kingdom* (Cambridge, 2013); E. Baptist, *The Half Has Never Been Told: Slavery and the Making of American Capitalism* (New York, 2014); S. Rockman, *Scraping By: Wage Labor, Slavery, and Survival in Early Baltimore* (Baltimore, 2009). For examples of slaves used as collateral, see R. Kilbourne Jr., *Debt, Investment, Slaves: Credit Relations in East Feliciana Parish, Louisiana, 1825–1885* (Tuscaloosa, 1995) and C. Schermerhorn, *The Business of Slavery and the Rise of American Capitalism, 1815–1860* (New Haven, 2015.) Other *antebellum* financial books that are crucial to understanding this period include J. Levy, *Freaks of Fortune: The Emerging World of Capitalism and Risk in America* (Cambridge, 2012). For the history of cotton as a global commodity, see S. Beckert, *Empire of Cotton: A Global History of Capitalism* (New York, 2014). M. Caires's forthcoming book on Civil War money with Harvard University Press will undoubtedly be the gold standard for any works detailing this pivotal piece of Civil War finance.
3   M. Wilkins, *The History of Foreign Investment in the United States to 1914* (Cambridge/London, 1989), pp. 76ff, 116, 118. Only six American railroads at this time had foreign ownership that exceeded 10 per cent.

American debt in Europe until 1848

Despite the importance of American-German financial bonds over the course of the nineteenth century, much of the early story of American debt centers around non-German actors. After all, it was Dutch, Spanish and French loans that helped to finance the Revolutionary War. Following the war of 1812 and the cessation of hostilities with the British, London financiers welcomed American debt issues for federal, state and municipal bonds, on top of larger public works and internal improvement projects such as the Erie Canal. The story is not one without German actors – some Germans did help finance the war of 1812 – but their involvement was on a much smaller scale compared to what was to come. Such an appetite for American debt abroad led to an overall increase in the quantity of American debt held in European hands in the 1820s and 1830s.[4]

But if American debt could be found in large quantities in Europe, the interest of the German states originally lagged behind. The Restoration period in France and the rise of the *haute banque* helped to facilitate the rise of private banks in the German states – entities that had a virtual monopoly on the German financial industry until 1870. These private banks centered around a series of predominantly Jewish families (perhaps none more famous than the Frankfurt-based Rothschilds), who originated as trading or merchant houses before shifting their focus more exclusively to finance. Frankfurt am Main became a financial center for the southern German states, precisely because of the concentration of German Jews in the city, its free city status, and its location at a relative crossroads for European commercial routes. International government loans became a focal point for German banks in Frankfurt, who sold and underwrote the various issues. To a lesser degree, such loans also found a home to the north in Hamburg. Among these government loans, American debt was no exception – but it took a series of financial events and political revolution for many Germans to shift their eyes across the Atlantic.[5]

---

4 For more on early American debt held by Europeans, see G. S. Callendar, 'The Early Transportation and Banking Enterprises of the States in Relation to the Growth of Corporations', *The Quarterly Journal of Economics* 17/1 (1902), pp. 111–62. See also D. C. North, 'The United States Balance of Payments, 1790–1860', *Trends in the American Economy in the Nineteenth Century*, The Conference on Research in Income and Wealth (Princeton, 1960), pp. 573–628, here pp. 582ff. For the Germans specifically, see S. Lentz, '"[E]ine viel wichtigere Persönlichkeit […] als der Präsident selbst": David Parish und die Finanzierung der US-Regierung im Krieg von 1812', *Die hanseatisch-amerikanischen Beziehungen seit 1790*, ed. C. Schnurmann and H. Herold (Trier, 2017), pp. 35–64.
5 G. Kurgan-van Hentenryk, 'Jewish Private Banks', *The World of Private Banking*, ed. P. Cottrell and Y. Cassis (Farnham, 2009), pp. 213–30, here p. 214.

By the 1830s, American state securities had become a valuable commodity in Europe – although still largely outside the German states. The fact that the United States had completely retired its national debt in 1836 meant that other American investment opportunities had become a necessity for European investors who wished to invest across the Atlantic. The British and Dutch, in particular, became interested in state securities. Amsterdam-based Hope & Co. marketed bonds of various American states and municipalities, such as New York City, Boston and even Mobile, Alabama. In London, the interest in American state securities was split between Baring Brothers and N. M. Rothschild. While most American securities sold abroad in the 1830s were initially sold in London, by the late 1830s these bonds could be found amongst the Dutch, but also the French, Portuguese, and increasingly the Germans and Swiss. In the summer of 1838, Congressman James Garland placed the amount of foreign debt held abroad at 65 million dollars.[6]

Speculation by American banks and a property bubble in the United States coupled with restrictive lending practices in Great Britain prompted the Panic of 1837 – a financial panic with transatlantic ramifications that ushered in a depression lasting into the middle part of the 1840s. The Panic of 1837 and its subsequent fallout proved to be one of the first real challenges for German investors in American indebtedness – but only after a flurry of increased debt sales abroad. The depression resulted in many American states looking to Europe to pursue new lines of capital. From 1837 to 1839, American state debt increased by more than 40 per cent, and some 100 million dollars of stocks and bonds found their way to London alone. This level of debt worried many European investors, however, and by the fall of 1839 the market for American state debt began to dry up across much of Europe. This, coupled with the failure of the Bank of the United States (operating under a state charter in Pennsylvania), resulted in a new, smaller panic in the fall of 1839. There was a quick rebound, however, and American state securities continued to flood markets throughout Europe – reaching the point by 1840 that every major European financial center had several financial houses selling American state securities. By 1841, many European banks (and politicians) had grown wary of language surrounding the reluctance of many states to honor their debts and called on the federal government to assume state debts. Such a practice – the brainchild of America's first Secretary of the Treasury, Alexander Hamilton – had occurred following the American Revolution, and many in Europe logically assumed that the federal government would not risk default on the part of numerous states within the Union. Missouri Senator Thomas Hart Benson, however, depicted the primary concern surrounding state debts, indicating that a federal assumption would be 'to the enormous and undue advantage of foreign capitalists'. Indeed, part of the 1840 presidential election entailed

6   Wilkins, *The History of Foreign Investment*, pp. 58f.

charges by the Democratic Party that a Whig victory would amount to foreign financiers taking over the federal government.[7]

By 1842, eight US states and one US territory (the future state of Florida) began to default on interest payments. While some states gave assurances that such actions were a temporary measure, others doubled down on the default as a way to 'punish' foreign investors. Governor Alexander McNutt of Mississippi specifically targeted the Jewish Rothschild family (with healthy Mississippi investments in the Frankfurt branch), commenting that 'the blood of Judas and Shylock flows' in their veins, and warning of a conspiracy on the part of the German family to 'mortgage our cotton fields and make serfs of our children'. By 1843, concerns over the level of American indebtedness in the hands of foreign creditors led to a Congressional investigation of the matter. The publication of a report on foreign debt projected 279 million dollars in total liabilities, of which 150 million dollars was held in Europe (of that 279 million dollars, 231 million was determined to be state debt). While almost every state began to resume their interest payments by the middle part of the 1840s (owing to the co-ordination of a wide array of European bankers in England, the Netherlands, and the German states), the actions of Southern states made some Europeans reticent to invest in the United States moving forward – even in United States federal debt and an emerging market for United States railroad stock.[8]

The turning point: 1848 and its aftermath

The reluctance to invest in American securities changed with the series of revolutions that swept through Europe in 1848. Specifically, the unrest in the German states stimulated capital flight. Coupled with the discovery of gold in California, many German investors began to wade into American markets to a degree never before seen. Germans began to invest at this point not only in state and federal debt, but also in large quantities of railroad bonds and shares. One estimate placed German acquisition between 1848 and 1851 at 42 million dollars. One investor in Bremen was alleged to have purchased over 40 different American securities by 1852. Increasingly, however, German emigrants found themselves purchasing American debt in part as a way to transfer their relative wealth across the Atlantic. On a whole, German immigrants brought greater wealth with them to the United States, and some opted to invest in the United States and its securities not only to ease their transfer of wealth, but also as a demonstration of loyalty to their new homeland.[9]

7   J. Sexton, *Debtor Diplomacy: Finance and American Foreign Relations in the Civil War Era, 1837–1873* (New York, 2005), pp. 25ff.
8   Sexton, *Debtor Diplomacy*, p. 27; North, 'United States Balance of Payments', p. 625 n. 81.
9   Wilkins, *The History of Foreign Investment*, p. 75.

A more profound ideological premise might have been afoot with German purchases – that of deeper anti-slavery ties that bound Americans and Germans together across the Atlantic. The American Revolution and constitution quickly found connections with European liberals who championed the new republic as an idealistic, even utopian, manifestation of the Enlightenment. In the minds of many German revolutionaries, the political liberalism of America stood in stark contrast to the repressive trends of Restoration Europe. For revolutionaries in 1848, the United States had become a symbol of political freedom – a great democratic experiment that all activists hoped to replicate back on the continent. To emulate the American federal system became an aspiration of many.[10]

The United States became a destination for many German Forty-Eighters. One of the earliest, Friedrich Hecker, arrived in New York City in the fall of 1848 to a crowd of some 20,000 people and an official delegation led by the mayor. Another leader, Carl Schurz, made the decision to sail from London, where he had been a part of the German exile community there. 'The ideas of which I have dreamed and for which I have fought I shall find there,' Schurz later recalled saying. All told, 130,000 Germans on average immigrated annually to the United States. Once in the United States, these immigrants took on active roles in civic and political organizations – and not just prominent educated leaders of the failed revolutions back in Europe. German Americans formed revolutionary societies to aid their brethren back across the Atlantic. In extreme cases, like the German Revolutionary League, there were even calls to annex portions of European states into the United States, thereby forming a world republic. Such a plan was laid out by Forty-Eighter Theodor Pösche in a book entitled *The New Rome: The United States of the World*.[11]

But if there was an idealistic notion of the United States and an enthusiasm for the American Republic, there ran a concurrent thread that championed the material gain one could achieve in this new America. Such hopes and aspirations quickly became one of the driving factors behind mass immigration to the United States and increased investment on the part of Germans in United States securities. Hundreds of guidebooks emerged for prospective travelers to America – detailing not only the great potential of this country on the other side of the ocean, but also the great stain of slavery in the eyes of many German liberals. This notion is one in further need of exploration, but certainly could go a long way towards explaining certain financial decision-making.[12]

10   These ideas – which are still in a very early stage for this project – rely heavily on the ideas of H. Keil that he explored in a 1999 talk entitled 'Race and Ethnicity: Slavery and the German Radical Tradition'.
11   A. Fleche, *The Revolution of 1861: The American Civil War in the Age of Nationalist Conflict* (Chapel Hill, 2012), pp. 22f, 27ff.
12   Therese Huber and Ottilie Assing provide two wonderful examples of German radicals who influenced anti-slavery sentiment. For more on Huber, see S. Lentz, 'Abolitionists in the German

Ideological motivations aside, the 1850s witnessed an increase in American state government debt exceeding 257 million dollars by 1860. Federal debt also increased over the course of this decade – especially in the second half of the 1850s, during the administration of President James Buchanan. At President Buchanan's inaugural address, he proclaimed, 'no nation has ever before been embarrassed from too large a surplus in the Treasury'. On the surface, evidence would support Buchanan's assertions. On 1 July 1857, the national debt stood at approximately 29 million dollars, with a cash balance in the Treasury of north of 17 million dollars. That being said, Buchanan's administration did a noble job in torpedoing the financial prospects of the United States. Issues over tariff policy and an increasing reliance on Treasury notes to fund the government resulted in a national debt of nearly 65 million dollars by 1 July 1860, with only 3.6 million dollars in cash reserves – a remarkable increase of 50 million dollars in financial liabilities for the country in a time of peace.[13]

For Germans, the 1850s ushered in a new era of American investment, reflected on the Frankfurt Börse specifically. In particular, municipal bonds took on a level of special importance. Between 1797 and 1848, not a single American security was listed on the Frankfurt Börse. Even by 1852, there was only federal debt and three other municipal bonds, in addition to a single railroad bond. But by 1854, American securities flooded Frankfurt – at least as far as listings. By 1854, there were 26 different American listings on the Frankfurt Börse foreign issues board. These included federal, state and municipal bonds (the Galena and Chicago Union Railroad being the only American railroad listed). With these dramatic gains came greater interest in American securities in Frankfurt specifically being publicized. One article in the summer of 1856 proclaimed: 'It is well known that a considerable amount of German capital is invested in American Bonds and Securities,' although the article did go on to note that many German investors had grown wary of several railroad bond and stock issues that had delayed payment.[14]

The election of Abraham Lincoln (supported by a large number of German immigrants) and the subsequent secession of seven Southern states ushered in a new era for transatlantic finance. German financiers and their clients watched with bated breath as a Civil War commenced on a scale never before seen. The exigencies of war required the United States to raise unprecedented amounts of capital to subdue the Confederacy – an area that geographically was the same

Hinterland? Therese Huber and the Spread of Anti-Slavery Sentiment in the German Territories in the Early Nineteenth Century', *Slavery Hinterland: Transatlantic Slavery and Continental Europe, 1680–1850*, ed. F. Brahm and E. Rosenhaft (Woodbridge, 2016), pp. 187–211.

13   E. Paxson Oberholtzer, *Jay Cooke: Financier of the Civil War*, 2 vols (Philadelphia, 1907), Vol. 1, pp. 121ff, 125ff.

14   H. Bohme, *Frankfurt und Hamburg: Des Deutsches Reiches Silber- und Goldloch und die Allerenglischste Stadt des Kontinents* (Frankfurt, 1968), pp. 156–61; 'American Securities in Europe', *The American Railroad Journal* 29 (1856), p. 458.

size as Western Europe. But this tells only part of the story of the successful execution of the financial war. The cause of the Union and emancipation relied upon a triumvirate of financial instruments: bond issues (more than two billion dollars' worth); the issuance of a new currency backed by the United States government, referred to as greenbacks and authorized by the Legal Tender Act of 1862; and a radical new taxation policy centered around the first income tax paved the way for Union success. But to tell the story of finance during the American Civil War, one must also consider the global dimension of the conflict – as Union bonds found takers on various continents, and especially among European investors.

American bonds in the German states during the American Civil War

Despite the successful efforts to sell bonds domestically among the Northern populace, international sales were important and indeed necessary for the success of the Union cause. In essence, international sales acted as a validation for the future success of Union securities – the mere act of European investment had an undeniable impact amongst financiers in the North, who shared their confidence with the general public. All told, several hundred million dollars' worth of these bonds made their way across the Atlantic during the war itself, finding investors in Britain, France, Belgium, Ireland, Russia, Switzerland, Austria, Italy, the German states and the Netherlands. Although Britain served as the perceived primary market for sales, in reality the under-appreciated continental sales in the Netherlands and especially amongst the anti-slavery population of the German states constituted the true market for international sales – revealing the political and economic pull of the continent, and reflecting the larger integration and sophistication of global capital markets by the middle of the nineteenth century. One estimate placed 250 million dollars of the 320 million dollars of wartime sales in the Netherlands and the German states.[15]

Nineteenth-century financial markets – and specifically the vibrant bond markets – are vital to understanding the political economy of this era. Bond issues and the market response to them reflected the political and diplomatic stakes of the time period. Established European houses such as the Rothschilds, Barings, and Hope & Co. (along with their correspondent banks) played as

---

15 Studying international bond sales during the American Civil War does not come without difficulty. Whereas the ledgers associated with the Bureau of Public Debt (housed at the National Archives) carry meticulous records of domestic primary purchases, secondary market sales (including to European banks) become much more difficult to trace. Additionally, many European firms' records have been lost to wars and time. Furthermore, Wall Street financial firms acting on behalf of international clients could hold bonds, so that the physical bonds never traveled overseas.

pivotal a role in politics as foreign ministers at times. Thus, by the time of the American Civil War, the Lincoln administration knew that an American bond issue that reached European markets played a crucial role in the fate of the Union abroad.

Many different German families forged connections between German financial centers and the emerging power of New York City. For example, Louis von Hoffman & Co. in New York shared partners with a German firm of the same name. Likewise, H. Gelpcke & Co. in New York conducted business with Breest & Gelpcke of Berlin. Philip Speyer of Frankfurt's Lazard Speyer-Ellissen formed Philip Speyer & Co. in the United States, while Darmstadter Bank opened a New York bank, G. von Baur & Co. In addition, firms just outside the German states (who nevertheless did extensive business with German customers) likewise set up American partners. New York bankers Adrian and John Iselin conducted extensive business, for instance, with Geneva-based Lombard Odier & Cie. Indeed, as Swiss bankers became more interested in American finance from the 1850s onward, they became incredibly active on the Frankfurt Börse in order to facilitate their purchases. Thus, the German financial industry, as we shall see, fostered a wide network of European trans-atlantic finance.[16]

All told, the United States government sold 2.27 billion dollars' worth of bonds during the American Civil War. These sales were through several dozen different loans authorized by Congress, and garnered between 5 per cent and 7.3 per cent interest. There were only three loan issues, however, that were of greatest interest to Europeans: the two 'National' 6 per cent loans of 1861 and 1865, and the most popular 6 per cent '5–20' loan. Congress passed the 500 million dollars '5–20' loan in the spring of 1862, and it earned its nickname because the bonds could be redeemed by the government after a minimum of five years but matured in 20 years. None of these bond issues were sponsored or underwritten by European banks. Rather, European banks acted as a secondary or tertiary market after purchasing the bonds, either directly from the United States government or from a financial partner in the States, most often in New York City.

The debate over international sales, however, began at home. While some criticized foreign sales and emphasized the political advantage of a purely domestic issue in wartime, others in Washington recognized the power of international support and foreign 'buy in' to the Union cause. Secretary of the Treasury Salmon Chase remarked that a foreign loan helped to ensure 'all hopes and all fears that the existing rebellion will result in a dismemberment of the American Republic are alike groundless'. Indeed, the passage of the first American loan bill in the summer of 1861 to finance the war included a provision for 50 million dollars of the bill in a direct European loan, if desired.

16 Wilkins, *The History of Foreign Investment*, pp. 98f.

Ultimately, the 50 million dollars provision was not enacted directly with any European banks, but Europeans began to purchase the bonds via American banking houses. Chase's successor, William Pitt Fessenden, demonstrated initial interest in pursuing an international direct loan, but by the fall of 1864 his opinion on the matter had soured, even leading him to declare in December 1864: 'This nation has been able, thus far, to conduct a domestic war of unparalleled magnitude and cost without appealing for aid to any foreign people.' While Fessenden's claim is certainly one of dubious validity, it was undoubtedly the case that at the highest levels of government the messaging on international bond sales (direct or indirect) was muddled at best.[17]

Civil War general and New York City Democratic Party politico Daniel Sickles also advocated for a foreign loan but emphasized the power of a widely held bond issue abroad. Writing from Union-occupied New Orleans, Sickles exclaimed:

> our bonds should be placed within the reach of <u>our friends in Europe</u> by a popular arrangement that will enable the <u>producing class</u> to buy them <u>in small amounts</u> – by means of pamphlets, friendly journals, and advertisements, the inducement of a fair commission held and to judicious agents – the excellence of the security and ample return in the way of interest would be made apparent to our friends and to all who like a proposition + safe investment ... The same could be done in Germany and probably in France.

Little did Sickles and others know that the United States government and financial houses abroad were already undertaking such activity.[18]

Despite the financial reputations of the London and Paris financial markets in the mid nineteenth century, in order to truly understand the primacy of Union sales abroad during the war, one must focus on the German states. The work of US minister William Murphy in Frankfurt offers a window into the breadth of these sales. Murphy, a fervent anti-slavery man, assumed the position of US Consul in June 1861, and once the war commenced he used his prominent position to host patriotic gatherings, which also doubled as multilevel marketing parties for Union bonds (his German guests were ready investors, given their deep anti-slavery ties). Murphy also reached out to editors of local newspapers to cover Union finances – and the Union cause more generally – in a very positive light. To be sure, the state of affairs in Frankfurt tracked the military fortunes of the Union army. The perceived setback at the Battle of Shiloh in

---

17   Salmon Chase to William Aspinwall, 30 March 1863, Salmon Chase Papers, Historical Society of Pennsylvania (hereafter: HSP), Philadelphia, Pennsylvania; Salmon Chase to Horace Greely, quoted in Sexton, *Debtor Diplomacy*, p. 128; William Pitt Fessenden quote, in Sexton, *Debtor Diplomacy*, p. 129.
18   Daniel Sickles to Salmon Chase, 5 July 1864, Salmon Chase Papers, HSP.

April 1862 had as much of an impact on finance as that of the great victory of the capture of New Orleans later that month.[19]

By 1863, such actions paid tremendous dividends, as Murphy reported to Secretary of State William Seward that the demand for bonds was 'so extensive as generally to exceed the supplies in the market'. Such interest in Germany accelerated following the Union victories at Gettysburg and Vicksburg in July 1863. 'The transactions in US bonds,' Murphy reported that summer, 'assumed, in fact, an astonishing extent.' The activity in Europe more broadly spiked beginning in the fall of 1863, largely owing to the rumor that a large German bank would float a loan to the federal government – something that would create a snowball effect of further financial support for the North. On 3 October 1863, Murphy wrote to Secretary Seward regarding the 10 million pounds sterling (slightly under 50 million dollars) 6 per cent loan that was potentially going to be offered by the Bank für Handel und Industrie in nearby Darmstadt. The bank was of 'good reputation and credit', as far as Murphy had uncovered, and had the potential to open the floodgates for European loans to the American government, causing some excitement on European exchanges. The efforts in Germany were fairly widespread – even Karl Marx reportedly purchased bonds in 1864. In addition, the efforts on the part of the French bank Erlanger to finance a cotton loan on behalf of the Confederacy can be seen in a somewhat different light when one realizes that Erlanger purchased Union bonds at the exact same time on the Frankfurt Börse.[20]

Alexander W. White, future co-founder and inaugural president of Cornell University, commented on the success of Murphy and Union securities during his travels through Germany in 1863. 'William Walton Murphy of Michigan,' remarked White, 'had labored hard to induce the Frankfurt bankers to take our government bonds, and to recommend them to their customers, and had at last been successful.' Upon his departure from Germany in late July 1863, White recalled one of his last experiences in Germany being a stroll with Murphy to the *Zeil* – a busy Frankfurt thoroughfare not far from the Börse (and currently the home to American fast-food restaurants and European retail chain stores) – where they encountered the Vice Consul, who handed Murphy a newspaper. Murphy 'tore it open, read a few lines, and then instantly jumped out into the middle of the street, waved his hat and began to shout. The public in general thought him mad ... but as soon as he could get his breath he pointed out the

---

19   For more on Shiloh and New Orleans impacting American securities in Frankfurt, see William Murphy to William Seward, 5 May 1862, RG 59, National Archives and Records Administration II, College Park, Maryland (hereafter: NARA II); William Murphy to William Seward, 19 May 1862, RG 59, NARA II; William Murphy to William Seward, 2 June 1862, RG 59, NARA II.

20   William Murphy to William Seward, 20 January 1863, RG 59, NARA II; Murphy to Seward, 27 July 1863, RG 59, NARA II; Murphy to Seward, 3 October 1863, RG 59, NARA II; Niall Ferguson, *The Cash Nexus: Money and Power in the Modern World, 1700–2000* (London, 2001), pp. 5f. For more on Murphy, see Sexton, *Debtor Diplomacy*, pp. 121ff.

headlines of the newspaper. They indicated the victories of Gettysburg and Vicksburg.'[21]

The '5–20' bond issues passed by the American Congress in 1862 were floated in Frankfurt and absorbed by some of the larger houses, such as Karl Pollitz, M. A. Gruenebaum & Ballin, Lazard Speyer-Ellisson, Metzler, and Seligman & Stettheimer, to name but a few of the banks. Murphy used the press to his advantage. Publications such as the *Neue Frankfurter Zeitung* and *L'Europe* championed Union bond sales while simultaneously downplaying efforts for a Confederate bond floated by Erlanger. The end result was the claim that 'hundreds of millions' of dollars were invested in American securities on the Frankfurt exchanges alone – a claim that seems on the surface to be quite credible.[22]

Keeping the war going: the final years

Various American government officials in the German states outside Frankfurt relayed the interest of the German people in American bonds as the calendar turned to 1864. Vice Consul W. Marsh of Hamburg wrote to Secretary of State Seward in July 1864, to communicate that: 'I had a call from Mr Hoffsteadt. The object of his visit was to inform me that he had had a consultation with eminent Bankers on the subject of a Premium Loan of 1,000 Million Dollars, as a preliminary step in support of his offer to the United States Government.' Marsh similarly relayed the impact of the successful re-election of Abraham Lincoln in the fall of 1864, and that proposals of international loans had tremendous impacts on international sales. 'At any rate I can truly say', remarked Marsh, 'that the German Loan which I was the promoter of had the effect here of selling millions of our Bonds.' Marsh similarly relayed the faith of German financiers when he remarked in the spring of 1865 (just a month before the Confederate surrender of forces at Appomattox Court House effectively ended the war),

---

21   Quoted in M. Sterne, 'From Jonesville to Frankfort on the Main: The Political Career of William Walton Murphy, 1861–1869', *Quarterly Review of the Michigan Alumnus* 65/18 (1959), pp. 251–61, here pp. 256f. Alexander White famously noted in his autobiography an instance while in London where he tried to exchange greenbacks for sterling and was sternly rebuked by the cashier: 'Don't offer us any of those things; we don't take them; they will never be good for anything.' A. D. White, *Autobiography of Andrew Dickson White* (New York, 1905), p. 194.

22   U. Heyn, *Private Banking and Industrialization: The Case of Frankfurt am Main, 1825–1875* (New York, 1981), pp. 274f; E. Korach, *Das Deutsche Privatbankgeschäft: Studien zu seiner Geschichte und heutigen Stellung* (Berlin, 1910), p. 31; Handelskammer Frankfurt, ed., *Geschichte der Handelskammer zu Frankfurt am Main (1707–1908)* (Frankfurt, 1908), pp. 1141f. For more on Austrian security depreciation, see D. C. M. Platt, *Foreign Finance in Continental Europe and the United States, 1815–1870* (Abington, 1984), pp. 90, 92ff; and D. Good, *The Economic Rise of the Hapsburg Empire* (Berkeley, 1984), p. 145.

'only we hear of Richmond falling you will see your stocks advance to 75 per cent of their value in Hamburg Change'.[23]

But perhaps one of the biggest contributing factors to the success of Union bonds in the German states stemmed from the personal and professional partnerships of banks in the United States and in Frankfurt. Indeed, the majority of these bonds surely made their way overseas via New York City houses that had German connections. One prime example is that of J. & W. Seligman & Co. Joseph Seligman originally immigrated from Germany to the United States in 1837 and quickly built a dry goods empire. By the time of the war, Seligman's company produced a large quantity of uniforms for the Union army. That being said, Seligman recognized the potential to become a significant player in international finance. As such, Joseph sent his brother Henry to Frankfurt in 1862 in the hopes of establishing a German house; Joseph subsequently followed him across the Atlantic, spending a significant amount of time in the region during the war. While the firm did not formally establish a banking house in Frankfurt until 1864, Joseph became active in the securities market during his visit. Seligman conveyed his confidence in American securities early on. 'Now I confess', admitted Seligman, 'that altho' I know the US to possess unparalleled resources, I sometimes doubt whether any people in any nation can successfully go on for years adding 1000s of millions to their National debt. If such a nation however does exist, there is no doubt but that the US are that nation.' While the exact total of Seligman's sales remains a mystery (owing to the likely destruction of pertinent materials by an archivist some 50 years ago), the firm undoubtedly played a critical role in financing Union bonds in the German states.[24]

One financial institution from Frankfurt that provides us with some of the most concrete numbers from this period is that of Bethmann Bankhaus. While more commonly associated with financing the Eiffel Tower in the 1880s, Bethmann actively traded in Union securities throughout the war. Beginning with National Loan '81 bonds (the first bond issues authorized by Congress, and so-called because they would reach full maturity in 1881), by the second quarter of 1864 the house rapidly advanced its position in 6 per cent 5–20 bonds (first issued by Congress in 1862). All told, the house purchased 620,000 dollars in 5–20 securities on the Frankfurt Börse between April 1864 and June 1865. Examining the Frankfurt stock quotations for Union bonds (known as

---

23   W. Marsh to Seward, 30 July 1864, RG 59, NARA II; W. Marsh to Seward, 23 November 1864, RG 59, NARA II; Marsh to Seward, 5 December 1864, RG 59, NARA II; W. Marsh to Seward, 8 March 1865, RG 59, NARA II.

24   Joseph Seligman Journal, Seligman Family Papers, New-York Historical Society, New York. The exact quantity of sales on the part of the Seligmans is a source of great debate. For more on Greenberg's questioning of the Seligman figure, see D. Greenberg, 'Yankee Financiers and the Establishment of Trans-Atlantic Partnerships: A Re-Examination', *Business History* 16/1 (1974), pp. 17–35.

the *Börsen-Kursblatt*) reveals the interest in American securities. While the National Loan had found its way onto the exchange by 1862, the 5–20 bonds were not listed on the exchange until 31 August 1863 and did not reflect prices until 8 September 1863. To demonstrate the volume of trading and general interest in 5–20 sales, by 1 August 1864, midday trading prices for 5–20s were being listed (the only non-German security listed aside from Austrian state securities, which eventually dissipated). A month later, the Kursblatt was also listing the price of the 5–20 on the Berlin exchange, one of only six securities quoted. Thus, by the late summer and early fall of 1864, American securities on the exchange were a remarkably popular commodity, rivaling any German state securities. The appeal of these securities made the German states the single most important international market for Union securities during the war – a feat that carried over into the post-war period as well.[25]

Wartime sales in Germany reached their height in February 1865, on the occasion of George Washington's birthday and the simultaneous report of the constitutional amendment to ban slavery in the American Congress. This important news, arriving on a symbolic holiday for Americans in Germany, led to the United States flag being flown over the American Consulate – an unusual occurrence at the time. While some sceptics were of the opinion that such an action was undertaken to bull the market, an official telegram from the United States confirming the passage of the Thirteenth Amendment led to a palpable energy permeating the entire exchange. Almost immediately, 5–20s rose 1 per cent on the Börse, and within two hours over 800,000 dollars of 5–20s had been sold. Additionally, rumors spread that the war had in fact concluded, leading to even further sales on the exchange in Frankfurt, as well as in Amsterdam, Munich and Berlin. In fact, Berlin sales of 5–20s reached a point that was 8 to 10 per cent above New York City price quotations.[26]

So, what quantity of bonds were sold in Germany by the end of the Civil War? A March 1865 *Philadelphia Daily Bulletin* article (ironically about the importance of keeping the loan domestic) stated that 200 million dollars of the loan could be found in Germany and nearly 100 million dollars in England, 'with a demand so rapidly increasing not only in these countries but in other parts of Europe that it is expected before long the aggregate total will exceed 500 million'. In June of 1865, former Secretary of the Treasury Robert Walker declared in a letter to Secretary of the Treasury McCulloch, 'more than 150 millions of our securities were sold, during less than two years in Europe'. In 1867, Robert Walker wrote of his exploits traveling through Europe. Accepting that 'any call for a loan would be defeated by the machinations of

---

25 Bethmann Bank Collection, Institut für Stadtgeschichte, Frankfurt, Germany; stock quotations drawn from Kursblatt records, Frankfurt Börse Papers, Hessisches Staatsarchiv, Darmstadt, Germany.
26 Oberholtzer, *Jay Cooke*, Vol. 1, p. 515.

France & England', Walker subsequently visited 'nearly every city of Holland and Germany, giving [an] opportunity to discuss the question personally with these bankers ... the result was that in a brief period the people of Germany, emphatically the great masses of the people, took several hundred millions of our loan at the same rates as our own citizens.' Similarly, years later, Otto von Bismarck could boast:

> It was reported to me that Lincoln could not keep the war going if he did not receive financial aid from Germany. His commissioners stated that they had been rebuffed in London & Paris. We wished the Union to be restored. The North seemed to me to be morally right, but, quite apart from that, we desired a strong prosperous and united Nation on the other side of the Atlantic.[27]

By March of 1865, it was estimated that 250 million of the 320 million dollars in US securities abroad were held in German and Dutch hands (a low estimation, in this author's opinion). Even many of the sales in Britain were on behalf of German and Dutch markets. While the Leipzig-based house of Knauth, Nachod & Kuhne provided the aforementioned estimate, they also pushed for a permanent American agent connected to a trustworthy banking house in Frankfurt, to ensure that sales of US securities remained honest on the exchange and did not devolve into pure speculation – a figure they put at 100 million dollars' worth of bonds at that time.[28]

Financial capitalism reoriented

If wartime sales were remarkable, it was the years immediately following the Civil War that revealed the evolving nature of global finance. For while London and Paris still retained important roles in investing in United States securities – especially as vital arbitrage markets – it was the Netherlands and the German states (eventually Germany) that took on a refined role. Berlin, Frankfurt and Hamburg all served as vital pieces in the American financial machine abroad. By contrast, the war represented a significant divergence for German markets towards American investments. Reflective of all of this, by the four-year anniversary of Appomattox, some one billion dollars in federal debt could be found in foreign hands.

---

27 *Philadelphia Daily Bulletin*, 29 March 1865; R. J. Walker, 'Our National Finances – An Open Letter to the American People', dated 30 November 1867 (Washington DC, 1867), quoted in J. Hawgood, 'The Civil War and Central Europe', *Heard Round the World: The Impact Abroad of the Civil War*, ed. H. Hyman (New York, 1969), pp. 145–76, here p. 151; ibid.
28 Sales estimate located in Knauth, Nachod & Kuhne to Jay Cooke, 30 March 1865, Jay Cooke Papers, HSP.

In order to examine these relationships, however, one must first understand the evolving demand for American debt in Europe by the late 1860s. By the summer of 1865, with the war for all intents and purposes over, European investors, most notably the Dutch and Germans, pushed foreign investment in the United States well beyond its pre-Civil War levels. Word quickly spread across the United States of the insatiable demand for federal debt in the German states. Just months after the war had ended, the *New York Times* republished a letter that had originally run in Altona. The letter concluded with the following passage: 'The Germans are a thrifty and safe calculating people, ever choosing the safest and best marks for their products, whether money or goods, and they seem to be now the war is over, perfectly satisfied to deposit their savings in American securities.'[29]

But what accounted for the interest in the German states that fed the demand? For some, the bonds were purchased in anticipation of European conflict between the French and German states. One report from Germany indicated, 'a real investment demand for 5–20s is now setting in from the peasantry and that class of people, especially since the war looks inevitable'.[30] For others, bonds took on geopolitical relevance. 'These bonds also invite a large immigration,' one article proclaimed:

> When the people of Europe receive that the great republic meets its interest promptly, and that too of so high a rate ... the emigrant carries with him his bonds, because he feels the confidence that he can realize upon them ... It seems to us that the missionary influence of those bonds in Americanizing Europe, in drawing its people to our government, and in making them as it were the constant watchers of American progress, is indeed boundless.[31]

Another letter written from an American in Germany reinforced this sentiment of the power of bonds on immigration:

> These bonds are the most powerful and influential emissaries you could have sent over to the Old Continent to convert the masses in republican principles. They never before heard so much talk about America; your means and resources, your future and your prospects, are discussed everywhere, and in such favorable terms that emigration is the leading topic among the sturdy masses; and the next year will bring you for every $1,000 of your bonds taken in Germany, at least one of her sturdy sons.[32]

29 'Five-Twenties Abroad', *New York Times*, 2 April 1867.
30 'American Bonds Hoarded Abroad', *Gettysburg Sentinel*, 26 June 1866.
31 'Our Bonds Abroad – A Powerful American Missionary', *Semi-Weekly Wisconsin* (Milwaukee), 28 February 1866.
32 Quoted in ibid.

Whatever the reason, the post-Civil War period marked a dramatic increase in interest in American debt on the part of German banks and their array of clients and partners across Europe.

In reality, the sale of Union securities during the war and in its immediate aftermath perhaps belied a starker transformation: that the national financial infrastructure created during the war took a national moment and portended an international revolution for American banks. Banking structures that had previously existed on local levels were now elevated to a national financial structure that took on transnational ramifications. Furthermore, the war and international markets for Union securities on such a large level took *antebellum* British structures and flipped them on their head. *Antebellum* British banking partnerships with American partners (not sending agents, as British banks were accustomed to doing) became a model that American banks took as they expanded into international markets. No longer subservient to British banks, the post-war period witnessed American finance wading into international (and especially continental) markets like never before, and fundamental to this were Union bonds. Just as important to this were German banks, working closely in concert with American partners to facilitate new routes of capital that relied less on the financial metropoles of London, Paris and Amsterdam.[33]

Thus, American finance had come full circle. The *antebellum* financial system predicated on British and (to a lesser degree) Dutch financial entities had witnessed a reversal by which American banks were projecting a new wealth overseas. A national financial transformation facilitated by the Legal Tender Act and National Banking Act had forced American banks to shed the *antebellum* financial world, only to expand a powerful sphere of influence abroad. The United States was not the world's creditor – yet – but the financial transformations of the Civil War era enabled Gilded Age finance to propel America in that pivotal direction. Key to this transformation was a new financial partner abroad – the emerging world of German finance that became deeply entwined with American bankers. New York, Frankfurt, Berlin and Hamburg all could now rightfully take their place on the world financial stage – true financial centers no longer operating on the periphery. A deeper exploration and further levels of analysis are vital to understand this story of the increasing financial ties between these two nations and how they contributed to the emergence of Germany and the United States as two economic powerhouses by the end of the century.

33 Such a notion of British bank inversion is addressed by J. Sexton in his recent work, 'International Finance in the Civil War Era', *The Transnational Significance of the American Civil War*, ed. J. Nagler, D. Doyle and M. Gräser (Basingstoke, 2016), pp. 91–106.

13

Afterword

GÖRAN RYDÉN

This is a book about connections, which is hardly a surprising thing in a collected volume bearing the title *Globalized Peripheries*. This is a volume creating a place for itself in the buoyant field of global history, and in doing so, the concept of connections is one of the first tools to be picked out of the historian's toolbox. This is hardly a new feature in global history. In his very influential *The Birth of the Modern World* (2004), C. A. Bayly added the subtitle *Global Connections and Comparisons*, and in his first paragraph, he stated that the 'revolutionary age' began in the 1780s and that this had to do with 'the interconnectedness and interdependence of political and social changes'. Four years earlier another mainstay of global history, Kenneth Pomeranz's *The Great Divergence*, had been published – and its first chapter featured the concepts of comparison and connection in the title. Pomeranz strove to both compare and relate China to Europe. It is fair to say that these 'double Cs' have figured prominently in all global history since the Millennium, even if some writers have preferred to use synonyms – like integration or interaction – when debating whether continents, countries, regions or other places belonged together. Global history has hovered over the question of belonging, and who or what belonged to whom and what.[1]

---

1 C. A. Bayly, *The Birth of the Modern World, 1780–1914: Global Connections and Comparisons* (Oxford, 2004); K. Pomeranz, *The Great Divergence: China, Europe, and the Making of the Modern World Economy* (Princeton, 2000); J. Osterhammel and N. P. Petersson, *Globalization: A Short History* (Princeton, 2003), pp. 13ff. It is interesting to note that the 'double Cs' have turned into 'treble Cs' or even 'quadruple Cs' by adding discussions about communities and circulations. See G. Rydén, 'Provincial Cosmopolitans: An Introduction', *Sweden in the Eighteenth-Century World: Provincial Cosmopolitans*, ed. G. Rydén (Farnham, 2013), pp. 22ff.

The present volume fits nicely into such a setting, of a 'double C paradigm', with its ambition of linking, connecting, Eastern and Central Europe to the Atlantic World, through 'trading practices', 'commodity flows', migration, financial systems, et cetera. But connection is a tricky concept, as are its various synonyms. A first problem is to decide what to connect – something that is seldom too obvious. Most global history has proceeded along a macro level, linking 'global' places with other 'global' locations, while others have attempted to integrate individuals and a micro perspective to their ambitions. Bayly, for instance, wanted to begin his treatment with 'bodily practices' before ascending to a more familiar macro perspective. This volume builds on this existing scholarship, but also considers the epistemological baggage that shaped it. The stated aim is 'to show on the basis of empirical findings that the historiography of the Atlantic World has created a misleading image of apparent "centers" and "peripheries" of the early modern world economy that should be called into question'. This volume thus tackles both theoretical and methodological questions.[2]

The theoretical ambition at work here is, on an abstract level, connected to the powerful model of center – semiperiphery – periphery, established by Immanuel Wallerstein and other world-systems theorists many decades ago; but on a more concrete plane, it is about the place of Eastern and Central Europe in such a way of ordering the world. The overarching ambition is thus to (re-)instate forgotten, or neglected, regions into the narrative of the emergence of the modern world. These theoretical ambitions are attached to the methodological approach permeating this volume; true to the German historiographical tradition, the empirical approach is highlighted in many of the chapters. To name just a few: the chapters by Wimmler and Gehrmann stress the importance of the Sound Toll Registers in monitoring the trade to and from the Baltic Sea, while dos Santos Arnold uses the *Admiralitäts- und Convoygeld-Einnahmebücher* to measure the trade to Hamburg. These chapters could not have been written without these sources – something that justifies the distinct methodological approaches of many of the chapters.

The 'forgotten region' ambition is a central feature in this volume, and it is so from two different angles. On the one hand, it is obvious that Eastern and Central Europe were closely attached to the Atlantic economy. The chapter by Steffen shows how Silesian linen became a staple in the early modern Atlantic trade, and that both the West African market and its Caribbean counterpart received large volumes of textiles shipped down the Elbe and then exported

2   Bayly, *The Birth of the Modern World*, p. 1. For an introduction to these different ways of approaching global history, relating to the Atlantic World, see J. P. Greene and P. D. Morgan, eds, *Atlantic History: A Critical Appraisal* (Oxford, 2009). The masterpiece in bringing the micro perspective into dialogue with the macro level is E. Rothschild, *The Inner Life of Empires: An Eighteenth-Century History* (Princeton, 2011).

through Hamburg. A similar story, but with a reverse commodity chain, is told by Wimmler and dos Santos Arnold. Large shipments of sugar arrived in Stettin and Hamburg. On the other hand, these narratives, together with the other chapters, make it possible to refute the Wallerstein theory; Wimmler and Weber strive in their introduction for something 'beyond Wallerstein', and the chapter by Kaps, for instance, points to the validity of such an ambition. In his analysis of Trieste as a gateway to the Spanish Empire, Kaps points to the problematic position of viewing both the port in the Adriatic Sea as well as producing centers within the Habsburg Empire as merely dependent semiperipheries.

The present volume is not the only project trying to attach Eastern, Central or Continental Europe to discussions about the Atlantic World or global history. At least two previous English published collections share the same agenda. *Slavery Hinterland: Transatlantic Slavery and Continental Europe, 1680–1850*, edited by Felix Brahm and Eve Rosenhaft (2016), is also about connections; but by emphasizing the term 'hinterland' in their title, a slightly different theoretical starting point is established. In their introduction to the volume, Brahm and Rosenhaft argue that this term, initially with a spatial meaning, has a contested history closely attached to a hierarchical thinking, in which the 'hinterland' was subordinated to a center. Still, the term could prove useful as a means of attracting attention to 'forgotten regions', and 'to identify an inland area that is economically or politically *related* to a port city'. The difference between the two approaches might just be one between a spatial outlook, the 'hinterland', and a theoretical approach, to move 'beyond Wallerstein'.[3]

Slavery and the slave trade in a German context is also the focus of the second collection published in English, in a thematic issue of *Atlantic Studies* from 2017; the 'colonial amnesia of Germans' is the starting point, and how this has 'contributed to a still persistent racism in German society'. The way to tackle this 'amnesia' and present-day racism is by more historical research. In the introduction to the volume, the editors Heike Raphael-Hernandez and Pia Wiegmink propose a connection between the early German encounters with slavery and the later German colonization of Africa. In their handling of these topics, the concept of 'entanglements' is crucial. On face value, we are once again dealing with a synonym for connections, but the concept of entanglement has previously been used in global history writing as a slightly more open-ended approach that enables scholars to look at a connection – or interactions – from two different angles, illustrating their interdependence.[4]

---

3   F. Brahm and E. Rosenhaft, 'Introduction: Towards a Comprehensive European History of Slavery', *Slavery Hinterland: Transatlantic Slavery and Continental Europe, 1680–1850*, ed. F. Brahm and E. Rosenhaft (Woodbridge, 2016), pp. 1–23, here p. 4 (my italics).

4   H. Raphael-Hernandez and P. Wiegmink, 'German Entanglements in Transatlantic Slavery: An Introduction', *Atlantic Studies* 14/4 (2017), pp. 419–35, here p. 420.

It is easy for me, as a Scandinavian global historian, to feel a kind of familiarity with this 'forgotten region' approach. Other regions experienced a similar
destiny. One such region, or perhaps better an empire, actually features in the
volume; in the chapter by Gehrmann we are told the story of how rhubarb
was brought from China to Europe via Russia. Another part of Europe, which
has largely been left out of the discussion about the Atlantic World and global
history, is Scandinavia and the Baltic provinces. Perhaps by overstretching the
meaning of Wallerstein's model it is possible to stress that the early modern
semiperiphery, in the guise of Scandinavia, has been relegated to a position in
the periphery in recent global history writing – surpassed by the early modern
periphery, in the guise of regions like the Caribbean, West Africa, et cetera.
The obvious centerpiece during both the early modern world and in most
global history writing has been the main Atlantic powers, with Britain at its
epicenter. The main interest of much of both global and Atlantic history has
been the connections between the center and the periphery; between Britain
and West Africa, the Caribbean, the North American colonies, et cetera, with
Scandinavia, along with Central Europe, left out.

Having said that, recent research indicates that Scandinavia, along with
Eastern and Central Europe, was closely connected to the Atlantic World
and has a place within global history. In one sense, Sweden and Denmark
were actually more closely tied to the early modern global development than
Continental Europe, and especially so as both countries established chartered
companies that traded with both Asia and within the Atlantic economy. Apart
from a short episode in the seventeenth century with an African company,
Sweden took part in the trade with China through its East India Company
from 1732. Denmark had a much longer tradition and traded in both Asia and
across the Atlantic, through an Asiatic Company and a Guinea and West India
Company. The Oldenburg monarchy actually established a powerful trading
station in India and West Africa, apart from the fully developed colonies in
the Caribbean. This also meant that the Danes became deeply involved in both
slavery and the slave trade, from the latter days of the seventeenth century until
the first years of the nineteenth century. The Danes also colonized Iceland and
Greenland.[5]

Apart from this direct Scandinavian involvement in global trade, the region
experienced a similar situation to Eastern and Central Europe, discussed in
the related literature above. To a large extent, it was Swedish and Norwegian

5   *Danmark og Kolonierne*, 5 vols: M. Venborg Pedersen, ed., *Danmark og Kolonierne –
Danmark: En Kolonimagt (Copenhagen, 2017); N. Brimmes, ed., *Danmark og Kolonierne – Indien:
Tranquebar, Serampore og Nicobarerne* (Copenhagen, 2017); P. O. Hernæs, ed., *Danmark og
Kolonierne – Vestafrika: Forterne på Guldkysten* (Copenhagen, 2017); P. E. Olsen, ed., *Danmark
og Kolonierne – Vestindien: St Croix, St Thomas og St Jan* (Copenhagen, 2017); H. C. Gylløv,
ed., *Danmark og Kolonierne – Grønland: Den Arktiske Koloni* (Copenhagen, 2017); L. Müller,
Sveriges Första Globala Århundrade: En 1700–Talshistoria (Stockholm, 2018).

metal-making that created the foundation for the Scandinavian participation in global trade. Norwegian silver, copper from Falun and Røros as well as Swedish iron were a much sought-after resource; they made up a large share of what the chartered companies brought from Scandinavia, but these metals were also exported through other channels. It is likely that Scandinavian copper found its way to both West African and Caribbean markets, as manillas and as equipment for the sugar plantations, and Swedish iron (voyage iron) was used as barter for slaves along the Guinea coast. The Scandinavian involvement in global trade was not only a supply-sided phenomenon, as the region also received large shipments of colonial goods. The volume of imported sugar increased in both the Danish and the Swedish realms, and consumption levels rose radically during the eighteenth century.[6]

It is clear that much of the Scandinavian research into this development can be characterized as a version of the 'forgotten region' paradigm. About 10 years ago, I was involved in a small project, together with Leos Müller and Holger Weiss, aiming for a kind of inventory of Swedish and Finnish global history research, resulting in a collected volume. In our introduction to the volume, we began by telling the story of how Swedish herring, salted with Portuguese salt, became food for Caribbean slaves, who in turn produced sugar for the European market. Our conclusion from that example was that Swedish developments had a place in the narrative of how Europe came to dominate a large part of the globe, and that it was essential that Swedish and Finnish scholars seriously adapted to this challenge. The narrative throughout the collection was centered on Sweden, and our plea was that the Swedish realm ought to have a place within global history.[7]

A decade later, things had gradually changed, and a kind of entanglement perspective was more pronounced. From a personal point of view, one can clearly detect a changing outlook from the arguments in *Baltic Iron in the Atlantic World in the Eighteenth Century*, published in 2007, to '"Voyage Iron": An Atlantic Slave Trade Currency, its European Origins, and African Impacts', published in 2018 (both written with Chris Evans). The former used an almost Wallersteinian model with Britain as its center, Sweden and Russia in the semiperiphery, and with West Africa and South Carolina as the periphery, and with the ambition of inserting Sweden into an analysis of the early modern Atlantic development. The latter text takes a different standpoint and views the development from an African angle. Even if iron was produced in West Africa, the output was smaller than the demand, which made the supply of Swedish

6   C. Evans and G. Rydén, '"Voyage Iron": An Atlantic Slave Trade Currency, its European Origins, and African Impacts', *Past & Present* 239/1 (2018), pp. 41–70; K. Rönnbäck, *Commerce and Colonisation: Studies of Early Modern Merchant Capitalism in the Atlantic Economy* (Gothenburg, 2009).
7   L. Müller, G. Rydén and H. Weiss, eds, *Global Historia från Periferin: Norden 1600–1850* (Lund, 2009).

iron important in the development of African agriculture.[8] A similar historiographical development can also be seen in Denmark. Studies about the Danish
colonial past have a long history, but for a long time they focused mostly on
trade to and from Copenhagen. Recently this has changed, and the five-volume
work *Danmark og Kolonierne* is an impressive example of an entangled global
history. In the volume on West Africa, to take just one example, the authors
have chosen the African viewpoint, and their treatment mainly concentrates
on what took place in and around Christiansborg, the Danish headquarter on
the Gold Coast. They deal with local politics and struggles, everyday life in the
castle, the slave trade, et cetera.[9]

Beyond a doubt, Scandinavia has been one of the 'forgotten regions' in the
rapidly developing field of global history. Another neglected region is Eastern
and Central Europe. At best, these two large parts of Europe have been characterized as 'global peripheries' in studies that have analyzed the transatlantic
slave trade, or trade in luxury goods like tea, sugar, coffee, et cetera. In recent
years, this neglect has been noticed by Scandinavian as well as Central European
scholars; an increasing number of studies have shown that both regions were
attached to the development of an Atlantic World, and that they both need to
be better integrated within global history writings. Early modern Scandinavia,
Eastern and Central Europe were connected to a wider world. Scandinavian
scholars have pointed to the importance of metals and metalwares from Sweden
and Norway in the Atlantic trade, and a similar argument has been put forward
about both metals and textiles from the Holy Roman Empire. Other studies
have also shown the importance of German merchants and capital, as well as
Scandinavian shipping, in this trade from port cities along the Atlantic coast.
These new findings from the last decade are, however, only a first step in order
to integrate these 'forgotten regions' into a fully developed analysis of the
early modern Atlantic World. It is also a mere beginning in a process of fully
recognizing Scandinavia, as well as Eastern and Central Europe, as equally
important parts in the field of global history. What is needed, after having
generated new empirical findings, is another step that begins to scrutinize the
theoretical foundations of the previous models of both the Atlantic World
and global developments more generally. What is needed is an attempt to go
'beyond Wallerstein'.

In what way do the individual chapters of this volume help us to go 'beyond
Wallerstein'? This is the simple question we have to ask, as it is the main
question addressed in the introduction by Wimmler and Weber. Before that,
however, a short characterization of the 11 chapters is necessary. It is obvious
that most of them remain close to the favorite topic of global history writing:

---

8   C. Evans and G. Rydén, *Baltic Iron in the Atlantic World in the Eighteenth Century* (Leiden,
2007); Evans and Rydén, '"Voyage Iron"'.
9   Hernæs, ed., *Danmark og Kolonierne – Vestafrika*.

that of trade. Anka Steffen analyzes linen from Silesia on the Atlantic market, followed by Jutta Wimmler's treatments of Prussian imports through the port of Stettin, and Torsten dos Santos Arnold's description of imports to Hamburg. Klemens Kaps concentrates on Trieste as a gateway for goods from the Habsburg Monarchy; Anne Sophie Overkamp studies textile merchants in the Wupper Valley, while Margrit Schulte Beerbühl follows German merchants to London and other European port cities. David K. Thomson's chapter could also be inserted under the 'trade' heading, although he deals with the financial sphere; Friederike Gehrmann also studies trade, but as noted above, she analyzes the Russian rhubarb trade. The remaining three chapters have a different agenda. Two of them could loosely be said to deal with migration. Josef Köstlbauer writes about the Moravian networks spanning the Atlantic, while Alexandra Gittermann's topic is the German migration to the North American colonies. The first empirical chapter of the volume, by Bernhard Struck, is really the odd one out, as it relates the partition of Poland in 1772 to political events and climatic changes in the Atlantic World.

In many ways, the contribution by Steffen could be seen as leading the way to move 'beyond Wallerstein'. She begins her chapter by posing the question of why previous studies of the Atlantic economy have concentrated on cotton rather than linen, even when studies have shown that the African market demanded both these textiles. Steffen's study adds to this picture that linen, like cotton, came in a wide variety of qualities and forms, and that African consumers knew what they wanted. Her analysis is mainly focused on the Atlantic, but a few words are spared for Silesia, the Central European region where the linen was manufactured, and the conclusion is that the Atlantic 'entanglement' actually strengthened the feudal bonds in the region at the same time as the linen merchants grew richer. The causality link in the text goes from the Atlantic World to Silesia, but could one – perhaps – not change the outlook and imagine that the developments in a 'landlocked' Central European region also affected what happened in West Africa?

In Wimmler's case, the focus is clearly on Prussia, as she is investigating trade from the Atlantic, aiming for a discussion about consumption of 'overseas products'. She can show that sugar was imported in large quantities and then transported to Berlin on newly built waterways. The port also received dyestuffs, which were highly sought after by textile and uniform makers in the capital. Prussia was thus connected to the Atlantic economy, but the question might be posed as one between a supply- and demand-sided explanation. Perhaps we might view the military demand for colored uniforms as a sign of the latter; in terms of military power, the eighteenth-century Prussian state cannot be viewed as a 'semiperiphery'!

With dos Santos Arnold's chapter, we leave the Central European 'hinterland' for a study mainly about the actual shipping of goods to Hamburg. The port on the Elbe was the main gateway into Central Europe, but little is said about that. Instead, the chapter is about the origin of the sugar, and which merchants dominated the sugar trade. One interesting feature is that these merchants were able to switch suppliers and acted thus from a rather powerful position, something that might make us curious about the position of Hamburg in Wallerstein's schema.

The chapter by Kaps is one of the few chapters in the volume that clearly picks up the theoretical discussion from the introduction; the question was whether 'the Habsburg Monarchy was ... marginalized from global markets and thus a semi-peripheral space'. Like Wimmler, he argues against it being marginalized. Trieste was transformed as a result of cameralist ideas that developed the port into an important node in the trade with the Spanish Empire. The Habsburg Monarchy was more of a core region than a periphery, and the reasons behind the expansion of trade are to be found in internal features within the monarchy.

Overkamp also has a theoretical beginning, as she adds a discussion about cartels to one about peripheries, and she does so in a study firmly located in a landlocked region of the Wupper Valley. She shows how merchants enhanced their position by collaborating, and that they thereby partly suspended the dependency of their region. In a direct criticism of Wallerstein, she states that his analytical framework lacks the 'individual agents', and that he therefore cannot anticipate a situation with a different set of power relations than stipulated by the model. The Wupper Valley merchants were hardly dependent agents on the Central European textile market.

Such a perspective is also accentuated by Schulte Beerbühl in her chapter on German merchants in London. The changing linen trade after 1660 is the foundation for her study, in which she shows how the novel situation, with new trade routes and supply chains, was greatly affected by the active ambitions of the merchants and their willingness to migrate to the major Atlantic ports, and London in particular. Once again, we are left with an implicit criticism of the center/periphery way of analyzing the world, as how should we characterize German merchants in London? Do they belong in the center or in the (semi-)periphery?

People on the move is also the topic of Köstlbauer's article, but movements are tricky to pin down as either for or against the hierarchical thinking of Wallerstein. Köstlbauer writes about the religious networks of the Moravian Brethren. In an interesting analysis, it is shown how they seem to have moved in a completely different social set-up. Men, women, children, slaves and slave owners moved around the Atlantic in circles not resembling other circuits, proving that the agents actually created their own destiny and social settings, as well as the mental and social outlook, in a fashion not envisaged by advocates of the World-System theory.

The migration perspective is even more accentuated in the chapter by Gittermann. She begins by stating that the Atlantic World was not only about goods on the move, and follows this up by stating that slaves were not the only humans who crossed the ocean in large numbers. Her chapter is about Germans leaving Europe for a new life in the North America colonies; once again, we are left with the question of how to categorize people, agents, in different spatial settings. Large numbers of Germans left their homes in peripheral parts of Central Europe for a new life in peripheral parts of Northern America. They were willing immigrants, but the process was also related to colonial ambitions, and thus part of much larger processes.

For Gehrmann as well, the question of how to categorize a region is paramount, and in her case the master question is whether Russia should 'remain' in the periphery, as world-systems theorists have decided, or not. She argues that Russia was well integrated in the global economy, not least as an intermediary of goods from Asia to Europe. The rhubarb trade is her focus, and that is linked to the fur trade, both in Siberia and North America.

Two of the chapters in this volume fall slightly outside the scope focused on by the other chapters. Thomson's chapter can be viewed in the light of trade, but it deals with a much later period than the others – he analyzes financial relations between Germany and the US, but during the nineteenth century – while Struck takes a geopolitical perspective in his chapter on the first partition of Poland. Concerning Thomson's text, it is tricky to make the same kind of comments about peripheries. By the nineteenth century, both investigated countries had begun the journey from the outskirts of the world to becoming something more along the lines of centerpieces in the geopolitical developments that followed the period studied by Thomson, although he does not deal with this change as such.

Arriving last at Struck's chapter, placed first in the volume, on the question of whether Prussia had an Atlantic history, it is striking to say that this chapter is in many ways the only one that debates with world-systems theorists with their own armaments; Struck really paints with large brushes and relates large historical processes to each other. His aim is to write a global history of the Polish partition, but his narrative starts in the Caribbean after the end of the Seven Years' War. The argument is that states in the second half of the eighteenth century strove to expand their realms, subjugating more people and resources. During the decades after the peace of Paris, many more hurricanes ravaged the Caribbean, making it more problematic to expand the plantation system. The outlook for a geopolitical strengthening was much better in continental Europe, and Prussia's power expanded while France and Britain lost power. Once again, we are left with an argument like Wimmler's, that it might not be wise to view eighteenth-century Prussia as part of the European periphery.

It is with new empirical studies that we can challenge, and ultimately modify, previous explanations of historical change. This volume set the agenda of moving 'beyond Wallerstein', and thus to challenge the theory of the Modern World-System that has reigned for so long within much global history writing. In particular, the aim was to (re-)instate Eastern and Central Europe into a constructive analysis of the early modern Atlantic World, as well as to claim a rightful place in future global history writings. The 11 empirical chapters of this volume have clearly shown that much of Europe has been neglected in such a discussion, and they have shown that Eastern and Central Europe were connected to the Atlantic World. In doing so they have also, together with similar studies, created a foundation for a critical discussion about the frames for analyzing the Atlantic World.

The most striking feature of these studies is the latent questioning of the preconditioned nature of the World-System approach; where Wallerstein implied a more or less constant power relation between the center and the peripheries, the contributors to this volume always wanted to investigate the concrete connections between the different nodes of the system. In doing so they established a much more complicated picture of the early modern Atlantic World. London, and the British economy, must still be seen as an indisputable center around which much activity and life orbited, but power, economic wealth and agency could also be found in other places; power and wealth were to be found in Eastern and Central Europe, as they were at other places outside the center.

A second important conclusion to draw from these empirical investigations is the importance of adding agency to the structural analysis of world-systems. Many of the chapters have shown the way in which people had the power to change and challenge the structures in which they lived and acted. It is important to note that, when this happened, it must be read as a sign that power relations were not always something that went from the center to the periphery. Several chapters have shown that they also went the other way round. A third feature is that not all connections of importance are economic links. Several chapters have indicated that it might be strange to view eighteenth-century Prussia – or even the Habsburg Monarchy – as a periphery, considering its military strength and ability to enforce its power on most of Europe.

If such critical assessments of previous theoretical explanations are to be seen as a second step in the process of (re-)integrating Eastern and Central Europe into a wider discussion about the early modern Atlantic World and global history writings, there are also more steps one should consider. On the one hand, global historians must begin to question their findings in relation to what it means and meant to state that a region was integrated into, or connected to, the Atlantic World. Many of the chapters in this volume have shown that Eastern and Central Europe were connected to the Atlantic World, but does that automatically imply that we can label these regions as Atlantic, or that they were global regions? The questions that must be posed after the steps taken here are about the impact on people, and how far we can approach along the line of connecting. It seems to me that, when we have moved 'beyond Wallerstein', we must approach global history also from below, and connect the macro perspective with a micro perspective that better enables us to link up with the lives of ordinary people. If agency should be taken seriously, one must make an effort to include the agency of all people.

On the other hand, it is also crucial that global historians – whether from Central Europe, Scandinavia, or any other place around the globe – integrate their deep and penetrating research into the present-day debates about problems commonly referred to as generated by the process of globalization. Germany is hardly the only country with a 'colonial amnesia'. On the contrary, this kind of oblivion seems to be pervasive. In what is one of the most important Scandinavian books on the early modern Atlantic World, *Slavhandel och Slaveri under Svensk Flagg*, Holger Weiss sets the tone with a thorough discussion of the political debate about Swedish slavery that occurred in 2007, the 200th anniversary of the British abolition of the slave trade. The historical narrative of Swedish slavery came after. We simply cannot forget that history matters today, and that the task of historians is to make that clear.[10]

10   H. Weiss, *Slavhandel och Slaveri under Svensk Flagg: Koloniala Drömmar och Verklighet i Afrika och Karibien 1770–1847* (Helsinki, 2016).

Bibliography of Secondary Works Cited

Aaslestad, K., and J. Joor, eds, *Revisiting Napoleon's Continental System: Local, Regional and European Experiences* (Basingstoke, 2015).

Adamczyk, D., *Zur Stellung Polens im modernen Weltsystem der frühen Neuzeit* (Hamburg, 2001).

Adelmann, G., 'Strukturwandlungen der rheinischen Leinen- und Baumwollgewerbe zu Beginn der Industrialisierung', *Vierteljahrschrift für Sozial- und Wirtschaftsgeschichte* 53 (1966), pp. 162–84.

Akademiia Nauk SSSR, ed., *Russko-Kitaiskie Otnosheniia 1689–1916: Ofitsialnye Dokumenty* (Moscow, 1958).

Alden, D., 'The Undeclared War of 1773–1777: Climax of Luso-Spanish Platine Rivalry', *Hispanic American Historical Review* 1/41 (1961), pp. 55–74.

Aldenhoff-Hübinger, R., C. Gouseff and T. Serrier, eds, *Europa Vertikal: Zur Ost-West-Gliederung im 19. und 20. Jahrhundert* (Göttingen, 2016).

Alpern, S. B., 'What Africans Got for their Slaves: A Master List of European Trade Goods', *History in Africa* 22 (1995), pp. 5–43.

Alpers, E. A., 'Indian Textiles at Mozambique Island in the Mid-Eighteenth Century', *Textile History* 48/1 (2017), pp. 31–48.

Andreozzi, D., 'Tra Trieste, Ancona, Venezia e Bologna: La Canapa e il Commercio nell'Adriatico del '700', *Trieste e l'Adriatico: Uomini, Merci, Conflitti* (Trieste, 2005), pp. 153–201.

——, 'From the Black Sea to the Americas: The Trading Companies of Trieste and the Global Commercial Network (18th Century)', *Mediterranean Doubts: Trading Companies, Conflicts and Strategies in the Global Spaces (XV–XIX Centuries)*, ed. D. Andreozzi (Palermo, 2017), pp. 65–87.

Armitage, D., and S. Subrahmanyam, eds, *The Age of Revolutions in Global Context, c. 1760–1840* (Basingstoke, 2009).

Armitage, D., 'The Atlantic Ocean', *Oceanic Histories*, ed. D. Armitage, A. Bashford and S. Sivasundaram (Cambridge, 2018), pp. 85–110.

Ashtor, E., 'The Volume of Mediaeval Spice Trade', *Journal of European Economic History* 9/3 (1980), pp. 753–63.

Augustyn, W., 'Friede und Gerechtigkeit – Wandlungen eines Bildmotivs', *Pax: Beiträge zu Idee und Darstellung des Friedens*, ed. W. Augustyn (Munich, 2003), pp. 243–300.

Aust, M., and J. Obertreis, eds, *Osteuropäische Geschichte und Globalgeschichte* (Stuttgart, 2014).

Aust, M., and J. Obertreis, 'Einleitung', *Osteuropäische Geschichte und Globalgeschichte*, ed. Aust and Obertreis, pp. 7–23.

Baasch, E., *Quellen zur Geschichte von Hamburgs Handel und Schiffahrt im 17., 18., und 19. Jahrhundert* (Hamburg, 1910).

Bade, K. J., 'German Transatlantic Emigration in the Nineteenth and Twentieth Centuries', *European Expansion and Migration*, ed. Emmer and Mörner, pp. 121–55.

Bagiński, H., *Polska i Bałtyk: Zagadnienie Dostępu Polski do Morza* (Warsaw, 1959).

Bailyn, B., *The Peopling of British North America: An Introduction* (London, 1987).

Bailyn, B., and P. L. Denault, eds, *Soundings in Atlantic History: Latent Structures and Intellectual Currents, 1500–1830* (Cambridge, 2009).

Bandyopādhyāya, S., *From Plassey to Partition: A History of Modern India* (New Delhi, 2004).

Baptist, E., *The Half Has Never Been Told: Slavery and the Making of American Capitalism* (New York, 2014).

Barcia, M., '"A Not-so-Common Wind": Slave Revolts in the Age of Revolutions in Cuba and Brazil', *Review* 2/31 (2008), pp. 169–93.

Batou, J., and H. Szlajfer, eds, *Western Europe, Eastern Europe and World Development, 13th–18th Centuries: Collection of Essays of Marian Małowist* (Leiden, 2009).

Bayly, C. A., *The Birth of the Modern World 1780–1914: Global Connections and Comparisons* (Oxford, 2004).

Beckert, S., *Empire of Cotton: A Global History* (New York, 2014 and 2015).

Beguelin, H. v., ed., *Historisch-kritische Darstellung der Accise- und Zollverfassung in den Preußischen Staaten* (Berlin, 1797).

Bell, W. P., *The Foreign Protestants and the Settlement of Nova Scotia: The History of a Piece of Arrested British Colonial Policy in the Eighteenth Century* (Toronto, 1961).

Bentham, D., *Memoirs of James Hutton: Comprising the Annals of his Life, and Connection with the United Brethren* (London, 1856).

Berend, I. T., *Central and Eastern Europe 1944–1993: Detour from the Periphery to the Periphery* (Cambridge, 1996).

Berg, M., ed., *Writing the History of the Global: Challenges for the 21st Century* (Oxford, 2013).

Beutin, L., *Der deutsche Seehandel im Mittelmeergebiet bis zu den napoleonischen Kriegen* (Neumünster, 1933).

Birmingham, S., *Our Crowd: The Great Jewish Families of New York* (New York, 1967).

Bittner, T., 'Kartelle und Wachstum im deutschen Kaiserreich: wirtschaftshistorische Erkenntnisse und industrieökonomische Forschungsperspektiven', *Jahrbuch für Wirtschaftsgeschichte* 43 (2002), pp. 137–58.

Blackbourn, D., *The Conquest of Nature: Water, Landscape, and the Making of Modern Germany* (London, 2006).

Boch, R., *Grenzenloses Wachstum? Das rheinische Wirtschaftsbürgertum und seine Industrialisierungsdebatte 1814–1857* (Göttingen, 1991).

Bockstoce, J. R., *Furs and Frontiers in the Far North: The Contest among Native and Foreign Nations for the Bering Strait Fur Trade* (New Haven, 2009).

Bohme, H., *Frankfurt und Hamburg: Des Deutschen Reiches Silber- und Goldloch und die Allerenglischste Stadt des Kontinents* (Frankfurt, 1968).

Boldorf, M., *Europäische Leinenregionen im Wandel: Institutionelle Weichenstellungen in Schlesien und Irland, 1750–1850* (Cologne, 2006).

Bömelburg H.-J., A. Gestrich and H. Schnabel-Schüle, eds, *Die Teilungen Polen-Litauens: Inklusions- und Exklusionsmechanismen – Traditionsbildung – Vergleichsebenen* (Osnabrück, 2013).

Brahm, F., and E. Rosenhaft, eds, *Slavery Hinterland: Transatlantic Slavery and Continental Europe, 1680–1850* (Woodbridge, 2016).

Brahm, F., and E. Rosenhaft, 'Introduction: Towards a Comprehensive European History of Slavery and Abolition', *Slavery Hinterland*, ed. Brahm and Rosenhaft, pp. 1–23.

Braudel, F., *Das Mittelmeer und die mediterrane Welt in der Epoche Philipps II*, Vol. 2 (Frankfurt, 1992).

Brewer, J., *The Sinews of Power: War, Money and the English State, 1688–1783* (London, 2002).

Brietzke, D., 'Schuback, Johannes', *Neue Deutsche Biographie* 23 (Berlin, 2007), pp. 601–2.

Brimmes, N., ed., *Danmark og Kolonierne: Indien – Tranquebar, Serampore og Nicobarerne* (Copenhagen, 2017).

Brinck, A., *Die deutsche Auswanderungswelle in die britischen Kolonien Nordamerikas um die Mitte des 18. Jahrhunderts* (Stuttgart, 1993).

Bruckmüller, E., 'Triest und Österreich im 18. Jahrhundert', *Österreichische Osthefte* 3 (1985), pp. 300–30.

Buchholz, W., *Pommern* (Berlin, 1999).

Buist, M. G., *Ad Spes non Fracta: Hope & Co. 1770–1815* (The Hague, 1974).

Burke, P., A. Mączak and H. Samsonowicz, eds, *East-Central Europe in Transition: From the Fourteenth to the Seventeenth Century* (Cambridge, 1985).

Burke, P., *Die europäische Renaissance: Zentren und Peripherien* (Munich, 1998).

Burleigh, M., *Germany Turns Eastwards: A Study of Ostforschung in the Third Reich* (Cambridge/New York, 1988).

Butel, P., *Les négociants bordelais, l'Europe et les iles au XVIIe siècle* (Paris, 1974).

Callendar, G. S., 'The Early Transportation and Banking Enterprises of the States in Relation to the Growth of Corporations', *The Quarterly Journal of Economics* 17/1 (1902), pp. 111–62.

Calloway, C. G., *One Vast Winter Count: The Native American West before Lewis and Clark* (Lincoln, 2003).

Canny, N., 'Atlantic History and Global History', *Atlantic History*, ed. Greene and Morgan, pp. 317–36.

Canny, N., and P. D. Morgan, eds, *The Oxford Handbook of the Atlantic World 1450–1850* (Oxford, 2012 and 2013).

Carney, J., *Black Rice: The African Origins of Rice Cultivation in the Americas* (Cambridge, 2001).

Carreira, A., *A Companhia Geral do Grão-Pará e Maranhão*, Vol. 2 (São Paulo, 1988).

Cattaruzza, M., 'Cittadinanza e Ceto Mercantile a Trieste (1749–1850)', *Österreichisches Italien – Italienisches Österreich*, ed. Mazohl-Wallnig and Meriggi, pp. 113–37.

Caviedes, C. N., 'Five Hundred Years of Hurricanes in the Caribbean: Their Relationship with Global Climate Variabilities', *GeoJournal* 23/4 (1991), pp. 301–10.

Cerman, M., *Villagers and Lords in Eastern Europe, 1300–1800* (Basingstoke, 2012).

Chakrabarty, D., 'The Four Climates of History', *Critical Enquiry* 2/35 (2009), pp. 197–222.

Charles, L., and G. Daudin, 'Eighteenth-Century International Trade Statistics: Sources and Methods', *Revue de l'OFCE* 140/4 (2015), pp. 7–36.

——, 'France, c. 1713 – c. 1821', *Revue de l'OFCE* 140/4 (2015), pp. 237–48.

Che-Chia, C., 'Origins of a Misunderstanding: The Qianlong Emperor's Embargo on Rhubarb Exports to Russia, the Scenario and its Consequences', *Asian Medicine* 1/2 (2005), pp. 335–54.

Christensen, A. E., 'Der handelsgeschichtliche Wert der Sundzollregister: Ein Beitrag zu seiner Beurteilung', *Hansische Geschichtsblätter* 59 (1934), pp. 28–142.

Clark, C., *Iron Kingdom: The Rise and Downfall of Prussia, 1600–1847* (Cambridge, 2006).

Clarkson, L., 'The Linen Industry in Early Modern Europe', *The Cambridge History of Western Textiles*, ed. D. Jenkins (Cambridge, 2003), pp. 473–92.

Clingingsmith, D., and J. Williamson, 'Deindustrialisation in Eighteenth and Nineteenth-Century India: Mughal Decline, Climate Shocks and British Industrial Ascent', *Explorations in Economic History* 3/45 (2009), pp. 209–34.

Coclanis, P. A., 'Atlantic World or Atlantic/World?', *William and Mary Quarterly* 63 (2006), pp. 725–42.

——, 'Beyond Atlantic History', *Atlantic History*, ed. Greene and Morgan, pp. 337–56.

Collet, D., *Die doppelte Katastrophe: Klima und Kultur in der europäischen Hungerkrise, 1770–1772* (Göttingen, 2019).

Collins, B., and P. Ollerenshaw, *The European Linen Industry in Historical Perspective* (Oxford, 2003).

Conrad, S., 'Doppelte Marginalisierung: Plädoyer für eine transnationale Perspektive auf die deutsche Geschichte', *Geschichte und Gesellschaft* 28 (2002), pp. 145–69.

Conrad, S., and J. Osterhammel, eds, *An Emerging Modern World 1750–1970* (Cambridge/London, 2018).

Cranz, D., *Historie von Grönland: Enthaltend die Beschreibung des Landes und der Einwohner &c. insbesondere die Geschichte der dortigen Mission der Evangelischen Brüder zu Neu-Herrnhut und Lichtenfels* (Barby, 1765).

——, *Alte und Neue Brüder-Historie oder kurz gefaßte Geschichte der Evangelischen Brüder-Unität in den älteren Zeiten insonderheit in dem gegenwärtigen Jahrhundert* (Barby, 1771).

Crespo, S. A., *Mercaderes Atlánticos: Redes del Comercio Flamenco y Holandés entre Europa y el Caribe* (Córdoba, 2009).

Cronshagen, J., 'Owning the Body, Wooing the Soul: How Forced Labor was Justified in the Moravian Correspondence Network in Eighteenth-Century Surinam', *Connecting Worlds and People: Early Modern Diasporas*, ed. D. Freist and S. Lachenicht (London/New York, 2016), pp. 81–103.

Cross, A., *By the Banks of the Neva: Chapters from the Lives and Careers of the British in Eighteenth-Century Russia* (Cambridge, 1997).

Crouzet, F., 'Wars, Blockade, and Economic Change in Europe, 1792–1815', *The Journal of Economic History* 24 (1964), pp. 567–88.

Curtin, P. D., *Economic Change in Precolonial Africa: Senegambia in the Era of the Slave Trade* (Madison, 1975).

Cusin, F., 'Precedenti di Concorrenza fra i Porti del Mare del Nord e i Porti dell'Adriatico: Saggio sul Commercio del Porto di Trieste nel Secolo XVIII (1760–1776)', *Annali della R. Università degli Studi Economici e Commerciali di Trieste* 3 (1931), pp. 3–68.

Dahlmann, D., *Sibirien: Vom 16. Jahrhundert bis zur Gegenwart* (Paderborn, 2009).

Dalos, G., I. Eörsi et al., *Die andere Hälfte Europas* (Berlin, 1985).

Damodaram, V., 'The East India Company, Famine and Ecological Conditions in Eighteenth-Century Bengal', *The East India Company and the Natural World*, ed. A. Winterbottom (Basingstoke, 2015), pp. 80–102.

Daniels, C., and M. V. Kennedy, eds, *Negotiated Empires: Centers and Peripheries in the Americas, 1500–1820* (New York, 2002).

Davies, K. G., *The Royal African Company* (London, 1957).

de Castelnau-L'Estoile, C., and F. Regourd, *Connaissances et Pouvoirs: Les Espaces Impériaux (XVIe–XVIIIe siècles): France, Espagne, Portugal* (Bordeaux, 2005).

de Lacy Mann, J., and A. Powell Wadsworth, *The Cotton Trade and Industrial Lancashire, 1600–1780* (Bristol, 1999).

de Marees, P., *Beschryvinghe ende historisch verhael van Gout Koninckrijck van Guinea [...]* (Amsterdam, 1602 and 1617).

Dejung, C., and M. Lengwiler, 'Einleitung', *Ränder der Moderne: Neue Perspektiven auf die Europäische Geschichte (1800–1930)*, ed. C. Dejung and M. Lengwiler (Cologne/Weimar/Vienna, 2016), pp. 7–35.

Denzel, M. A., ed., *Gewürze: Produktion, Handel und Konsum in der Frühen Neuzeit* (St Katharinen, 1999).

Denzel, M. A., 'Der seewärtige Einfuhrhandel Hamburgs nach den Admiralitäts- und Convoygeld-Einnahmebüchern (1733–1798)', *Vierteljahresschrift für Sozial- und Wirtschaftsgeschichte* 102/2 (2015), pp. 131–60.

Desrochers, R. E., 'Slave-for-Sale Advertisements and Slavery in Massachusetts, 1704–1781', *The William and Mary Quarterly* 59 (2002), pp. 623–64.

Dietz, W., *Die Wuppertaler Garnnahrung* (Neustadt/Aisch, 1957).

Doerflinger, T. M., *A Vigorous Spirit of Enterprise: Merchants and Economic Developments in Revolutionary Philadelphia* (Williamsburg, 1986 and Chapel Hill/London, 2001).

dos Santos Arnold, T., 'Central Europe and the Portuguese, Spanish and French Atlantic: 15th to 19th Centuries', *European Review* 26/3 (2018), pp. 421–9.

Dufournaud, N., and B. Michon, 'Les Femmes et le Commerce Maritime à Nantes (1660–1740): Un Role Largement Méconnu', *Clio: Femmes, Genre, Histoire* 23 (2005), pp. 1–16.

Dunn, R. S., *Sugar and Slaves: The Rise of the Planter Class in the British West Indies, 1624–1713* (Williamsburg, 2000).

DuPlessis, R. S., *The Material Atlantic: Clothing, Commerce, and Colonization in the Atlantic World, 1650–1800* (Cambridge, 2016).

Elliott, J. H., *Empires of the Atlantic World: Britain and Spain in America 1492–1830* (New Haven/London, 2006).

Emmer, P. C., and M. Mörner, eds, *European Expansion and Migration: Essays on the Intercontinental Migration from Africa, Asia and Europe* (New York/ Oxford, 1992).

Emmer, P., and W. Klooster, 'The Dutch Atlantic, 1600–1800: Expansion without Empire', *Itinerario* 2 (1999), pp. 48–69.

Enthoven, V., 'An Assessment of Dutch Transatlantic Commerce, 1585–1817', *Riches from Atlantic Commerce*, ed. Postma and Enthoven, pp. 385–445.

Epstein, S. R., *Freedom and Growth: The Rise of States and Markets in Europe, 1300–1750* (London/New York, 2000).

Evans, C., and G. Rydén, *Baltic Iron in the Atlantic World in the Eighteenth Century* (Boston, 2007).

Evans, C., and G. Rydén, '"Voyage Iron": An Atlantic Slave Trade Currency, its European Origins, and African Impacts', *Past & Present* 239/1 (2018), pp. 41–70.

Faber, E., *Litorale Austriaco: Das österreichische und kroatische Küstenland* (Trondheim/Graz, 1995).

Feest, C. F., ed., *Indians and Europe: An Interdisciplinary Collection of Essays* (Lincoln/London, 1999).

Fenwick Jones, G., *The Georgia Dutch: From the Rhine and Danube to the Savannah, 1733–1783* (Athens/London, 1992).

Ferguson, N., *The Cash Nexus: Money and Power in the Modern World, 1700–2000* (London, 2001).

Ferreiro, L. D., *Brothers at Arms: American Independence and the Men of France and Spain who Saved It* (New York, 2016).

Finzi, R., L. Panariti and G. Panjek, eds, *La Cittá dei Traffici 1719–1918: Storia Economica e Sociale di Trieste*, Vol. 2 (Trieste, 2003).

Fischer, C. E., 'Die Geschichte der deutschen Versuche zur Lösung des Kartell- und Monopol-Problems', *Zeitschrift für die gesamte Staatswissenschaft/ Journal of Institutional and Theoretical Economics* 110 (1954), pp. 425–56.

Fischer, U., 'Die Entwicklung des Ortes Herrnhut bis 1760', *Graf ohne Grenzen: Leben und Werk von Nikolaus Ludwig Graf von Zinzendorf*, ed. P. M. Peucker, S. Augustin, W. Langerfeld and D. Meyer (Herrnhut, 2000), pp. 32–6.

Fischer, W., and A. Kunz, eds, *Grundlagen der Historischen Statistik von Deutschland: Quellen, Methoden, Forschungsziele* (Opladen, 1991).

Fisher, J. R., *Commercial Relations between Spain and Spanish America in the Era of Free Trade, 1778–1796* (Liverpool, 1985).

Fisher, R. H., 'Finding America', *Russian America*, ed. Smith-Sweetland, pp. 17–31.

Fleche, A., *The Revolution of 1861: The American Civil War in the Age of Nationalist Conflict* (Chapel Hill, 2012).

Flügel, A., *Kaufleute und Manufakturen in Bielefeld: Soziale und wirtschaftliche Entwicklung im proto-industriellen Leinengewerbe von 1680 bis 1850* (Bielefeld, 1993).

Foust, C. M., *Rhubarb: The Wondrous Drug* (Princeton, 1992).

——, *Muscovite and Mandarin: Russia's Trade with China and its Setting, 1727–1805* (Chapel Hill, 2012).

Fradera, J. M., *Indústria i Mercat: Les Bases Comercials de la Industria Catalana Moderna, 1814–1845* (Barcelona, 1987).

Fradera, J. M., and C. Schmidt-Nowara, eds, *Slavery and Antislavery in Spain's Atlantic Empire* (New York, 2013).

Frank, A. G., *ReORIENT: Global Economy in the Asian Age* (Berkeley, 1998).

Freist, D., and S. Lachenicht, eds, *Connecting Worlds and People: Early Modern Diasporas* (London/New York, 2016).

Frigo, D., 'Le "Disavventure della Navigazione": Neutralità Veneziana e Conflitti Europei nel Primo Settecento', *Attraverso i Conflitti: Neutralità e Commercio fra età Moderna ed età Contemporanea*, ed. D. Andreozzi (Trieste, 2017), pp. 53–74.

Füllberg-Stolberg, C., 'Die Herrnhuter Mission: Sklaverei und Sklavenemanzipation in der Karibik', *Sklaverei und Zwangsarbeit*, ed. Herrmann-Otto, Simonis and Trefz, pp. 254–80.

Garner, G., ed., *Die Ökonomie des Privilegs: Westeuropa 16.–19. Jahrhundert/ L'économie du privilège: Europe occidentale XVIe–XIX siècles* (Frankfurt, 2016).

Gasser, P., 'Triests Handelsversuche mit Spanien und die Probleme der Österreichischen Schiffahrt in den Jahren 1750–1800', Part 1, *Mitteilungen des Österreichischen Staatsarchivs* 36 (1983), pp. 150–87.

——, 'Triests Handelsversuche mit Spanien und die Probleme der Österreichischen Schiffahrt in den Jahren 1750–1800', Part 2, *Mitteilungen des Österreichischen Staatsarchivs* 37 (1984), pp. 172–97.

Gaziński, R., *Handel Morski Szczecina w Latach 1720–1805* (Szczecin, 2000).

Gebhard, W., 'Bericht des Hof-Kammerrats Friedrich Heinrich Jacobi über die Industrie der Herzogtümer Jülich und Berg aus den Jahren 1773 und 1774', *Zeitschrift des Bergischen Geschichtsvereins* 18 (1882), pp. 1–148.

Gerbner, K., *Christian Slavery: Conversion and Race in the Protestant Atlantic World* (Philadelphia, 2018).

Gerhard, H.-J., and K. H. Kaufhold, eds, *Preise im Vor- und Frühindustriellen Deutschland: Nahrungsmittel – Getränke – Gewürze – Rohstoffe und Gewerbeprodukte* (Stuttgart, 2001).

Gibson, C., *Empire's Crossroads: A New History of the Caribbean* (London, 2014).

Gill, C., *The Rise of the Irish Linen Industry* (Oxford, 1925).

Glamann, K., *Dutch-Asiatic Trade 1620–1740* (s'Gravenhage, 1981).

Gobel, E., 'The Sound Toll Registers Online Project, 1497–1857', *International Journal of Maritime History* 22/2 (2010), pp. 305–24.

Good, D., *The Economic Rise of the Hapsburg Empire* (Berkeley, 1984).

——, *Der wirtschaftliche Aufstieg des Habsburgerreichs 1750–1918* (Vienna/Cologne/Graz, 1986).

Gorißen, S., 'Der Preis des Vertrauens: Unsicherheit, Institutionen und Rationalität im vorindustriellen Fernhandel', *Vertrauen: Historische Annäherungen*, ed. U. Frevert (Göttingen, 2003), pp. 90–118.

——, 'Gewerbe im Herzogtum Berg vom Spätmittelalter bis 1806', *Geschichte des Bergischen Landes*, ed. Gorißen, Sassin and Wesoly, pp. 407–67.

——, 'Interessen und ökonomische Funktionen merkantilistischer Privilegienpolitik: Das Herzogtum Berg und seine Textilgewerbe zwischen 16. und 18. Jahrhundert', *Die Ökonomie des Privilegs: Westeuropa 16.–19. Jahrhundert/L'économie du privilège: Europe occidentale XVIe–XIX siècles*, ed. G. Garner (Frankfurt, 2016), pp. 279–329.

Gorißen, S., H. Sassin and K. Wesoly, eds, *Geschichte des Bergischen Landes*, Vol. 1 (Bielefeld, 2014).

Gräf, H., and R. Pröve, *Wege ins Ungewisse: Reisen in der Frühen Neuzeit 1500–1800* (Frankfurt, 1997).

Greenberg, D., 'Yankee Financiers and the Establishment of Trans-Atlantic Partnerships: A Re-Examination', *Business History* 16/1 (1974), pp. 17–35.

Greene, J. P., and P. D. Morgan, eds, *Atlantic History: A Critical Appraisal* (Oxford, 2009).

Greene, J. P., and P. D. Morgan, 'Introduction: The Present State of Atlantic History', *Atlantic History*, ed. Greene and Morgan, pp. 3–34.

Grubb, F., 'The Market Structure of Shipping German Immigrants to Colonial America', *The Pennsylvania Magazine of History and Biography* 111 (1987), pp. 27–48.

——, 'The Auction of *Redemptioner Servants*, Philadelphia, 1771–1808: An Economic Analysis', *The Journal of Economic History* 48 (1988), pp. 583–603.

Gylløv, H. C., ed., *Danmark og kolonierne – Grønland: Den Arktiske Koloni* (Copenhagen, 2017).

Häberlein, M., *Vom Oberrhein zum Susquehanna: Studien zur badischen Auswanderung nach Pennsylvania im 18. Jahrhundert* (Stuttgart, 1993).

——, 'Migration and Business Ventures: German-Speaking Migrants and Commercial Networks in the Eighteenth-Century British-Atlantic World', *Transnational Networks: German Migrants in the British Empire*, ed. S. Manz, J. R. Davis and M. Schulte Beerbühl (Leiden, 2011), pp. 19–57.

Hackmann, J., and M. Kopij-Weiß, *Nationen in Kontakt und Konflikt: Deutsch-polnische Verflechtungen 1806–1918* (Darmstadt, 2014).

Haggerty, S., *'Merely for Money'? Business Culture in the British Atlantic, 1750–1815* (Liverpool, 2012).

Haid, E., S. Weismann and B. Wöller, 'Einleitung', *Galizien: Peripherie der Moderne – Moderne der Peripherie?*, ed. E. Haid, S. Weismann and B. Wöller (Marburg, 2013), pp. 1–10.

Halecki, O., 'Why was Poland Partitioned?', *Slavic Review* 22/3 (1963), pp. 432–41.

Hamer, P. M., ed., *The Papers of Henry Laurens*, 2 vols (Columbia, 1968/70).

Hancock, D., *Citizens of the World: London Merchants and the Integration of the British Atlantic Community, 1735–1785* (Cambridge, 2005).

——, 'The Intensification of Atlantic Maritime Trade (1492–1815)', *The Sea in History: The Early Modern World*, ed. C. Buchet and G. Le Bouëdec (Woodbridge, 2017), pp. 19–29.

Handelskammer Frankfurt, ed., *Geschichte der Handelskammer zu Frankfurt am Main, 1707–1908* (Frankfurt, 1908).

Hardtwig, W., and P. Müller, eds, *Die Vergangenheit der Weltgeschichte: Universalhistorisches Denken in Berlin 1800–1933* (Göttingen, 2010).

Hassinger, H., 'Der Außenhandel der Habsburgermonarchie in der zweiten Hälfte des 18. Jahrhunderts', *Die wirtschaftliche Situation in Deutschland und Österreich an der Wende vom 18. zum 19. Jahrhundert*, ed. F. Lütge (Stuttgart, 1964), pp. 61–98.

Hatje, F., 'Libertät, Neutralität und Commercium: Zu den politischen Voraussetzungen für Hamburgs Handel', *Hamburger Wirtschafts-Chronik* 7 (2007/08), pp. 213–47.

Hausmann, G., *Universität und städtische Gesellschaft in Odessa, 1865–1917: Soziale und nationale Selbstorganisation an der Peripherie des Zarenreiches* (Stuttgart, 1998).

Hawgood, J., 'The Civil War and Central Europe', *Heard Round the World: The Impact Abroad of the Civil War*, ed. H. Hyman (New York, 1969), pp. 145–76.

Hawthorne, W., 'The Cultural Meaning of Work: The "Black Rice Debate" Reconsidered', *Rice*, ed. Marton, pp. 279–90.

Heller, K., *Der russisch-chinesische Handel von seinen Anfängen bis zum Ausgang des 19. Jahrhunderts* (Erlangen, 1980).

———, 'Der russisch-chinesische Handel in Kjachta: Eine Besonderheit in den außenwirtschaftlichen Beziehungen Rußlands im 18. und 19. Jahrhundert', *Jahrbücher für Geschichte Osteuropas* 47/29 (1981), pp. 515–36.

Henkel, M., *Zunftmissbräuche: 'Arbeiterbewegung' im Merkantilismus* (Frankfurt, 1989).

Herberts, H., *Alles ist Kirche und Handel: Wirtschaft und Gesellschaft des Wuppertals im Vormärz und in der Revolution 1848/49* (Neustadt/Aisch, 1980).

Hernæs, P. O., ed., *Danmark og Kolonierne – Vestafrika: Forterne på Guldkysten* (Copenhagen, 2017).

Herrmann-Otto, E., M. Simonis and A. Trefz, eds, *Sklaverei und Zwangsarbeit zwischen Akzeptanz und Widerstand* (Hildesheim, 2011).

Heyn, U., *Private Banking and Industrialization: The Case of Frankfurt Am Main, 1825–1875* (New York, 1981).

Hobsbawm, E., *Age of Revolution 1789–1848* (London, 1999).

Hochedlinger, M., *Austria's Wars of Emergence: War, State and Society in the Habsburg Monarchy 1683–1797* (London, 2003).

Hodson, C., 'Exile on Spruce Street: An Acadian History', *The William and Mary Quarterly* 67/2 (2010), pp. 249–78.

———, *The Acadian Diaspora: An Eighteenth-Century History* (Oxford, 2012 and 2017).

Hoth, W., *Die Industrialisierung einer rheinischen Gewerbestadt – dargestellt am Beispiel Wuppertal* (Cologne, 1975).

Hroch, M., 'Die Rolle des zentraleuropäischen Handels im Ausgleich der Handelsbilanz zwischen Ost- und Westeuropa 1550–1650', *Der Außenhandel Ostmitteleuropas 1450–1650*, ed. I. Bog (Böhlau, 1971), pp. 1–27.

Huang, A., *Die Textilien des Hanseraums: Produktion und Distribution einer spätmittelalterlichen Fernhandelsware* (Cologne, 2015).

Hull, W. H., *Benjamin Furly and Quakerism in Rotterdam* (Lancaster, 1941).

Hüsgen, J., *Mission und Sklaverei: Die Herrnhuter Brüdergemeine und die Sklavenemanzipation in Britisch- und Dänisch-Westindien* (Stuttgart, 2016).

Hyden-Hanscho, V., *Reisende, Migranten, Kulturmanager: Mittlerpersönlichkeiten zwischen Frankreich und dem Wiener Hof 1630–1730* (Stuttgart, 2013).

Imbusch, P., *'Das moderne Weltsystem': Eine Kritik der Weltsystemtheorie Immanuel Wallersteins* (Marburg, 1990).

Industrie- u. Handelskammer Wuppertal and W. Köllmann, eds, *Industrie- und Handelskammer Wuppertal, 1831–1956: Festschrift zum 125 jährigen Jubiläum am 17. Jan. 1956* (Wuppertal, 1956).

Irwin, J., and P. R. Schwartz, *Studies in Indo-European Textile History* (Ahmedabad, 1966).

Jeggle, C., 'Pre-Industrial Worlds of Production: Conventions, Institutions and Organizations', *Historical Social Research* 36 (2011), pp. 125–49.

Johnson, L. R., *Central Europe: Enemies, Neighbors, Friends* (Oxford/New York, 2002).

Johnson, M., *Anglo-African Trade in the Eighteenth Century: English Statistics on African Trade 1699–1808*, ed. J. T. Lindblad and R. Ross (Leiden, 1990).

Johnson, S., 'El Niño: Environmental Crisis and the Emergence of Alternative Markets in the Hispanic Caribbean, 1760s–1770s', *The William and Mary Quarterly* 62/3 (2005), pp. 365–410.

——, *Climate and Catastrophe in Cuba and the Atlantic World in the Age of Revolution* (Chapel Hill, 2011).

Johnson, W., *River of Dark Dreams: Slavery and Empire in the Cotton Kingdom* (Cambridge, 2013).

Jones, A., *German Sources for West African History 1599–1669* (Wiesbaden, 1983).

——, *Brandenburg Sources for West African History 1680–1700* (Stuttgart, 1985).

Jones, D. W., *London Overseas-Merchant Groups at the End of the Seventeenth Century and the Moves against the East India Company* (Oxford, 1970).

——, *War and Economy in the Age of William III and Marlborough* (Oxford, 1988).

Jordan, J. W., 'Moravian Immigration to Pennsylvania, 1734–1767', *Transactions of the Moravian Historical Society* 5/2 (1896), pp. 51–90.

Kaltenstadler, W., 'Der österreichische Seehandel über Triest im 18. Jahrhundert', Part 2, *Vierteljahresschrift für Sozial- und Wirtschaftsgeschichte* 56 (1969), pp. 1–104.

Kalus, M., *Pfeffer – Kupfer – Nachrichten: Kaufmannsnetzwerke und Handelsstrukturen im europäisch-asiatischen Handel am Ende des 16. Jahrhunderts* (Augsburg, 2010).

Kamenskij, A. B., *The Russian Empire in the Eighteenth Century: Searching for a Place in the World* (Armonk, 1997).

Kanstrup, J., 'Svigagtig Angivelse: Øresundstolden i 1700-tallet', *Tolden i Sundet: Toldopkrævning, Politik og Skibsfart i Øresund 1429–1857*, ed. O. Degn (Copenhagen, 2010), pp. 371–454.

Kapp, F., *Geschichte der Deutschen im Staate New York bis zum Anfang des neuzehnten Jahrhunderts* (New York, 1869).

Kaps, K., 'Entre Servicio Estatal y los Negocios Transnacionales: El Caso de Paolo Greppi, Cónsul Imperial en Cádiz (1774–1791)', *Los Consules Extranjeros en la Edad Moderna y a Principios de la Edad Contemporánea (Siglos XV–XIX)*, ed. M. Aglietti, M. Herrero Sánchez and F. Zamora Rodríguez (Madrid, 2013), pp. 225–35.

——, 'Zwischen Zentraleuropa und iberischem Atlantik: Mailänder Kaufleute in Cádiz im 18. Jahrhundert', *Annales Mercaturae* 3 (2017), pp. 85–105.

Kaps, K., and A. Komlosy, 'Centers and Peripheries Revisited: Polycentric Connections or Entangled Hierarchies', *Review Fernand Braudel Center* 36, 3/4 (2013 [de facto: 2017]), pp. 237–64.

Kaufhold, K. H., *Das Metallgewerbe der Grafschaft Mark im 18. und frühen 19. Jahrhundert* (Dortmund, 1976).

Kellenbenz, H., 'Der Lutherische Gottesdienst und die Niederlassung Hamburger Kaufleute in Lissabon im Anfang des Achtzehnten Jahrhunderts', *Hamburger Wirtschafts-Chronik* 1 (1950), pp. 31–40.

——, *Unternehmerkräfte im Hamburger Portugal- und Spanienhandel, 1590–1625* (Hamburg, 1954).

——, 'Review of Immanuel Wallerstein: The Modern World-System, Vol. 1', *Journal of Modern History* 48/4 (1976), pp. 685–92.

Kelly, J., *America's Longest Siege: Charleston, Slavery, and the Slow March toward Civil War* (New York, 2013).

Kermann, J., *Die Manufakturen im Rheinland 1750–1833* (Bonn, 1972).

Kilbourne Jr., R., *Debt, Investment, Slaves: Credit Relations in East Feliciana Parish, Louisiana, 1825–1885* (Tuscaloosa, 1995).

Kisch, H., 'The Textile Industries in Silesia and the Rhineland: A Comparative Study in Industrialization', *The Journal of Economic History* 19/4 (1959), pp. 541–64.

——, 'From Monopoly to Laissez-faire: The Early Growth of the Wupper Valley Textile Trades', *Journal of European Economic History* 1 (1972), pp. 298–407.

Kizwalter, T., *O Nowocześnosci Narodu: Przypadek Polski* (Warsaw, 1999).

Klíma, A., 'Glassmaking Industry and Trade in Bohemia in the 17th and 18th Centuries', *Journal of European Economic History* 13/3 (1984), pp. 499–520.

Klooster, W., 'Curaçao and the Caribbean Transit Trade', *Riches from Atlantic Commerce*, ed. Postma and Enthoven, pp. 203–18.

Knitter, M., 'Verifizierung von Schifffahrtsstatistiken des Stettiner Hafens in der zweiten Hälfte des 18. und Anfang des 19. Jahrhunderts', *Studia Maritima* 25 (2012), pp. 23–50.

Knittle, W. A., *Early Eighteenth Century Palatine Emigration: A British Government Redemptioner Project to Manufacture Naval Stores* (Baltimore, 1965).

Knudsen, A.-C., and K. Gram-Skjoldager, 'Historiography and Narration in Transnational History', *Journal of Global History* 9 (2014), pp. 143–61.

Kobayashi, K., 'Indian Textiles and Gum Arabic in the Lower Senegal River: Global Significance of Local Trade and Consumers in the Early Nineteenth Century', *African Economic History* 45/2 (2017), pp. 27–53.

Köllmann, W., *Sozialgeschichte der Stadt Barmen* (Tübingen, 1960).

Komlos, J., *Die Habsburgermonarchie als Zollunion: Die wirtschaftliche Entwicklung Österreich-Ungarns im 19. Jahrhundert* (Vienna, 1986).

Komlosy, A., *Grenze und ungleiche regionale Entwicklung: Binnenmarkt und Migration in der Habsburgermonarchie* (Vienna, 2003).

Korach, E., *Das Deutsche Privatbankgeschäft: Studien zu seiner Geschichte und heutigen Stellung* (Berlin, 1910).

Kotilaine, J. T., *Russia's Foreign Trade and Economic Expansion in the Seventeenth Century: Windows on the World* (Leiden, 2005).

Krawehl, O.-E., 'Quellen zur Hamburger Handelsstatistik im 18. Jahrhundert', *Grundlagen der Historischen Statistik von Deutschland: Quellen, Methoden, Forschungsziele*, ed. W. Fischer and A. Kunz (Opladen, 1991), pp. 47–69.

Kriedte, P., H. Medick and J. Schlumbohm, *Industrialisierung vor der Industrialisierung: Gewerbliche Warenproduktion auf dem Land in der Formationsperiode des Kapitalismus* (Göttingen, 1977).

Kriedte, P., *Taufgesinnte und grosses Kapital: Die niederrheinisch-bergischen Mennoniten und der Aufstieg des Krefelder Seidengewerbes (Mitte des 17. Jahrhunderts–1815)* (Göttingen, 2007).

Kriger, C. E., *Cloth in West African History* (Lanham, 2006).

——, '"Guinea Cloth": Production and Consumption of Cotton Textiles in West Africa before and during the Atlantic Slave Trade', *The Spinning World: A Global History of Cotton Textiles, 1200–1850*, ed. G. Riello and P. Parthasarathi (Oxford, 2009), pp. 105–26.

Kröger, R., 'Die Erstlingsbilder in der Brüdergemeine', *Unitas Fratrum* 67/68 (2012), pp. 135–63.

Kühn, S., *Der Hirschberger Leinwand- und Schleyerhandel von 1648 bis 1806* (Aalen, 1982) [Breslau, 1938].

Kula, W., *An Economic Theory of the Feudal System: Towards a Model of the Polish Economy 1500–1800* (Bristol, 1976).

Kunz, A., 'Der Zittauer Leinengroßhandel im 18. Jahrhundert', *Zittauer Geschichtsblätter* 6 (1930), pp. 43–8.

Labuda, G., *Dzieje Szczecina Wiek X–1805* (Warsaw, 1963).

Labuda, G., ed., *Historia Pomorza: Tom II: Do Roku 1815; Część 3: Pomorze Zachodnie w Latach 1648–1815* (Poznań, 2003).

Lachenicht, S., ed., *Europeans Engaging the Atlantic: Knowledge and Trade, 1500–1800* (Frankfurt, 2014).

Lachenicht, S., 'Europeans Engaging the Atlantic: Knowledge and Trade, c. 1500–1800: An Introduction', *Europeans Engaging the Atlantic*, ed. Lachenicht, pp. 7–21.

Landes, D. S., *Bankers and Pashas: International Finance and Economic Imperialism in Egypt* (New York, 1958).

Landesverband Rheinland Industriemuseum and C. Gottfried, eds, *Cromford Ratingen: Lebenswelten zwischen erster Fabrik und Herrenhaus um 1800* (Ratingen, 2010).

Landwehr, A., *Die anwesende Abwesenheit der Vergangenheit: Essay zur Geschichtstheorie* (Frankfurt, 2016).

Law, R., ed., *Correspondence of the Royal African Company's Chief Merchants at Cabo Corso Castle with William's Fort, Whydah, and Little Popo Factory, 1727–1728* (Madison, 1991).

——, *The English in West Africa: The Local Correspondence of the Royal African Company of England 1681–1699*, Vol. 1 (Oxford, 1997).

Lemire, B., *Fashion's Favorite: The Cotton Trade and the Consumer in Britain, 1660–1800* (Oxford, 1991).

——, 'Transforming Consumer Custom: Linen, Cotton, and the English Market, 1660–1800', *The European Linen Industry*, ed. Collins and Ollerenshaw, pp. 187–207.

——, 'Distant Cargoes and Local Cultures in the Material Atlantic', *William and Mary Quarterly* 73/3 (2016), pp. 543–8.

Lentz, S., 'Abolitionists in the German Hinterland? Therese Huber and the Spread of Anti-Slavery Sentiment in the German Territories in the Early Nineteenth Century', *Slavery Hinterland*, ed. Brahm and Rosenhaft, pp. 187–211.

Lesiński, H., *Handel Morski Kołobrzegu w XVII i XVIII Wieku* (Szczecin, 1982).

——, 'Kształtowanie się Stosunków Rynkowych pod Wpływem Merkantylistycznej Polityki Państwa', *Historia Pomorza*, ed. Labuda, pp. 681–98.

——, 'Rozwój Handlu Morskiego Miast Zachodniopomorskich', *Historia Pomorza*, ed. Labuda, pp. 699–728.

Leutzsch, A., *Geschichte der Globalisierung als globalisierte Geschichte: Die historische Konstruktion der Weltgesellschaft bei Rosenstock-Huessy und Braudel* (Frankfurt/New York, 2009).

Levy, J., *Freaks of Fortune: The Emerging World of Capitalism and Risk in America* (Cambridge, 2012).

Lewicki, P., *EU-Space and the Euroclass: Modernity, Nationality and Lifestyle among Eurocrats in Brussels* (Bielefeld, 2017).

Lisanti, L., ed., *Negócios Coloniais: Uma Correspondência Comercial do Século XVIII*, 5 vols (Rio de Janeiro, 1971).

Liss, P. K., *Atlantic Empires: The Networks of Trade and Revolution, 1713–1826* (Baltimore, 1983).

Liva, G., 'L'Archivio Greppi e l'Attività della Filiale di P. G. a Cadice nella Corrispondenza Commerciale (1769–1799)', *Archivio Storico Lombardo* 122 (1995), pp. 431–87.

Löffler, U., *Lissabons Fall – Europas Schrecken: Die Deutung des Erdbebens von Lissabon im deutschsprachigen Protestantismus des 18. Jahrhunderts* (Berlin/New York, 1999).

Ludovici, C. G., *Eröffnete Akademie der Kaufleute, oder vollständiges Kaufmanns-Lexicon*, Vol. 1 (Leipzig, 1767).

Ludwig, J., *Der Handel Sachsens nach Spanien und Lateinamerika 1760–1830: Warenexport, Unternehmerinteressen und Staatliche Politik* (Dresden, 2014).

Łukowski, J., *The Partitions of Poland: 1772, 1793, 1795* (London, 1999).

Machado, P., *Ocean of Trade: South Asian Merchants, Africa and the Indian Ocean, c. 1750–1850* (Cambridge, 2014).

Maier, C. S., 'Transformations of Territoriality, 1600–2000', *Transnationale Geschichte: Themen, Tendenzen und Theorien*, ed. G. Budde, S. Conrad and O. Janz (Göttingen, 2006), pp. 32–55.

——, *Once within Borders: Territories of Power, Wealth, and Belonging since 1500* (Cambridge/London 2016).

Makin, J. H., and N. J. Ornstein, *Debt and Taxes* (Washington DC, 1994).

Mallinckrodt, R. v., 'There are No Slaves in Prussia?', *Slavery Hinterland*, ed. Brahm and Rosenhaft, pp. 109–31.

——, 'Verhandelte (Un-)Freiheit: Sklaverei, Leibeigenschaft und innereuropäischer Wissenstransfer am Ausgang des 18. Jahrhunderts', *Geschichte und Gesellschaft* 43 (2017), pp. 1–34.

Małowist, M., 'Śląskie Tekstylia w Zachodniej Afryce w XVI i XVII wieku', *Przegląd Historyczny* 55 (1964), pp. 98–9.

——, 'The Foundations of European Expansion in Africa in the 16th Century: Europe, Maghreb, and Western Sudan', *Western Europe, Eastern Europe and World Development*, ed. Batou and Szlajfer, pp. 339–69.

——, 'Portuguese Expansion in Africa and European Economy at the Turn of the 15th Century', *Western Europe, Eastern Europe and World Development*, ed. Batou and Szlajfer, pp. 373–93.

Martínez Shaw, C., 'Bourbon Reformism and Spanish Colonial Trade, 1717–1778', *Atlantic History: History of the Atlantic System 1580–1830*, ed. H. Pietschmann (Göttingen, 2002), pp. 375–86.

Marton, R., ed., *Rice: A Global History* (London, 2014).

Mason, J. C. S., *The Moravian Church and the Missionary Awakening in England, 1760–1800* (Woodbridge/Rochester, 2001).

Mauruschat, H. H., *Gewürze, Zucker und Salz im vorindustriellen Europa: Eine preisgeschichtliche Untersuchung* (Göttingen, 1975).

Mazohl-Wallnig, B., and M. Meriggi, eds, *Österreichisches Italien – Italienisches Österreich: Interkulturelle Gemeinsamkeiten und nationale Differenzen vom 18. Jahrhundert bis zum Ende des Ersten Weltkrieges* (Vienna, 1999).

McCusker, J. J., and R. R. Menard, *The Economy of British America, 1607–1789* (Chapel Hill/London, 1985).

McNeill, J. R., *Mosquito Empires: Ecology and War in the Greater Caribbean, 1620–1914* (Cambridge, 2010).

Meriwether, R. L., *The Expansion of South Carolina, 1729–1765* (Kingsport, 1940).

Mettele, G., *Weltbürgertum oder Gottesreich: Die Herrnhuter Brüdergemeine als globale Gemeinschaft 1727–1857* (Göttingen, 2009).

——, 'Identities across Borders: The Moravian Brethren as a Global Community', *Pietism and Community in Europe and North America, 1650–1850*, ed. J. Strom (Leiden/Boston, 2010), pp. 155–77.

Meyer, D., *Zinzendorf und die Herrnhuter Brüdergemeine 1700–2000* (Göttingen, 2009).

Middell, M., 'Universalgeschichte, Weltgeschichte, Globalgeschichte, Geschichte der Globalisierung – ein Streit um Worte?', *Globalisierung und Globalgeschichte*, ed. M. Grandner, D. Rothermund and W. Schwentker (Vienna, 2005), pp. 60–82.

Middell, M., and K. Naumann, 'The Writing of World History in Europe from the Middle of the Nineteenth Century to the Present: Conceptual Renewal and Challenge to National Histories', *Transnational Challenges to National History Writing*, ed. M. Middell and L. Roura (Basingstoke, 2013), pp. 54–139.

Millo, A., 'The Creation of a New Bourgeoisie in Trieste', *Social Change in the Habsburg Monarchy / Les transformations de la société dans la monarchie des Habsbourg: l'époque des Lumières*, Das achtzehnte Jahrhundert und Österreich (Internationale Beihefte), Vol. 3, ed. H. Heppner, P. Urbanitsch and R. Zedinger (Bochum, 2011), pp. 215–28.

Mittelberger, G., *Journey to Pennsylvania in the Year 1750 and Return to Germany in the Year 1754*, ed. Carl Theodore Eben (Philadelphia, 1898).

Mittenzwei, I., *Zwischen Gestern und Morgen: Wiens frühe Bourgeoisie an der Wende vom 18. zum 19. Jahrhundert* (Vienna/Cologne/Weimar, 1998), pp. 206–15.

Molin, G. T., 'Internationale Beziehungen als Gegenstand der deutschen Neuzeit-Historiographie seit dem 18. Jahrhundert: Eine Traditionskritik in Grundzügen und Beispielen', *Internationale Geschichte: Themen – Ergebnisse – Aussichten*, ed. W. Loth and J. Osterhammel (Munich/Oldenburg, 2000), pp. 3–30.

Moltmann, G., 'The Migration of German *Redemptioners* to North America, 1720–1820', *Colonialism and Migration: Indentured Labour Before and After Slavery*, ed. P. C. Emmer (Dordrecht, 1986), pp. 105–22.

Monahan, E., *The Merchants of Siberia: Trade in Early Modern Russia* (Ithaca/London, 2016).

Morgan, P. D., 'A Comment', *Europeans Engaging the Atlantic*, ed. Lachenicht, pp. 151–60.

Moskalewicz, M., and W. Przybylski, 'Making Sense of Central Europe: Political Concepts of the Region', *Understanding Central Europe*, ed. M. Moskalewicz and W. Przybylski (New York, 2018), pp. 1–22.

Müller, L., G. Rydén and H. Weiss, eds, *Global Historia från Periferin: Norden 1600–1850* (Lund, 2009).

Müller, L., *Sveriges Första Globala Århundrade: En 1700-Talshistoria* (Stockholm, 2018).

Müller, M., H. R. Schmidt and L. Tissot, eds, *Regulierte Märkte: Zünfte und Kartelle/Marchés Régulés: Corporations et Cartels* (Zurich, 2011).

Naumann, K., 'Osteuropäische Geschichte und Globalgeschichte: Ein Kommentar', *Osteuropäische Geschichte und Globalgeschichte*, ed. Aust and Obertreis, pp. 317–30.

Newman, E. K., 'Anglo-Hamburg Trade in the Late Seventeenth and Early Eighteenth Centuries' (unpublished Ph.D.: London, 1979).

Newton, R. A., '"Good and Kind Benefactors": British Logwood Merchants and Boston's Christ Church', *Early American Studies* 11 (2013), pp. 15–36.

Nolte, H.-H., 'The Position of Eastern Europe in the International System in Early Modern Times', *Review* 4/1 (1982), pp. 25–84.

——, 'Zur Rezeption des Weltsystemkonzepts in Deutschland', *Comparativ* 5 (1994), pp. 91–100.

North, D. C., 'The United States Balance of Payments, 1790–1860', *Trends in the American Economy in the Nineteenth Century*, The Conference on Research in Income and Wealth (Princeton, 1960), pp. 573–628.

Nunes Dias, M., 'Fomento Ultramarino e Mercantilismo: A Companhia do Grão-Pará e Maranhão, 1775–1778', *Revista de História* 32 (1966), pp. 367–415.

O'Brien, P., 'Historiographical Traditions and Modern Imperatives for the Restoration of Global History', *Journal of Global History* 1/1 (2006), pp. 3–39.

Oberholtzer, E. P., *Jay Cooke: Financier of the Civil War*, 2 vols (Philadelphia, 1907).

Ogilvie, S., *Institutions and European Trade: Merchants' Guilds, 1000–1800* (Cambridge, 2011).

Oldendorp, C. G. A., *Geschichte der Mission der evangelischen Brüder auf den caraibischen Inseln S. Thomas, S. Croix und S. Jan* (Barby, 1777).

Olsen, P. E., ed., *Danmark og Kolonierne – Vestindien: St Croix, St Thomas og St Jan* (Copenhagen, 2017).

Olszewski, K., 'The Rise and Decline of the Polish-Lithunian Commonwealth due to Grain Trade', *Munich Personal RePEc Archive*, 13 January 2016, Paper No. 68805.

O'Reilly, W., 'Working for the Crown: German Migrants and Britain's Commercial Success in the Early Eighteenth-Century American Colonies', *Journal of Modern European History* 15 (2017), pp. 130–52.

Osterhammel, J., *Die Entzauberung Asiens: Europa und die asiatischen Reiche im 18. Jahrhundert* (Munich, 1998).

——, *Unfabling the East: The Enlightenment's Encounter with Asia* (Princeton, 2018).

Osterhammel, J., and N. P. Petersson, *Globalization: A Short History* (Princeton, 2003).

Overkamp, A. S., 'Of Tape and Ties: Abraham Frowein from Elberfeld and Atlantic Trade', *Europeans Engaging the Atlantic*, ed. Lachenicht, pp. 127–50.

——, 'A Hinterland to the Slave Trade? Atlantic Connections of the Wupper Valley in the Early Nineteenth Century', *Slavery Hinterland*, ed. Brahm and Rosenhaft, pp. 161–85.

Palmer, R. R., *The Age of the Democratic Revolution*, 2 vols (Princeton, 1959 and 1964).

Panjek, G., '"Una Commercial Officina" fra Vie di Mare e di Terra', *La Cittá dei Traffici*, ed. Finzi, Panariti and Panjek, pp. 235–348.

Pape, R., 'Anton Fürstenau: Ein Kaufmann und Diplomat der Reichsstadt Herford im 17. Jahrhundert', *Herforder Jahrbuch* 22/14 (1771/72).

Parker, G., *Global Crisis: War, Climate Change and Catastrophe in the Seventeenth Century* (New Haven, 2013).

Patel, K. K., 'An Emperor without Clothes? The Debate about Transnational History Twenty-Five Years on', *Histoire@Politique* 26 (2015), pp. 1–16.

Pearson, M. N., ed., *Spices in the Indian Ocean World* (Aldershot, 1996).

Pearson, M. N., 'Introduction', *Spices*, ed. Pearson, pp. xv–xxxvii.

Pettigrew, W. A., *Freedom's Debt: The Royal African Company and the Politics of the Atlantic Slave Trade, 1672–1752* (Chapel Hill, 2013).

Peucker, P., 'Aus allen Nationen: Nichteuropäer in den deutschen Brüdergemeinden des 18. Jahrhunderts', *Unitas Fratrum* 59/60 (2007), pp. 1–35.

——, 'In the Blue Cabinet: Moravians, Marriage, and Sex', *Journal of Moravian History* 10 (2011), pp. 7–37.

Philipp, G., 'Integrationsprobleme im 18. Jahrhundert: Ein Türke am Weimarer Hofe und bei den Herrnhutern', *Pietismus und Neuzeit* 33 (2007), pp. 99–127.

Pieper, R., 'Zur Anbindung Innerösterreichs an die atlantischen Märkte in der Frühen Neuzeit (1670–1758)', *Kuppeln – Korn – Kanonen: Unerkannte und unbekannte Spuren in Südosteuropa von der Aufklärung bis in die Gegenwart*, ed. U. Tischler-Hofer and R. Zedinger (Innsbruck/Vienna/Bozen, 2010), pp. 175–86.

Pierce, R. A., 'Russian America and China', *Russian America*, ed. Smith-Sweetland, pp. 73–9.

Pinkard, S., *A Revolution in Taste: The Rise of French Cuisine 1650–1800* (Cambridge, 2010).

Pitz, E., *Die Zolltarife der Stadt Hamburg* (Wiesbaden, 1961).

Plank, G., *An Unsettled Conquest: The British Campaign against the Peoples of Acadia* (Philadelphia, 2003).

Platt, D. C. M., *Foreign Finance in Continental Europe and the United States, 1815–1870* (Abington, 1984).

Podmore, C., *The Moravian Church in England, 1728–1760* (Oxford/New York, 1998).

Poettering, J., 'Hamburger Sefarden im atlantischen Zuckerhandel des 17. Jahrhunderts' (MA thesis: University of Hamburg, 2003).

——, 'Kein Banghase sein: Hamburger Kaufmannslehrlinge im katholischen Lissabon des 17. Jahrhunderts', *Portugal und das Heilige Römische Reich (16.–18. Jahrhundert) – Portugal e o Sacro Império (séculos XVI–XVIII)*, ed. A. Curvelo and M. Simões (Münster, 2011), pp. 207–16.

——, *Handel, Nation und Religion: Kaufleute zwischen Portugal und Hamburg im 17. Jahrhundert* (Göttingen, 2013).

Pomeranz, K., *The Great Divergence: China, Europe, and the Making of the Modern World Economy* (Princeton, 2000).

Postma, J., and V. Enthoven, eds, *Riches from Atlantic Commerce: Dutch Transatlantic Trade and Shipping, 1585–1817* (Leiden/Boston, 2003).

Prado, F., *Edge of Empire: Atlantic Networks and Revolution in Bourbon Río de la Plata* (Oakley, 2015).

Prestholdt, J., *Domesticating the World: African Consumerism and the Genealogies of Globalization* (Berkeley, 2008).

Price, J., ed., *Joshua Johnson's Letterbook, 1771–1774: Letters from a Merchant in London to his Partners in Maryland* (London, 1979).

Prigge, W., ed., *Peripherie ist überall* (Frankfurt, 1998).

Rabuzzi, D. A., 'Cutting out the Middlemen? American Trade in Northern Europe, 1783–1815', *Merchant Organization and Maritime Trade with the North Atlantic, 1660–1815*, ed. O. U. Janzen (St Johns, 1998), pp. 175–99.

Rachel, H., ed., *Die Handels-, Zoll- und Akzisepolitik Preußens 1740–1786: Dritter Band, Erste Hälfte, Acta Borussica*, Reihe 2, Abteilung C (Berlin, 1928).
——, *Die Handels-, Zoll- und Akzisepolitik Preußens 1740–1786: Dritter Band, Zweite Hälfte, Acta Borussica*, Abteilung C (Berlin/Frankfurt, 1928/1986–87).
Radeff, A., 'Gewürzhandel en détail am Ende des Ancien Régime: Handeln und Wandern', *Gewürze*, ed. Denzel, pp. 187–204.
Raeff, M., 'Some Observations on the Work of Hermann Aubin', *Paths of Continuity: Central European Historiography from the 1930s to the 1950s*, ed. H. Lehmann and J. Van Hörn Melton (Cambridge, 1994), pp. 239–49.
Raphael-Hernandez, H., and P. Wiegmink, 'German Entanglements in Transatlantic Slavery: An Introduction', *Atlantic Studies* 14/4 (2017), pp. 419–35.
——, 'The Right to Freedom: Eighteenth-Century Slave Resistance and Early Moravian Missions in the Danish West Indies and Dutch Suriname', *Atlantic Studies* 14/4 (2017), pp. 457–75.
Ravalli, R., *Sea Otters: A History* (Lincoln/London, 2018).
Recker, M.-L., ed., *Von der Konkurrenz zur Rivalität: Das britisch-deutsche Verhältnis in den Ländern der europäischen Peripherie 1919–1939* (Stuttgart, 1986).
Reininghaus, W., 'Wirtschaft, Gesellschaft und Staat in der alten Grafschaft Mark', *Preußen im südlichen Westfalen*, ed. E. Trox (Lüdenscheid, 1993), pp. 11–41.
Renne, E. P., *Cloth that Does Not Die: The Meaning of Cloth in Bùnú Social Life* (Seattle, 1995).
Riello, G., and P. Parthasarathi, eds, *The Spinning World: A Global History of Cotton Textiles, 1200–1850* (Oxford, 2009).
Riello, G., and T. Roy, eds, *How India Clothed the World: The World of South Asian Textiles, 1500–1850* (Leiden, 2009).
Riello, G., *Cotton: The Fabric that Made the Modern World* (Cambridge, 2013).
Riemann, H., *Geschichte der Stadt Colberg: Aus den Quellen dargestellt* (Colberg, 1873).
Riley, J. C., *The Seven Years War and the Old Regime in France: The Economic and Financial Toll* (Princeton, 1986).
Risch, E., 'Joseph Crellius, Immigrant Broker', *The New England Quarterly* 12 (1939), pp. 241–67.
Rockman, S., *Scraping By: Wage Labor, Slavery, and Survival in Early Baltimore* (Baltimore, 2009).
Romaniello, M. P., 'True Rhubarb? Trading Eurasian Botanical and Medical Knowledge in the Eighteenth Century', *Journal of Global History* 11 (2016), pp. 3–23.
Rönnbäck, K., *Commerce and Colonisation: Studies of Early Modern Merchant Capitalism in the Atlantic Economy* (Gothenburg, 2009).
Röskau-Rydel, I., *Kultur an der Peripherie des Habsburger Reiches: Die Geschichte des Bildungswesens und der kulturellen Einrichtungen in Lemberg von 1772 bis 1848* (Wiesbaden, 1993).

Rössler, H., '"Die Zuckerbäcker waren vornehmlich Hannoveraner": Zur Geschichte der Wanderung aus dem Elbe-Weser-Dreieck in die britische Zuckerindustrie', *Jahrbuch der Männer vom Morgenstern* 81 (2002), pp. 137–236.

Rothermund, D., *Geschichte als Prozess und Aussage: Eine Einführung in Theorien des historischen Wandels und der Geschichtsschreibung* (Munich, 1995).

Rothschild, E., 'A Horrible Tragedy in the French Atlantic', *Past and Present* 192 (2006), pp. 67–108.

——, *The Inner Life of Empires: An Eighteenth-Century History* (Princeton, 2011).

Rumpler, H., 'Economia e Potere Politico: Il Ruolo di Trieste nella Politica di Sviluppo Economico di Vienna', *La Cittá dei Traffici*, ed. Finzi, Panariti and Panjek, pp. 55–124.

Rushforth, B., and P. W. Mapp, eds, *Colonial North America and the Atlantic World: A History in Documents* (New Jersey, 2009).

Rydén, G., 'Provincial Cosmopolitans: An Introduction', *Sweden in the Eighteenth-Century World: Provincial Cosmopolitans*, ed. G. Rydén (Farnham, 2013), pp. 1–32.

Sampaio, A. C. Jucá de, 'A Economia do Império Português no Período Pombalino', *A 'Época Pombalina' no Mundo Luso-Brasileiro*, ed. F. Falcon and C. Rodrigues (Rio de Janeiro, 2015), pp. 31–58.

Samsonowicz, H., *Późne Średniowiecze Miast Nadbałtyckich: Studia nad Dziejami Hanzy nad Bałtykiem w XIV–XV wieku* (Warsaw, 1968).

Sassen, S., 'Bordering Capabilities versus Borders: Implications for National Borders', *Michigan Journal of International Law* 30/3 (2009), pp. 567–95.

Saunier, P.-Y., *Transnational History* (Basingstoke, 2013).

Schelbert, L., and H. Rappolt, eds, *Alles ist ganz anders hier: Auswandererschicksale in Briefen aus zwei Jahrhunderten* (Olten/Freiburg, 1997).

Schenk, F. B., 'Lemberg and Wolff revisited: Zur Entstehung und Struktur des Konzepts "Osteuropa" seit dem späten 18. Jahrhundert', *Europa Vertikal*, ed. Aldenhoff-Hübinger, Gouseff and Serrier, pp. 43–62.

Schermerhorn, C., *The Business of Slavery and the Rise of American Capitalism, 1815–1860* (New Haven, 2015).

Schivelbusch, W., 'Spices: Tastes of Paradise', *The Taste Culture Reader: Experiencing Food and Drink*, ed. C. Korsmeyer (Oxford, 2007), pp. 123–30.

Schlögel, K., *Die Mitte liegt ostwärts: Die Deutschen, der verlorene Osten und Mitteleuropa* (Berlin, 1986).

Schmidt, H., *Die Entwicklung der Bielefelder Firmen E. A. Delius, E. A. Delius & Söhne und C. A. Delius & Söhne und die Betätigung ihrer Inhaber im Rahmen des Ravensberger Wirtschaftslebens, 1787–1925* (Lemgo, 1926).

Schmidt, T., 'Beiträge zur Geschichte des Stettiner Handels: Der Handel unter Friedrich dem Großen', *Baltische Studien* 20 (1864), pp. 165–273.

Schmitt, E., 'Europäischer Pfefferhandel und Pfefferkonsum im Ersten Kolonialzeitalter', *Gewürze*, ed. Denzel, pp. 15–26.

Schmitt, E., 'The Brandenburg Overseas Trading Companies in the 17th Century', *Companies and Trade: Essays on Overseas Trading Companies during the Ancien Regime*, ed. L. Blussé and F. Gaastra (Leiden, 1981), pp. 159–76.

Schmitz, E., *Leinengewerbe und Leinenhandel in Nordwestdeutschland, 1650–1850* (Cologne, 1967).

Schmoller, G., 'Studien über die wirtschaftliche Politik Friedrichs des Großen und Preußens überhaupt von 1680–1786: Die Erwerbung Pommerns und der Handel auf der Oder und in Stettin bis 1740', *Jahrbuch für Gesetzgebung, Verwaltung und Volkswirtschaft im Deutschen Reich* 8/2 (1884), pp. 69–78.

Schmoller, G., W. Naudé and A. Skalweit, eds, *Die Getreidehandelspolitik und Kriegsmagazinverwaltung Preußens 1740–1756*, Acta Borussica, Reihe 2, Abteilung A, Band 3 (Frankfurt, 1986/87).

Schneider, E. A., *The Occupation of Havana: War, Trade and Slavery in the Atlantic World* (Chapel Hill, 2018).

Schneider, J., O.-E. Krawehl and M. A. Denzel, *Statistiken des Hamburger seewärtigen Einfuhrhandels im 18. Jahrhundert: Nach den Admiralitäts- und Convoygeld-Einnahmebüchern* (St Katharinen, 2001).

Schönfeld, E., *Herford als Garn- und Leinemarkt in zwei Jahrhunderten, 1670–1870* (Bielefeld, 1929).

Schramm, P. E., 'His, Pierre', *Neue Deutsche Biographie* 9 (Berlin, 1972), p. 248.

Schroeder, P. W., *The Transformation of European Politics, 1763–1848* (Oxford, 1994).

Schröter, H. G., 'Kartellierung und Dekartellierung 1890–1990', *Vierteljahrschrift für Sozial- und Wirtschaftsgeschichte* 81 (1994), pp. 457–93.

Schui, F., 'Prussia's "Trans-Oceanic Moment": The Creation of the Prussian Asiatic Trade Company in 1750', *The Historical Journal* 49/1 (2006), pp. 143–60.

Schulte Beerbühl, M., *Deutsche Kaufleute in London: Welthandel und Einbürgerung (1660–1818)* (London, 2007).

——, 'Internationale Handelsnetze Westfälischer Kaufleute in London (c. 1660–1815)', *Kultur, Strategien und Netzwerke: Familienunternehmen in Westfalen im 19. und 20. Jahrhundert*, ed. K.-P. Ellerbrock et al. (Dortmund, 2014), pp. 153–74.

——, *The Forgotten Majority: German Merchants in London: Naturalization and Global Trade, 1660–1815* (New York, 2015).

Schulte Beerbühl, M., and K. Weber, 'From Westphalia to the Caribbean: Networks of German Textile Merchants in the Eighteenth Century', *Cosmopolitan Networks in Commerce and Society 1660–1914*, ed. A. Gestrich and M. Schulte Beerbühl, Bulletin Supplement No. 2 (London, 2011), pp. 53–98.

Schwartz, S. B., 'The Economy of the Portuguese Empire', *Portuguese Oceanic Expansion, 1400–1800*, ed. F. Bethencourt and D. Ramada Curto (Cambridge, 2007), pp. 19–48.

Sensbach, J. F., *Rebecca's Revival: Creating Black Christianity in the Atlantic World* (Cambridge, 2006).

——, '"Don't Teach My Negroes to be Pietists": Pietism and the Roots of the Black Protestant Church', *Pietism in Germany and North America 1680–1820*, ed. J. Strom, H. Lehmann and J. Van Horn Melton (Leiden, 2009), pp. 183–98.

Serrier, T., 'Veröstlichung der Barbaren: Die symbolische Verwerfung des Anderen hinter Rhein und Oder im deutsch-französischen und deutsch-polnischen Kontext', *Europa Vertikal*, ed. Aldenhoff-Hübinger, Gouseff and Serrier, pp. 102–20.

Sexton, J., *Debtor Diplomacy: Finance and American Foreign Relations in the Civil War Era, 1837–1873* (New York, 2005).

——, 'International Finance in the Civil War Era', *Transnational Significance of the American Civil War*, ed. J. Nagler, D. Doyle and M. Gräser (Basingstoke, 2016), pp. 91–106.

Shannon, T. J., 'Uniformity and Fashion in the Atlantic World', *William and Mary Quarterly* 73/3 (2016), pp. 549–54.

Sheridan, R. B., 'The Jamaican Slave Insurrection Scare of 1776 and the American Revolution', *The Journal of Negro History* 61/3 (1976), pp. 290–308.

Sieber, R., *African Textiles and Decorative Arts* (New Haven, 1972).

Smith, H. R., 'Reserving Water: Environmental and Technological Relationships with Colonial South Carolina Inland Rice Plantations', *Rice*, ed. Marton, pp. 189–211.

Smith-Sweetland, B., ed., *Russian America: The Forgotten Frontier* (Tacoma, 1990).

Soderlund, J. R., ed., *William Penn and the Founding of Pennsylvania, 1680–1684: A Documentary History* (Philadelphia, 1983).

Stanziani, A., ed., *La Qualité des Produits en France, XVIIIe–XXe siècles* (Paris, 2003).

Stanziani, A., 'Revisiting Russian Serfdom: Bonded Peasants and Market Dynamics, 1600s–1800s', *International Labor and Working-Class History* 78/1 (2010), pp. 12–27.

Statt, D., *Foreigners and Englishmen: The Controversy over Immigration and Population, 1660–1760* (London, 1995).

Steffen, A., and K. Weber, 'Spinning and Weaving for the Slave Trade: Proto-Industry in Eighteenth-Century Silesia', *Slavery Hinterland*, ed. Brahm and Rosenhaft, pp. 87–107.

Steffen, A., 'A Cloth that Binds – New Perspectives on the 18th-Century Prussian Economy' (unpublished working paper: Boston, 18th World Economic History Congress, 29 July 2018 to 3 August 2018), *Slavery & Abolition: A Journal of Slave and Post-Slave Studies* (2021, forthcoming).

Sterne, M., 'From Jonesville to Frankfurt on the Main: The Political Career of William Walton Murphy, 1861–1869', *Quarterly Review of the Michigan Alumnus* 65/18 (1959), pp. 251–61.

Strassburger, R. B., and W. J. Hinke, eds, *Pennsylvania German Pioneers: A Publication of the Lists of Arrivals in the Port of Philadelphia from 1727 to 1808*, Vol. 1 (Norristown/Pennsylvania, 1934).

Straubel, R., 'Stettin als Handelsplatz und wirtschaftlicher Vorort Pommerns im spätabsolutistischen Preussen', *Jahrbuch für die Geschichte Mittel- und Ostdeutschlands* 50 (2004), pp. 131–89.

Struck, B., *Nicht West – nicht Ost: Frankreich und Polen in der Wahrnehmung deutscher Reisender 1750 und 1850* (Göttingen, 2006).

Struck, B., K. Ferris and J. Revel, 'Introduction: Space and Scale in Transnational History', *The International History Review* 33/4 (2011), pp. 573–84.

Styles, J., 'An Ocean of Textiles', *William and Mary Quarterly* 73/3 (2016), pp. 531–7.

Szücs, J., *Die drei historischen Regionen Europas: Mit einem Vorwort von Fernand Braudel* (Frankfurt, 1994).

Taenzer, U., *Kernprobleme der Marktwirtschaft, Unternehmenskonzentration: Ein Lehr- und Arbeitsbuch* (Stuttgart, 1981).

Tamaki, T., 'Hamburg as a Gateway: The Economic Connections between the Atlantic and the Baltic in the Long Eighteenth-Century with Special Reference to French Colonial Goods', *The Rise of the Atlantic Economy and the North Sea/Baltic Trade, 1500–1800*, ed. L. Müller, P. R. Rössner and T. Tamaki (Stuttgart, 2011), pp. 61–80.

Tarrade, J., *Le Commerce Colonial de la France à la Fin de l'Ancien Régime*, 2 vols (Paris, 1972).

The Colonial Records of the State of Georgia, Vol. 21 (New York, 1970).

Thornton, J., *Africa and Africans in the Making of the Atlantic World, 1400–1800* (Cambridge, 1999).

Thum, G., 'Die kulturelle Leere des Ostens: Legitimierung preußisch-deutscher Herrschaft im 19. Jahrhundert', *Umkämpfte Räume: Raumbilder, Ordnungswille und Gewaltmobilisierung*, ed. U. Jureit (Göttingen, 2016), pp. 263–86.

Thun, A., *Die Industrie am Niederrhein und ihre Arbeiter* (Leipzig, 1879).

Tilly, C., *European Revolutions 1492–1992* (Cambridge, 1993).

Tomich, D. W., *Slavery in the Circuit of Sugar* (Albany, 2016).

Treue, W., *Wirtschaftszustände und Wirtschaftspolitik in Preußen 1815–1825* (Stuttgart, 1937).

Trivellato, F., *The Familiarity of Strangers: The Sephardic Diaspora, Livorno, and Cross-Cultural Trade in the Early Modern Period* (New Haven/London 2009).

Tucci, U., 'Die Triestiner Kaufmannschaft im 18. Jahrhundert: Ihre Ausrichtung, ihre Gutachten', *Beiträge zur Handels- und Verkehrsgeschichte*, ed. P. W. Roth (Graz, 1978), pp. 121–33.

Tyler, J. W., 'Foster Cunliffe and Sons: Liverpool Merchants in the Maryland Tobacco Trade, 1738–1765', *Maryland Historical Magazine* 73 (1978), pp. 246–79.

Unger, R. W., 'Income Differentials, Institutions and Religion: Working in the Rhineland or Pennsylvania in the Eighteenth Century', *Working on Labor: Essays in Honor of Jan Lucassen*, ed. M. van der Linden and L. Lucassen (Leiden, 2012), pp. 269–95.

van Bel, J. G., *De Linnenhandel van Amsterdam in de XVIIIe Eeuw* (Amsterdam, 1940).

van Deusen, N. E., *Global Indios: The Indigenous Struggle for Justice in Sixteenth-Century Spain* (Durham/London, 2015).

van Ruymbeke, B., 'Minority Survival: The Huguenot Paradigm in France and the Diaspora', *Memory and Identity: The Huguenots and the Atlantic Diaspora*, ed. B. van Ruymbeke and R. J. Sparks (Columbia, 2003), pp. 1–25.

Vassallo, C., *Corsairing to Commerce: Maltese Merchants in XVIII Century Spain* (Malta, 1997).

Veluwenkamp, J. W., and W. Scheltjens, 'Baltic Drugs Traffic 1650–1850: Sound Toll Registers Online as a Source for the Import of Medicines in the Baltic Sea Area', *Social History of Medicine* 31/1 (2017), pp. 140–76.

Venborg Pedersen, M., ed., *Danmark og Kolonierne – Danmark: En Kolonimagt* (Copenhagen, 2017).

Vilar, P., *La Catalogne dans l'Espagne Moderne: Recherches sur les Fondements Économiques des Structures Nationales: Vol. 3: La Formation du Capital Commercial* (Paris, 1962).

Vogel, Bürgermeister zu Wolgast, 'Inwiefern gehört die Provinz Pommern zu den wichtigsten Erwerbungen des Hauses Hohenzollern', *Archiv für Landeskunde der Preußischen Monarchie* 5 (1858), pp. 219–75.

Vogt, P., 'Die Mission der Herrnhuter Brüdergemeinde und ihre Bedeutung für den Neubeginn der protestantischen Missionen am Ende des 18. Jahrhunderts', *Pietismus und Neuzeit* 35 (2009), pp. 204–36.

——, 'Zinzendorf's "Seventeen Points of Matrimony": A Fundamental Document on the Moravian Understanding of Marriage and Sexuality', *Journal of Moravian History* 10 (2011), pp. 38–67.

Volz, G., ed., *Die Werke Friedrichs des Großen*, 10 vols (Berlin, 1912–1914).

Voss, K., *Sklaven als Ware und Kapital: Die Plantagenökonomie von Saint-Domingue als Entwicklungsprojekt, 1697–1715* (Munich, 2016).

Wake, C. H. H., 'The Changing Pattern of Europe's Pepper and Spice Imports, c. 1400–1700', *Spices*, ed. Pearson, pp. 141–84.

Wallerstein, I., *The Modern World-System*, 4 vols (New York, 1974–2011).

——, *Der historische Kapitalismus* (Berlin, 1984).

——, 'Hold the Tiller Firm: On Method and the Unit of Analysis', *The Essential Wallerstein*, ed. I. Wallerstein (New York, 2000), pp. 149–59.

Walsh, L. S., 'Liverpool's Slave Trade to the Colonial Chesapeake: Slaving on the Periphery', *Liverpool and Transatlantic Slavery*, ed. D. Richardson, S. Schwarz and A. Tibbles (Liverpool, 2007), pp. 98–117.

Wandycz, P. S., *The Lands of Partitioned Poland, 1795–1918* (Seattle, 1974).

Wareing, J., *Indentured Migration and the Servant Trade from London to America, 1618–1718: "There is a Great Want of Servants"* (Oxford, 2016).

Weaver, J., *Red Atlantic: American Indigenes and the Making of the Modern World 1000–1927* (Chapel Hill, 2014).

Weber, K., 'Les livres douaniers de l'Amirauté de Hambourg au XVIIIe siècle: une source de grande valeur encore inexploitée', *Bulletin du Centre d'Histoire des Espaces Atlantiques*, New Series 9 (1999), pp. 93–126.

——, 'Die Admiralitätszoll- und Convoygeld Einnahmebücher: Eine wichtige Quelle für Hamburgs Wirtschaftsgeschichte im 18. Jahrhundert', *Hamburger Wirtschafts-Chronik* 1 (2000), pp. 83–112.

——, *Deutsche Kaufleute im Atlantikhandel, 1680–1830: Unternehmen und Familien in Hamburg, Cádiz und Bordeaux* (Munich, 2004).

——, 'Boué, Pierre', *Hamburgische Biografie* 5 (Göttingen, 2010), pp. 59–60.

——, 'Zwischen Religion und Ökonomie: Sepharden und Hugenotten in Hamburg, 1580–1800', *Religion und Mobilität: Zum Verhältnis von raumbezogener Mobilität und religiöser Identitätsbildung im frühneuzeitlichen Europa*, ed. H. P. T. Jürgen and T. Weller (Göttingen, 2010), pp. 148–64.

——, 'Hamburg, 1728–1811', *Revue de l'OFCE* 140 (2015), pp. 265–8.

Weber, K., and M. Schulte Beerbühl, 'From Westphalia to the Caribbean: Networks of German Textile Merchants in the Eighteenth Century', *Cosmopolitan Networks in Commerce and Society 1660–1914*, ed. A. Gestrich and M. Schulte Beerbühl (London, 2011), pp. 53–98.

Weiss, H., *Slavhandel och Slaveri under Svensk Flagg: Koloniala Drömmar och Verklighet i Afrika och Karibien 1770–1847* (Helsinki, 2016).

Wendland, A. V., 'Randgeschichten? Osteuropäische Perspektiven auf Kulturtransfer und Verflechtungsgeschichte', *Osteuropa* 58/3 (2008), pp. 95–116.

Wheeler, M. E., 'The Origins of the Russian American Company', *Jahrbücher für Geschichte Osteuropas* 32/14 (1966), pp. 485–94.

White, A. D., *Autobiography of Andrew Dickson White* (New York, 1905).

Wilkins, M., *The History of Foreign Investment in the United States to 1914* (Cambridge, 1989).

Wimmler, J., *Centralized African States in the Transatlantic Slave Trade: The Example of 18th-Century Asante and Dahomey* (Graz, 2012).

——, *The Sun King's Atlantic: Drugs, Demons and Dyestuffs in the Atlantic World, 1640–1730* (Leiden/Boston, 2017).

——, 'Dyeing Woollens in Eighteenth-Century Berlin: The *Königliches Lagerhaus* and the Globalization of Prussia through Colouring Materials', *Cotton in Context: Manufacturing, Marketing and Consuming Textiles in the German-speaking World (1500–1900)*, ed. K. Siebenhüner, J. Jordan and G. Schopf (Vienna/Cologne/Weimar, 2019), pp. 195–221.

——, 'Incidental Things in Historiography', *Cambridge Archaeological Journal* 30/1 (2020), pp. 153–6.

Wittmütz, V., *Kleine Wuppertaler Stadtgeschichte* (Regensburg, 2013).

Wokeck, M. S., *A Tide of Alien Tongues: The Flow and Ebb of German Immigration to Pennsylvania, 1683–1776* (Ann Arbor, 1983).

Wokeck, M. S., *Trade in Strangers: The Beginnings of Mass Migration to North America* (University Park, 1999).

——, 'Expanding the Paths of Immmigration: The Role of German Pioneers in Regional Settlements in North America', *Atlantic Migrations: Regions and Movements in Germany and North America/USA during the 18th and 19th Century*, ed. S. Heerwart and C. Schnurmann (Hamburg/Münster, 2007), pp. 83–109.

Wolff, L., *Inventing Eastern Europe: The Map of Civilization on the Mind of the Enlightenment* (Stanford, 1994).

Wollstadt, H.-J., *Geordnetes Dienen in der christlichen Gemeinde* (Göttingen, 1966).

Wong, R. B., 'Possibilities of Plenty and the Persistence of Poverty: Industrialization and International Trade', *An Emerging Modern World*, ed. Conrad and Osterhammel, pp. 251–409.

Zarycki, T., *Ideologies of Eastness in Central and Eastern Europe* (London/New York, 2014).

Zeuske, M., 'Preußen und Westindien: Die vergessenen Anfänge der Handels- und Konsularbeziehungen Deutschlands mit der Karibik und Lateinamerika 1800–1870', *Preußen und Lateinamerika: Im Spannungsfeld von Kommerz, Macht und Kultur*, ed. S. Carreras and G. Maihold (Münster, 2004), pp. 145–215.

Zeuske, M., and J. Ludwig, 'Amerikanische Kolonialwaren und Wirtschaftspolitik in Preußen und Sachsen: Prolegomena (17./18. und frühes 19. Jahrhundert)', *Jahrbuch für Geschichte von Staat, Wirtschaft und Gesellschaft Lateinamerikas* 32 (1995), pp. 257–301.

Zündorf, L., *Zur Aktualität von Immanuel Wallerstein: Einleitung in sein Werk* (Wiesbaden, 2010).

Zwanowetz, G., 'Zur wirtschaftlichen Lage Tirols und Vorarlbergs gegen Ende der Regierungszeit Kaiser Josephs II', *Erzeugung, Verkehr und Handel in der Geschichte der Alpenländer*, ed. F. Huter, F. Mathis and G. Zwanowetz (Innsbruck, 1977), pp. 417–47.

Index

Page numbers in **bold** refer to illustrations

PEOPLE, MARKETS, GOODS:
ECONOMIES AND SOCIETIES IN HISTORY

ISSN: 2051-7467

Printed and bound by CPI Group (UK) Ltd, Croydon, CR0 4YY

09/06/2025

14685705-0002